Victoria's Daughters

Also by Jerrold M. Packard

Farewell in Splendor
Neither Friend Nor Foe
Sons of Heaven
Peter's Kingdom
American Monarchy
The Queen & Her Court

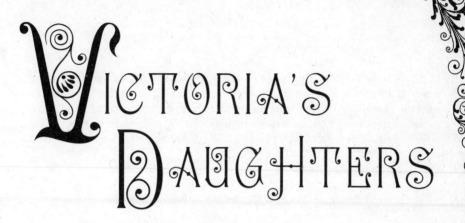

VICTORIA'S DAUGHTERS

Jerrold M. Packard

St. Martin's Griffin ❦ New York

Design by Nancy Resnick

Library of Congress Cataloging-in-Publication Data

Packard, Jerrold M.
    Victoria's daughters / Jerrold M. Packard.
        p.   cm.
    Includes bibliographical references and index.
    ISBN 0-312-19562-1 (hc)
    ISBN 0-312-24496-7 (pbk)
    1. Victoria, Queen of Great Britain, 1819–1901—Family. 2. Marriages of royalty and nobility—Great Britain—History—19th century. 3. Victoria, Empress, consort of Frederick III, German emperor, 1840–1901. 4. Alice, Grand Duchess, consort of Ludwig IV, Grand Duke of Hesse-Darmstadt, 1843–1878. 5. Helena Augusta Victoria, Princess Christian of Schleswig-Holstein-Sonderburg-Augustenburg, 1846–1923. 6. Louise, Princess, Duchess of Argyll, 1848–1939. 7. Beatrice, consort of Prince Henry of Battenburg, 1857–1944. 8. Mothers and daughters—Great Britain—History—19th century. 9. Great Britain—History—Victoria, 1837–1901—Biography. 10. Women—Great Britain—History—19th century. 11. Princesses—Great Britain—Biography.   I. Title.
DA554.P33   1998
941.081'092'2—dc21   98-21116
[B]   CIP

17 16 15 14 13

For Sara

Contents

The Children and Grandchildren of Victoria and Albert

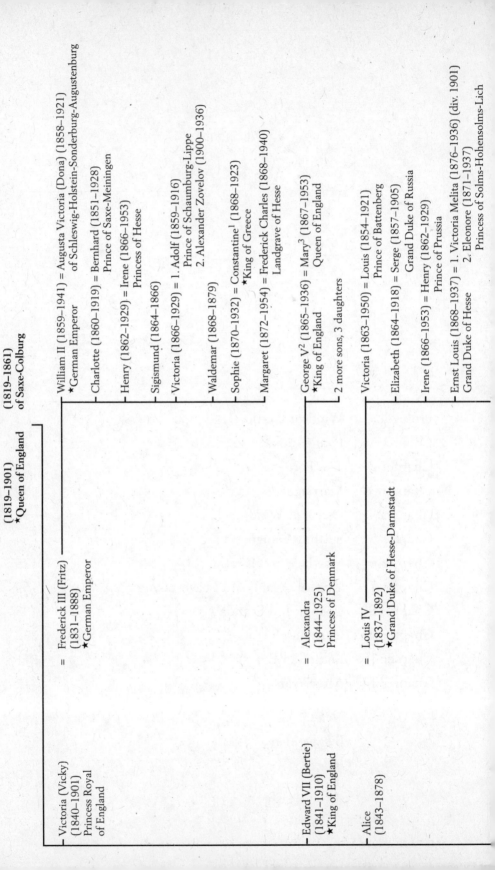

Alfred (1844–1900)
Duke of Edinburgh and Saxe-Coburg-Gotha
= Marie (1853–1920) Grand Duchess of Russia
- Frederick William (1870–1873)
- Alexandra (Alix) (1872–1918) = Nicholas II[4] (1868–1918) Tsar of Russia ★Tsarina of Russia
- Mary Victoria (1874–1878)
- 1 son, 4 daughters

Helena (Lenchen) (1846–1923)
= Christian (1831–1917) Prince of Schleswig-Holstein-Sonderburg-Augustenburg
- Christian Victor (1867–1900)
- Albert (1869–1931) Duke of Schleswig-Holstein-Sonderburg-Augustenburg
- Helena Victoria (1870–1948)
- Marie Louise (1872–1957) = Aribert (1864–1933) Prince of Anhalt-Dessau (div. 1900)

Louise (1848–1939)
= John (1845–1914) 9th Duke of Argyll
- Frederick Harald (1876)
- (Stillborn son, 1877)

Arthur (1850–1942)
Duke of Connaught and Strathearn
= Louise (1860–1917) Princess of Prussia
- 2 daughters, 1 son

Leopold (1853–1884)
Duke of Albany
= Helena (1861–1922) Princess of Waldeck-Pyrmont
- 1 daughter, 1 son

Beatrice (1857–1944)
= Henry (Liko) (1858–1896) Prince of Battenberg
- Alexander (1886–1960) = Lady Irene Denison (1890–1956) Marquess of Carisbrooke
- Victoria Eugenie (Ena) (1887–1969) = Alfonso XIII[5] (1886–1941) Queen of Spain ★King of Spain
- Leopold (Lord Leopold Mountbatten) (1889–1922)
- Maurice (Prince of Battenberg) (1891–1914)

[1] Uncle of Prince Philip, husband of Queen Elizabeth II of England
[2] Grandfather of Queen Elizabeth II of England
[3] Great-granddaughter of King George III of England, Queen Victoria's grandfather
[4] Blood-nephew of Queen Alexandra, wife of King Edward VII
[5] Grandfather of Juan Carlos, who became King of Spain when its monarchy was restored in 1975

NOTE: stars indicate sovereignty. Titles and names shown were not necessarily the title & name at the time of marriage.

Principal Characters

THE SISTERS

VICTORIA (Vicky): Crown princess of Prussia, German empress
  born: November 21, 1840, Buckingham Palace
  created princess royal: January 19, 1841
  married: January 25, 1858, Chapel Royal, St. James's Palace
  husband: HIM Emperor Frederick III, died June 15, 1888
  died: August 5, 1901, Friedrichshof

ALICE: Grand duchess of Hesse-Darmstadt
  born: April 25, 1843, Buckingham Palace
  married: July 1, 1862, Osborne House
  husband: HRH Grand Duke Louis IV of Hesse-Darmstadt,
    died March 13, 1892
  died: December 14, 1878, Darmstadt

HELENA (Lenchen): Princess Christian
  born: May 25, 1846, Buckingham Palace
  married: July 5, 1866, Private Chapel, Windsor
  husband: HSH Prince Christian of Schleswig-Holstein-
    Sonderburg-Augustenburg (created HRH by
    Queen Victoria), died October 28, 1917
  died: June 9, 1923, Schomberg House, London

LOUISE: Marchioness of Lorne, later duchess of Argyll
    born: March 18, 1848, Buckingham Palace
    married: March 21, 1871, St. George's Chapel, Windsor
    husband: 9th duke of Argyll (marquess of Lorne), died May 2,
      1914
    died: December 3, 1939, Kensington Palace

BEATRICE: Princess Henry of Battenberg
    born: April 14, 1857, Buckingham Palace
    married: July 23, 1885, Whippingham Church, Osborne
    husband: HSH Prince Henry of Battenberg (created HRH by
      Queen Victoria), died January 20, 1896
    died: October 26, 1944, Brantridge Park, Balcombe, Sussex

ALBERT (1819–1861), father, prince consort
ALBERT (1869–1931), son of *Helena* (natural father of Valerie,
    duchess of Arenberg, 1900–1953)
ALBERT EDWARD (Bertie) (1841–1910), brother, prince of Wales,
    later King Edward VII, married Princess Alexandra of
    Denmark
ALEXANDER (Drino) (1886–1960), son of *Beatrice,* prince of
    Battenberg, later marquess of Carisbrooke
ALEXANDRA (Alix) (1844–1925), sister-in-law, princess of
    Denmark, princess of Wales, and queen to Edward VII
ALEXANDRA (Alix, Alicky) (1872–1918), daughter of *Alice,*
    princess of Hesse-Darmstadt and empress to Nicholas II of
    Russia
ALFRED (Affie) (1844–1900), brother, duke of Edinburgh, married
    Grand Duchess Marie of Russia
ARTHUR (1850–1942), brother, duke of Connaught, married
    Princess Louise of Prussia
AUGUSTA (1858–1921), mother-in-law to *Vicky,* princess of
    Weimar, queen of Prussia, German empress to William I
AUGUSTA VICTORIA (Dona) (1858–1921), daughter-in-law to *Vicky,*
    princess of Schleswig-Holstein-Sonderburg-Augustenburg,
    German empress to William II
BATTENBERG, PRINCE ALEXANDER of (Sandro) (1857–1893), reign-
    ing prince of Bulgaria

BATTENBERG, PRINCE HENRY of (Liko) (1858–1896), married
   Beatrice

BATTENBERG, PRINCE LOUIS of (1854–1921), married Princess
   Victoria of Hesse (daughter of *Alice*), later marquess of
   Milford Haven

CHARLOTTE (1860–1919), daughter of *Vicky*, princess of Prussia,
   married Prince Bernhard of Saxe-Meiningen

CHRISTIAN (1831–1917), married *Helena*, prince of Schleswig-
   Holstein-Sonderburg-Augustenburg

CHRISTIAN VICTOR (Christle) (1867–1900), son of *Helena*, prince
   of Schleswig-Holstein-Sonderburg-Augustenburg

ELLA (1864–1918), daughter of *Alice*, princess of Hesse-
   Darmstadt, married Grand Duke Serge of Russia

ERNEST II (1818–1893), uncle, brother to prince consort, grand
   duke of Coburg

ERNEST (1868–1937), son of *Alice*, grand duke of Hesse-Darmstadt

FREDERICK III (Fritz) (1831–1888), married *Vicky*, German emperor

FREDERICK (Frittie) (1870–1873), son of *Alice*, prince of Hesse-
   Darmstadt

GEORGE V (1865–1936), nephew, son of Edward VII, king of England

HELENA VICTORIA (1870–1948), daughter of *Helena*, princess of
   Schleswig-Holstein-Sonderburg-Augustenburg

HENRY (1862–1929), son of *Vicky*, prince of Prussia, married
   Princess Irene of Hesse-Darmstadt (daughter of *Alice*)

IRENE, daughter of *Alice*, princess of Hesse-Darmstadt, married
   Prince Henry of Prussia (son of *Vicky*)

LEOPOLD (1853–1884), brother, duke of Albany, married Princess
   Helena of Waldeck-Pyrmont

LEOPOLD (1889–1922), son of *Beatrice*, prince of Battenberg, later
   Lord Leopold Mountbatten

LORNE (John/Ian) (1845–1914), married *Louise*, marquess of
   Lorne and duke of Argyll

LOUIS (1838–1892), married *Alice*, grand duke of Hesse-
   Darmstadt

MARGARET (Mossy) (1872–1954), daughter of *Vicky*, princess of Prussia, married Prince Frederick of Hesse-Cassel

MARIE LOUISE (1872–1956), daughter of *Helena*, princess of Schleswig-Holstein-Sonderburg-Augustenburg, married Prince Aribert of Anhalt (divorced)

MAURICE (1891–1914), son of *Beatrice*, prince of Battenberg

SIGISMUND (Sigi) (1864–1866), son of *Vicky*, prince of Prussia

SOPHIE (1870–1932), daughter of *Vicky*, princess of Prussia, married Prince, later King Constantine (Tino) of Greece

VICTORIA (1863–1950), daughter of *Alice*, princess of Hesse-Darmstadt, married Prince Louis of Battenberg

VICTORIA (Moretta) (1866–1929), daughter of *Vicky*, princess of Prussia, married Prince Adolf of Schaumburg-Lippe

VICTORIA (1819–1901), mother, queen of England

VICTORIA EUGENIA (Ena) (1887–1969), daughter of *Beatrice*, princess of Battenberg, married King Alfonso XIII of Spain

WALDEMAR (Waldy) (1868–1879), son of *Vicky*, prince of Prussia

WILLIAM I (1797–1888), father-in-law to *Vicky*, king of Prussia and German emperor

WILLIAM II (Willy) (1859–1941), son of *Vicky*, prince of Prussia, German emperor

Prologue

Windsor Castle

FRIDAY, NOVEMBER 3, 1944

Death had come as gently as sleep to Victoria and Albert's last child. Princess Beatrice, ninth born and fifth daughter, had always been "the baby" to her august mother, but now her name recalled only the haziest of memories for most. The world she symbolized was buried beyond recall, first in Flanders mud, more lately in a Europe being laid waste a second time. Yet at her passing, a distinguished company of Beatrice's countrymen broke off from their urgent wartime duties to gather and to remember what this woman had once been to their kingdom.

Shortly before noon on this late autumn morning, the Blitz having painfully returned to Britain in the form of pilotless German rockets, a bone-weary King George VI led the mourners—mostly members of Europe's extended royal clan—in bidding his great-aunt Bee a subdued good-bye. The scene was played out at St. George's Chapel, for centuries the de facto parish church to England's royal family, and where only a few emblems of the usual splendor associated with this renowned place of worship were in evidence this morning. But there was no question of the high rank of the deceased: not only did the archbishop of Canterbury and the

1

dean of Windsor lend their eminence to the ceremony, but the dozens of brilliantly emblazoned Garter knights' banners, since 1939 removed from the stalls because of the danger from air raids, had at the monarch's command been returned as a mark of respect to the dead princess.

Joining the sovereign at the side of the coffin were members of most of Europe's royal families, including the kings of Norway and of the Hellenes, the deceased's nieces Princesses Helena Victoria and Marie Louise, and—as chief mourner—the long-exiled queen of Spain, Beatrice's daughter, Victoria Eugenia. The congregants displayed little grandeur, most of the men dressed in the winter uniforms of the armed services—the British king was attired as a fleet admiral—while the women were hidden in the plain and somber black of mourning.

With the failing light of an autumn sun only just illumining the medieval setting, Britain's queen consort led her Spanish counterpart to the edge of the exposed vault. The two women dropped low curtsies over the coffin. A future queen, the eighteen-year-old Princess Elizabeth, watched solemnly from a few feet away as her parents presided over the homage to a spent generation.

Even though many of the mourners had passed their own lifetimes in Europe's palaces, only a few—only the very oldest—could know the endless splendors that had passed before Princess Beatrice's eyes over her eighty-seven years, the first half of which had been spent at the elbow of the nineteenth-century's greatest monarch and the woman for whom a long era had been named. The titles of Her Royal Highness Princess Beatrice Mary Victoria Feodore were read aloud by the Garter King of Arms, then slowly the gathering turned and left the chapel to face the dangers and uncertainties of a country—a world—at war and yearning for peace. But the last of Queen Victoria's illustrious daughters was already at peace.

1

Foundations

Since neither the queen nor her new husband had the first idea how pregnancy might be avoided, only weeks after her wedding the amazed Victoria found herself, not particularly happily, with child. The expectant mother suppressed her horror of what she called the "shadow side" of marriage and resolved to look upon the approaching event with something like equanimity. Both parents were determined to give their kingdom a male heir, such production representing the most fundamental duty of sovereign mother and consort father. Thus it happened that in the early hours of November 21, 1840, a rainy day Victoria remembered most clearly for the smoking chimneys outside her bedroom windows, the young queen's labor pains began, a week or two earlier than her doctors had predicted.

Because of the low state of medicine in the early nineteenth century, childbirth was still a largely primitive undertaking. Though royal deliveries were conducted with a degree of care far exceeding that received by most of her kingdom's mothers, the effort had, in truth, killed the queen's aunt, a tragedy most responsible for putting Victoria on the throne. This unique position she now filled with a prideful mix of noblesse oblige and the assuredness that it had been God's own plan. Indeed, it did appear that divine facilitation had led some three and a half years earlier to the accession of the eighteen-year-old princess to Britain's throne.

To understand how Victoria became queen of England, it is necessary to look back a few decades, to the reign of her grandfather, King George III, and his queen, Charlotte. George, the prince of Wales, the couple's eldest child, had to the surprise of many fulfilled his dynastic duty by contracting for a lawful marriage, relatively late in life—he was already in his thirties when he went to the altar. Others, however, accurately foresaw the failure of that enterprise, since his bride-to-be was a woman whose tastes differed in almost every particular from those of her reluctant fiancé.

To complicate the situation, the royal groom had already been married—although his first marriage, to the Roman Catholic widow Maria Fitzherbert, was officially kept secret: marriage between any heir to the British throne and a Catholic was impermissible under the law as it then stood, and to this day continues so. Because of its illegality, George's marriage to Mrs. Fitzherbert had been contracted in an essentially morganatic state (though Britain didn't and still legally doesn't recognize this either),[1] which meant that his wife could not assume rank as princess of Wales, nor could any children of that union have inherited rank, titles, or rights to the throne from their father. Though on becoming king George could have made Mrs. Fitzherbert his queen—she was already widely called "Princess Fitz"—such an act would have brought disapprobation from every European court, as well as grave constitutional questions as to the legitimacy of Britain's crown, a matter taken by royalty of the early nineteenth century with massive seriousness, and therefore not a course likely to have been followed by a fourth King George.

Mrs. Fitzherbert's star began to be overshadowed in the mid-1790s when George took a sudden passion for new lovers, first Lady

Jersey, later Lady Hertford. It was actually debts incurred during his illegal marriage that most directly prompted the prince to contract an approved marriage as a means of regularizing his purse. George abruptly divorced Mrs. Fitzherbert, even though he swore he still loved her. He surely was mollified, however, by Parliament's promise that in return for making a dynastically valid union, it would pay off his vast debts *and* generously increase his state allowance.

In 1794, George asked Lady Jersey, his hitherto standby mistress, to see what she might be able to find him by way of a suitably Protestant princess. It is perhaps understandable that she did not wish to recommend anyone who would diminish her own standing with the prince. In view of the results—Lady Jersey's intervention proved catastrophic—George would have been better off asking the help of a less personally interested intermediary.

What she came up with turned out to be one of Europe's least appealing princesses. Caroline of Brunswick was royal—in fact, George's first cousin (her mother was the sister of his father)—but that about covered her commendable qualities, aside from the prospective groom's belief the connection would please her uncle, his father. On the negative side, Caroline's speech was uncouth, her appearance astoundingly unregal, her bodily hygiene verging on the barbaric. George's cultured tastes clearly stood diametrically opposed to the princess's general lowness. The courtier Lord Malmesbury was nonetheless dispatched to Germany to inspect and negotiate. When in 1795 Caroline arrived in England and George first saw what his ill-luck had brought him, he immediately called out to his valet for a brandy.

Remaining insensibly drunk even on his wedding night, the prince nonetheless performed conjugally, the result being a daughter whom he named Charlotte, after his own mother. The infant was destined to be—given the father's lack of regard for its mother—George's only heir. Caroline was, unsurprisingly, discarded almost immediately after Charlotte's conception, never again to spend a night with her husband, nor even to pass many more days under his roof.

George would soon formally separate from a woman chiefly distinguished for being one of the most ill-used princesses in British history.

Eighteen years later, Princess Charlotte, by then a young woman, was herself ready to mate. Understandably, she was leery of marriage, having seen her own childhood ruined by the aftermath of her parents' ill-assorted union. Though she was loyal to her father, Charlotte was nonetheless perfectly sensible to the prince of Wales's many and varied shortcomings—she once confided that "my mother was bad, but she would not have been so bad if my father had not been much worse still." But now grown, the all-but-certain heiress to the kingdom in which George was serving as regent for his mentally incapacitated father had all Europe from which to choose a husband.

Leopold of Coburg was the eventual winner of Charlotte's hand and of future status as consort to a British monarch. Likely the handsomest prince in Europe, Leopold already boasted a distinguished career as a major general in the Russian Army during the Napoleonic War, and—what gave him his eligibility to marry Charlotte—he was the younger son of the reigning duke of an insignificant if picturesque German duchy. Coburg claimed little more than sixty thousand subjects and was almost entirely unremarked upon in Europe's affairs except for the extraordinary good looks borne by a high proportion of the sons of its reigning house; even the great Napoleon himself once called Leopold the "handsomest young man I ever saw at the Tuileries."

Of ponderous personality, and apt to measure every word with razor-edged precision, Leopold's somber character stood in notable contrast to Charlotte's; the princess, though dignified and imperious, was outspoken and romantic, possessed of impulsive spirits and a generous heart. As for Leopold, he was cautiously quiet, not noticeably passionate, and had too little money to be generous. But in May 1816 the couple married, and the still-gangly princess almost immediately became pregnant. She miscarried this first child, but quickly conceived again. On November 3, 1817, three weeks overdue in her second pregnancy, Charlotte's waters broke and her doctors put her to bed.

Had those doctors been less timid in their ministrations, the subsequent history of the world might have been greatly altered. But dealing with royal births tended to make even otherwise-aggressive physicians think twice before applying necessary measures. Sir Richard Croft, Charlotte's obstetrician, examined the princess—without, of course, the slightest effort to employ sanitary methods, the medical implications of asepsis not then being understood. Judging that birth was near, the doctor called in the great officers of state to observe the event—a ritual long required at royal accouchements to ensure that no substitute baby was inserted into the royal line. But Croft and the witnesses were to be disappointed: the child refused to be born.

Following a full day of labor, Charlotte's pains lessened in their intensity; but though her cervix had dilated, she grew too weak to provide the final effort needed to push her baby into the doctors' waiting arms. The princess had been bled several times during her pregnancy in the accepted maternity treatment of the age (the reasoning being this would "prevent hemorrhage or the child growing too large") and had thus by the time of her labor been rendered dangerously anemic. After another twenty-four hours during which she still failed to expel the child (her doctors were unwilling to apply forceps, though a pair was standing by and the technique had been in use for over a century), it became obvious that a medical disaster was occurring. Finally, at the end of a total of fifty hours of labor, the all-but-expended princess managed to deliver a son—stillborn. Though her attendants frenziedly attempted every known remedy to bring breath into the child, it had evidently been dead for hours.

Valiant but tragically overdue efforts were now hurriedly put into play to save the life of the mother. Charlotte's loss of blood over the two days had been substantial, and a clumsy manual removal of the placenta only depleted her little remaining strength. The princess was in the end overcome by the combined effects of

anemia, a likely pulmonary embolism, and perhaps even a por-
phyria attack (the disease having long manifested itself as madness
in her grandfather, King George III). She succumbed at 2:30 A.M. on
November 6, 1817, and with her died the Hanoverian succession.

With the recent and frightening shadow of the French Revolution's menace to the governing precepts of society, few Britons
could envision a secure state without a monarch to lend it legitimacy. In consequence, the quest to produce a legal heir to King
George's creaking throne represented serious business.

The eventual victor in the sweepstakes would be determined by
the mathematical rules that governed (and still govern) succession to
the British throne. The United Kingdom had never been subject
to the so-called Salic succession, the disbarring of female succession
to the throne that was the customary practice in the German and
most of the Catholic states. Inheritance of the throne went to the
sons of the sovereign in the order of their birth, followed by daughters in their birth order. Legitimate children of each heir succeeded,
according to the same rules, directly after their royal parent, noting
most importantly that the daughters of the higher heir preceded
any child of his (or her) younger siblings. Thus, for example, a
daughter by the older brother Kent would precede both the
younger brother Cumberland *and* any of his children, even sons.

All of the prince of Wales's sisters were childless, and meno-
pause had removed them from future childbearing. Some of his
brothers had to date sired children, but all such offspring were,
without exception, illegitimate, and thus ineligible to accede to the
throne. Still, the stakes were high: several were anxious to receive
the prospective parliamentary allowance of £25,000—then a vast
amount in terms of its purchasing power—that all of King George's
sons would receive upon making proper dynastic marriages; with
the gambling and high-living debts that were the hallmark and
shame of the Hanoverian princes, these aging and largely spent men
found themselves in the unseemly position of being run to ground
by creditors, and the allowance would go far in ameliorating this an-

noyance. Thus several of Charlotte's uncles (George himself had apparently given up any thought of remarriage and the production of an heir), all of whom were well into the time of life when most men were greeting not new children but new grandchildren, undertook to perform their dynastic duty by making a run at the inheritance sweepstakes. Unfortunately, they were to many of their nation little more than scoundrels; Shelley characterized them, with biting pith, as "the dregs of their dull race."

Listed by their order of succession rights following George, the prince of Wales, the surviving uncles at the time of Charlotte's death were the dukes of York, Clarence, Kent, Cumberland, Sussex, and Cambridge. The eldest, York, was already married, but the union was childless and looked to stay that way; his wife, even if not yet barren, found her menagerie of monkeys and dogs far more congenial company than she did her racing-obsessed husband. Sussex, of literary inclinations, lived with a nonroyal lady with whom he was very much in love; he refused to put her aside, and thus for all practical purposes excluded himself from the succession. (Years later, Queen Victoria would allow the couple to marry legally, dynastically speaking.) Cambridge, who affected a blond wig and lived in Hanover, in 1818 married legally, again dynastically speaking, but as the youngest son, his odds of either succeeding to the throne or siring the successor to it were held to be imposingly long. Thus it was Clarence, Kent, and Cumberland who joined the fray in earnest.

Passing by Clarence and Kent for a moment, Cumberland, whose facial scars combined unpleasantly with a distorted eye, was not only a national bogeyman whose name was invoked by British mothers to keep their children in line, but was also reputed (admittedly gossip rather than fact) to have murdered his manservant and committed incest with his sister, Sophia. In 1815, Cumberland married a divorced German princess, herself a reputed murderess, who was never welcomed into her husband's family.[2]

Of the three, Clarence stood closest to the throne, preceded only by Wales and York. Though by all accounts genuinely in love with his longtime mistress, Clarence quietly but firmly put the kindly mother of his houseful of ten strapping bastards out the back door. Queen Charlotte quickly chose an eligible German for him, one Princess Adelaide of Saxe-Meiningen, a woman many years younger but evidently willing to marry a plausible heir to the British crown.

Kent, too, had kept a mistress—one of twenty-seven-years' standing. His companionship with this Madame St. Laurent was reputed as happy, though it was childless. A complex individual, ignored in childhood by a mother absorbed with an almost lunatic progression of birthings, Kent grew into a man capable of ferocious cruelty (to military underlings) and loving kindness (especially to Madame St. Laurent).

Like his brother Clarence, Kent too dismissed his true love for the sake of his dynastic duty. His choice for a bride was the thirty-two-year-old widowed Princess Victoire of Leiningen, who had been born a princess of Saxe-Coburg, had been married to the prince of Leiningen,[3] and was sister to the bereft Prince Leopold. Kent and Victoire were married in May 1818, in Coburg, and again in the rites of the Church of England, at Kew, two months later. The latter rite was a double wedding: Clarence took his Adelaide to wife alongside his younger brother. The prince regent gave both brides away. The chief celebrant was the aged Queen Charlotte, her husband locked away, blind and insane, in the stone bosom of Windsor Castle's venerable walls.

As it happened, four of the royal wives brought forth children at nearly the same time, 1819 witnessing a kind of group confinement. In March, both Clarence and Cambridge became fathers, Clarence for the first time legitimately; sadly, neither his daughter nor her sister born two years later long survived. Cambridge's new son, George, was healthy, but a long way down the line. Cumberland's duchess then gave birth in late May to a son who, but for the arrival of a cousin, would have become the eventual ruler not only of Hanover but of the United Kingdom as well.

Little Cumberland's usurper to such power was a fine and lusty daughter born to Kent and Victoire on May 24, 1819. The glittering destiny for this little girl—named Victoria after her mother—was, however, by no means clear at this point, since any number of future Clarence cousins, or a brother of her own, or even, God forbid, a product of George IV's fagged-out loins would have displaced her. But, to her good fortune, it wouldn't be long before any rivals were either eliminated or made redundant.

The removal of the first block in Victoria's path to the throne came a few months after her birth, when in January 1820 the infant princess's father died, and thus the possibility of being preceded by a younger brother vanished. Six days after Kent expired, the death of her grandfather, King George III, put her rakehell uncle Wales, the prince regent, on the throne as King George IV. Her future grew stronger yet as Uncle York died in 1827. The king himself died in 1830, succeeded to the throne by Clarence as William IV; but by this time the new Queen Adelaide was exceedingly unlikely to produce any more children.

Finally, in the spring of 1837, William IV, the only person between Victoria and the throne, was dying. William had been not exactly a bad king, only a stupid and uninspiring one, who did little if anything to repair the damage to the crown's reputation wrought by his immediate predecessors. The British people now realized that the dynasty was on the verge of taking a crucial turn with the accession of a chaste and well-liked princess, one who would become the first sovereign queen since Anne Stuart had died more than twelve decades earlier. Under the late Hanoverians, the monarchy's repute had sunk to its lowest ebb in the nation's modern history, and the vision of the young and promising Princess Victoria inheriting the throne was one all Britain held most earnestly to its collective heart.

The sole snag in this happy scenario was Victoria's mother's "adviser," the widely detested Sir John Conroy, the man to whom the duchess had entrusted the administration of her household as well as the education of her daughter. Conroy was, moreover, popularly thought to be Victoire's lover, and would thus likely control Victoria until she turned eighteen. And depending on Victoria's wishes or degree of ambition, his influence could persist for a good deal longer.

As for the dying King William, his fondest hope was that his niece would grow up safely before he left the world; at eighteen, according to the constitution, a monarch could rule by herself, without the supplementary regent required for a minor on the throne. Since the duchess of Kent had been named regent-designate for her minor daughter, and William hated Victoire, and Conroy would be the power behind the duchess, and William hated him more, the sick king determined, *steeled* himself, to last through May 1837, the month of his niece's coming of age. Meanwhile, Victoria's tutor embroiled Victoire in unseemly quarrels with the king, apparently in an effort to isolate the princess and thus keep her out of the monarch's reach and interference.

As it happened, the girl at the center of these collective ambitions despised Conroy as much as did her uncle William. Observing what she construed to be her mother's unseemly dependence on Conroy hardened the heiress presumptive, adding to her long-festering detestation of a man she regarded as a worthless and treacherous interloper who had been raised far too high by her mother.

William would indeed live just long enough to see Victoria turn eighteen. From the moment of her accession only days after her milestone birthday, the new queen unequivocally demonstrated that she intended to be her own mistress, brooking absolutely no interference from her now-irrelevant mother. Having never been allowed to pass a night away from her mother, on the day she became queen she icily informed the unnerved Victoire that from now on she would sleep alone, in her own bedroom. Moreover, Victoria made it clear that Sir John Conroy would not be allowed to contribute so much as a word about how she would conduct herself as Britain's sovereign.

Upon her accession to the throne, Uncle Leopold of Coburg entered Victoria's life as a major force, completely replacing Victoire's maternal influence. After Princess Charlotte's death in 1817, the mourning but suddenly redundant Leopold had decided to remain in England, partly to ward off any political threat to the allowance Parliament had awarded him on his marriage to Charlotte. He made his home at Claremont House, in Surrey, where he had once lived with Charlotte. There the Coburg prince acted as an important financial supporter to his sister, Victoire, while in the meantime serving as a surrogate father to Princess Victoria. In later years, Claremont House and the security it had afforded in those parlous times would represent the locus of many of Queen Victoria's most pleasant childhood memories. But in 1831, Leopold had been chosen by the newly independent Belgians to reign as their new king,[4] unhappily leaving Victoria in her last six years as a princess solely in the hands of the duchess of Kent's ambition and Conroy's avarice.

Although Victoria as queen quickly made it clear to Leopold that she would not be governed in her political duties by his advice, counsel he offered on a frequent basis via the Brussels-to-London post, she *would* eventually give in to his matchmaking. His greatest ambition was to marry off his English niece, a regnant queen, to his nephew, the near-penniless younger son of his brother, the reigning sovereign in Coburg. It seemed to Leopold that the young man in question, named Albert, had no good reason not to go to England and forge Coburg influence at the elbow of the ruler of the richest and most powerful nation in the world.

Victoria first met her first cousin when he came to England still in his teens to be looked over as future consort material; Albert had for some time been aware that his uncle Leopold savored the notion of his niece and nephew reigning together under his tutelage. But this initial visit produced no sparks, Victoria being far too enthralled with the power and independence that had so recently fallen to her like a perfectly ripened peach. In fact, the young queen at first concluded that she might not even marry at all, ever, fearful that in so doing she would see the exhilarating wonders of her sovereignty threatened. Further, the specter of marriage raised not-quite-savory considerations of bodily functions, a topic that had always rather nauseated her. Soon enough, though, she began to tire of the elderly company that represented the coterie around which her duties turned, finding that she had "no scope," as she put it in her diary, for her "very violent feelings of affection."

Two years later, when a more mature Prince Albert came again to visit the young queen, serendipity and hormones took over, and Victoria fell passionately in love with her now "embellished" (her phrase) cousin, truly one of the handsomest possessors of a royal title in Europe: tall, blue-eyed, a face enticingly framed by light brown hair and "delicate mustachios," slim legs shown off by tight breeches that served as a dramatic counterweight to his broad shoulders and slender waist—all in all, a vision that sent the tiny monarch reeling. It was she who formally proposed marriage—the gender reversal required since she outranked her cousin—and on February 10, 1840, the couple was married in St. George's Chapel, Windsor.

Uncle Leopold had expected a peerage for Albert, but Prime Minister Lord Melbourne regretfully informed his sovereign that Parliament wouldn't take willingly to the proposal of an alien becoming a member of the House of Lords. The question was suspended pending a supposedly more propitious time, but it was never seriously raised again. Victoria herself thought the title of "King-Consort" would be perfect for Albert, but that too was discarded as "un-English." Her husband thus remained plain "Prince Albert," and would wait eighteen years to be honored by his wife with the titular dignity of "Prince Consort."

With her marriage, the girlish virgin queen who had stayed up all night dancing every dance transferred all of her passion to her husband. For twenty years, until the end of his life—and then for forty more until the end of her own—Victoria's obsession with Albert would fill her heart to a point where all else would vie, often unsuccessfully, for what very little space remained.

Late on the evening of November 20, 1840, ten months after her wedding, the twenty-one-year-old queen went into labor. Victoria was only a bit older than her aunt, Princess Charlotte, had been during confinement. Her child, assuming it wasn't stillborn, would be the first direct heir born to a reigning British monarch in almost eight decades. She of course had no way of knowing whether the child would be the fervently hoped-for male—a matter of considerably dynastic moment.

Just after noon the next day, November 21, when the unanesthetized delivery finally produced an apparently perfect infant (when asked if she wanted a sedative, the queen bravely claimed she could "bear pain as well as other people"), Victoria's physician Dr. Charles Locock famously declared to his exhausted sovereign, "Oh, Madam, it is a princess." Quick to show a deep understanding of where her monarchial duty stood, Victoria piped the immortal reply in a high and girlish voice: "Never mind, the next will be a prince." Nonetheless, for safely interposing an heir between Victoria and Uncle Cumberland (by now sixty-nine years old and king of Hanover), Locock was paid £1,000, a princely sum in 1840.[5]

In spite of the infant's less than desirable sex, husband and wife both appreciated Victoria's good fortune in getting through what was at the time an exceedingly dangerous enterprise for any woman. And both were equally pleased in the knowledge that the queen could, indisputably, produce healthy babies and navigate the process with relatively minor trauma. Little doubt existed in either's mind that the next would be the boy who should rightly occupy the throne after his mother. That cleared up, Victoria and Albert got down to simply enjoying the fact of a healthy new baby in the palace.

Referred to, with regal brevity, as "the Child" until its christening, during which ceremony Albert declared it had "behaved with great propriety, and like a Christian," the tiny princess was given the name Victoria, after her mother, and, unavoidably, after her mother's mother, with whom the queen was still not fully congenial. The little princess soon became known in the family as "Vicky," or, most familiarly, "Pussy"; two months after her birth she officially became the "Princess Royal." The title, a dignity bestowed by the monarch at his or her personal preference, had first been employed by King Charles I for his daughter some two centuries earlier. It signified the sovereign's eldest female issue, though in reality it added nothing in constitutional terms to the bearer's stature.[6]

Faced with the probability that their daughter's adult life would most likely be passed as ornament and breeder in some Continental court, the parents—particularly Albert—set about deciding how to capitalize on these circumstances, which is to say how this princess might best further her father's deeply held liberal political ideals. But while this future bearer of the Albertine vision remained an infant, Albert simply reveled in the joys of a father who truly and unabashedly loved his child.

His hopes for this child had their roots in Albert's own earliest days growing up in Coburg. The duchy was small and, in the larger scheme of European affairs, insignificant, and thus its royal family was removed from both the pleasures and the dangers of international affairs. Only Prince Leopold's union with Princess Charlotte of Wales had brought excitement and fame to Coburg, before Leopold's sister again brought a connection with the British royal family through her own marriage to the duke of Kent. Perhaps as a result of its isolation from larger neighbors and issues, some of the ducal family—virtually the only populace resembling "society" that Coburg possessed—desired a more liberated community, one less constrained by the conservative precepts that had for centuries formed the outlook of the larger and more powerful European courts. Young Prince Albert especially grew up conjuring a broad-minded vision of the relationship between those who govern and those who are governed, his model being the state of social affairs as they were developing in parliamentary Britain.

An early trauma in Albert's life was the disappearance of his mother, a family tragedy that occurred when he was four. Duchess Louise, unable any longer to suffer alone her aged husband's gross infidelities, sought comfort in the arms and sympathies of a young officer in Coburg's army. Though she deeply loved her two young sons (Albert's brother Ernest was a year older), the pressures of an empty and ill-matched marriage overcame her wedding vows, and Louise ran away with the officer. Duke Ernest divorced his wife in absentia, and neither Albert nor his brother ever saw their mother again. She would die eight years later, in 1831. The duke remarried. Both boys formed a happy relationship with their new stepmother (Princess Marie of Würtemberg, who also happened to be their cousin), yet Albert would never cease to cherish his mother's memory, romanticizing her escape if at the same time deploring her injury to a royal "system" that was meant to keep the thrones of Europe on sturdy foundations.

Musically talented—a gift two of his own daughters would inherit—and a scholar from his youth, Albert possessed an intelligence more ordered and far better grounded than that of his future wife. From earliest schooldays he willed himself to soak up as much as he could of the scholarly disciplines: ancient and modern history, English, mathematics, French, Latin composition, the natural sciences, music—all of which was interspersed with "bodily exercises . . . and amusement." His learning revolved around an unvaried schedule, from 6:00 A.M. until 8:00 P.M. his day a blueprint of orderly and substantive study. Unfortunately, a habit of early retiring became so thoroughly a part of this routine that for the rest of his life he greatly disliked the late hours that were the norm of European court life.[7]

As the British queen's consort, Albert became irrevocably tied to his adopted country's liberal government—albeit a liberalism that was still a very long way from late twentieth-century notions of what constitutes enlightened government—and he began planning in earnest how his future children might realize his ideal, wherein parliamentary government was presided over by constitutional, nonreactionary, fair-minded monarchs who would as a cardinal virtue of their station remain above party politics. The prince knew that for any boys born to him and Victoria, their destinies most likely would be tied to Britain, the eldest as heir, the younger sons in high positions in the army and navy. But daughters, he recognized, could be instruments for spreading British enlightenment to the Continental courts in which they would almost certainly marry.

The queen maintained a certain distance from her firstborn, in the manner of mothers of her class. But despite any disappointment Albert may have initially felt at being presented with a girl child, he unequivocally took Vicky into the center of his heart. It was a rapture that would last the rest of his lifetime, and one reciprocated for every day of his daughter's own lifetime as well. The depth of the prince's adoration for his firstborn would not be repeated with any of the eight children who came after Vicky, a girl who started out and always remained truly extraordinary, her amazing future capabilities by all accounts apparent to her enchanted father from her earliest days.

The degree of Albert's involvement with his children first became evident in the prince's early criticism of the nursery routine to which Vicky was subjected. Few upper-class wives in nineteenth-century Britain provided their offspring with what we now fatuously refer to as "quality" time, and the proposition that a regnant queen would or could sublimate her substantive official duties to the mundane requirements of child care would never have been considered by Victoria. She saw her new baby twice a day—at bath time and in her own dressing room while she changed for dinner—as well as at a smattering of family gatherings. The monarch took pride in her first infant and having produced her, but was far too busy to give herself over to actually rearing Vicky.

Both parents actively attempted to instill a sense of cultivated breeding in their children, not least to guide their treatment toward those not of their own rank, particularly servants, of whom a galaxy invariably cosseted the family from the impositions of ordinary life. Victoria and Albert wanted as well to ensure that their offspring would understand why their exalted positions existed at all in the order of society. They were prohibited from the casual friendships children normally form with other children, Albert's justification being that such relations could all too easily ricochet with importunings on their intimacy. Victoria always thought and wrote of herself as being "above" matters of rank; but in fact, nothing is further from an accurate interpretation of her deepest held views. In the first place, the sovereign understood precious little of the lives of her humblest subjects. Furthermore, she considered the poor virtually another race from her own. She and Albert expended vast amounts of energy in physically separating themselves from common mortals, and in her widowhood such separation would become a four-decade-long obsession. Such thinking must inexorably have permeated her children's consciousnesses, keeping them essentially ignorant of the real workings of ordinary humankind over so many of whom their mother reigned.

Albert cleaved not nearly so tightly to Victoria as she to him. Though he was throughout their married life unquestionably in love with Victoria—never did any of the sexual opportunities at court cause him to step down from the plane of perfect marital fidelity, not so much as even to engage in a flirtation—he was able to find the emotional room for his children that always eluded his wife. It seemed to many who observed the family that Victoria's happiness in her children was more for the joy they brought Albert than for any deep attachment of her own. The sovereign's own deepest ties to her offspring were for whatever help they could bring to assuaging the broad and endless demands that came with her unique position.

The queen's imperfections as a mother—real though perhaps unfairly magnified because of her enormous role in history—were not returned in bitterness or in any lack of love on the part of her children. But they would be manifested by what happened in her offsprings' own lives as a result of Queen Victoria's too-often malign influence.

For the less busy Albert, Vicky's care was another matter. Politically speaking, he was not much more than an ornament in the earliest days of his marriage; his wife flatly refused his offers to help with any of her real work, instead delegating to him such inconsequentialities as blotting the signature she applied to state papers. The queen calculated, tersely but in the realistic way in which she often judged such things, that "Albert is in my house and not I in his." Though during her first pregnancy the queen began to discover how useful Albert could be to her, his days still held many empty hours, and he thus found time, and was so inclined, to attend lovingly to his daughter, even in her nursery. But his presence there itself created problems, when the women charged with overseeing nursery procedures outspokenly resented what they characterized as the prince's "interference" in their previously unchallenged domain.

Albert's particular nemesis in his domestic life was the queen's own former governess, Baroness Louise Lehzen,[8] who as Victoria's intimate was general factotum and de facto, if not titular, head of the royal home. For many years, this formidable German lady had stood between Victoria and the political tug-of-war to which the duchess of Kent and Conroy had subjected her adolescent charge. Kept by the duchess from any unsupervised contact with the outside world, Victoria clung to the loving and sympathetic Lehzen with a touching ferocity. After her accession to the throne, neither Victoria nor Lehzen relaxed the closeness of their relationship, which in the early days of the queen's marriage meant that Albert often came out on the short end of his wife's considerations.

Before her daughter's birth, the only duties Victoria had officially assigned to Albert amounted to little more than titular supervision over the private domestic arrangements of Buckingham Palace and Windsor Castle, the couple's two homes. But the prince's authority was often thwarted by resentful functionaries, the palace and castle having for centuries represented the uncontested fiefdoms of a vast panoply of chamberlains, officials, stewards, high servants, and free-floating hangers-on.

With Albert's ascendancy over the monarchy's domestic affairs, which would shortly spell the end of Lehzen's regime, the nursery and its precious cargo was elevated into what became virtually a department of state. To oversee all those responsible for the care of his babies, Albert wrote detailed job descriptions for each staff position, including the various nurses, nurserymaids, assistant nurserymaids, and wet nurses (Queen Victoria most emphatically did *not* breast-feed her babies). The extraordinarily stringent security arrangements that the prince devised would soon mean the introduction of convoluted hallways, secret passages, manned guardrooms blocking access to the nursery, and elaborate locks—the master keys kept, with delicious exclusivity, by Albert himself. The most fundamental rule governing this new, military structure was that the infant princess royal and her future siblings must never, under any circumstances, be left alone—an irony in that the queen herself had so resented that status as a child. And as a reminder that court etiquette held sway here as much as it did in the palace's public rooms, the rules specified that the wet nurse must remain standing while feeding any royal child, obviously in recognition of the infant's exalted station.

It was during her first pregnancy and postnatal recovery that the queen initially suspected Albert's potential talent for dealing with her *official* business. Her condition caused her to feel unwell at this time[9] and thus often indisposed to attend to concerns of state, so Victoria hesitatingly began to ask Albert to write memos and minutes to the relevant ministers. "The Prince's observations," as Prime Minister Lord Melbourne came to characterize Albert's efforts, soon earned the respect of the men who managed Britain's complex enterprises.

The queen, too, came deeply to appreciate Albert's abilities, his stock soaring when she grasped that he could with growing effect put forward her positions and prejudices with the ministers to whom she daily gave audiences. Victoria's premarital fondness for and dependence on her first prime minister, Lord Melbourne, had been thought a dangerous thing, leading to serious difficulties between the sovereign and Melbourne's successor when Melbourne lost office. It was Albert who diplomatically, and with unarguable logic, taught his wife that the breaking of ties to any minister had to be faced to prevent constitutional injury to the monarchy. In keeping with the passionate nature of her personality, Victoria soon thereafter came under the almost complete tutelage of her prince. One official would write of Albert as "in fact, tho' not in name, Her Majesty's Private Secretary." Another minister went further, stating that the queen had turned Albert into a virtual "King-Consort," which had, ironically, been the title she suggested for him when the marriage negotiations first got underway.

As the queen was not a woman to cast her passions over wide waters, so Lehzen fell once Albert sought to implement his nursery controls. The baroness, accepting her defeat and unwilling to assume a lesser position in court, returned in 1842 to her native Hanover. The queen was saddened by the loss, but showed little real distress. Albert was, of course, elated at his rival's departure. He wrote of Lehzen as "a crazy, common, stupid intriguer," adding that "all the disagreeableness I suffer comes from one and the same person and that is precisely the person whom Victoria chooses for her friend and confidante." With Lehzen's retreat Albert lost his major domestic adversary, and was in an unopposed position to exercise control over the nursery staff. And his wife found the prize she would come to treasure more than anything else in the world: her own and Albert's near self-sufficiency from intellectual or emotional dependence on anyone else in the world.

A year after Vicky's birth, the already precocious tot found herself joined by another baby in the nursery. This time it was a boy—the heir apparent to the throne, christened Albert Edward, and for the next seven decades to be known as "Bertie" by his family. The royal couple and most of their subjects rejoiced in the knowledge that the nation's sovereignty would revert to a king and the "natural" order of things would thereby someday be restored. In 1841, no one could have guessed just how long that was going to take, nor how totally both Britain and the world would become accustomed to the idea of Queen Victoria representing the "natural" order of things.

However Queen Victoria's political life is judged—and if in the assessment there is much for her detractors to deplore, there is also much for her admirers to praise—her conduct as a mother started out as wanting and ended up as a tragic record of lost opportunities, unforgivable interference, and self-centered demands—especially that her own interests and needs invariably be placed before those of her children. These deficiencies were almost impossible for her children to ignore or challenge because of the all but unassailable position their mother held as the head of a larger family that would by the end of her reign encompass a quarter of the earth's people.

Victoria didn't dislike children, as the low points of her relationships with her own might suggest. It was more a case of not actively *liking* them. The permutations of her own personality, and her unshakable appreciation of the position she held, kept her from loosening her dignity enough to give them, especially the older ones, the kind of natural affection children thrive on. Her eldest daughter would claim always to remember the "unclouded happiness" of her youth; but the sources of the shortcomings that would mar Vicky's adult life began during her earliest years, and many of these problems were maternal in genesis. A year after the princess royal's birth, Victoria wrote to her uncle Leopold that Vicky was "quite a dear little companion . . . [but] is sadly backward." Perhaps the queen's comments simply reflected her inability to understand, or empathize with, a child—*any* child. Perhaps they sprang from a possessive love for Albert that would tolerate little interference from any other quarter. Possibly they were an early sign of awareness that Victoria could see the dark places in her daughter's personality. Understanding what led the queen to this appraisal of a little girl almost universally admired for her lively intelligence lies at the heart of understanding the course of Vicky's calamitous life.

Early on, it seemed that Albert's infatuation with Vicky was such that Victoria's presence was neither particularly needed nor wanted in his molding of a perfect daughter. He was to sculpt in his daughter an unwavering confidence in herself, from her earliest days. As all those around her—courtiers, nursemaids, relatives, visitors to whom she was shown off by her proud parents—fawned over the young princess royal, this sense of superiority, or, perhaps more precisely, the inability to believe she could be wrong, was inexorably buttressed. From those earliest years, the little girl stored up constant approbation, in reserve for the day when she would turn it disastrously loose in her adult life.

Soon after Bertie's birth, Albert's chief political, moral, and personal adviser and fellow Coburger, Baron Stockmar, a man as convinced of his own rightness as he was that the sun would rise each morning, devised at his master's behest an educational plan for the eighteen-month-old Vicky and her newborn brother. Designed along lines that he knew would gratify his royal employer, Stock-mar's forty-six-page memorandum informed the queen and the prince that, as difficult as it would be adequately to educate two children of such exalted station and futures, "a dereliction of their most sacred Duties" would be the result if they did not try. Since Stockmar himself understood this would be a near-impossible task for parents so young, he volunteered that it would be his pleasure to take on the hard work involved in this mission. Victoria and Albert speedily assented. In Stockmar's undertaking to "strengthen the good [and] subdue . . . the evil dispositions of our Nature," Vicky would come through relatively psychologically intact. Her brother Bertie would not be so fortunate.

2

The Forties

Victoria and Albert's third baby came hard in the wake of the first and second. Alice Maud Mary was born at Buckingham Palace at the dawn of a pleasant spring morning in April 1843. With her lifelong penchant for recording the minutiae of her life in her diary, the queen characterized the labor preceding Alice's birth as severe but gratefully brief. The whole thing had taken about four hours after her waters broke an hour or two after midnight. Fortunately, none of the difficulties that had marred the prince of Wales's birth were repeated—Victoria recalled that experience as the most arduous of her deliveries. The queen expressed some irritation that no high officers of state except Lord Liverpool had seen fit to present themselves for the occasion, but it had been the short labor and the inconveniently early hours that were responsible for the paucity of official witnesses to the baby's authenticity as a real princess. To the mother's gratification, the high and mighty did begin to flow into the palace in the hours following the infant's safe delivery.

Neither parent seemed to mind that the child was another girl. Bertie already safely represented the normal heir to the throne, and though another male would have been appreciated in an era when disease routinely carried off even babies born to the highest, both queen and prince knew more children could surely be expected. However, a handful of critics publicly sniffed at the child's sex, one of them clearly intimating the mother had some control in the matter by characterizing Alice's sex as a "disappointment . . . and I think there was a general wish in the country that the succession should have been strengthened by another male descendant. . . ." Even the Privy Council appeared to concur in the mild sense of regret, sending Albert an address of both "congratulation and condolence."

Public scolds aside, one of the queen's happiest subjects at Alice's birth was Lord Melbourne. The former prime minister and passionate admirer of the queen, now two years out of Downing Street, had recently suffered a crippling stroke. But harder on him than his new physical limitations was the fact that he no longer enjoyed near-daily intimacy with the young sovereign, a liaison that had long been his by right of office. With the thoughtfulness that formed an underpinning of Prince Albert's personality, the queen's husband ordered that Melbourne be immediately notified of the expected child's safe delivery wherever he might be at the time. When word reached him at his country estate that the baby was born and was to be named Alice, the former premier was beside himself with joy. It seemed that he and Victoria had once carried on a discussion in which they ranked the intrinsic beauty of female names, and it was "Alice" that he had liked best. The young sovereign, who still venerated the elder statesman, had tucked away the fact, and by giving the name to her second daughter, honored the man who had taught her to be a queen.

Alice's birth was soon to lead Victoria and Albert to the startling deduction that their living quarters in Buckingham Palace had grown insufficient, "cramped," as the queen now began to characterize them. Though a multitude of her humble subjects might have fitted into the immense palace with unimagined comfort, the kingdom's preeminent figure required a setting more suited to glorifying the living symbol of the nation and her family.

In fairness to Victoria's discontent, the design of Buckingham Palace was not, in fact, especially well suited to the needs of a large family, regardless of the undoubted splendors of its vast state rooms and the passages that were wider than many of London's thoroughfares. Much of the U-shaped building (the fourth wing—the east front—wouldn't be built until 1847, turning the U into an enclosed quadrangle) was taken up by grandiose chambers of state never meant to provide homely comforts. The several thousand square feet of less palatial apartments in the north wing were required for Victoria and Albert's own social and official use, and adequate nurseries could not be squeezed in. The attic rooms used for the royal children were fairly commodious, but Mr. Blore, the architect called in to advise how those quarters might be increased, reported that unhealthy smells of oil and glue from the basement had hopelessly permeated the palace's interstices to the top floor. What was more, anything described as an attic was held by the royal infants' parents to be out of keeping with its tiny occupants' exalted status. Blore suggested adding the east front, and that the palace engineers be allowed to "alter the drains." Since something in the range of £1 million had been spent on this palace alone only twenty years earlier by Victoria's uncle George IV, the British taxpayer and the taxpayers' representatives in Parliament reacted to Blore's suggestions with a predictable outburst of fiscal indignation.

As it happened, lack of space was of only secondary concern to the queen. What really upset Victoria were the nearby horrors of an Industrial Age metropolis, the squalid slums of Pimlico that oozed over the Thames floodplain virtually bang up against the palace: the sooty and leaden air, fouled by countless stoves and fireplaces, and the smoldering garbage tips that released a Stygian pall of smoke over and under and through every corner of the capital; not to mention the multitudes of noisy, inquisitive, and unclean people, some of whom had unapologetically broken into the palace in search of relief from their degraded state.

The royal family's usual escape from such disagreeableness was found at Windsor. Compared with Buckingham Palace, the Thames-side castle was regarded by Victoria and Albert as a paradise. This venerable home of British monarchy, a fortress whose stone walls had since the eleventh century sheltered the nation's sovereigns from enemies and the elements, had at the behest of King George IV (while still regent) been transformed into a palace whose French Rococo and mock-Gothic splendors overwhelmed residents and visitors alike. The castle's romantic associations were especially pungent for Victoria: it was at the top of the splendorously named Sovereign's Stairs where in 1839 she first looked upon Albert.

Unfortunately, Windsor's delightfully endless space, sumptuously decorated chambers, and blessed twenty-mile remove from Pimlico's grit, were offset by a number of disagreeable factors, not least the primitive sanitary arrangements that often caused a nearly overpowering stink, particularly when rainstorms overtaxed the drains. Randomly sited cesspits and foul odors in the summer from the sludgy Thames served only to increase Victoria's impatience to get away from everything that was old. Windsor wouldn't, alas, do. What she and Albert coveted for themselves and their growing family was cleanliness, space, and—very high on her wish list—privacy.[1]

Money was never much of a barrier to the monarch's doing as she wished. A financially cautious monarch when compared to her immediate predecessors, her parliamentary income of £385,000 a year (not to mention vast personal property) nevertheless permitted indulgences. With the wherewithal to make their desires reality, within months of Alice's birth Victoria and Albert began to search for a suitable place to which they could escape from London and Windsor when they felt cramped, or when the weather was bad, or simply when the mood struck. Though they set no mandate that their retreat be located near to the sea, Victoria had long been predisposed to finding a haven along her island kingdom's shores. Thus, when an estate on the Isle of Wight's northern coastline conveniently came on the market, bringing to the surface memories of sun-filled days she had spent on the island as a young girl, there began a series of sharp negotiations by Albert with the seller. Soon the couple found themselves the owners of Osborne, a word which throughout the queen's life she would preface with "dear."

Though because of the new occupants' position Osborne House

was to grow into an unmistakably "royal" residence, it remained relatively unostentatious: the family's own quarters were compact and (compared with Buckingham Palace or Windsor Castle) *gemütlich*. Many of the furnishings were bought from London's commercial emporia, and special delights were installed for the children—including a full-size "Swiss Cottage" where the young princes and princesses could practice some of the household pursuits their mother's humbler subjects would know. Here, too, they began at early ages to learn responsibility, the girls to clean the place and prepare simple teas for their parents, the boys to see to it that the gardens were kept in trim.

It was at Osborne that the royal children would run and frolic to their hearts' content, nearly free from etiquette and rules, courtiers, instructors, and governesses. In this enchanted place they would play on their private beach, dig for shells and build fragile castles in the white sand, and pass privileged childhoods within the secure walls of England's most sequestered royal home.

Already, though, the relationships between the queen's three children were being shaped by pressures whose consequences would be felt throughout their lives. Vicky, the cynosure of unbounded praise from within the royal household, was growing into a young girl both proud of her singularity and unwilling to share it with a younger brother she knew was destined to have a future far more consequential than her own, despite her unique rank as princess royal. Her childish jealousy of Bertie—a resentment that was both reluctant and guileless, while he never less than adored her—was obvious early on. She called him "the Boy" and flaunted her obvious intellectual gifts over a child not nearly so blessed as herself.

The educational regimen that Baron Stockmar had set out for the children, with the parents' approval, was one designed above all else to oversee "the Child's natural Instincts" and "keep its Mind pure." Vicky and Bertie, to whom this directive would most stringently be applied in the coming years, would react to it in very different ways. Bertie, whose natural bent was not academic, resisted. But Vicky became her tutor's perfect vessel and, in the doing, her parents' pride,

Stockmar having instilled in the girl from the start a militant, some-times heedless, self-assurance. The potential dangers of their daugh-ter's brilliance were, of course, unseen by her proud and delighted parents. To her father, Vicky soon seemed a paragon of perfection. Vicky's brother suffered in his mother's evaluation the misfortune of coming up short in intellectual comparisons. Many bitter weeds would go into the brew that poisoned more than a half century of relations between Victoria and this son. But one of the vilest was the early and invidious contrasting of Bertie and Vicky, the latter in-evitably prevailing in their mother's eye. Victoria never viewed her eldest son in the light of his own merits and substantial qualities, but rather in comparison to his siblings' strengths and, even more cruelly, to how far his intellect stood below that of his father.

Throughout her childhood, Vicky's egotism represented one of her least admirable traits, a sense of superiority that would for years have her lording her natural authority over her sisters and brothers as well as the servants, and even, sometimes, her mother's ministers. It would lead Bertie into developing a closer relationship with Alice; when he first began to talk, his speech was stigmatized by a minor stutter, which made him appear even more disadvantaged when compared to his eldest sister. From Alice's earliest days, she possessed the ability to soothe the prince of Wales's frustrations and draw out the best in him, a quality of innate kindness his siblings would long remember. The bright but overindulged Vicky found great pleasure in impressing her mother's courtiers, while Alice would develop a sense, almost completely missing in the princess royal, of when to retreat—one of Vicky's most profound failings in adult life.

This first trio of nursery inmates was joined in August 1844 by a fourth royal child. Prince Alfred—his family diminutized it to "Affie," a name that stuck for all fifty-six years of his life—was from birth preordained for a non-English adulthood. In a joint decision with Albert's childless brother, Ernest (who succeeded to Coburg's throne the year Affie was born), Victoria and Albert designated this son as his uncle's heir. Bertie would have been the normal successor (after Albert himself), but as prince of Wales his future sovereignty

of the kingdom was, of course, already set. The family firmly believed Coburg required a full-time monarch. And so Affie would
from earliest childhood be taught to love, as his mother would put
it, "the dear small country to which he belongs in every respect, as
does his papa." He grew up far the handsomest of Victoria's sons,
little suspecting that time would bring a strange, ultimately ruinous
mixture of adventure and tragedy, and a life more distant from his
mother than that of any of his siblings.

With the regularity of a metronome, the royal family continued to
multiply. Vicky and Bertie, Alice and Affie, were shortly joined by
another sister. The fifth child—born in 1846, one day after the
queen's twenty-seventh birthday—was named Helena, in honor of
Hélène, the duchess of Orléans, her godmother. For the whole of
her life, Helena would be called "Lenchen." The Germanized pet
name—the diminutive German ending *chen* added to her fore-
shortened given name—was, of course, her father's idea. In common
with all the children born after Vicky and Bertie, Lenchen would
cause her parents far less concern, both personal and dynastic, than
did their first two. Even in obstetrical terms, Lenchen's arrival was
relatively little distinguished: though the labor was protracted, both
mother and child recovered swiftly. What did set Lenchen apart in
the family was that among her female siblings she would grow into
the healthiest, most robust, and least remarkable of them all.

By the time of her arrival, Lenchen's royal rank had been
rendered dynastically unimportant, comparatively speaking. The
succession was already well seen to, what with Bertie and Affie in-
terposed against any plausible chance that one of the queen's odi-
ous uncles or cousins might ever occupy the throne. Vicky clearly
had tremendous things in store for her, her parents already beginning to hint at with which future mate she would choose to shape
a brilliantly democratic European world. It seemed Alice might
even make a match approaching Vicky's in its furthering of their father's dream. But little thought was given to Lenchen in Albert's
ambitious reveries; she didn't, in fact, really seem needed toward

any political end. Her realization of this would first be a lead weight pulling her down to mediocrity; later it became her very means of freeing herself from a world that all but overwhelmed her.

At her christening, held at Buckingham Palace, Lenchen cried throughout, disgracing herself in the estimation of those who held that royal babies were expected to behave more worthily than ordinary infants. Gaslight, then novel and thought very modern, was used for the first time at a royal christening, the device's nozzles ventilated—as the queen approvingly noted—by Professor Faraday's wonderful technique of drawing off the fumes down the stems of the candelabras.

Lenchen's birth prompted another of her parents' domestic memoranda, this one officially dividing their brood into two categories. Vicky and Bertie would now graduate from nursery status into a new classroom category, named for the "Development of [Their] Character." The younger trio of Alice, Affie, and Lenchen comprised the official "Nursery" genus.

In her new prestige shared with Bertie, the princess royal—now six years old—was assigned the Victorian equivalent of a standard work week. Her studies in the classroom, supervised by a new governess named Sarah Hildyard, were in the morning hours made up of arithmetic, poetry, history, and dictation, with geography, more history, and the study of her royal progenitors completing the afternoon. Occasional lessons in music and art, dancing and scripture added to Stockmar's blueprint for filling her august head and formidable future. To no one's particular surprise but everyone's pleasure, Vicky excelled in almost everything. Her ability in art showed a special faculty, clearly inherited from a mother whose gift with watercolors approached professional command.

When eventually Alice left the nursery category for the classroom, her relationship with Vicky began to deepen into a dependence of the younger sister on the older, a closeness that would help both get through their difficult and connected futures. Now sharing a bedroom and clothes, the two became confidantes in a world where nonservant outsiders were so rare as to be almost nonexistent. What strains did develop between them stemmed from Alice's being put off by her sister's adroitness at almost everything. Vicky, on the other hand, was to learn the occasional lesson in humility from Alice's far gentler and less imperious nature. In later life the princess royal would fondly recall Alice's early diplomatic skills within the family and with their governess, proficiency that would be a long time coming to Vicky herself.

Few things excited Queen Victoria as much as death. Mourning in all its permutations and intricacies was one of the great constants of her life, eventually becoming for the monarch something near obsession. The year 1848 started off with a big death in the family, when Albert's step-grandmother died on February 23. "My poor Albert is quite broken down by this and is so pale and sad it breaks my heart," the queen, once again pregnant, wrote; but the conclusion probably reflected more her own growing fixation than her husband's grief. Nonetheless, since it made him sad, it made her wretched. The death came on the cusp of the Continent's troubles, which she took to be a threat to her throne in what came to be called the Year of Revolutions. In Britain, it did seem to some that the threat from the so-called Chartists might have an outside chance of sweeping the monarchy aside in favor of a republic, and thus her concerns weren't entirely without substance.

The events unfolding at a startling pace in Europe seemed to confirm Victoria's fear. Three days after Albert's grandmother died, revolution erupted in Paris, ordinary workers protesting a government that had become every bit as distasteful as the pre-guillotine *ancien régime*. The target of the wrathful French was the debased and disreputable rule of the Orléans monarchy, headed by the "Citizen-King" and self-styled liberal, Louis-Philippe of the House of Bourbon and line of Orléans. When a throng marched on the Tuileries to demand his head, the monarch had just enough time to disguise himself as a woman and scurry out the back door before the mob smashed in his front door. So too did Uncle Leopold's throne in Brussels come under severe threat, but the Belgian crown luckily held, leading a relieved Leopold to write his niece wondering "what will become of us."

When the bedraggled remains of the French royal family came streaming into England toward the end of February (Louis-Philippe now traveled under the name "Mr. Smith," wore a cap and goggles, hadn't shaved for some days, and looked no more royal than the skipper of the fishing smack that had transported him away from French soil), Victoria became so agitated that Albert feared she might lose the baby whose time was almost on her. The seven-year-old princess royal remembered in later years her amazement at seeing her father collect clothing and other necessities of life for the refugees, who had arrived with little more than the (admittedly expensive) clothes on their backs. Even Vicky's young siblings were old enough to recognize the spectacle as a blow to their caste's dignity.

The Parisians' revolt was the explosion that would set off more revolutions and insurrections all over the Continent. Even heretofore-secure Britain would not escape the storm unscathed, the crisis abroad not long in generating seriously popular resentment at the social inequities that were rampant in Victoria's kingdom. Trade disruptions throughout Europe soon resounded in Britain, causing unemployment to mount to frightening levels. The reaction of the Whig government was not to adopt fiscal measures directed at overcoming the worst effects of this unemployment, but instead to increase spending on a militia prepared to combat public unrest. The result among disaffected workers was predictable and swift, their resentments quickly threatening to turn into what might end in catastrophic disorder.

On Saturday, March 18, the usual throng of courtiers and government ministers had gathered for the queen's sixth birthing. By coincidence, on that day the House of Commons was debating what should be done about the appalling conditions of childbirth among the poor (which is to say, most) mothers of the nation; the safety and comfort for these humbler of the queen's subjects were dropping toward crisis levels.

Interrupting her book—*The Letters of W. von Humboldt to a Female Friend*, recommended by the solicitous Stockmar as "being written specially for ladies"—Victoria had early that day taken to her lying-in. The obstetrician Dr. Locock was the chief physician in attendance. Mrs. Lilly the midwife was in attendance also, as was always the case—in fact, the thoughtful Prince Albert now routinely sent the royal carriage around to her home in Camberwell whenever his wife's time rolled around again, meaning that the midwife's neighborhood, and soon enough the whole city, would know another prince or princess was about to come into the world.

As twenty-one blasts from guns at the Tower of London and in Hyde Park announced that the queen had been delivered of a princess (101 shots would have betokened a prince), news was just coming into the city of startling events in Berlin. The Prussian king's arch-reactionary government had come under attack from the mobs in the capital's streets, and the monarch and his family had been forced to lie "flat on [their] bellies inside the Palace as bullets whistled about outside." News of this sort was likely to cause the weakened Victoria near as much distress as had the birth of her baby.

At the end of the day Albert noted with reverent thanks in a letter to Stockmar that both mother and daughter had come through "perfectly well." He added that this deliverance of his wife, who had suffered "many moral shocks" of late, had served to increase his gratitude at having fathered another healthy daughter. In the House of Lords, the Marquess of Lansdowne begged his colleagues' concurrence in a motion of commendation for the queen's recovery, and in the Commons Lord John Russell begged much the same thing. No dissenters were noted on either motion.

The new princess was called Louise Caroline Alberta, names that were most meaningful to and revered by the prince, rather than by his wife, who had chosen all the earlier children's names. Louise was for Albert's own mother (who had, of course, also been Victoria's aunt), of tragic life but now tender memory. Caroline commemorated his step-grandmother, the dowager duchess of Gotha, who had died a few days before his daughter's birth. Alberta, the third name, was for himself, which greatly pleased the queen, Louise being the only one of his daughters so named. Until the infant princess left the nursery, the family would call her "Loo-Loo."

Unsettled by the insurgencies preceding Louise's appearance, to Albert's orderly mind even the birth order of his children seemed to be a sign of trouble. Up to now it had been girl boy, girl boy, girl. . . . Number six wasn't the expected male child to make everything neat and even, lending the new babe's beginnings in life a slight fillip of paternal annoyance. Unfortunately, Princess Louise would annoy her family, particularly her mother and her sisters, for a very large part of the rest of their lives.

As the new mother recuperated, the frightening din of the Chartists' tumbrels shadowed Victoria's joy at her baby's safe delivery, especially when those tumbrels began to head not only toward the political bastions of the country but against the walls of Buckingham Palace as well. April 3, the day Victoria left her confinement bed, she was given word that in one week these homegrown revolutionaries, who were called after the "Chart" of mass signature petitions they wished to deliver to Parliament, planned to mount a mass demonstration at Kennington Common. The protesters meant their actions to be law-abiding, but the first real specter of *any* substantive lower-class challenge to the establishment terrified those who believed that to have been born at the top of the social order was an act of divine planning. Ostensibly representing a mass plea for parliamentary reform—votes for all adult males, abolition of property qualifications for the vote, secret ballot, equal electoral districts—the Chartists fatally stirred their ideas with the stick of socialism, the philosophy still damp from the blood of the guillotine and anathema to the queen and the higher orders at whose head she symbolically stood.

Buoyed by the events across the Channel, the Chartists claimed to have gathered 6 million signatures—a figure (had it been anywhere near accurate) that would have represented a stunningly high proportion of Britain's male population. The actual chart weighed 584 pounds, and was ferried to the House of Commons spread over three cabs. Though most of those who signed would not have supported the tiny minority of revolutionaries advocating actual violence to achieve their objectives, the government was nonetheless sufficiently frightened to enlist 70,000 special constables charged with maintaining "social order." In the end, parliamentary officials would dismiss the Chartists with the sneer that they had turned in "only" 2 million signatures. (In fact, the chart turned out to have contained 23,000 signatures.) Though the upper classes viewed all this through the prism of a Europe that was in many places really on fire (though on the Continent, too, the revolutionaries' aims were mostly successfully thwarted by the established governments), soon the prevailing mentality said that Britain's immutable institutions survived because they were superior to those of their foreign counterparts. Notwithstanding, the bitterness left from this affair would after not too many years turn into an attack on the British status quo by a far more sophisticated and successful proletarian political movement.

The queen observed this drama with barely concealed alarm. Sheltering the French royal family at the estate of Claremont, in Surrey, and the more recently arrived prince and princess of Prussia at Buckingham Palace, she suffered one more shock when in the middle of it all her ministers privately advised Albert to take his family to the countryside for their own safety. Victoria not surprisingly resented that her baby, only two weeks old, should be subjected to this indignity. As for her own medical condition, postnatal women of the higher classes were expected to go no farther than their couch for six weeks. Two days before the Chartists were due to have their gathering on Kennington Common, the royal family set off for the Isle of Wight and Osborne, the departure guarded by scores of special police constables. The public was informed that the trip represented nothing more than a rest for the queen; in reality it was an escape from a threat by the sovereign's own subjects. Worried that her flight might be seen by the public for exactly what it was, Albert sent an equerry to London to measure the feelings of his wife's ordinary subjects. The aide reported back to the prince that most people seemed relieved that the queen had been removed from harm's way, declaring that he "never heard one person express a belief that her departure was due to personal alarm."

Even when the worst had passed and the Chartists melted away like spring snow after the Kennington episode, the prince of Wales was still each night put to bed as near his parents as possible. When a group of unidentified but worrisomely scruffy men disembarked from the ferry at Cowes, the island's port nearest the royal estate, Osborne's menservants were ordered to take arms to defend their queen. Though it turned out the shabby visitors had simply been merrymakers on a seaside pleasure trip, the sovereign thought the whole business a close shave. What the queen would always refer to as "our revolution" provided her and her family not so much a lesson in democracy as one in the dangers of letting democracy get out of hand.

Making the best of a bad business, the royal family was determined to enjoy an untimely holiday at the new seaside villa which Albert's own cleverness was playing such a large part in turning into the family's dream home. The sweeping terraces designed by the prince, together with the magnificent new trees—bays and corks and evergreen oaks—were lending the still-unfinished estate a beauty it hadn't known before. As for the newest child, the infant Princess Louise proved to be a placid soul, giving neither her parents nor her nurses much trouble. The queen was even so pleased with her that the baby was, unusually, brought in to join her siblings at family teatime.

But the days of escape ended, and Louise was due to be christened, and such christening had to be carried out in London. The prince of Prussia had been wanted as a godparent, but the queen's ministers reasoned it might not do to employ a member of a foreign family whose throne might yet be swept away. The Prussians were likely hurt by Victoria and Albert's acquiescence in this unwonted interference, but as refugee-guests they held their tongues.

The baby's christening went off almost without incident, with little other than Princess Alice's fidgetiness of which to make note. Near the end, though, the queen's elderly and probably senile aunt Mary of Gloucester, evidently forgetting where she was but assuming it was her niece's coronation, suddenly threw herself to her knees before the queen in a florid act of obeisance. Victoria's shock was profound: "Imagine our *Horror!*" she confided to her diary.

3

Marriage

Though the English seemed to take relatively little notice of the fact that their sovereign was also queen of Scotland, Victoria never for a moment allowed herself to forget it. No sooner had she and Albert begun their first visit together to Scotland in 1842 than she contrived a passionate regard for her northern kingdom, in her inimitable way wanting to embrace all that was new and invigorating in that land of her Stuart ancestors. Her next visit, in 1847, convinced Victoria that the deep recesses of the Highlands would make the perfect setting for a second holiday home, a secluded Scottish retreat whose very existence would do honor to the branch of her patrimony that Britain's Hanoverian sovereigns had, for the most part, long and egregiously shunned.

Valleys reminiscent of his native Thuringia irresistibly drew Albert northward, while the potential privacy was for Victoria nearly as esteemed as life itself. For both, the attraction was buttressed by what she perceived as simple unpretentiousness on the part of Scotland's inhabitants. And finally, the scales were more than tipped by the practical recognition that the nation's new railways could quickly carry them to a country that only a few years earlier had been impossibly distant from England's capital. In 1848, the year of Louise's birth, Victoria and Albert happened upon a small baronial-style castle called Balmoral in Aberdeen County, set in the romantically alluring valley bordering the Dee River. The couple took a lease on the blessedly isolated property and soon introduced their children to its charms.

It is difficult today to imagine the degree of remoteness that Balmoral represented to the mid-nineteenth-century consciousness, regardless of the railways that had made the place even thinkable for a never-off-duty monarch. Albert described it to the duchess of Kent as an "un-come-at-able place," though his mother-in-law was to be generously given her own neighboring mansion, called Abergeldie, a picturesque dwelling within an easy drive from the larger castle. The new royal estate would eventually form what was in effect a small community, a cottage-based weaving industry for the families of Balmoral's servants complemented by a savings bank, shops, and a library. A nearby small mansion called Birkhall would serve as housing for the overflow of the queen's guests.

Four years after first settling into her rented Highland retreat, the monarch would possess the property outright when she bought the lease for £31,500. As with Osborne, the original residence was then torn down, to be replaced by a far larger structure in whose design and construction Albert again took a prominent role. Victoria set the foundation stone in September 1853. Like the original Balmoral, the rebuilt dwelling simulated a Scottish baronial look, all turrets and crenellated battlements and flag towers. But the interiors reflected not so much the ancient Stuarts as the middle-class *Gemütlich* beloved of both sovereign and consort. The furniture, upholstery, rugs, and many of the wall coverings took the royal Stuart tartan as their chief element, the motif so overdone that it induced in many visitors a torpor that wags called "tartanitis." Albert justified the surfeit of plaid with his usual sense of social utility, explaining that its production had helped to revive the failing local industry.

Again as with Osborne, the royal couple bought up surrounding lands to further guarantee their privacy, in the end possessing one of the most valuable estates in Scotland. In short order, their Deeside holidays—with riding expeditions on stalwart Highland ponies, picnics and fishing, shooting and wildflower collecting—represented a beloved annual tradition for the nation's first family, and it was here that soon blossomed the love affair of Victoria and Albert's eldest daughter.

By the mid-1850s, when the oldest children were approaching maturity, Louise looked likely to be the queen's last daughter. In 1850, a third son had been born, whom Victoria decided to name Arthur after the victor of Waterloo. Naturally the old duke of Wellington— a national hero who beguiled the queen—was chosen to stand as godfather at his namesake's christening, assuring his sovereign that the gesture meant more to him than any of his galaxy of military honors.[1] The unique tie with a man who had been through much of the nineteenth century as Britain's greatest hero would settle deeply into young Arthur's psyche, and all his life the prince would be fascinated with anything military. When he was still barely able to talk, he put his family on notice that "Arta is going to be a soldier."

In April 1853, a fourth son appeared, Leopold George Duncan[2] Albert—Victoria's first child to be born under the blessed deliverance of chloroform. Again, Mrs. Lilly was present, as she had been with the baby's seven siblings. Joining the midwife was the well-known Edinburgh anesthetist Dr. John Snow, who had been asked by the queen's personal physician to administer a pain reliever; that Dr. Snow was famous for his competence in the procedure probably eased any doubts Victoria may have had about his providing what was at the time a still highly experimental palliative. The ounce of the chemical she was given was not, however, enough at any time to render the patient unconscious. The monarch was, as she later confided to her diary, "greatly pleased with the effect."

This medical novelty attracted a fair amount of notoriety. With the medical and religious worlds composed entirely of men, and highly conservative men at that, the idea of the queen receiving any anesthetic designed to relieve the agony of childbirth created a the-

ological and social thunderstorm. Opponents to the use of chloroform cited biblical antecedents for their disapproval, asserting that
birthing women were *meant* to suffer, this view supported by close
reading of the book of Genesis. What was more, went the argument,
a painful delivery supposedly ensured that the mother would want
to take better care of her children, though the logic of this latter
proposition was, at best, murky. The popular press took the editor-
ial stance that the administration of choloroform was a danger to
the queen's health, and was being performed solely in the name of
scientific experimentation. Many people swallowed this last absurdity and worried very much about their sovereign's safety. Notwithstanding, it was Victoria's approval of the best sedative available at
the time that eventually broke both the clerics and the dissenting
learned on the issue. The queen later professed some pride in having served as a role model in this issue.

Unfortunately, the ease with which Leopold came into the world
did not translate into similarly happy prospects for his future. The
first sign to the queen that something was terribly wrong with her
new son was the unusual thinness of this child as compared with
the generally fat babies she had been yielding so regularly: Leopold
was at birth by far the smallest of her eight babies. Victoria also
frankly described her fourth son as "the ugliest," typical of the sin-
gular candor with which she would all her life discuss her offspring—to her diary, to the children's siblings, to other family
members. But in this case she seems to have been genuinely put off
by the baby's appearance, so much so that weeks would pass when
she saw little of Leopold, who was left to the care of a Scottish wet
nurse.

The seriousness of the infant prince's problems far transcended
scrawniness. When only months old, ominous bruises, large and ab-
normally dark, began to appear all over his body, even slight falls
producing discolorations. Hemophilia was quickly diagnosed. The
shock devastated the parents, with the realization that this frightening condition had entered the royal family. How it got there, from
which side of the family, was a mystery to Albert and the queen,

both understandably asserting that his or her family had been free of such taint.

When Leopold was born, the route by which hemophilia passes through families was understood, though the laws of genetics themselves were only slowly being comprehended—most precisely and accurately by a monk named Gregor Mendel. But in the secure and almost unimaginably privileged universe inhabited by the British royal family, this particular disease was almost literally the last thing that would have been considered a danger to the queen's children or to her future descendants.

As the succession to Britain's throne is invariable in its regularity, so too hemophilia is governed by its own strict rules of inheritability. The formula can be stated succinctly. Except in circumstances so rare as to be negligible, women are not themselves hemophiliacs, which is to say they are not themselves bleeders.[3] They are, however, the primary transmitters, or carriers, of the hemophilia gene. Of a female carrier's sons (and assuming the father is not a hemophiliac himself), on average half will be hemophiliacs, though it is possible that *all* such sons would be nonhemophiliacs.[4] Of her daughters, on average half will in their turn be carriers, though *all* could be. Of a hemophiliac man's sons (and assuming the mother is not a carrier), none can have the condition, but *all* his daughters will be carriers.

The disease can come from either parent—either ancestral line can be the taproot of hemophilia. Somewhere in each familial line of hemophilia a defect in the blood-coagulating gene happens, right out of the blue. But just as the disorder is extremely rare, so of course have these genetic mutations been rare. It is estimated that 80 percent of all cases of hemophilia spring from an identifiable family source.

There is every reason to conclude that Queen Victoria was a hemophilia carrier, not in a spontaneous mutation of her own chromosomes, as the commonly accepted assumption would have it, but rather from her parents. If such was the case, we cannot know whether it was passed down from her father, the duke of Kent.

What *is* known is that the duke sprang from one of the best documented, most public families in history. Since the disease is unmistakably obvious in its victims, and has been to medical observers for centuries, it is highly unlikely that he was a "secret" hemophiliac. But had he been, all of his daughters would have been carriers.

The duchess of Kent could herself have undergone a spontaneous mutation in her genetic makeup, thus making her the begetter of the disease. But the chances of this happening are small—somewhere between one in 25,000 and one in 100,000 people in a generation. The duchess could have been a carrier from earlier generations of Coburgs. But lengthy and meticulous research into her medical history has failed to find any ancestor who might have bequeathed the defective gene.[5] Even more meticulous records, carried down to the present day, of the duchess's two Leiningen children and their descendants, fail to uncover a single instance of hemophilia.

The likeliest source of Queen Victoria's hemophiliac gene would be her father. But not necessarily her legal and presumed father, the duke of Kent. The inference that can of course be drawn is that she is possibly *not* descended paternally from the royal family of the greatest empire the world has ever known, but rather only maternally from that of the tiny and inconsequential duchy of Coburg. Leopold of Coburg himself lost the chance to sire Britain's future kings when his son and his wife died at Claremont in 1817; but his family's blood strain might, ironically, be the only *royal* blood strain from which Queen Victoria's children are descended.

Victoria's son remained an invalid all his short life, though he would marry and father two children—the second, a son, born posthumously. While Victoria's distancing herself from her son—mainly by leaving him behind after family holidays at Balmoral and Osborne—was justified in the name of protecting the boy from injury, Leopold could have been, and was, safe in any of the queen's homes. More likely, the monarch was ashamed of and embarrassed by Leopold's condition; her coolness toward him, sometimes crossing the line into psychological cruelty, was probably the result of both emotions. Her feelings represented a mixture of the attitudes of the times—nineteenth-century beliefs with respect to dread disease were far from enlightened—and the growing fear that *she* (surely Albert was too pure) had been the responsible party.

When Leopold grew into young manhood, his qualities of intellect were far the greatest of any of Victoria's four sons; only Vicky approached him in cleverness. The queen would raise Leopold to become what was in effect a kind of extra-confidential secretary, a turn of events at which the prince of Wales would take deep offense, and with good reason. By that time, though, Bertie would be so scorned by his unbalanced mother than any injury to her oldest son's sensibilities had become immaterial to her.

As Vicky entered young womanhood, the fulfilling of the family's long-standing intimations as to her future began to rise in the queen and prince consort's[6] order of priorities. And those intimations were momentous: the allying of their own happy island kingdom with the increasingly powerful but resolutely illiberal Prussia.

Albert's vision of a "liberalized" Prussia did not in any way contemplate displacing its Hohenzollern monarchy. Vicky's pragmatic father viewed Europe through the lens of the nineteenth century's values. He would no more countenance the unseating of a legitimate royal house than he would have espoused the ideals that had driven the French Revolution: Albert didn't want a new order, but rather the existing order improved upon. Scion of a dynasty that had since its founding obsessed itself, sometimes to the point of farce, with the hegemony of the military over the civil state, the current Prussian sovereign, Frederick William IV, was, alas, an absolutist defender of his kingdom's political character. But, Albert reasoned, if this monarch was hopelessly reactionary in his adherence to absolute rule by God-anointed kings, surely his successors might be amenable to a more liberal future for Prussia and for Europe.

Before Germany finally became politically unified in 1871, what had gone by that name was two big kingdoms, a few lesser ones, and an almost preposterous patchwork of smaller and even close to indiscernible principalities, duchies and grand duchies, city-states, and other oddments of jealously maintained autonomy. Most of these bits represented the residue of the long-moribund Holy Roman Empire, but every one of them obstinately guarded its independence, only reluctantly yielding fragments of sovereignty to the various loose unions that had been created in Napoleon's revolutionary wake. The two leading states were the lusty and almost purely German Prussia under its Hohenzollerns, and the magisterial but nearly spent Austria under the Hapsburgs.

Austria's eminence was abiding, proud, and of centuries-long standing. But by the mid-nineteenth century its ruling dynasty had grown arthritic, unable to placate an empire that was composed, except for the Germanic core, of non-Germanic elements agitating for freedom from Vienna's grip. Prussia, too, boasted a proud history, even if the Hapsburgs viewed their neighbor's royal family as a clan of barracks-obsessed parvenus. Prussia was both jealous and contemptuous of Austria, and its soldiers had over the last century appropriated valuable bits of Hapsburg land, most importantly the ore-rich Silesia.

Thanks to the single-mindedness of the military-obsessed kings in Berlin, by the 1850s, Prussia wielded the trump hand over Austria. The tempests of 1848 disabused Prussia's king, Frederick William—one-time possessor of some scant reputation as a liberal because he had granted, at gunpoint, a few reforms—of any lingering notions of governing in a liberal, which is to say parliamentary, fashion. In the event, by 1857 Frederick William had gone insane,[7] and a year later his younger brother William became regent in his stead.

Prince Albert had gotten to know William relatively well, having established a kind of working friendship with him when, during the Prussian royal family's asylum in England in 1848, the prince lobbied the Hohenzollern prince on how British-style parliamentary rule could serve as a model for a united Germany. Albert considered that he had made headway with William, even talking him out of allying Prussia with the hopelessly reactionary Austrian and Russian governments. But the prince consort had misjudged his guest. William's taciturn bent had allowed Albert to preach with very little interruption, and while the prince continued making his case, he took his guest's lack of response for acquiescence. In fact, the idea of German unity horrified William, who was sickened by the vision of a lot of unruly non-Prussian Germans becoming part of the patrimony his Hohenzollern predecessors had created.

While Albert and William expatiated over the future of European civilization, their wives were forming an alliance of their own. Augusta had been a princess of Weimar before her marriage to William, and took pride in the liberal constitutionalism for which that small state had long been associated. Her political views, taken together with her aggressive and vivacious personality, had since direly strained relations with her dour husband. But her friendship with Victoria would be of long standing, and would one day prove useful to the British queen in dealing with Vicky.

Augusta and William's son, the Hohenzollern prince Frederick William, born in 1831, had always by his family been called "Fritz." There is no certainty who first conceived the pairing of the obvious eventual heir to the Prussian throne with the English princess royal. Most likely, the idea had first been seriously considered by Victoria's forever-plotting uncle Leopold. The Belgian king would have had a good reason for doing so, judging a Prussian-British connection as one likely to guarantee his country's security from its traditional antagonist, the French.

Whether Leopold was actively involved in furthering an alliance between his grand-niece and a future Prussian monarch is incidental to the identity of the real instigator of what was potentially the most important royal match of the nineteenth century. It was unquestionably the perspicacious Albert who most clearly saw the extent of the possibilities in such a union, and who must have been nurturing the prospect in his innermost thoughts as early as his engagement to Britain's queen.

Three years after the Prussian royal family's visit, Victoria's husband found himself reaping widespread praise for the most spectacular material accomplishment of his entire two decades as consort. It was he who conceived of the Great Exhibition of 1851 and what was, in effect, the first of the giant international fairs. The extravaganza's phenomenal success was in great measure due to both the vision and deep involvement the prince brought to it. Housed in Joseph Paxton's futuristic glass palace—known as the Crystal Palace—the exhibition represented a colossal ingathering and showing off of the world's manufactured wares, with British industry proudly and prominently displayed at the forefront in a paean to the glories of empire, its trade and commerce. There had been nettlesome grumbling over the project, particularly its cost, and a few soreheads even suggested that the show would end up as little more than an avenue for aliens to enter England disguised as tourists, set up their own republic, and bring down the established order. Paranoia aside, Albert's spectacular was probably the greatest entertainment success of the mid-Victorian era, earning millions of pounds in paid admissions during its run in Hyde Park.[8]

Even while Albert busied himself with the exhibition, in the back of his mind the vision of his daughter's future hummed quietly but persistently. Stockmar, intimately aware of his master's interest in an Anglo-Prussian alliance, proposed a dexterous way to set the matter in motion. If the queen would graciously invite the family of Prince William of Prussia to tour the exhibition, the opportunity to let the two family's children get to know each other would naturally present itself. When the invitation went off to Berlin, William quickly accepted what he imagined as an opportunity to further strengthen his ties with the United Kingdom. At the end of April 1851, he and Augusta duly arrived in England. Accompanying the parents were their two children: twenty-year-old Fritz—tall, blue-eyed, and already wearing light blond-brown mustachios—and his shy and still-awkward sister, thirteen-year-old Louise.

Vicky and Fritz first caught sight of each other in the dazzling setting of Buckingham Palace's Chinese Drawing Room. On the evening the Prussians arrived, they came to the palace to join Victoria and Albert on a drive to the exhibition. Ten-year-old Vicky was being afforded the highly unusual treat of inclusion in an adult excursion, ostensibly to keep Fritz's little sister company on the tour. Though her parents did not, of course, expect any romantic flickers from so young a child, they nevertheless hoped that she might make a felicitous impression on Fritz, who well knew by this time that his own future might be linked with that of the British queen's daughter.

The vivacious Vicky not only created the desired impression but dominated the evening. Where Fritz's already bashful sister said few words, in accordance with the demure passivity expected of a Prussian princess, the chatterbox Vicky was a marvel who amazed her visitor. Like her mother when she was young, the princess royal had early developed an innate naturalness and lack of guile, qualities wholly different from all Fritz had known in Berlin's turgid and etiquette-bound court. What was more, since Vicky had been raised in what was essentially a bilingual home, her German was fluent, a skill she quickly and with obvious pride exhibited when responding to Fritz's faltering English. Loving her own stage and an audience even more than she did her father's wonderful exhibition, she answered questions, explained, pointed out, and discoursed on nearly everything the two families were seeing. Only when her parents refused her piteous pleas to be allowed to attend the evening's opera did Vicky's egocentric petulance become embarrassingly apparent to the young German prince.

But that was the first day. Over the next two weeks, Vicky and Fritz were allowed to spend many hours in each other's company—something that, ironically, would not have been permitted had she been a few years older. During her days with him, Vicky learned a great deal about the young Prussian, and there was almost nothing of which the delighted ten-year-old disapproved. That he had been a student in Bonn she thought especially admirable because her father had also once attended the same university. That Fritz almost swooned over the degree of familiarity and openness displayed between members of Britain's royal family amazed Vicky, unaware that life could be, in fact almost always was, vastly different in the Continental courts.

Fritz was also much attended to by Albert himself. Having taken the young man down to Osborne along with the rest of the family, the prince consort wasted little time in bombarding him with long, heartfelt, and probably wearying political discussions. When Fritz had to take his leave at the end of the two-week visit, he asked his host to write in his autograph book. The prince consort's words—typically Albertine in their earnestness—were meant to impress his own liberalism and pan-Germanism into the mind of the younger man: "May Prussia be merged in Germany, and not Germany in Prussia." When Germany was born, precisely the reverse would prove true.

While most of the family's dynastic marital attention remained focused on Vicky after Fritz returned to his homeland, Alice, too, was nearing the age when her parents would have to start seriously considering her future. In 1854 the Crimean War started, and Victoria and Albert's second daughter, now eleven, first tasted of the cause that would become her life's work. Alice was already far the most emotionally sensitive of the princesses, her sympathies with other people's burdens notably marked for a child so young. When she was taken by her mother to visit the war wounded streaming back from Russian battlefields to hospitals in Britain, the horrifying scenes she witnessed, no matter how circumspectly masked for the queen's presence, burned indelible pictures on Alice's sense of compassion. The girl's tenderness toward the unfortunate was, however, counterbalanced by a dark side, a temper that could be easily triggered by innocuous events, quarrels in the sisters' schoolroom springing from her response to a careless word from a sibling. More damaging was the trait that would one day all but estrange Alice from Queen Victoria: the propensity to sharpness of tongue, to quick criticisms of those she found uncongenial, or who didn't share her sense of duty, or of concern, or of compassion. Alice's zeal to do good, to relieve the suffering of others, acquired at the foot of an altruistic father whom she worshipped, would in later life render her woundingly intolerant of others who hadn't been endowed with such a generous allotment of humanity.

Alice contracted scarlet fever in 1855, permanently weakening her constitution. It was a presentiment the queen seemed not to appreciate, possibly because of her own deep-seated unease with illness of any kind, even that in her own family. Added to the girl's difficulties during adolescence were looks that elicited one of the queen's most blunt assessments of her shortcomings when, in a letter to her half sister, Princess Feodore of Leiningen, Victoria commented, "I dare say [Alice] will improve. . . ." Whereas Alice's severely sharp face might in our age of anorexic role models have been esteemed, combined with a severe mid-Victorian hair arrangement and intensity of expression it cast her into unfavorable comparison with the doll-like elder sister, who received universal praise. Not only was Alice grave in expression; her personality settled ever more into a rigidity that many found offputting. She hadn't the art to make life easy for herself.

As close as Alice had been to Vicky up until now, no two of the sisters would ever achieve a depth of childhood intimacy to match the extraordinary bond that Alice shared in these years with the prince of Wales. Like Alice, as an adolescent, Bertie too found little that would lighten his journey through a trying relationship with his parents. Constant and demeaning comparisons to Albert only reinforced Bertie's determination to resist maternal entreaties to conform, to follow Vicky's example. The following admonition from a mother couldn't have been easy for any of the queen's children: "*None* of you can *ever* be proud enough of being the *child* of SUCH a father who has not an equal in this world . . . so great, so good, so faultless." Where his younger brothers and sisters were able psychologically to jettison most of this nonsense, Bertie could not.

Ever since the prince of Wales's tutors had taken over from his governesses at his seventh birthday, daily existence often became a trial for the boy. Constantly reminded at home by both parents and instructors that he was destined for greatness as the nation's future king, the young prince was neither intellectually nor emotionally up to achieving the challenge his sex and birth order had placed upon him. Bertie's qualities of generosity and good-heartedness—when parental demands didn't send him into furors of temper—were typically overlooked. Albert's notions of making a "pure" prince of his son ran, sadly and with tragic portent for the future, counter to the material at hand.

While Bertie was being molded into a man who would his entire life shun intellectual pursuits, his sister Alice was turning deeply introspective, a girl ill at ease with the bizarre mix of assured prerogatives and stifling constrictions that marked her uniquely privileged life. Vicky blithely continued her self-confident dash toward what she knew would be a momentous future. But Alice saw no shining horizon to match the princess royal's. And instead of advancing herself, she concentrated on encouraging and motivating Bertie, for whom in these youthful years she continued to harbor a deep and mature fondness. When their mother criticized the one, the other would be the first to take his or her sibling's part. If Alice were sent to her room, Bertie would very soon sneak up to see her, his purpose as he put it, "to give Alee a morsel of news." And it was this sister who could, more than anyone else in the family, gently criticize the heir to the throne without wounding his feelings, her aim often to help him learn how to cushion himself from his family's barbs. Despite the monarch's own inability to empathize with him, Victoria at least gave credit to Alice for the wonders this daughter alone worked upon her very unpredictable Bertie.

In the early 1850s the personalities of Lenchen and Louise were being steadfastly forged into bearing characteristics that would mark their adult lives: Lenchen becoming the dutiful, lusterless, and muted daughter to a taxing and demanding mother; Louise going the opposite direction into a rebelliousness founded on sizable talent, a piercing tongue, and the most striking physical appearance of any member of her immediate family.

If Lenchen was to fade into being the most placid of the sisters to date, she also appeared outwardly the least complicated. With neither Vicky's remarkable intelligence and precocious maturity nor Alice's propensity to turn everything into a mission, Lenchen in girlhood gave her parents little cause for concern—except as to how one day to settle her in a suitable match. The children's physical characteristics always being a matter of emphatic candor for their mother, this third daughter's plainness caused her distress from Lenchen's early youth. This princess simply had a tendency toward fat, a susceptibility Victoria could ignore in herself but never in her children.

A tomboy daughter rarely engendered good-natured pride in Victorian parents of any class or condition. Lenchen excelled at less feminine pursuits—swimming, racing against her siblings—activities a princess wasn't expected to engage in, let alone show up her brothers. As an adolescent, she once expressed a wish to be a boy so she could chuck her awkward sidesaddle and ride astride. She enjoyed youthful tinkering with the fabulous apparatuses that highlighted this era of elaborate mechanical doodads and gigamarees. Poking at the engines far below the glistening decks of the family yachts enticed Lenchen far more than did her sisters' ever so serious tea parties. As long as she still retained the cover of childhood and the presence of like-minded brothers, Lenchen's existence seemed natural to her, despite maternal carping as to its unsuitability for a princess. Only when she lost this innocence during her teens would her life take on its coloring of apathy and, in the transition, the forfeiting of her authentic voice.

Far apart in temperament from Lenchen's rough-and-tumble and eventual sedate nature, it was always Louise who was the recipient of praise from courtiers and governesses for her radiance even while in infancy—Lady Augusta Bruce's adulation typical in calling her "the delicious Baby . . . a delight and beautiful creature." The girls had been taught to put out their hands to be kissed by those with whom they came in contact (excluding, of course, those impossibly far below them in rank), and Louise even from her earliest days took with little prodding to this particular observance. In 1849 General Charles Grey, one of the queen's courtiers, wrote in evident surprise that he had "just seen the Princess Louise in the gallery, and kissed her hand, 16-months-old and a bit—toddling along." The object of this stately servant's astonishment learned early that royal etiquette would serve well for a lifetime of receiving others' obeisances.

There was no question of "free time" for Louise—nor, for that matter, for any of the children. Their lives were regimented according to Stockmar's directives, and progress reports in arithmetic, history, geography, and grammar were carefully noted by their father. Louise's highs and lows were both found in foreign languages: she loved and did well in French, but the German lessons under Fräulein Bauer were the least pleasurable of any of her early studies. Fortunately, nonacademic pursuits were never held entirely at bay. Likely the most pleasurable were the picnics at Balmoral on which all the children would be offered "wee drams" of Scotland's most famous spirits, by the estate's crofters, which they were expected to down.

As for nearly all upper-class families in nineteenth-century Britain, Queen Victoria's children didn't really *live* with their parents. Instead, rigidly scheduled and usually short visits would be planned throughout the day—sometimes the parents to the children in their nursery, schoolroom, or bedrooms, the places where they were expected to remain, away from adult eyes except those of servants; at other times the children to the parents, at tea, or breakfast, in the formal and otherwise off-limits precincts of adults. This regimen served until the age of confirmation, when the young princes and princesses would become quasi-participants in their parents' adult lives and partial members of their social circles.

The strictly controlled school regimens to which all the queen's offspring were subjected had inflicted the greatest strain on the older children. By the early 1850s, when Louise began her schooling, Albert had to a degree come to his senses about the inflexibility of Baron Stockmar's system, and its hitherto invariable elements began to be modified to each child's inclinations and abilities. Unfortunately for the younger siblings, the prince consort had become so much the surrogate monarch in his wife's kingdom that, by the time Louise was approaching adolescence, he retained only a small fraction of the time to spend with her that he had with Vicky. It might be noted that the queen was complaining of how little even *she* enjoyed of Albert's not otherwise-occupied hours.

The royal children were not immune to physical punishment to help mold them into the decorous and accomplished individuals their parents meant them to be. But while Vicky rarely merited so much as a swat, Louise received more than her share, her natural rebelliousness leading the queen or her nursery substitutes to subject this daughter to routine spankings for misbehavior. When Victoria's own mother commented on how difficult it was to hear a child scream during such treatment, the monarch rejoined, "not when you have eight, Mama—that wears off!"

Victoria was determined to make sure that the children didn't for a moment forget that their mother was also their queen and they therefore must not expect the familiarities from her that a child might receive from an ordinary mother. Her severities were apparently meant to help the children keep this fact in mind. But Albert recognized the lack of logic in this attitude, telling his wife that "it is impossible to be on happy friendly terms with people you have just been scolding." Years later Victoria would admit to her eldest daughter that "too great care, too much constant watching leads to those very dangers hereafter, which one wishes to avoid." By that time, Vicky was already subjecting her own eldest child to a rerun of her childhood experiences.

One of the most important skills expected of the queen's daughters was the ability to seize the social initiative, to be the center of attention and automatically maintain one's dignity, to remember people (and their titles and positions and accomplishments), to grace the courts to which they were born, would be married into, or would visit on their constant travels from one European capital to another. To make sure these skills were ingrained in her girls, the monarch saw to it that all were trained in the arcane talent of making the *cercle*—walking around a room and dispensing polite nothings, as they would do for those thousands who would over their lifetime be presented to them. As an adult, Louise would remember her sisters and herself practicing the art by strewing chairs around their schoolroom and addressing the appropriate words to each, as if they were meeting ambassadors or nobles or fleet admirals.

For the queen's eldest daughter, adult life began in the middle of September 1855. Britain was still fighting its war in the Crimea, and this was just after the fall of Sebastopol. Albert had received a telegram from the commanding general informing him that "the city is in the hands of the Allies," the news thrilling the royal family as much as it would the rest of the nation. Vicky had three weeks earlier returned from a state visit to Paris with her parents, one in which for the first time in her life she had in her estimation been treated as a genuine grown-up. A spirited duo whose outsized personalities the princess royal had fallen madly in love with, both the French emperor and his empress had doted on her in turn.

At the invitation of her parents, Fritz came back to England, this time for a visit to Balmoral. Physically, the young Prussian prince was now significantly changed from his introductory appearance four years earlier. His newly noticeable "high forehead, noble brow and clear blue eyes" made an instant and special effect on Vicky. Though Fritz was rendered sophisticated by a handsome mustache that looked as though it had been fashioned of molten gold, he remained at twenty-four friendly and unaffected, still quick to marvel at the relative informality practiced at the holiday home of the British queen. Now in the gloriously wild setting of the Scottish Highlands, a landscape that reminded the young prince of his beloved Nordic sagas, he had come to the most romantic surroundings imaginable for the job at hand.

The object of his attention was herself far more mature as well. Though not yet fifteen, the princess royal stood poised to assume the attributes of womanhood, her physical appearance much altered, so much *prettier*, Fritz thought, than the girl he had seen at the Great Exhibition. Vicky's intellect, too, not surprisingly had sharpened; only her bell-like laughter was the same as that he had remembered.

Fritz now knew, of course, precisely what was expected of him at Balmoral. Even though it was clearly too early for the couple to marry, the princess royal not much past having entered puberty, both the British and Prussian royal families expected that the prospect should be decided one way or another. "The visit makes my heart break, as it *may* and probably *will* decide the fate of our dear eldest child"—Victoria was presciently correct about how things stood, just as she was delighted at how much more grown up Fritz seemed than when he had last visited. From the first day of this visit, Fritz stood clearly on the verge of making the queen of England a very happy woman.

What the Prussian prince couldn't tell Vicky—or, for that matter, her family—was what life would be like for her should they marry and she return with him to the rigors of court etiquette in Berlin and Potsdam. There had, after all, been ample reason for Fritz's surprise at the relative informality of Vicky's life. Though the British court was bound by an inflexible minuet of convention and custom meant to maintain the dignity of state and crown—an inflexibility Victoria would have been the last to relax—it was nonetheless remarkably relaxed as compared to the rules that governed life for the Hohenzollerns.

The Prussia that Fritz would one day govern existed as a military-controlled state, a sort of open-air barracks where not everyone necessarily wore a uniform. This mind-set took roots at the country's very beginnings, planting itself powerfully in virtually every member (male and female) of the ruling House of Hohenzollern, a mentality that would last until the end of the Prussian monarchy in 1918.

By the early fifteenth century this family of warrior-kings had gained control of Brandenburg, the area centering on Berlin that would become the political heart of latter-day Prussia. The ruling dynasty would link their Brandenburg with the ancient duchy of Prussia that lay eastward, along the Baltic, lands that had been originally Germanized by the Teutonic knights, a caste of crusading warriors who had conquered the indigenous natives of Baltic stock. During these times, colonies of Germans settled in towns all along the Baltic coast, hunkering in as far as the Gulf of Finland, instilling all along the way their language, culture, traditions, and—often foremost—their energy. The Germans even appropriated for themselves the name of the original Balts—the *Prusiaskai*.

What emerged in the east was the nucleus of modern "Prussia," which might have remained just another minor East European–oriented state but for the Peace of Westphalia in 1648. That concord divvied up the spoils of the Thirty Years' War, and Brandenburg-Prussia was handed additional lands in the center of Germany, providing it with an invaluable toehold in the more sophisticated Western-directed parts of Europe. Its young ruler and the fount of its future greatness, the elector Frederick William[9]—five generations ahead of Fritz and known to history as the Great Elector—devoted his reign to turning his state into a perfectly honed military weapon and its dynasty into the model of an absolutist monarchy. Successful to a remarkable degree, the Great Elector also saw to it that Prussia would be a central player in European power politics.

Frederick William's son, Frederick I, upgraded his own royal position from elector to king. Next in line was Frederick William I, who famously collected outlandishly tall soldiers with which to beautify and amplify his regiments.[10] To history, Frederick William I is best known for the almost inconceivable cruelty to which he subjected his son and heir.

Frederick II—the Great—represented the apogee of the Hohenzollern dynasty, at least in terms of his own unambiguous brilliance and his often-brutal exercise of Prussian self-interest. Shaped by the loathsome treatment meted out by his twisted father, he was in his private life the antithesis of Frederick William I. So cultured was he that his closest companion was Voltaire, and so musically talented that he himself composed compositions played to this day. Hence his court assumed a quality and grace found only in the sybaritic *luxe* of the Versailles of the later French Bourbons. To underline the point, the monarch openly eschewed his native language in favor of French, and the literature of his own Germany—including the glories of Goethe—for that of France.

Frederick industriously enlarged his armies from 90,000 to 150,000 men, and then, demonstrating to Europe that true German power now resided not in Vienna but in Berlin, shamelessly tore the rich Austrian duchy of Silesia from Hapsburg empress Maria Theresa in the War of the Austrian Succession. When she was joined by half of Europe in an attempt to get it back, Frederick allied with England and managed to retain it despite the imbalance of greater forces arrayed against him. For good measure, he also thumbed his nose at Vienna by upgrading his dynasty's title from king *in* Prussia to king *of* Prussia, putting him on a formal par with Europe's mightiest sovereigns.

Without a son of his own—this homosexual monarch's marriage to Elizabeth of Brunswick-Wolfenbüttel had been childless—Frederick was succeeded by his weak and licentious nephew, Frederick William II, who, in league with Russia's tsar, dismembered and then obliterated Poland, after having safeguarded (or so he thought) Prussia's western flank by making peace with Napoleon. But Frederick William II's successor, Frederick William III, harvested the catastrophe of his father's ill-placed faith in the Corsican menace: in 1806, at Jena, Napoleon annihilated the Prussian Army. After the little would-be emperor triumphantly marched into Berlin, Bonaparte vindictively desecrated Frederick the Great's tomb as a lesson in the reality of the new order. Frederick William III's opting out of the alliance against Napoleon had permitted the French dictator first to defeat Austria and then to bowl through Central Europe. All that kept the monarch's reputation from total demise were the efforts of his wife, Queen Louise, a resourceful consort who managed to wheedle relatively lenient terms from Napoleon.

When Frederick William III was restored to his throne after Napoleon's defeat, the final years of his reign were devoted chiefly to the restoration of the nation's prestige, specifically through a massive Berlin building spree carried out in large part through the genius of the architect Karl Friedrich Schinkel. This master of classical design accomplished for the Prussian capital much the same as John Nash was doing for London at about the same time. Though political reforms would occur, at heart this reborn Prussia remained the garrison state of its Hohenzollern founders.

Fritz's uncle, Frederick William IV, succeeded to the throne in 1840. For awhile, it looked as though the kingdom might be ruled by the most liberal monarch in the dynasty's history, which attribute would have been no great stretch given the reactionary governance of his predecessors. But just as the events of 1848 altered much of the European landscape, they also eliminated any chance that a Prussian king would bend to popular demands, entreaties that Frederick William IV considered little more than constitutional camouflage designed to overthrow the God-given order.

During their balmy days of courtship under the clear Highland skies, Vicky and Fritz might have had premonitions that marriage between them would not be universally popular in either of their countries: many Britons volubly distrusted all foreigners and believed no prince of any Continental court could ever be good enough to marry the eldest daughter of their sovereign; and many rather more thoughtful Prussians believed it foolish in the extreme for the heir to their own throne to marry the daughter of England's queen—especially now, when such an alliance would antagonize the tsar, the leader of a powerful Russia at that moment very much at war with Great Britain.

Regardless of such misgivings, after the Balmoral idyll the engine of love made marriage unstoppable. In the first place, Fritz was now simply besotted with the peppy fourteen-year-old. Vicky herself was probably too young to understand the extent of the commitment she was making, or to foresee the physical demands of a husband. But when Fritz squeezed her hand, and she squeezed back, given the extremely limited field from which either could choose mates, they said yes to each other for life, and meant it with all their hearts, and thus was made one of the most momentous and passionate matches in royal history.

After each had actually committed to the other, reality demanded that the onrushing pace of events be brought down to a more reasonable speed. Following Fritz's presentation to his intended parents-in-law of the news that their daughter had agreed to his proposal, and after Victoria and Albert exuberantly "kissed and pressed the poor dear child in our arms," daylight was let in on the magic. Vicky's parents stipulated that marriage would have to wait until the bride turned seventeen, some two years hence, and that their promises could only be seen as the families' private business, the agreement to be hidden from the public until the greater part of the waiting period had run its course.

Then as now, news concerning members of the royal family was of enormous interest in Britain—although there was then, of course, a good deal less of it published. *The Times* got wind of the facts, probably because the prince consort told Foreign Minister Lord Clarendon and gave his leave for Clarendon to pass the tidings on to the prime minister, Lord Palmerston, all of which allowed the intelligence to leak to the press. Editorializing over the union began almost immediately, and much of the commentary decried Vicky marrying a member of a dynasty that was not especially popular in Britain. The editor of *The Times* opined that Fritz's family was a "paltry one" and Prussia a "wretched State." A large part of the Prussian aristocracy returned the sentiments precisely in kind, meaning that Vicky had to look forward to a formidably unfavorable tide of comment from her adopted countrymen before her engagement even became official.

After the queen assured Fritz that he would "be almost closer to us parents than our own son"—the son she undoubtedly had in mind was Bertie—the young prince was sent home to wait.

The following summer, England's murderous little war in the Crimea was finally drawing to a close. The queen's soldiers had suffered appalling difficulties—largely because of knuckle-headed generalship abetted by unchecked and virtually untreatable cholera—but she was nonetheless heartened that the unpleasant foreign business was finished. Both Russia, her longtime personal nemesis (Victoria had written that the whole thing was the fault of *"one man,"* the tsar, whom she intensely disliked), and Austria had been seriously weakened. France and England had fought on the same side for the first time in centuries, principally because they believed Russia was threatening their interests in the eastern Mediterranean. If anything of lasting value came of the Crimean adventure, it was that women established their importance in nursing, doing so magnificently under the historic leadership of Florence Nightingale. As for the monarch, the thirty-eight-year-old Victoria now found out she was going to give Albert another baby. Providing her husband with this pleasure was, she reasoned, the one sure safety valve from a morning-to-night work schedule she thought was wearing him out, the concern that now darkened her thoughts as did no other.

The next spring—on April 14, 1857—Beatrice Mary Victoria Feodore arrived, a child who would, for the biblical allusion of the youngest offspring, often be referred to as "my Benjamina" by her mother. Beatrice's delivery was again accompanied by the welcome relief of anesthesia, again administered by Dr. Snow of Edinburgh. The infant's birth preceded by sixteen days the death of Princess Mary, the last surviving child of King George III, whose demise was seen by Victoria as a kind of final royal break with the eighteenth century. The queen's confinement passed without any great trouble, but her doctors warned her that this ninth child should be her last. When Prince Albert was told that both his wife and newborn daughter were free of any danger, he attended a meeting of the Privy Council to see it order prayers of thanks for the sovereign's safety; the archbishop of Canterbury himself set to writing the resolution, which would be offered at the following Sunday's service, the first after Easter.

Beatrice's siblings were little aroused by the arrival of their newest sister. The princess royal, whose thoughts now centered almost exclusively on Fritz, mused that "she [Beatrice] will hardly know me . . . I shan't seem like a sister to her when we meet. I shall be more like a cousin or an aunt." But a group of American citizens took the new princess's birth with some degree of gravity, and, in the process of founding a town on the Nebraska plains, they decided to name it Beatrice, perhaps in the hope that some of the luster of the British crown might find its way to their remote corner of the New World.

While their new little sister passed her days in the glorious golden cradle in which all the royal children had been safely sheltered dur-

ing their first months of life, the four eldest girls continued their sin-
gular educations as daughters of Queen Victoria. Vicky was now
separated a bit from the others, as a more grown-up treatment was
thought only right by her mother now that she was an engaged
woman. Most affected by Vicky's happy elevation and impending
marriage was fourteen-year-old Alice.

The older girls had been made to understand that the queen intended to rely heavily on them. In prosperous nineteenth-century
families, the presumption strongly existed that one of multiple sisters could well be expected to remain permanently at home in the
role of companion to her mother, sometimes even as companion to
her father. The designated daughter would give up a large share of
her chances to marry, since in this era once past her mid-twenties a
woman was considered a nearly unmarriable old maid. The social
convention of this kind of indentured daughter was adamantly defended by Queen Victoria, and must have made her constant childbearing very much more tolerable, with the knowledge that she was
producing a crutch for her later years.

Alice could now reasonably judge that such a melancholy fate
would be passed to one of her three younger sisters. And she was,
indeed, to be spared spinsterhood, for even as Beatrice was being
fed by a wet nurse, Albert and Victoria were busy planning their
second daughter's marital future. As early as May 1856, the queen
had begun writing her uncle in Brussels for his views on the suitability of the heir to the Dutch throne for Alice, echoing Leopold's
candidature of the young man's father for herself a generation earlier. The prince in question was three years older than Alice, and
Protestant, a religious qualification of paramount importance. Victoria wanted to find out as much as possible about his "entourage
and disposition," knowing that a spoiled prince was capable of "ru-
ining" himself, and she wouldn't have a scoundrel marrying into the
family. Problematically, Victoria wasn't sure Alice would quite do as
the queen of the dour and overenthusiastically democratic Dutch,
but discreet inquiries pending future action couldn't, in any case, go
amiss.

Concerns about Alice's appropriateness as a queen weren't altogether misplaced. It wasn't that the girl hadn't the flamboyant intellectual quickness of her older sister; princesses were not, in fact, expected to be much more than ornamental, and Vicky's vaunted braininess was already seen as a liability of some gravity amongst Prussians. But unmistakable signs were in evidence of Alice's defiance of the golden chains that limited her horizons. At Balmoral, where she seemed happiest because of the freedom the secure world of the estate gave her, the princess was eager to visit the tenants in their cottages. The experience gave her early and unmistakable evidence that the whole world didn't pass its days in the splendor she had always known, and she earnestly spoke of these things to the family. Once she escaped her governess while at chapel at Windsor, slipping into the public pews so she might better understand people not hostage to the same protocol that bound her so tightly.

Though the self-starting Vicky's abilities had always been very much in evidence—she had never been in the least hesitant to show them off—Alice didn't far trail her older sister in brainpower and ability to reason once her own education had gotten underway. One of her youthful friends was Fritz's sister, Princess Louise, who would later write that Alice always seemed to inhabit Vicky's shadow, "occupying a subordinate place to her very gifted and distinguished sister," as she put it. But Alice's gifts were only dormant, awaiting freedom from constant comparison with the star of the family. A material difference between the first of Victoria's daughters would be Alice's mature staying power: Vicky always cast her own undeniable talents over wide waters, while Alice would plumb a small pool to greater depths and often to a greater prize.

In 1855, when Alice contracted scarlet fever, the illness's effects fused with the vague melancholia that distinguished the girl from her less emotional siblings. From her early teen years she began to stand out within her family for what would seem to be a martyrlike fortitude in the face of adversity. The realization that she would soon lose Vicky—in effect the loss of her closest companion—and the concomitant knowledge that more adult duties would now be expected of her in the family circle were heavy burdens for a girl of perilously changeable temperament. Daydreams might have transported a normal girl in preparation for a future away from the difficulties of familial loyalty and obedience. For one in Alice's place in life, whose mother was her sovereign, no such ready escape existed.

The two years between Vicky and Fritz's troth-plighting and their marriage passed in a blizzard of preparation. The time was Albert's last truly profitable opportunity to instill in his daughter the knowledge about how to be an effective queen consort, and he devoted two hours every evening to the training of the most important pupil he would ever have. (Oddly, the prince consort seems never to have considered his eldest son's future with the same overwhelming significance as Vicky's.) Passionately believing in the certitude of everything her father had to pass on to her, Vicky in turn soaked up his directives in the conviction that they represented the best advice any royal bride-to-be had ever received. But the father's lessons—at least as they were understood by the daughter—understressed the vast differences in outlook and beliefs between nations. Vicky became convinced that all she would have to do to be successful in her new home was to parrot her understanding of Albertine truths, and the devils of injustice and ignorance could surely never prevail. Almost from the moment she set foot on Prussian soil, that conviction would frustrate her life. Had she possessed her father's ability to winnow chaff from the grain—the unimportant from the essential, the matters of the heart from those of the head—the damage to Vicky's and Germany's future might not have been so devastating.

Contrasting with the solemnity passing between father and eldest daughter, the princess's mother would suffer only one noteworthy, however trivial, indignity before she got Vicky safely married. Though the bride's home was generally considered the sole appropriate setting for a young woman's wedding, in this case the bride was marrying the future sovereign of his respective nation. Not without justice did Prussian officials thus expect Fritz to marry in Berlin; his wife would be the junior partner in this marriage, not her husband's equal in importance. When Victoria heard of these expectations, her response was almost farcical: "The assumption of its being *too much* for a Prince Royal of Prussia to *come* over to marry *the Princess Royal of Great Britain* IN England is too *absurd*, to say the least. . . . Whatever may be the usual practice of Prussian Princes, it is not *every* day that one marries the eldest daughter of the Queen of England. The question must therefore be considered as settled and closed. . . ." Rarely did Queen Victoria have trouble finding the right words to express the heights of her own sense of majesty.

Vicky and Fritz's wedding was celebrated on January 25, 1858, in the modest Chapel Royal of St. James's Palace, a stone's throw down the Mall from Buckingham Palace. Royal wedding ceremonies were not in the nineteenth century treated as great public spectacles, and the suggestion that Westminster Abbey or St. Paul's Cathedral be employed would have been considered by the queen nearly as aberrant as holding the service in Berlin. Nonetheless, the setting still erred on the side of being really too small. Court officials allocated the pews so that the men had twenty inches on which to sit; the women received four more inches, but this still meant that some of the more lavishly hoop-skirted dresses got badly squashed. All of Vicky's sisters except Beatrice took prominent roles in the ceremony. Alice walked directly behind the queen in the processional, and since she was about to become the oldest unmarried daughter was given the significant privilege of carrying a wreath, while Lenchen and Louise were only permitted bouquets with which to adorn their girlish toilettes.

As still happens today, after the ceremony the bride and bridegroom appeared on Buckingham Palace's balcony. There, with both sets of parents, they acknowledged the cheers and good wishes of an enormous crowd that flowed down what was then still a parklike Mall. Vicky's sisters clung to the doorway opening onto the balcony, peeking at the populace pressing against the palace's railings, all probably hoping their own weddings would be just as wonderful as Vicky's had been.

The twenty-six-year-old groom and his seventeen-year-old bride, now officially Prince and Princess Frederick William of Prussia,[11] spent their honeymoon at Windsor, where a throng of Etonians from across the Thames had unhitched the bridal carriage from its traces and in high spirits dragged it and its occupants up to the castle. Though she had been at ease among adults all her life, Vicky was nervous with the husband who was in so many ways unknown to her. Their wedding night was actually the first time she had as a woman been alone with Fritz. Finally, at the end of the momentous day, Fritz came over to the settee where his young wife was sitting, still in her white velvet going-away dress, bent next to her, took her hand in his, and kissed it, very gently.

4

Death at Windsor

Following her marriage, Vicky might have been a very happy young woman. Unfortunately, from the day she arrived in Berlin, events coursed downward for a princess who could never forget her Englishness and would never become a Prussian.

There had been a window after Vicky arrived, a few months perhaps, when she might conceivably have managed to get off to a better and happier start. On the February morning in 1858 when with Fritz she rode into the capital, tens of thousands of the city's residents packed the icy streets to embrace the young couple—ordinary Prussians showing unfeigned enthusiasm in welcoming both to their nation and into their affection the eldest daughter of the English monarch. On that freezing but sunny day Vicky wore no wrap over her low-cut gown, following established Prussian court etiquette. Still she insisted her carriage windows remain lowered to enable the crowds to see clearly the face of their future queen. Vicky drank in the sights of a city that was, compared to London, raw and only beginning its development as a world capital, and it was well the day was freezing lest the princess be overpowered by the odor of raw sewage that ordinarily permeated the city—not too unlike what she had known in her own London.

As the horses drew up before the forbidding gray mass of the Royal Palace squatting at the end of Unter den Linden, the city's principal street, lined with its eponymous lime trees, she for the first time beheld the man who would be an immensely influential component of her and her new country's life for the next three decades. William—the prince of Prussia still only serving as regent for his unhinged brother—glowered down from the top of the steps at his new daughter-in-law. On leaving the carriage, Vicky dropped into an impressively deep curtsey, one that her mother would have been proud of. As she slowly stood up and raised her face to the already elderly behemoth, she expected no more than to be politely kissed. Instead, William quickly glanced away to greet his son. The nature of the relationship would never get much better.

Perhaps if the untested princess had been initially welcomed into the Prussian household with even a modicum of warmth, perhaps if Prince William had shown her but a fraction of the respect that her own illustrious father had always paid her, perhaps if she herself had understood she needed to earn her way into Fritz's family, then the sad pages that unfolded in Vicky's lifelong confrontation with Prussia might have read differently. But being taken, at the age of seventeen, into a strange environment where all that she was—a woman, a foreigner, a liberally educated person—mitigated against her, her only retreat was into what she had known in her past, which is to say into her own family, into England and Englishness, and into a new husband who, fortunately for her but perhaps unfortunately for Germany, loved her very much.

The big ugly palace looming behind her new family was where she was going to live for the time being, like it or not. Andreas Schlüter had designed most of the Baroque structure at the end of the seventeenth century, though a few of its rear-facing bits were even older. One of Vicky's new maids-of-honor characterized the Royal Palace as "endless, dark corridors connecting huge mysterious rooms, hung with large pictures of long-forgotten Royal personages." If not particularly beautiful or graceful, it was unquestionably vast. The latter quality, along with the building's lack of any modern fixtures whatsoever, were conditions that its new occupant would soon come to despise.

Beyond these inconveniences, Vicky would also have to accustom herself to daily treks through gloomy chambers, most depressingly the one in which Frederick William III had died. There was no central corridor, but instead an enfilade of adjoining rooms—no other route existed to serve as conduit between her sitting room and new boudoir. Though a smaller *Schloss* that had been the Berlin home of Fritz's grandfather stood a few yards down Unter den Linden, it was still under renovation to become the couple's eventual city residence. Thus, Vicky and Fritz would live in the larger, ceremonial home of the Prussian monarchy until this so-called Crown Prince's Palace was completed.

Besides an off-putting father-in-law and a hideous barn of a home, the new bride's incessant family letterwriting between London and Berlin further helped to get Vicky's future as a Prussian princess off to a labored start. As much as the princess held her own strong opinions about everything from politics and society to the appropriate time to have dinner—the British royal family's time, of course—and as much as she was her liberal father's daughter, it was her parents', particularly her mother's, constant postal hectoring that was responsible for keeping Vicky from adjusting to the realities of her new life. The father strove to guide his daughter's political attitudes and opinions, while the queen, certainly at first, seemed more intent on controlling her daughter's personal life.

Only a month after her marriage, Albert sent his daughter a letter that could be described as a master plan for her married life. At its heart was the following counsel: "Your place is that of your husband's wife, and of your mother's daughter. You will desire nothing else, but you will also forego nothing of that which you owe to your husband and to your mother," adding the warning that "the public . . . will now become minutely critical and take you to pieces anatomically." The prince consort's advice and cautionary note to his daughter was doubtless well meant, that she should strive to become the wife appropriate to a nineteenth-century prince, and in a society more conservative than that in which she had grown up. As to Vicky's remaining "your mother's daughter," Albert could only have meant to advise the seventeen-year-old that British royal probity would serve her well in Berlin. But if such was her father's meaning, it wasn't echoed by Queen Victoria, and nor was it how Vicky understood her father, even though the remark would be the compass by which she directed her new life.

Queen Victoria, for her part, was determined that Vicky, utterly inappropriately, would remain the British princess royal despite her new position as Fritz's wife and a princess of Prussia. Yet if Vicky were to hope to effect the sort of political change she had come to believe in, and that her father had trained her to accomplish, and if she desired a harmonious relationship with the family of which she was now a member, she had to become in Prussian eyes a *Prussian* princess, the wife of the man who would one day be king, the mother of the king who would follow her husband. But from the beginning she could never stop thinking of England as "home," nor would she temper her unalterable view that just about anything British was better than just about everything Prussian. Though this flaw was understandable in a seventeen-year-old, its consequences were to be enormous.

Victoria not only demanded frequent return letters—by "frequent" the queen meant "daily," which was generally how Vicky responded—but, intensely curious about how other royal families lived, she constantly sought her daughter's views on her new relatives. Vicky obliged, blithely telling her mother how appalled she was by the ignorance that was everywhere displayed by the extended Prussian royal family, how military affairs were the only deep interest on the part of the men (her father-in-law freely boasted of his lack of interest in almost anything else), how the women cared for little except the most mundane minutiae of domestic life. Even her mother-in-law, Princess Augusta, a woman raised in the relatively liberal atmosphere of Weimar, was, according to Vicky, a bluestocking who personally censored her reading material. One of Fritz's uncles—Frederick Carl—was reported to have beaten his wife's ears while she was in her delivery bed, for having produced a third daughter in a row without a male heir. Though likely justified in these assessments, one of Vicky's faults would be the too-quick and sometimes facile judgments she made of those she met. Not only would she lose those who might have been supporters because of a single negative comment; she sometimes thoughtlessly became over-enamored of some whose friendship would later cause her harm.

Though many of her new relatives led lives that were in Vicky's estimation bizarre—especially as they contrasted with the modest and unimaginative existences of most of the English court—the constant reporting of intimate details to her mother, who relished receiving them, tended to make it difficult for the young princess to think of the Prussian royals in a respectful way. Furthermore, she found it hard to hide these emerging beliefs, in either personal or political matters. When she told her mother that she was adhering to the somewhat more fulsome mourning rituals practiced in the Prussian court (just as she should have), the queen shot off an absurd demand that it was Vicky's duty "as *my daughter* and Princess Royal," to stick to the English way of doing things, regardless of the resentment it would cause in Berlin. In justice to Vicky, for a daughter used to a lifetime of following the dictates of her particular mother, it would have been a leap to ignore such ultimatums.

Shortly after marriage, Vicky found herself pregnant. Predictably, the news upset her mother. Because the queen had herself as a new wife become pregnant so quickly—before she had "a year of *happy* enjoyment *with* dear Papa, to myself"—she thought her daughter foolish not to wait longer. Victoria was no less reluctant to inform Fritz of her disappointment, admonishing him in a letter that "you men are far too selfish!" Vicky's pregnancy was attended by the normal discomfort women endure at such time, prompting the queen, who believed husbands should concede a large responsibility in the matter, to "*hope* that Fritz is *duly shocked* . . ."

While a member of the future generation of Hohenzollern royalty was growing in her womb, Vicky began life in two new homes. As her eighteenth birthday present, the princess and her husband moved into the newly refurbished Crown Prince's Palace on Unter den Linden, not only Berlin's most renowned street but its busiest as well. Here they finally escaped the unpleasantness of the Royal Palace, and they quickly put its royal ghosts behind them. But even more consequential to their future, with the king's formal permission they took occupancy of the Neues Palais—three stories, two hundred rooms—that filled one end of Potsdam's Sans Souci Park. The latter became the true home of their hearts for the entire three decades of their marriage, during which Vicky would turn Frederick the Great's Versailles-like confection—so long neglected that upon first moving in the princess discovered rooms full of bats—into one of the most sumptuous residences of royal Europe.

Meanwhile, Vicky's impending delivery elicited well-intentioned advice and assistance from Queen Victoria. But despite her good objectives, serious harm was done to Vicky's position in her new family, resentments being created from which trouble would flow as freely as a floodtide. In what was beyond question a genuine concern for her daughter's undergoing the trial that still killed many women in the mid-nineteenth century, Queen Victoria nonetheless injected into the standards and practices of the Prussian court her own demands surrounding the birth of her first grandchild.

In January 1859, Vicky reached her pregnancy's full term. Eager to ensure her daughter's safety, the queen sent a pair of medical attendants from home: James Clark, her personal physician, and a midwife, Mrs. Innocent. The two brought along with them a bottle of chloroform, which, thanks to the queen's custom, had become an accepted anesthetic in British deliveries. Not so in Prussia.

At midnight on the 26th, Vicky's doctors put her to bed, the princess in hard labor. Throughout that night, the labor pains were agonizing but unyielding. Her German physician, Dr. Wegner, finding himself in dire need of assistance, called a colleague, Dr. Eduard Martin, to come to the palace; he arrived at 10:30 A.M., eleven hours after Vicky's labor began. (Clark, the English physician, was apparently doing little more than observing, likely realizing that if he interfered he would as a foreigner be blamed if anything went wrong.) Martin immediately began a manual internal examination.

He felt that the baby was turned in the breech position, and at once realized that if it couldn't be turned, it would have to be pulled out as is. Any other course, or any further delay, could well mean Vicky's death. Meanwhile, the other observers were so sure that both the princess and the baby were already doomed that notices were quietly sent to the Berlin newspapers announcing their deaths.

Martin set to work. First he requested Clark to give Vicky a few drops of the chloroform that the Englishman had brought with him. This was done, however, over Dr. Wegner's objection against giving the patient any anesthetic whatever. As Vicky kept screaming and crying out for pardon—apparently for the trouble she felt she was causing—Martin began to pull the baby out.

At 2:45 on the afternoon of the 27th—nearly fifteen hours into labor—the baby started to emerge. First its rear end appeared, and then the legs, which had been folded up against its stomach and chest. Following another dose of chloroform, the doctor surgically stretched Vicky's uterus, after which the baby finished descending, though with its left arm folded up behind its head. During the enormously difficult birth, the considerable force used to pull this arm free severely damaged the limb—whether from the application of forceps is unclear. The newborn baby did not immediately seem to be breathing. What is very likely, and would go far in explaining the future personality of the infant, was that long moments—perhaps some minutes—were passed until its first breath was taken, with some brain damage plausibly the result of the delay. The attendants rubbed the baby, possibly causing yet further unintentional damage to the already injured arm; the doctors evidently believed that a perfect baby had been born despite the horrifying circumstances of the delivery, and the severity of the injury to the limb was not even realized until three days later.

Except for the arm, the health of the baby, who was named Wilhelm—and would be called "Willy" in the family—seemed normal enough. But from the first days of his life, when the left arm was seen to be nearly paralyzed, Vicky and Fritz began attempts to strengthen the wrenched part. However, within months it became apparent that, no matter what anyone did, the slower-growing arm was going to be shorter, and the left hand far weaker than its right counterpart. Into childhood, Willy would be forced to wear gruesome apparatuses designed to "fix" his injury; and at the age of four, doctors put him in a machine for an hour each day hoping to correct the head droop caused by the imbalance between one good arm and one bad one. Galvanic and electroshock "treatments" followed, as did agonizing riding lessons designed to prepare him for the inevitable equine future that awaited all Hohenzollern princes. Willy would soon learn to keep the afflicted limb stuffed into specially heightened pockets, lending an appearance of equality. Though the boy's father never experienced insuperable trouble accepting the injury as something that couldn't be changed, his mother was appalled that she had brought a far less than perfect future Prussian king into the world. The princess's attempts to mold Willy, both physically and psychologically, into something he couldn't be very soon set the disastrous course on which mother and son would travel, to the despair of both.

Louise had been deeply saddened when Vicky went off with her new husband to life in Prussia, but the news from Berlin that she and her sisters and brothers had been transformed into aunts and uncles thrilled the eleven-year-old. When the momentous telegram reached the palace, Louise began to race around telling anyone who would listen that "we are not royal children, we are uncles and aunts." Her younger siblings would have been justified in thinking of Willy as more like just another brother—Beatrice, Victoria's last child, was just twenty-one months older than her nephew. "Baby" would soon enough insist that Willy call her "Aunt Beatrice," though, in full deference to her heightened status.

Alice now stepped up into Vicky's vacated role as her father's private pupil. Though he wouldn't give the same intensity to any of the other children as he had bestowed on his eldest, Albert diligently tutored the fifteen-year-old every evening in his study. Unhappily, the strain of having assumed virtually all of the queen's important work had begun to drag down his health. Never a robust man, he was always prey to whatever stray infections or ailments were traveling the formidably contaminated tide of daily Victorian life. Furthermore, Vicky's physical absence took a serious toll on his well-being. Albert's self-absorbing relationship with his eldest daughter had been severed by the reality of the very union he had prepared her for: not only had Fritz now become the principal intimate male in his daughter's life, but there was the significant distance between England and her new home. Correspondence thus became an important link between father and eldest daughter: the first letters between them were posted before the sun had gone down on the princess royal's wedding day. As Alice watched the transformation of the man who formed the heart of her universe, she tried in every way she knew to fill that emptiness. And it was she who, while coming to the prince consort every evening for her instruction, first clearly saw her father's physical—and psychological—downturn.

While Albert was captaining the monarchy with the authority that the queen had abdicated to him (and a voice her ministers gladly listened to in lieu of that of his wife, who was as often guided by emotion as by intellect), Victoria now had time to map not only Alice's future but the matrimonial prospects of all her children coming up on adulthood. Of far the greatest importance in dynastic terms to Britain itself was, of course, Bertie's marriage. The choice of wife for the heir to the throne was a matter that the queen could not haphazardly allow to just happen or to be decided by Bertie's undirected feelings alone. Though Victoria sensibly recognized and promoted the conviction that her children should marry for love, as she herself had so successfully and happily done, this conviction did not mean that the choice of spousal candidates could ever extend beyond an extremely limited range.

At this relatively early point in her reign, these limitations effectively translated into Continental Protestant princes and princesses for her daughters and sons. Britons—her own subjects—no matter how high their rank, were ineligible on at least three counts: there weren't any royal cousins among the British Hanoverian relations that the monarch thought especially well of (cousinship itself, even in the first degree, was not an eliminating factor for prospective royal spouses anywhere in Europe); marrying a fellow Briton wasted the opportunity to make some kind of useful foreign alliance; and raising one of her own nonroyal (even if noble) subjects through marriage into the royal family was held to be politically objectionable.

So, for Alice, Victoria had only a tiny number of names to work with. Other than the prince of Orange—Willem—the list of eligible suitors for her second daughter featured only one or two other obvious candidates. Prussian Prince Albert figured as a possibility, and Vicky was asked for her advice on this candidate. Vicky in turn questioned Fritz, who candidly volunteered that his cousin wouldn't likely do for "one who deserves the very best." All in all, the Dutch boy retained the inside track, though disturbing word had been received at Windsor that Willem was smitten by a pretty Austrian archduchess—a Catholic, the latter intelligence especially upsetting to the queen. This discounted Holland for Victoria, who didn't like even to hear the word "Catholic," let alone countenance having as son-in-law a prince who had actually been linked with one. Uncle Leopold, also no admirer of the Dutch royal family, noted that it was unfortunate having to exclude the Catholic Pedro of Portugal simply because of his religion, a matter that hadn't stopped Leopold himself from ascending the throne of the predominantly Catholic Belgians.

Nonetheless, aware of his prospects as the queen of England's second son-in-law, Prince Willem decided on coming to London to let Victoria look him over. She thought the visit precipitate, and soon regretted ever having let the matter of her daughter's future reach Dutch ears, Vicky agreeing with her mother that such a match would be disastrous for "poor dear Alice." Victoria and Albert even resolved, when Willem came to England, to keep him away from Bertie, on the rationale that the prince of Wales was already becoming objectionable enough and didn't need the bad example of a prince who was courting a Catholic princess.

But in January 1860, Willem duly arrived at Windsor, and though he seems to have behaved decorously enough, promptly proved himself unpalatable to Alice herself, who very likely had been influenced by her parents' prejudgment. He left unbetrothed. Far from disappointed, Victoria's family considered Alice fortunate to have been saved from an unattractive and inappropriate young man. Willem would die, debauched, within months after Alice's own death in 1878.

Compared to the imagined glories of Vicky's life in Prussia, the sisters at home enjoyed few special events in their circumscribed existence. But in 1860, Alice—now the product of her increasingly exhausted father's special tutoring—made her formal debut. This entry into society ordinarily signified that a girl of the aristocracy or upper classes had come of age to enter fashionable society's round of parties and balls and dinners, where she would be introduced to potential husbands. Virtually no other expectations were available to young women of that class and period. But for Alice, the daughter of parents who had long shunned the high society of which the queen nominally stood as head, her debut signified little other than that her parents would now speed up their search, albeit in private, for a suitably lofty husband for the seventeen-year-old princess.

In June 1860, with memories of Prince Willem of Orange put behind by everyone, another young prince—Louis of Hesse-Darmstadt—arrived at Windsor. The visit was ostensibly meant for Louis to enjoy the Ascot Races in the company of the royal family, but it was really a matrimonial inspection by the queen.

Since the collapse of an Orange candidacy, Vicky had been heavily consulted by her mother on finding a husband for Alice. Indeed, for the remainder of her siblings' quests for spouses, their eldest sister would take a leading, and highly pro-German, role, and it was she who now took up the banner for Louis, in spite of the fact that such really minor German states as Hesse-Darmstadt were not ordinarily looked upon in Prussia with any great degree of marital interest. Vicky, already absorbed in her unalloyed adoration of Fritz, frankly considered a Prussian prince as most suitable for Alice, which would have the added advantage that her sister might join her in Berlin. But Prussia was just at the moment depleted of much in the way of brother-in-law material, and in any case Queen Victoria had already begun to be intrigued over the slightly titillating Hesse family for Alice.

Though blood of the House of Hesse-Darmstadt traditionally was deemed only the palest shade of purple, it was nevertheless among the Continent's most venerable in terms of antiquity. What was more, in recent decades that blood had substantially, very substantially, strengthened through the efficacious vehicle of inter-marriage with mightier, richer, and infinitely more consequential dynasties.

The acorn of the reigning Hesse-Darmstadt family had first fallen from the mighty oak of Charlemagne, a thousand years before young Prince Louis faced Victoria's scrutiny as a mate for her second daughter. Inheritance and marriage and wars had led to near-countless divisions of lands and titles over that millennium, from the days of Count Giselbert thirty generations before Louis, and of Aubris and Ydulf and Brunulf, and St. Elizabeth of Hungary, who had reputedly healed a blind man in Pressburg, and from the dukes of Brabant and Lorraine, who in recent centuries had come to reign over a part of Hesse, which were, broadly speaking, the lands of western Germany that fanned out from the ancient city of Frankfurt, on the tributary of the Rhine called the Main. One shoot of the Hessian branch inherited as its own fiefdom the little landgravate (meaning a county ruled by sovereign counts) that would become known as Hesse-Darmstadt. Its small but picturesque capital city, Darmstadt, tidily housed the landgravate court, which after having been raised to the status of a grand duchy at the end of the six-teenth century formally changed its political designation to "Hesse and the Rhine." It and its three-quarters of a million people were headed by a grand duke. At the end of 1860, when the grand duchy's heir was bidden to Windsor to be perused, that reigning grand duke was Louis III.

Louis III, a giant just two inches short of seven feet, was the old-est of a trio of brothers and one sister. Their aunt, Elizabeth, had the good fortune to marry Tsar Alexander I of Russia, and as the dowager tsarina after her husband's death, she retained her strong interest in the art and science of royal matchmaking—an art and a science that had certainly served *her* well—for not only her imperial family in Russia but that of her grand ducal relatives in Darmstadt as well. Of particular interest to Elizabeth was her niece, the beautiful young Hessian princess, Marie. And as in a fairy tale, her nephew, the Tsarevitch Alexander Nicolaievitch, the twenty-year-old heir to the Russian throne (who boasted of an earlier connection with Britain's royal family in that he had once instructed the young Queen Victoria in the intricacies of the Polish mazurka), came to Darmstadt, fell in love with his lovely fifteen-year-old cousin, and became engaged to her. The tsarevitch invited his fiancée's brother, also called Alexander, to come with Marie to St. Petersburg, where she was to be married and make her home, believing that a sibling's presence at the court would help staunch any homesickness on Marie's part. To make the offer palatable to the dashing young Hessian prince, the tsarevitch offered Alexander a captaincy in the enormously glamorous Russian *Chevaliers Gardes*. The future tsar's brother-in-law's prospects in Russia looked to be endless.

Alexander, a major general at twenty, alas soon proved a handful for his sister's family. Yet his drunken boisterousness and lack of any sense of serenity would quickly seem relatively minor deficiencies as he was about to commit an act so inimical to his caste and rank that its offense to the jealously upheld principles of royal behavior would horrify every court in Europe. Alexander fell in love with and decided to marry a woman whose lack of high rank not only disqualified her to be his wife but, far more important, disqualified her as a sister-in-law for the future tsarina. The woman's name was Julie Hauke. She was of Polish birth, a countess of fairly recent family creation, and of good but not overly impressive German, French, and Hungarian ancestry. Her occupation was lady-in-waiting to Marie. Julie was said to have an "almost masculine mind," which translated into a streak of steel in her character that would serve her well in the ordeal she would soon undergo.

The affair was a long while in coming to a head. Three years after the couple met and declared their love and intention to marry, and were forcibly kept from doing so by the tsar's fury at such cheek, Alexander's brother Louis inherited the grand ducal throne back home in Darmstadt. Alexander and Julie continued their relationship, clearly with no thought of ending it. Upon St. Peterburg's demand that Louis—as both Alexander's firstborn sibling and sovereign—use his influence to bring the affair to a halt, the new grand duke did strongly warn his brother of the consequences should he and Julie marry. But the Hessian prince's sense of his personal honor had long since taken over what should have been a young prince's dynastic concerns, and knowing that Julie expected they should be married, Alexander convinced himself he had no option but to head for the altar. In October 1851, the couple was married in Breslau. The price Alexander paid was banishment from the Russian court and, indeed, from Russia itself, as well as the deprivation of all the honors his sister's family had bestowed on him; a dishonorable discharge from the Russian Army; and, for good measure, the status of pariah in every royal court in Europe where the assorted sovereignties concentrated a great deal of energy toward keeping parvenus like Julie Hauke from entering their midst as equals.

Though furious about his brother's breach of the rules, Louis knew that he would have to find some kind of appropriate status and title for his new sister-in-law, who could not, after all, be hidden from the public in his own tiny grand duchy. But Julie's morganatic marriage to Alexander unarguably meant she could not be a princess of Hesse, nor could she assume her husband's rank; any children would be, of course, ineligible to succeed to the Hessian throne. Finding a half-forgotten village along the Eder River in the northern part of his grand duchy, Louis gave Julie its name, and she henceforth became known as the countess of Battenberg, which rank would eventually be upgraded by the kindly Louis to princess of the same, with the quality of serene highness.[1]

Though Louis had meanwhile married a Bavarian princess, he and his wife were to have no children. His heir was thus his next younger brother, Charles. Charles's wife, Princess Elizabeth of Prussia—who had, incidentally, been born on the day of the Battle of

Waterloo and was honored with its heroes, the duke of Wellington and Prince Blücher, as godfathers—was the mother of three sons and a daughter. The first of these—Prince Louis—was, following his father, heir presumptive to the grand duchy. It was this young man who had just arrived at Windsor and was being looked at very carefully by Victoria as her prospective second son-in-law.

Louis appeared at the magisterial seat of English royalty with his younger brother, Henry. The queen found the pair exceedingly congenial, fortunately for Louis far more so than she had thought the prince of Orange. But of greater importance, her daughter Alice concurred that the elder of the pair was *enormously* congenial, apparently falling in what she considered to be love with the twenty-three-year-old Louis almost as soon as she set eyes on him. The only impediment to immediately settling the question of a match was that Louis was rumored to be in love with another princess, Marie of Baden. But the more the young man saw of Alice, the less he thought of Marie, and the more smitten he became with the princess within arm's reach. He determined that his own parents, whose blessings he wished to have, should think well of her, too.

Both of the principals were at their most attractive. Alice wasn't exactly pretty, but neither was she the pinched woman she would become in middle years. Youthful enthusiasm softened her countenance, despite the severe, center-parted hairstyle peculiar to the period and the matronly clothes all the daughters of the queen wore in contrast to the more youthful, fluffier styles favored by their upper-class contemporaries. Louis was quietly handsome, tall and still slender, his softly wavy light brown hair set off by side whiskers and a mustache. The Hessian prince's English was rudimentary, far less usable than Alice's near-perfect German, the language which the couple would use for their courtship and throughout their married life. Though "love" soon was professed on Alice's part, the couple in reality barely knew each other, being allowed to spend virtually no time alone together. But Alice clearly liked what she saw of Louis, and assumed his good manners boded well for future companionship. She hadn't yet any signals that the Hessian prince's intellectual bent was far below her own, and that his ability to show or bestow emotional support was equally limited. As for Louis, he perceived Alice as a decorative ornament in the palace of a future reigning grand duke, and in this he badly misjudged what drove the English princess. But on his return to Darmstadt he was understandably filled with wondrous expectations.

Alice was, of course, still innocent of the physical realities of marriage. Both of her parents believed that this side would somehow make itself magically evident on the wedding night, and thus needn't be discussed with any of their daughters; the queen also seemed to believe that no one else's sex life could ever achieve the heights of ecstasy hers and Albert's had reached, and there was therefore no reason to invite comparison. Further, for a girl whose family stood at the very peak of the British social order, Alice's knowledge of the world of men and women was extraordinarily circumscribed, her education limited in large part to family and academic matters: after the queen's children reached school age, not even brothers and sisters were ever again permitted to be alone in the same room together. The lubricious reasons for this absurdity must somehow have sunk into the young minds as their parents enforced their appalling prudishness, even in an age of relative prudishness, through conduct that was extreme. The princes were likely to have shucked off its effects the moment they left home for careers. The princesses were likely to have done no such thing, instead becoming gravely confused over the subject of sex.

Meanwhile, Vicky had been deeply involved in an important search, for a wife for Bertie. Louis's sister Anna seemed to Vicky a possible mate for the prince of Wales, though she didn't like the Hessian girl's figure and thought her teeth "nearly all spoilt." But time to examine the *Almanach de Gotha*, the stud book of European royalty, was limited by the fact that Vicky had had another child—a daughter, Charlotte. Charlotte proved a further thrill for the infant's young aunt Beatrice, who begged to be excused from her own nursery routine on the reasoning that she now had "no time . . . I must write to my niece." The prince consort sent his congratulations to Vicky: ". . . the little daughter is a kindly gift from heaven, that will (as I trust) procure for you many a happy hour in the days to come." To the contrary, Charlotte would in her mother's lifetime produce for her considerably more miserable moments than she would happy ones.

Louis returned to England in November 1860, on what the queen frankly wished to be a "decisive" visit. Five days after his arrival, he and Alice finally were able to have a talk "almost undisturbed," with only one lady-in-waiting hindering their ability to try genuinely and privately to understand each other's expectations. Throughout, Alice's family was all atwitter, her siblings understanding what was happening, the prince consort anxious for Louis to decide the matter, and the queen not especially liking having to go through the same nervous palpitations she had experienced during Vicky and Fritz's courtship. Even if Louis were to have had second thoughts about Alice's suitability for her future role in Darmstadt (where, by the way, the reason for their young prince's trip to England was known to nearly everyone), or about his own physical attraction to her, the pressure of Europe's most royal royal family on him to perform must have been well nigh unbearable.

Taking the plunge, on November 30, Princess Alice of Great Britain and Prince Louis of Hesse and the Rhine became officially engaged. Louis asked for his mother-in-law-to-be's blessing, though he was disappointed when she informed him that he and Alice must still wait a year until the wedding. Alice was bidden to her father's study, where Albert explained something of the physical side of marriage to his daughter—it is not known to what degree of technicality. The queen reported that Alice received her father's explanation "with joy."

Victoria invited Louis to stay in England for Christmas. The weather was horrible, with freezing rain, Christmas Day itself the coldest the island had experienced in half a century. For Alice it got warmer when Louis gave her a brooch and a cast of her hands, the latter just then a stylish gift. Her fiancé left three days after the holiday, Alice crying her eyes out at his departure.

The queen was not heartbroken at the thought of Alice's remove from her life. More practically, she viewed the union as the acquisition of another son—fully expecting Alice and Louis to spend a substantial part of their time in England, with her, after their marriage. In a letter to Uncle Leopold, she justified this expectation on the principle that since Louis didn't have any real work in Darmstadt other than to wait for the throne to be vacated (as she blandly put it, "Louis [is] not having any duties to detain him much at home at present"), he could just as well spend the time in England. Alice would be near to hand, her babies would be born in a civilized country, and God would be in His heaven.

Though she of course couldn't know it, this was the apogee of Queen Victoria's life, the high place from which she was soon to fall into the oncoming blackness of near dementia. Her eldest daughter was happily married to a noble husband who looked sure to fulfill Albert's cherished vision of a united, liberal Germany, and now the mother of a son and a daughter. Bertie had just returned from a successful tour of North America, acquitting himself commendably and becoming in his parents' eyes—sadly for but a short time—a son to be admired. The queen's second daughter was engaged to a winning young man, and it seemed as though Alice wouldn't even have to leave hearth and home except for annoying, but probably only short, visits to her husband's country. Six more children were available to fulfill various parental wants.

The queen had made up with her own semi-estranged mother, with whom her ties had been eroded almost to the point of breaking a few years earlier, in the prolonged wake of what Victoria held to be the duchess's unbecoming, possibly even indelicate, affiliation with Sir John Conroy. But largely through Albert's truly solicitous efforts, queen and duchess had in recent times been brought back together, their relationship restructured into the mature closeness that is one of the glories of an adult's union with a respected parent. Though the duchess of Kent commanded no political influence over her daughter, and made no effort to do so, Victoria and Albert and their children had come to treat her as a beloved matriarch. And, finally, the prince consort, God bless him, had become a king save only the title, admired by all her ministers, loved and depended upon to an inconceivable depth by herself. Only a fiend could have predicted that such bliss would, starting in a few weeks, begin to turn to choking dust.

Eighteen-sixty-one: the dreadful sound of that date would for the remaining forty years of her life bring back overpowering pain to Queen Victoria. It would always be recalled as the year in which her existence went from well-being and happiness and the will to live to the very depths of despair. It was the queen's forty-second year, just middle age, really only the end of being young. The opening chord of this *annus horribilis* for Britain's royal family actually came late on the last day of 1860.

Vicky and Fritz had been awakened in the bedroom of the Crown Prince's Palace early that morning. A telegram from Sans Souci, twenty miles to the west in the royal park at Potsdam, told them that the mentally disabled King Frederick William was dying in the same room that had once been occupied by his immeasurably nobler predecessor, Frederick the Great. In company with the regent Prince William and Princess Augusta, the young couple rushed to Sans Souci, there to find the aged Queen Elizabeth tending her dying husband. An hour after the chiming clocks ushered in the new year, Frederick William IV died. William and Augusta were now king and queen, Fritz and Vicky crown prince and crown princess.

After the telegram announcing the news reached Windsor, Victoria was distraught at word of a fellow sovereign's death. But what really worried the queen was the thought of what this meant for Albert. Her husband's attentions would be turned to guiding Fritz and Vicky through the added duties inevitably coming to a direct heir and his wife. By now, she knew too that all was not well with Albert. Not only had he become seriously lacking in physical vigor at forty-one, but it seemed that every ailment on the horizon effortlessly settled on him. Swollen glands and dental problems caused him almost constant pain, making it extremely difficult for him to keep up with the wide-ranging workload he had undertaken in his wife's name. No amount of wifely pleas that he slow down had the slight-est effect on Albert's determination to involve himself in most of the major policy issues facing the country, and in the doing to prove to England that it got the best of the bargain when he came from Coburg two decades earlier.

On March 16, 1861, this and every other matter was swept aside for Victoria in the first truly personal trial of her life. The duchess of Kent died, while holding her heartbroken daughter's hand, at Frog-more House in the grounds of Windsor Home Park. The only per-son Albert sent for was Princess Alice, to whom he gave a single simple instruction: "Go and comfort Mama." Alice had spent a good part of her days during the previous winter as a companion to her ailing grandmother, playing the piano in Frogmore's drawing room, and eventually nursing the old woman, in an early demonstration of the princess's abilities to care for the sick that would play so im-portant a role in her married life. Albert was wise to choose this daughter to help the monarch get past the tragedy.

But on the duchess's death, Queen Victoria almost immediately fell into a nervous breakdown, the first of two she would endure in this one year. Her initial response was to order that her mother's rooms be left exactly as they were, an ominous sign of obsessions to come.

It is hard today to understand Queen Victoria's loss of control and the near derangement that overcame her at this time. There had been long stretches of Victoria's earlier life—especially in the years immediately following her accession—when she doubted her mother's affection for her. "I don't believe Ma ever really loved me" (an entry in Victoria's journal) may have represented the pique of a moment, but it also likely reflected something of her deepest suspi-cion of her mother's true feelings for her. After the reconciliation of recent years, Victoria's need for her mother's love and companion-ship brought the two women closer together. What was more, the duchess represented the one woman in her close sphere whom Vic-toria did not feel she socially outranked. Queen Victoria never nec-essarily felt restricted by all the social rules that bound other women in her kingdom, particularly those of the higher classes. She believed, characteristically, that the depth of her love for her husband exceeded that of any other woman. She allowed no one to gainsay her, except Albert. She never, not for an instant, forgot her rank and position, regardless of her disingenuous professions of how little such matters meant. The result of these factors translated into a license to mourn that exceeded ordinary standards, right up to the point of her actually losing control of herself and of her usual finely honed sense of what best served her as monarch. Word of the queen's frenzy over the duchess's death even led to political implications. Vicky wrote her father of "monstrous reports" heard in Germany of Continental physicians having been called to the queen's bedside to attend her breakdown. Fortunately, the news heightened Albert's efforts to bring his wife out of her self-indulgent grief.

During the mean months that followed the duchess of Kent's death, a dismal succession of domestic worries and burdens occupied the sagging and depressed queen. Vicky wrote that she was having troubles with her parents-in-law, "quarrels without end," as the princess put it. What was more, the new King William was clearly going to be a problem: at his recent coronation in Königsberg, he declared that his crown had come from "the hand of God," a notion whose literality appalled Victoria and Albert.

Bertie's bachelorhood was also of worrisome gravity. Though his recently completed North American trip had elevated the prince in his parents' eyes (even if Albert churlishly told his twenty-year-old son that the real and sole reason for this success had been the fact that he was his mother's son), at heart both parents believed the only thing that would keep Bertie from being a disappointment in life was the steadying influence of an appropriately versed consort. After Victoria's and Vicky's minute perusal of the *Almanach de Gotha*, the most likely candidate appeared to be one Princess Alexandra of Denmark, the daughter of the heir to that kingdom's throne. Vicky would have preferred a German, but the queen didn't object to a Danish candidate as long as whoever it was could keep Bertie on an even keel. Victoria would have *liked* her son to find his wife-nominee desirable, but that wasn't something that couldn't, if necessary, be overcome.

Alice's situation also raised certain difficulties. Though it seemed that Alice and Louis were settled, the question of where the couple would live in Darmstadt hadn't been worked out by the groom-to-be's family; Hesse-Darmstadt was a poor country, and the grand duke couldn't conjure funds out of a threadbare treasury. Through her prime minister, Lord Palmerston, Victoria had managed to persuade Parliament to provide a £30,000 dowry for Alice, an amount that seemed generous, but as Albert knowingly remarked, "she will not be able to do great things with it." Compared to the vast riches expected someday to come Vicky's way on her accession as queen of Prussia, Alice's fiscal situation seemed almost bleak. But as Victoria viewed matters, the small-minded burghers of Darmstadt's niggling over building Alice a new palace was an unnecessary annoyance alongside the more important matters with which the British monarch had to deal. In fact, where the controversy over the couple's future palace did the most damage was in the resentment it caused her future countrymen even before Alice got to Hesse.

Louis again returned to Britain late that spring, joining his fiancée and her family for another holiday at their beloved Balmoral. The somewhat improved Victoria confessed that Louis's presence was largely responsible for her feeling better—her near-endless sobbing had finally started to abate—and she was, in fact, so much enamored of the young man that she took it into her head to raise him to a royal highness (though at home British elevation of his rank had no effect and there he remained a serene highness). But a disaster of monstrous proportions to the future of Britain's royal family and its monarchy was beginning to germinate in a much-ignored corner of Victoria's kingdom.

The Curragh was a name that would always torment Queen Victoria. Set on the plains of County Kildare in Ireland, the Curragh camp represented one of Britain's principal military training centers, the headquarters of the island's southeastern army district. Bertie had recently been sent there by his parents to receive training in his future role as head of the nation's armed forces. He was attached to the second battalion of the elite Grenadier Guards, his fellow officers coming almost exclusively from Britain's highest classes. In an episode of youthful high spirits, a group of these officer friends sneaked a young woman named Nellie Clifden into the prince's rooms, where Bertie had what was very likely his first experience with full-blown sex—where he was "introduced to dissipations," as one biographer nicely phrased it. Though the tryst remained secret for a few months, word of this indiscretion by the heir to the British throne eventually leaked out and got to Stockmar, the professional tittle-tattle, who thought such intelligence might, if widely known, ruin the young man's chances with Princess Alexandra because of her father's puritanical views on such matters. Stockmar told Albert on November 12. The news deeply affected the equally prudish prince consort, who was certain his son would go on to occupy his mother's throne as befouled as any Hanoverian *débauché*—and who worried that the young woman involved might even be pregnant and thus able to force his son into court on paternity charges.

Albert shared the story with his wife, who nearly came undone, in large part because of how badly she saw that it affected her husband; Victoria would later claim that she believed it was really this matter that killed the prince. Alice, by this time her mother's closest confidante aside from Albert, may have been told of Bertie's behavior; Vicky was not, only being informed by her parents that "bad news" had been received.

Albert decided to thrash out the matter with the prince of Wales, who had enrolled in university classes after leaving Ireland. What the prince consort couldn't have known when he left for Cambridge was that he had very likely already contracted typhoid, whose provenance was probably the plumbing at Windsor (the disease cannot, of course, be traced with certainty). Weak already, the prince was further troubled at recently received news that Coburg relatives in the Portuguese royal family were dying of typhoid; he had harbored great hopes that the liberal Coburg influence in Lisbon might bring that nation some relief from its backwardness. It was at the height of all these woes that he set out, in miserable rainy and cold weather, on a mission whose nature must have been as trying as it was overblown in both parents' minds.

While walking alone together through the sodden streets of the ancient university town, Albert tried to impress on the surprised Bertie how disappointed he was with this lapse in morals, misconduct to which the younger man freely admitted. When Albert said he nonetheless forgave his son, and that the queen did not know of the incident (which was untrue), the episode might have ended there rather than becoming the nucleus for a mother's unremitting antagonism that would fester for four long decades. But tragically, within days of Albert's return to Windsor, the doctors found that his health had deteriorated alarmingly.

Typhoid fever was one of the great levelers in the Victorian world. Caused principally by sewage carelessly disposed of and by impure water supplies, the surest preventive measure against the scourge was simple cleanliness. The illness is marked by headache and fatigue, accompanied by the inability to sleep, as well as a very high fever. In its early stages, it progresses to intestinal bleeding, with eruptions and blotches on the skin. The victim becomes emaciated, with a dry tongue, quickened pulse, and abdominal distention. Still not at this point necessarily fatal, death comes in the second or third week principally from exhaustion, or from uncontrollable internal bleeding, or from fever literally cooking the brain. The susceptibility to typhoid differed greatly among its victims, with men considerably more at risk than women, and, not surprisingly, physically weakened individuals at highest risk. Albert was just about the optimal victim.

On his return to Windsor, he was able—just—to fulfill one final, extremely important state duty: to redraft the government's communication in the *Trent* affair, which, by ameliorating Britain's harsh response to Washington on this early Civil War contretemps, helped to avert the very real possibility of military action between Britain and the United States. But by the end of the first week of December, he had grown too weak to stand, and had to be put to bed. To keep from frightening the queen, the royal doctors did not tell her (or Albert, for that matter) that they now knew typhoid fever to be the cause of the prince's illness, using instead the term "gastric fever" in hopes that Victoria, who was unavoidably involved with the day-to-day business of the monarchy, wouldn't worry quite so much.

At this point Alice stepped in as principal family caregiver. At eighteen, the princess's maturity would astound witnesses to the unfolding tragedy. She dropped every other pursuit of interest, including writing anything frivolous to Louis, informing her fiancé only of the facts surrounding the prince consort's illness and of her mother's needs: "I only hope that I am really useful to them . . . and I would still more gladly bear everything, if it were possible. . . ." One observer, Lady Lyttelton, called Alice "the angel in the house."

Alice would read to Albert, or play the piano in the room adjoining Windsor's Blue Room (the same room in which both George IV and William IV had died), where the prince now lay. She moved her own bed into the connecting room, rising at all hours of the night to comfort her declining father. Though her presence at his side unquestionably eased the torments of Albert's last days, her careful ministrations were powerless to check the progress of disease in a man who had already abdicated the will to live. The pregnant Vicky was kept in Berlin by her doctors, who feared that a winter journey across the Channel to England might endanger the baby she was carrying. Fifteen-year-old Lenchen and thirteen-year-old Louise, both confined mainly to their classroom, understood something of the danger their father was in, but were too young to in any way emulate Alice's remarkable nursing skills; furthermore, their mother did not want them to risk contracting his disease. Beatrice, only four, was, thankfully for all, oblivious to the drama.

December 14 brought this great family tragedy to a horrifying close. Alice wrote to Louis that morning, informing him that "everything would be decided" in the next twenty-four hours. She had also sent a telegram to Bertie the night before, telling him he must come home immediately; unbelievably, his mother evidently had no plans to bid him to the scene. The prince of Wales arrived at three in the morning on the 14th, appalled, and still unaware that his mother knew the causes of his father's unusual visit to him in Cambridge three weeks earlier. When Victoria saw him, she shuddered.

The queen was in and out of her husband's room all that day. Alice carried on steadily with her nursing activities, her ministrations to her dying father remarkably intimate for the age in which these horrors were playing out. While the princess oversaw everything lest Albert panic at her absence, between eight and nine o'clock in the evening—the latest hour Beatrice had ever been allowed to be up—her siblings were led into the room to bid their father a final good-bye. Sadly, the prince was unaware of the children's presence, depriving them of any real farewell on his passing. At 10:00 P.M., all realized—all that is except for Victoria, who was in denial over what was happening—that the end would be but moments in the coming. When Albert made a terrible sound in his throat, Alice calmly said to a lady-in-waiting next to her that "this is the death rattle." The queen, who had stepped out of the room for a momentary respite, was called back in. At 10:45 on the night of December 14, 1861, the prince consort died.

Victoria collapsed onto the floor. Alice just sat there beside her, looking up at the bed where the still-warm body lay. Lenchen was violently wracked with sobbing. Bertie stood silently at the foot of the bed, barely comprehending what had happened. Louise was awakened with the news, at which she cried out: "Oh! why did not God take me? I am so stupid and useless." The queen ended the worst day of her life when she went into Beatrice's nursery to comfort the one member of the family who was too young to know anything other than that everybody was so sad. Victoria, who had been given an opiate, picked up the sleeping four-year-old, stumbled down the corridor to her own bedroom, wrapped the child in Albert's nightclothes, and lay there, sleepless, while she waited for the dawn.

5

Settling Daughters

"Why may the earth not swallow me up?" Writing to her eldest daughter for the first time since Albert's death, Queen Victoria's lament expressed what would for a very long time be her unfeigned and wholehearted wish. The loss of a cherished spouse is perhaps the deepest horror a human being can suffer, a cutting off of a proud shared identity. For most people in such circumstances, however, even this great pain will fade with the physic of time. But Victoria was not most people; nor were the circumstances of her life governed by ordinary rules.

This widow was the peak, the unassailable pinnacle of British society and, beyond Britain, of much of a closely intertwined European royal caste. In the near quarter century since she had come to the throne, the sole supporter to whom she could turn unreservedly to help with her enormous burden had been her husband. Since their marriage, Albert had become infinitely more to the sovereign than her consort and the father of her children. Though Victoria's position in a constitutional monarchy largely circumscribed her actions and authority to figurehead status—the physical embodiment of a state in which parliamentarians governed—the monarch's desire to monitor and advise her government's actions was to an amazing extent acceded to by her ministers, men who permitted her to review and comment on their deliberations and decisions to any degree she chose. Her participation was, in the main, always treated with near-religious respect, and her views granted as much deference as possible.

Victoria regarded her role as a trust requiring her own unequivocal seriousness, immutable labor, and faithworthy probity; and she strove to fulfill that trust over any interest in personal gain or what would make life more comfortable for herself. Her entire existence reflected that outlook, whether it took the form of seemingly bizarre relations with her children or the demands she unflinchingly placed on her ministers. As for her official capacities, her closest adviser—eventually closer even than her prime ministers—was her husband, an adviser whose term was furthermore not fettered by any electorate. In the last years of their marriage, the prince consort spoke openly for a monarch whose grasp of national affairs came nowhere near matching his own, and who to her credit recognized her shortcomings and her husband's concomitant strengths. Lord Granville would write of the sovereign after her loss: "Having given up [for] 20 years, every year more, the habit of ever deciding anything, either great or small, on her own judgment . . . who has she upon whom she can [now] lean?" Gone was what one biographer called "an ever open encyclopedia on the desk beside her."[1] When Albert died, not only did the normal physical and emotional love that passes between spouses vanish with him, but so did the one person over whom this queen did not want to reign.

Savaged by grief, Victoria's mental state crashed into another breakdown. Not only was it was the second collapse within a year, its depth and duration would far overshadow the one that had come in the wake of her mother's death.

On December 14, 1861, Princess Alice ceased to be her father's nurse, and on the following day assumed that role for her remaining parent. Thoughts of Louis and life in Darmstadt would for a long time be relegated to a further corner of Alice's thoughts.

The ordeal that the queen underwent was in reality deeply shared by Alice. The younger woman would later write of her amazement that either she or her mother managed to survive the experience of Albert's death with their reason intact. Sleeping nightly in Victoria's room, keeping constant watch over the keening monarch, running interference with the ministers whose business with the sovereign remained as urgent as it had been before the prince consort's death—never did the princess flag, even when her own need for her father's counsel seemed almost unbearably urgent. It was Alice who ordered and then administered the opium that enabled her mother to get enough rest during those first nights so that Victoria's descent into madness never quite became irreversible. Many witnessing the scene at Windsor came away with the impression that if Princess Alice had herself broken down in the first days after Albert's death, she might have taken the queen with her, so precariously did the latter's health hang on the thread of her daughter's stamina.

When Louis came over from Darmstadt for Albert's funeral, he found the Alice he had left behind now another woman: a gaunt and hollow face replacing the pink-cheeked visage he had known, mourning-reddened eyes instead of the happy smile normal for a bride-to-be. Louis wasn't even sure that the Alice he was now seeing still wanted to marry, so absorbed was she not only in caring for her mother but in handling her own grief as well. The larger question the Hessian prince must have asked himself was whether this obsessed young woman would be suitable as the future grand duchess of his small realm.

Signs of change came within a few weeks, as Victoria's mind grew steadier and hope began to seep into the shadow world of the court. Most important, the recovering monarch was able to think out a blueprint to guide the remainder of her reign. Though she repeatedly expressed a wish that her life would soon be ended so she could join Albert in death, in the absence of such release she knew exactly how to carry on—at least as a queen. Victoria would henceforth treat *all* of Albert's views and dicta and opinions as holy writ, trying for the four remaining decades of her life to follow them as if they were a constitution—rules that she might interpret to shifting circumstances but could never fundamentally alter. But where her husband had been strong-willed and sometimes even mulish, he at least possessed the intellectual capacity to consider other views, to change his mind, to tack to the direction of the wind. His widow's values and opinions virtually froze in December 1861.

Though the cause of Victoria's grief of course grew more distant in time, the funereal obsequies grew ever more exacting, as did the queen's insistence that they be observed with an unremitting punctilio. None of the children was ever again allowed to talk about their father in easy, normal phrases, simply expressing that they *missed* him and wished he were still there. The queen expected every reference to the prince consort to be pious, but perforce artificially pious. Victoria turned her homes into great mausoleums devoted to Albert's memory, all of his private rooms treated as shrines: not a stick of furniture or a picture on the walls or even one of the countless Victorian doodads that decorated Albert's rooms was to be moved; his clothes were set out for the next day, as though he were alive and waiting for them; his shaving and toiletry needs were changed daily, valets filling basins each morning with fresh, warm water. This homage to a dead man continued virtually unabated for the next forty years, and no one ever challenged Victoria's right that it should be thus.

Of gravest domestic consequence, Victoria's relations with her eldest son following his father's death descended into an irrational and sometimes astonishing dichotomy of love mixed with loathing, respect with disparagement. She flatly determined to exclude Bertie from any but the most insubstantial social duties, while she herself retained undivided authority over the empire's political business. The prince of Wales, with his future consort, would be permitted to show himself socially, and she would insist that he always be accorded the highest respect for his own position as heir apparent (and thus for who his mother was). But Victoria never routinely shared ministerial intercourse with Bertie, dialogue in which her son Leopold would one day partake.

The immediate family issues that had to be resolved when she

began to emerge from deepest mourning were the marriages of
Bertie and Alice. Since Albert had approved Louis for Alice and
Alexandra for Bertie, Victoria concluded that nothing should inter-
fere with either of these unions. As she viewed matters, Bertie as
heir *had* to be married soon, and Alice's Hessian union would further Albert's vision of a future liberalized Germany. Her personal
opinion of Louis was a bit shaky, but she wrote to Vicky that although he was far less of a man than Fritz (since Victoria wasn't
given to flattering the crown princess, one can assume this as her
vouchsafed opinion), the monarch was nonetheless certain that the
young man's innate kindness would serve Alice well.

During the months after Charlotte's birth, Vicky had been con-
sumed by the task of helping to find a wife for her brother Bertie.
Assigned the job by her parents, the crown princess had proved the
perfect matchmaker. Intimately aware of her brother's shortcomings, thoroughly knowledgeable about the eligible princesses available for Bertie, and highly motivated to find a German—which she
knew would make her parents happiest—Vicky had set to her mission with a relish. She had traveled all over Germany looking for
someone suitable, aware that her brother was going to be hard to
please and furthermore that he would likely be heavy sledding for
any young woman. But the prospect of being queen of England was,
Vicky knew, a prize that gleamed brightly and would in the end result in any number of willing candidates.

Eventually it was Vicky's lady-in-waiting and close personal
friend, Walpurga "Wally" Hohenthal, who suggested the Danish
princess Alexandra. Wally's husband had served in the British Em-
bassy in Copenhagen, where she first met Alexandra, who was in
the opinion of many the loveliest princess of Bertie's age in Europe.
A photo of her that was sent to the queen and prince consort whet-
ted their inquisitiveness, especially with Vicky's appended note that
Alexandra was "just the style Bertie admires." Vicky's approval of a
non-German must have been hard for her, knowing how it might
alienate her further from Fritz's family, and clearly showed the love
she held for her brother. Though not entirely without hope that a
suitable German might still be found, the queen arranged that her

son and the Danish princess should meet in Speyer, ostensibly on a sightseeing trip to its famous cathedral.

In putting Alexandra forward, Vicky was indisputably taking a very real risk that her own position in Prussia would be made even more precarious. Besides the fact that Alexandra wasn't German, another contentious matter centered on the duchies of Schleswig and Holstein, lands disputed between German national interests and Denmark's crown. But trusting—perhaps too much so—in Wally's judgment, and certain that her brother would be drawn to the Danish princess's stunning good looks, as well as solicitous that he should be as happy with his wife as she was with her husband, Vicky wholeheartedly endorsed Alexandra. As it happened, the still-callow Bertie was apparently not fully sold on his elder sister's choice after the Speyer encounter, telling his parents that he needed time to think over such a momentous undertaking.

Busy as Victoria was with her older offspring, Louise and Lenchen were also coming up fast on marriageable age, and soon some part of the queen's energies would have to be turned to their needs, which meant, of course, finding husbands for them both. Vicky's marriage had been brilliant, about as important a liaison as possible in Europe, always excepting any that involved the occupants, present or future, of England's throne. Alice was going to make not a grand but certainly an important union with her Louis; Hesse wasn't Prussia, but in Albert's vision a liberal reigning prince in the small state couldn't be a bad thing. But after Vicky and Alice, Lenchen's and Louise's futures weren't likely to be nearly so important.

Lenchen was, unhappily, turning out to be a problem. Though the girl was so obedient as to sometimes seem nearly mindless, Victoria recognized that her middle daughter was not going to sweep any of the sons of Europe's Protestant houses off their feet, regardless of the girl's provenance as a daughter of the British queen. Already chunky and double-chinned, shy to the point of perpetual near terror and hard-pressed to hold up her end of any kind of halfway substantial conversation, the fifteen-year-old might prove very challenging to place favorably. One of the few members of Victoria and Albert's family not to possess any real degree of artistic talent—though she was proficient at the piano—Lenchen instead continued in her teens to invest her passions in animals, outdoor pursuits, and the cultivating of girlfriends beyond the secure and loving but stultifyingly limited circle of her sisters.

Five days before the black December Saturday that devastated her family, Lenchen had written to a friend, Emily Beauclerk, the daughter of a royal household official. Her letter had gone on about all the things that matter to any girl just coming into womanhood. She asked Emily for a photograph of herself, knowing that a picture of a nonfamily friend would represent for her a rare symbol of independence. She promised she was wearing the locket Emily gave her, every day, and told her friend how happy the family was to be getting favorable reports on Leopold, who was "delighted" with Cannes, where he had been sent to help him recover from his latest round of hemophilia-caused debility. In the middle of the letter, she mentioned that "darling Papa" was unwell, but that he was "going on as satisfactorily as possible." She explained that the prince consort was suffering from a "feverish attack brought on by influenza," and that the family was now "quite easy about him, all we have to do is be patient."

A month and an era later, Lenchen's first letters to Emily after Albert's death afforded some of the most poignant impressions of the blow that had traumatized the nation's first family. Having to describe what she called the "dreadful calamity" to Emily must have been wrenching for a sheltered girl so much of whose happiness vanished with her beloved father's death. In her dispatch of January 14, 1862, Lenchen wrote, "What we have lost nothing can ever replace, and our grief is *most, most* bitter . . . oh! if you knew how miserable I am." She described the prince consort's role in hers and her sisters' lives: "I adored Papa, I loved him more than anything on earth, his word was a most sacred law, and he was my help and adviser. . . . Those hours were the happiest of my life, and now it is all, all over." Assuming these words represented not merely the charged atmosphere of the moment, then clearly Lenchen had been closer to her father than to her mother.

In the first months of their mother's bereavement, it was four-year-old Beatrice who more than any other member of her family at home could make Victoria lay aside—however fleetingly—the mantle of royalty for that of unadorned motherhood. All the other children were now expected fully to share with their mother the dark gloom that had descended over the royal homes. Any sign of playfulness, or laughter, or forgetting for a moment the funereal rules that the monarch had laid down would draw a reproof from the queen, or, at the very least, a wounded expression implying that her grief wasn't being taken seriously. Even Beatrice was dressed, like her older sisters, in the voluminous mourning costumes that now shrouded every female at court, though she was yet too young to be fully bound by the regimen, and Victoria was willing to excuse her youngest child's occasional exuberant outbursts. Nonetheless, the environment weighed heavily on the four-year-old. The following apology was made by the princess to a lady of the court: "I had such a funny thought today, just for my own amusement, but it turned out an *unproper* thought so I would not let it think." Beatrice's sentiments were expressed in childish (if precocious) terms, but this reflection on the requirements of her new life was almost eerie in its glimpse of her future. Bright and vivacious as a young girl, Beatrice was to have her spirits slowly depressed by all this unnaturally perpetuated gloom, until she turned into the tongue-tied, backward young woman that only marriage would one day requite.

The royal children's social lives had come to a virtual halt in December 1861, the six still at home denied even those contacts with outsiders that had sometimes been allowed before their father's death. Lenchen told Emily that "it will be a long time before I shall see you again, but I shall think constantly of you." But on February 10, 1862, the princess wrote once more to her friend, in words suggesting the youthful buoyancy that was already bringing the younger members of the family back to some kind of normal life: "Today is dear Mama's wedding [anniversary]. I am afraid it will be a very trying day for her. Dear Pussie, I should be so delighted if you would let me have the bookmarker you made for me a long while ago. . . . I am going out riding this morning."

Louise became Alice's chief lieutenant in the first months after their father's death. Though the older Lenchen would in the normal course have become the next responsible daughter, her inability to go long without breaking down in tears reduced her usefulness. Instead, it was Louise who backed up Alice, and did so competently; this fourth daughter possessed much of the spirit that also characterized the second. All the sisters, though, concurred in the queen's demands that their father's plans be carried out without demur, including even those more ephemeral intimations that were interpreted as having been their father's wishes. First was physically getting rid of Bertie—out of the house and their mother's sight. Since Albert had planned a trip to the Near East for his eldest son, the queen packed her heir off in early February 1862, his departure undoubtedly a psychological relief to a still barely functional sovereign.

If any kind of gap was left by Bertie's departure, Vicky's arrival on Valentine's Day filled it. Alice went to meet her sister's ship at the pier, enabling the two to have a long cry together before their mother greeted the crown princess of Prussia. There was some concern that Vicky might upset the queen by not displaying the requisite degree of despair, since her sisters knew that the princess had decided she couldn't in the stern atmosphere of the Prussian court afford to give herself over to unrestrained emotions. But the visit was successful, as Vicky managed to tamp her instinctive perkiness to the muted tones that Victoria now demanded of everyone permitted her presence.

For the half year after her father's death, Alice had been the physical representation of the monarch to much of Britain's official world. Since the "Terrible Fourteenth," it was through this daughter that the great majority of the queen's communications passed to her government's ministers. Queen Victoria concealed herself in almost total seclusion, refusing to come into public at all since the disaster, and except that Albert had willed it should be so, Alice's planned July wedding would very likely have been canceled. There can be little doubt that any such celebration of normal life would have been anathema to Victoria without the Albertine sanctioning.

But Albert *had* plainly desired that Alice should go to Darmstadt, and thus the marriage had to go forward. To help get herself through the ordeal, Victoria focused on the thought that Alice and Louis would spend a substantial part of their married life in England, with her; by this time, the queen saw to it that her needs and wishes superseded those of anyone else, and even newlyweds would have to bend to that reality. Good, faithful Alice would be, thank God, available to share in and sympathize with every one of the queen's paroxysms of tears and now-routine spells of joyless brooding.

Osborne was where Victoria's early mourning had been carried out. Long a central symbol of happiness for Alice and her sisters and brothers, it had now been transformed by the queen's command into a kind of seaside mausoleum. But there Victoria felt safest from prying eyes, and it was at this shrine to her husband's memory that she decided Alice's marriage ceremony would be celebrated.

Not exactly celebrated, but rather performed. The widow would allow none of the usual happiness associated with a wedding to supersede her grief, regardless of the effect this would have on the bridal couple. Victoria rationalized the ceremony as essentially a religious rite rather than an occasion for revelry. And except for the white of Alice's wedding gown, the event that transpired bore far more the hallmarks of a wake then those of a wedding.

While at Balmoral in May, Victoria wrote in her diary that "the Angel of Death still follows us." She nonetheless expended considerable effort in helping Alice—who was just turning nineteen—to get her trousseau together; fortunately, its contents had been settled before Albert's death. The queen even seemed to get a modicum of enjoyment out of helping her daughter with the details of the ceremony, perhaps reminded of the happiness she herself had enjoyed twenty-two years earlier.

The event was to be conducted in Osborne's dining room. Though vastly grander than the chambers in which all but a tiny minority of her subjects took their own dinners, by royal standards the room was fairly runty. Of course, Alice's service was not to be the kind of a holiday event that had characterized Vicky's wedding at St. James's Palace, marked by a contingent of governmental personages and foreign royalty. Even a flock of bridesmaids, chosen like the trousseau before Albert's death, were now told their roles were to be curtailed so as not to create a spectacle. Alice would be principally attended by her three younger sisters and Louis's sister, Princess Anna of Hesse. A few weeks before the ceremony, the grand duchess of Hesse—Louis's aunt and the consort of the duchy's sovereign—died, throwing just that much more cold water over everyone's already damp spirits.

What should have been a festive and joyous day, July 1, 1862, was instead, as the queen described it to Lord Tennyson, "the saddest I remember." Indeed, the wedding could have been a funeral. Alice's sisters began the day in their black mourning dresses, changed at midday into white bridesmaids gowns, and returned to their black the minute the newlyweds departed for the honeymoon. A photograph of Alice taken that morning shows her draped in an elaborate white gown hemmed with orange blossom, with still more of that fragrant Victorian wedding flower crowning her head and shoring up a Honiton lace veil. But her face couldn't hide a sadness that seemed to speak more of tragedy than it did the beginning of a newly wedded life. To add to the disheartening air, the summer skies over the island were dull, with winds bearing down on Osborne from the Channel.

The guests were almost all family members, masses of Cambridges and Hesses, and a single Coburg—Albert's brother Ernest, who would give the bride away. (Vicky had been kept in Berlin by another pregnancy, this time of her second son.) A small posse of ministers and bishops and officers of state and court came down from London, a few family friends filling in the remainder of the guest list. Conspicuously absent from any socializing before the ceremony, the queen wasn't about to let herself be stared at by curious or pitying eyes. In the gloom, Baby Beatrice seemed to the crowd a little whirlwind trying to chase away the demons.

The altar was set up directly under Winterhalter's great 1846 portrait of the royal family, a picture placed in this position on the queen's birthday in 1849: it depicted the young Alice at her father's foot, Albert presiding over his painted family, his image on the canvas looking now to be watching over his daughter's wedding. The archbishop of York entered first as the ceremony got underway. The congregation then rustled expectantly when the doors to the hallway opened to admit the queen. Encircled by her four sons acting as a kind of living screen around their mother, Victoria walked to and then sat in the corner where Albert's painted eyes peered directly at his widow. The queen's returning gaze seldom left the portrait. Affie never stopped crying; tears even rolled down the archbishop's cheeks while reading the service. After Alice and Louis took their vows, the guests left for their luncheon in the Council Room. Victoria did not, of course, join them, instead hurrying with Beatrice next door into the little Horn Room to join Alice and Louis for their meal, the groom having just been created a British royal highness by his mother-in-law. After the bride redressed in black, the couple left for a honeymoon in which, Alice must have fervently prayed, the grief and gloom would be purged by a few degrees in her first hours as Louis's wife.

As for so many in her family, Albert's death left a substantial void in Vicky's life. Her mourning mother continued to write her the letters that arrived in Berlin nearly every day, for which in return Victoria expected a similar tide of correspondence. Where the advice Albert offered in his letters had shown a political understanding of the German character, sadly the mother's often missed her late husband's subtle but vital restraint. Instead, the queen continued to urge, even demand, that the crown princess act like an English princess in a court to which Vicky now owed, if not for her own sake then for Fritz's, an undivided *Prussian* allegiance.

Vicky had even more reason now to avoid expressing liberal-leaning opinions that could only aggravate her position. Her father had possessed some ability to make King William consider at least a relatively progressive view toward European politics. But shortly after Albert's death, the Prussian king would acquire a new prime minister—a man whose political orientation was about as far removed from Albert's as possible in the partisan world of nineteenth-century Europe. When William appointed Otto von Bismarck to direct the Prussian government, the tragically naive Vicky neither ameliorated nor cushioned her outspoken views against her father-in-law's new chief servant. Almost from the day this Prussian aristocrat entered into office, both she and Fritz would descend into a deadly and irreversible spiral of immateriality.

For a woman who believed her abilities were limitless if only she tried hard enough and believed strongly enough, Vicky's inability to find a cure for her firstborn's affliction was both unfathomable and unacceptable. And instead of diminishing, the injury to Willy's arm and shoulder had grown more prominent. Fritz had learned to accept the situation, but Vicky found that impossible. The "treatments" that had begun soon after birth had in the early 1860s become a nightmare in the family's life. The boy was continually subjected to painful harnesses and heat regimens, to compresses and muscle manipulations, to having his good arm tied down an hour each day so as to force him to use the unyielding one. The minutest details of these tortures Vicky forwarded on to her mother as the stuff of her daily correspondence; in one letter she included her own drawing of a splintlike body device that the harassed court physicians had engineered for the boy. An anguished mother, who felt guilt over providing her adopted country with an imperfect future king, she nearly smothered Willy with attention, initiating a tumultuous love-hate relationship that would in the coming years serve both poorly.

Two years before the pregnancy that had kept her from Alice's wedding, Vicky and Fritz had become parents for a second time in July 1860, to a baby girl born perfect in form and health. Less perfect would be the relationship between the mother and her daughter, whom the parents named Victoria Elizabeth Augusta Charlotte; she would always be Charlotte in the family. Their relationship would eventually sink into a cold and distant antipathy, although unlike the difficulties with Willy, its significance would be principally of a personal family nature.

Meanwhile, the entire Hohenzollern clan had begun openly to disdain Fritz's wife, inflicting every kind of snub and slight on the English princess that they could conjure. On the anniversary of Frederick William III's death, Vicky was actually turned out of her sitting room in the Neues Palais, the chamber emptied of her furniture and used for a memorial wake—all because that particular room had "always" been utilized for this purpose. King William's compassionless behavior toward his daughter-in-law can perhaps be rationalized as that of a sixty-four-year-old man who feared that his son was anxious to gain the throne for himself and his English wife. But particularly hurtful to Vicky was the startlingly unfriendly behavior of Queen Augusta, her mother's constant correspondent and the supposedly "liberal" member of the family. Now that her husband was king, Augusta was determined to have her way in all things social, and particularly resented any possibility that the eldest daughter of the queen of England might usurp any part of her limelight. As much as Vicky loved her husband and he her, Fritz was not a man to demand anything from his august parents, not respect or even respectful treatment for his wife.

Although these essentially personal family problems were troublesome enough, Vicky's political difficulties were magnified enormously by Bismarck, who had become prime minister at a moment when the thwarted King William had been actually on the verge of abdicating his throne to Fritz. What led to William's extraordinary near abdication was the monarch's almost monomaniacal obsession with his country's army—the instrument to which Prussia owed its status as one of Europe's few real power players.

The issue centered on a bill William had submitted for Parliament's approval of what he thought of as a routine change in the army's draft requirements. The king wanted an increase in the draft period from two years, which he considered too short, to three years; "discipline, blind obedience, are things which can be inculcated and given permanence only by long familiarity" was the gist of his argument. Further, William believed the character of the army would be weakened if the balance swung to a badly trained reserve force. Parliament for its part considered that the extension on enlistments would cost more than it was worth and, since that body's only real power was its control over national spending, was in a position to thwart its monarch. The legislature refused to bow to William's wishes. After more than two years of wrangling on the issue without a change in either's position, he considered that his only honorable recourse was to hand over the throne to Fritz.

In the one circumstance that would have vastly changed his, Prussia's, and Europe's destiny, Fritz made the most spectacular mistake of his life. His father's intention to resign the throne was no mere threat, the king coming to within a hair of carrying out this fateful action over such a preposterously nonessential matter. Despite his wife's urging to accept the crown that dangled over his head, Fritz begged his father to reconsider and, in effect, refused to accept it. Historians have judged that Fritz was primarily motivated by his respect for the monarchy and the "natural" order of succession—meaning only on his father's death should sovereignty come to him. Fritz furthermore agreed with his father on the army issue, relatively inconsequential as that may have been. But it is as likely that the twenty-nine-year-old crown prince was frightened of what would face him as sovereign: a truculent legislature that his personal instincts would be reluctant to tackle, an ex-king hovering in the background, and a wife mistrusted by the middle classes and disliked by the court and upper classes. Liberal as Fritz may have fancied himself, this scenario was one he had little stomach for.

Vicky, upon her return from visiting her newly widowed mother, had continued to plead with her husband to reconsider. Though no one expected William to live to a great age, Vicky knew he could well reign for several years more, years that would be deducted from Fritz's and her own chance to restructure Prussia. But Fritz refused. Instead, William invited the autocratic and reactionary Prussian nobleman Bismarck to attempt to resolve the impasse between crown and Parliament and to serve as his combined minister-president and foreign minister. An ultraroyalist to whom liberalism was anathema, who believed the might of the state came not from the will of the people but from the end of a finely rifled cannon barrel, thus became in September 1862 the highest servant of the crown and of the state. Bismarck would see to it that Fritz and his English wife were never again presented with such an opportunity while King William I remained alive.[2]

Back in England, grief still shrouded the royal residences like cobwebs in an attic. During the year after Albert's death, the queen's wailing would start up at the least provocation—walking into a room in which her husband had worked, or moving to a residence where his absence tore the fragile scab off her wound. After a time—a long time—the monarch's fits of hysterics began to descend into simple surliness. But Victoria seemed incapable of going forward into a new life, and her power and authority were such that she was allowed to maintain an almost impenetrable pall over the monarchy. Expected to ignore the joy inherent in their own youth, her children were among the principal victims of this regime, all bound instead to the cheerless routine that best suited their mother's new persona.

At sixteen, the just-confirmed Lenchen was considered to be, if not yet a woman, at least out of the schoolroom—too much formal education not held to be necessary or even quite fitting for the younger girls. Her mother found her thoughts turning to a husband for this middle daughter, the one she so frankly held to be the least promising. With typical candor, Victoria wrote that "poor dear Lenchen, though most useful and active and clever and amiable, does not improve in looks and has great difficulty with her figure and her want of calm, quiet, graceful manners."

With little sign of arresting her tendency toward stockiness, Lenchen ate in compensation for want of anything to do in the post-Albertine gloom. No more intellectually curious than she had been when in the schoolroom, and frightened of her imperious mother, the princess nonetheless possessed praiseworthy qualities that would serve her well in life: a kindness toward nearly everyone she encountered on a personal basis, and a loyalty to family and friends that was far from universal in the hothouse atmosphere of the court. Furthermore, her plumpness was offset by beautiful wavy brown hair and a face that, with oncoming maturity, boasted a fine straight nose and attractive amber eyes. Her talent at the piano was growing into a genuine command. And because Alice hadn't come back to England with anything like the regularity that her mother had expected, Victoria called on Lenchen with increasing frequency to help her with the official side of her life. The queen wrote to her uncle Leopold: "Lenchen is so useful, and her whole character so well adapted to live in the house, that . . . I could not give her up, without sinking under the weight of my desolation. A sufficient fortune to live independently if I died, and plenty of good sense and high moral worth are the only necessary requisites [for Lenchen's future husband]. He need not belong to a reigning house." He wouldn't.

In the fall of 1862, a somewhat rebalanced Victoria took her children on a long trip through Germany. The central purpose was to visit the late prince consort's boyhood homes in Coburg, where the queen showed her children the places that had been beloved by their father. Even here, she would be offended by any sign of overt joy: keeping childish chatter to a minimum even while eating, Victoria complained of "what I suffer often at dinner when jokes go on and my heart bleeds."

While visiting Uncle Leopold at Laeken Palace in Brussels, Lenchen and her sister Louise were introduced to Prince and Princess Christian of Denmark, who were accompanied by their daughters, Alexandra and Dagmar. The four girls, all close in age, became immediate friends, boding well for young Alexandra's forthcoming engagement to the prince of Wales.

On another visit to Germany three years later with her mother, the now twenty-year-old Lenchen met (except for a forgotten chance encounter in childhood) the man she was to marry, yet another Prince Christian, of Schleswig-Holstein-Sonderburg-Augustenburg. As with the spousal choices of nearly all of Victoria's children, this one raised its own political difficulties. On the plus (albeit slightly exotic) side, his mother, descended from a noble Danish family, was the former Countess Daneskyold. He was also kin to British royalty, his grandmother having been a granddaughter of Frederick, son of King George II and father of King George III.

However, fifteen years in age separated the prematurely musty Christian from the still-girlish Lenchen. Christian indisputably looked far older than he really was. In contemporary photographs, he could be mistaken for forty; this misfortune would in fact come to obsess the queen's present and future attitude toward him. Regrettably, he bore neither the intelligence nor the savoir-faire to make up for his old-fogyishness. He was not ambitious to any detectable degree, nor was he any kind of amiable raconteur. Especially troubling was the fact that, notwithstanding the expectations inherent in his caste, Christian possessed nothing remotely approaching a fortune and was, unhappily, near penniless, at least in royal terms. And he was jobless as well, since he had recently left the Prussian Army. A princess of the United Kingdom might reasonably have aimed for something more. Yet to Lenchen, Christian seemed just fine, and she determined that she was absolutely going to have him.

Since the queen had by now settled on Beatrice as the crutch of her old age, she resigned herself to losing Lenchen. Yet Victoria wasn't a woman to forfeit a daughter without gaining something in return. When it became clear that Lenchen had decided on the pauper prince, the monarch informed Christian that he would be acceptable as her son-in-law only if he agreed to live permanently in England, and moreover quite nearby to wherever she would be. Since his range of options appeared limited, and since he furthermore seems to have genuinely liked Lenchen, he readily consented. It must have all appeared very exciting to the German, but then Christian couldn't have been aware just how stupefyingly boring life at Queen Victoria's elbow was going to be.

Before anything could be finally decided, the one fly in this particular ointment had to be taken account of. As a prince of one of the branches of the elaborate Schleswig-Holstein family tree, Christian was a part of perhaps the most convoluted political controversy in Europe, one that had recently been at the root of a clever little war by which Bismarck gained control, at Denmark's expense, of the disputatious provinces of Schleswig and Holstein. An affair poorly understood then as now, Prussia's 1864 war with Denmark over Schleswig and Holstein (the latter's border came up to the very gates of the great northern German city of Hamburg) had just been fought in the expectation that it would provide an avenue for eliminating Austria from Prusso-German affairs, even though in the war Austria was, paradoxically, Prussia's ally. In creating the circumstances he believed would lead to Prussian hegemony on the Continent, Bismarck demonstrated a brilliance that would soon transform his tough little state into one of the world's great military powers—and himself into an adversarial behemoth with whom the rest of Europe would struggle for the next quarter century.

The Prusso-Danish war had been precipitated by Denmark's ill-considered political annexation of Schleswig, which had been the personal property of the Danish king since 1815, though not a part of Denmark itself. It and Holstein were, however, claimed by the home-grown duke of Augustenburg, a former schoolmate of Fritz's and now his and Vicky's close friend. Though Bismarck claimed he wanted only to maintain the status quo, his larger motives were, one, to annex the duchies to Prussia, and, two, to confirm Hohenzollern Prussia's leadership over German affairs at the expense of Hapsburg Austria. The Prussians and the Austrians together invaded Schleswig and Holstein, quickly defeating the Danes' toy army and then ambiguously occupying the two duchies. Vienna now held that Schleswig and Holstein should be governed by the indigenous Augustenburg family—Christian's family. But Bismarck, who had long been looking for the chance to eliminate Austria from a voice in North German affairs, would two years later use Vienna's growing discontent with Prussia's occupation of the duchies to make war on Austria, thereby paving the way for the political creation of a so-called *Klein-Deutschland*—a "small Germany," which is to say a Germany without Austria.

These events would have a profound impact on Queen Victoria's third daughter as the Augustenburg family became a second casualty in all this *Realpolitik*. A younger son of the Augustenburgs, who were a branch of the Schleswig-Holstein family, Christian recognized that his family were no longer practical candidates for a throne of the duchies. This signified that his own future was pretty much bereft of recognizable landmarks, and specifically that he was free from any dynastic responsibility at home. Yet even with the issue of Christian's political liabilities largely obviated by his family's loss to Bismarck's scheming and Prussia's strength, his own personal lack of desirability would drive a wedge between members of Lenchen's family.

Vicky strongly supported Christian to be her sister's husband, whose family had long been warmly welcomed at the Neues Palais, the crown prince and princess firmly supporting their friend's claims to the duchies in defiance of Bismarck. Vicky wrote to her mother of her disgust at the "small but powerful party which now reigns [Bismarck and his supporters] which does the mischief to present and future . . . and are at present mixed up with the fate of the family to which Lenchen is to belong. . . ." According to Vicky, Christian "is our *Hausfreund*. He comes and goes when he likes. . . . He is the best creature in the world."

But if Victoria's firstborn approved of Christian, her second-born was horrified when his mother announced to the family that Lenchen and Christian's marriage negotiations were formally underway. Though this may have been secondarily motivated by the prospect of a brother-in-law whose royal status was notably meager, the prince of Wales's more serious problem concerned Alexandra, whom he had married in 1863. The Augustenburgs were not only the enemies of Prussia, but of Denmark as well. The new princess of Wales, daughter of the Danish monarch at whose expense Christian's family would have taken Schleswig and Holstein, endlessly blubbered that "the Duchies belong to Papa." To confirm the seriousness of his reservations, Bertie dramatically threatened to estrange himself from involvement with his family if his and his wife's objections were ignored.

Louise, meanwhile, sided with Vicky in support of Christian, knowing that Lenchen wanted very much to get out from under the immediate control of their mother. But the Waleses had an ally in Alice, who declared against the match. Her grounds were typically rational. First, she reasoned that the marriage would infuriate the Hohenzollerns, who viewed the Augustenburgs as politically liberal, and Alice was smart enough to realize that unnecessarily riling Vicky's powerful in-laws was a stupid idea. She thought as well that Christian was too old for Lenchen, although Christian's age wasn't really any of her business, particularly since Lenchen seemed happy enough with him. But most importantly, Alice suspected that her sister was being pushed into a marriage in order to always be near at hand for the personal and selfish needs of the queen.

Alice freely expressed these reservations, setting in motion a serious breach between herself and her mother. When the princess heatedly defended herself, the road was paved for near-permanent estrangement between the two. Victoria would write of Alice's behavior in the matter as "jealous, sly and abominable." The queen loathed being thwarted in her matrimonial machinations (or, for that matter, in almost anything else), and when it was her own daughter who was doing the thwarting, her anger rose to stunning proportions.

This rift between the queen and Princess Alice quickly took on amazingly dark undertones. Having apparently forgotten that it was this daughter who had made herself sick nursing her mother through her grief less than five years earlier, Victoria's venomous anger at Alice over Christian of the Schleswig-Holstein affair was disseminated widely among her far-flung family. Writing to Uncle Leopold, she complained that "Alice (to my great sorrow for she used to be such a great comfort to me) is very unamiable and altogether not changed to her advantage. But the contrary in many ways—sharp and grand and wanting to have everything her own way." To Vicky she wrote that "our good Al. is like a distinguished lady of society but nothing more!" Rarely contradicted, Victoria was clearly incapable of brooking criticism of what she felt were her inalienable prerogatives as head of the family.

Still Alice tried to remain the peacemaker, no matter how strongly she opposed Lenchen's marriage. When the unmollified

Bertie declared his intention to boycott the ceremony, it was Alice who persuaded him to attend, writing him: "Oh, darling Bertie, don't let you be the one who cannot sacrifice his *own feelings* for the welfare of Mother and Sister." The princess would also remind her eldest brother that their mother had risked offending Berlin through her strong backing of his own marriage to Alexandra, whose Danish heritage had found little favor with the Hohenzollerns. Alice would also try to help patch up the rift Christian's parentage caused between her mother and the princess of Wales. If only her judgment had been used so wisely when she first decided to voice her own objections to the match.

Louise found a way to inject a touch of humor into all this grim business, suggesting that "Lenchen like Herodias should ask for Bismarck's head" as a wedding present from the king of Prussia. Victoria found the proposal amusing, and so repeated it to the crown princess in Berlin. Even Affie, who regarded Lenchen as his favorite sister, weighed in with good-humored advice to the effect that Christian not be looked at "with a prejudiced eye, for he is really a very good fellow, though not handsome."

Two years passed between gestation and realization of the marriage. Unhappily, the wedding came in the middle of the Austro-Prussian War, Bismarck's follow-up to his Danish war and the conflict that cleared the way for final Prussian dominance in Europe's German-speaking world. On a family level, this second of Bismarck's wars split Victoria's progeny and their spouses between the belligerents, Fritz commanding Prussian troops, Alice's husband leading Hessian forces in support of the Austrian Army. The state of affairs kept both Vicky and Alice away from the wedding, which, in all likelihood, was for the best.

Despite the bitter feelings over Christian's entering her family, Lenchen's wedding day—July 5, 1866—represented a personal triumph for this the most timid of the five sisters, and one that would happily spare the bride the political trials her two already married sisters were to endure in their more consequential marriages. What was more, these nuptials were not celebrated with the deafening gloom that overlaid those that had joined Alice and Louis. For a site, the queen consented to Windsor Castle's Private Chapel, admittedly a step down from St. George's Chapel, in the castle's Lower Ward, but a healthy step up from Osborne's dining room.

The bridal procession formed up in the castle's Grand Corridor, the interior passage that gives entry to all the principal private chambers in the palace part of the oldest occupied royal residence in the world. The leading participants stepped off toward the chapel to the strains of Beethoven's Triumphal March, creating a spectacle marred only slightly by the sudden disappearance of the duke of Cambridge, who suffered an attack of gout, which misfortune required a speedy reshuffling of celebrants. Christian, having just been naturalized and taken the oath of allegiance, was dressed as a major general in the British army, the recent commission reflecting an appropriate station for a son-in-law of the sovereign. *The Times* circumspectly noted that the groom's appearance was that of a "tall, military-looking man, apparently between 35 and 40 years of age, with a good forehead." Christian was attended by his "supporters"—Prince Frederic of Schleswig-Holstein and Prince Edward of Saxe-Weimar.

In the interests of relieving her habitual black dress with something to reflect the temporary joy she was permitting herself, Victoria ordered a new moiré gown, shot through with silver thread. On her head she wore a diamond tiara, the tail of her white widow's cap streaming down the back. The queen herself gave the bride away, answering the officiating archbishop's question with a gesture described as "full of dignity and determination."

Like many royal brides of the period, Lenchen was frankly outshone by the spectacular uniforms and court dress of many of the male guests. Still, she made a fine impression with her white satin gown speckled all over with orange blossoms and myrtle, hooped in the crinolined style of the period, and her diamond and opal jewelry glinting under the chapel's flickering candles. A flock of eight unmarried daughters of the higher nobility lined up behind Lenchen as her bridesmaids. Unfortunately, more than one guest commented that the princess appeared to be marrying an aged uncle. Lenchen and Christian spent their first night as husband and wife at Osborne, before setting off to honeymoon in Paris, Interlaken, and Genoa.

The Darmstadt into which Alice had followed Louis was very different from the neoclassical grandiosity of Vicky's Berlin, and unlike most European cities with their twisted lanes built over ancient footpaths, Darmstadt's streets had been evenly laid out, albeit at a loss in charm for such mechanical regularity. Only a small nucleus surrounding the antique palace remained to indicate the ancient-most parts of the town, but even that kernel was, compared to the beauties of the places in which Alice had been raised, dark and of limited attraction.

The closest similarity in royal life between Darmstadt and Berlin was the notion that any fiddling with tradition was nearly taboo, which precept ran headlong into Alice's inclination to change for the sake of change. Her unfortunate determination to remain a princess of Great Britain in her new home—a course already taken by Vicky—would serve Alice as poorly in grand ducal Hesse as it did her sister in Berlin. Though her German was fluent thanks to its having been spoken at home in her youth, enabling her to communicate freely with her husband's subjects-to-be, Alice from the outset followed paths that would lead to difficulties and mark her for most of her tenure in Hesse as hopelessly foreign.

At first, it was petty though closely held customs against which Alice rebelled. When, for example, she changed the early dinner hour—four o'clock, which she found absurd in contrast with the more "civilized" eight o'clock to which she had been accustomed at home—upper-class tongues wagged all over Hesse. She would often ask a lady-in-waiting to join her on what were considered to be "daring" private walks through the streets of Darmstadt, during which many passersby failed to recognize their new princess, or else showed surprise at the simplicity of Alice's plain dresses and democratic manner.

Considerably more controversial was the princess's choice of guests in hers and Louis's home: unable to abide a steady diet of sanctimonious and boring courtiers, Alice invited people who had never before seen the insides of the duchy's palaces, even bidding middle-class citizens to enter, provided only that those invited were doing something interesting or had something interesting to say. While this behavior perhaps endeared her to ordinary Hessians, it dismayed the government officials who had always monopolized the court and royal family. But whether the duchy's courtiers approved of her notions of inclusiveness wasn't something that Alice worried much about, except insofar as it affected Louis's position in the grand ducal family itself.

The question of housing for the couple had been a contentious one when they were still only engaged, the grand duke (Louis's uncle) having been loathe to spend his duchy's meager resources on a new setting appropriate to what he expected might be demanded for Queen Victoria's daughter. The question of a fitting residence remained on a low simmer during Alice's breaking-in period as Louis's wife, during which the couple made their first home in a little house in one of the dark streets of the town's Old Quarter. This seemed to suit the newlywed Alice just fine. The meager house was a far cry from anything she had ever known in her former life, and from its windows she could look out directly at carts rumbling along the cobbled streets—streets whose panoply of noises easily penetrated the royal couple's decidedly unpalatial walls.

Though Queen Victoria was free with invitations to return to England for visits, Alice was determined to stay in Hesse and try to accustom herself to its different way of life. Much of her new existence was highly pleasurable, as when she and Louis could escape the urban noisiness of Darmstadt by retreating to the family holiday home at Auerbach, a villa outside the town, lent them by her husband's uncle. In this bucolic setting, she found the greatest happiness in her married life, at this point in her relationship with Louis still blissfully and contentedly in love. Worrying about how her widowed mother was faring in England meant some of her new life was tucked in shadow, but in the main Alice loved Hesse, her position as a married woman, and a husband she delighted in getting to know.

Alice reveled in the bustle of the restoration of the wonderful old castle at Kranichstein, which the grand duke was giving to Louis. And beyond the pleasure of creating new nests for herself and her husband, the princess had also started a family with which to fill those nests. In April 1863, a little less than a year after her marriage, Alice's first child was born. It was for her, just as it had been for Vicky, a very difficult first delivery. As the mother-to-be went to Windsor for Bertie and Alexandra's wedding, the baby was born not in Hesse but in England, although the Darmstadt court chaplain came over for the christening; the infant was named Victoria Alberta Elizabeth Matilda Marie.[3]

In the summer after little Victoria's birth, Kranichstein was finished and became the house Alice and Louis considered the home of their dreams. Located in the hills a few miles northeast of Darmstadt, the castle called up a storybook kind of German charm: gray stone walls and turrets in a forested setting, its own lake, and wild boar roaming the surrounding parkland. The couple's first summer in this splendid setting provided the most idyllic days of their life together.

A year after their daughter's birth, Alice and Louis became parents again, and again of a girl, Elizabeth, always to be known to her family as "Ella." Alice's decision to breast-feed her new baby ran squarely into her mother's derision, exacerbating the growing split between the queen and the princess.[4] Furthering the rancor was Queen Victoria's awareness that Alice had found true happiness in Darmstadt with her young and handsome husband, the peevish mother realizing this would translate into fewer visits from her daughter and son-in-law.

Alice's growing self-confidence had by the mid-1860s made her the recognized arbiter of Darmstadt's social affairs, putting the grand duke's court and her parents-in-law's demicourt in the shade. But her attentions aimed beyond the concerns of upper-class society. As might be expected for a young woman who had nursed both her parents through life-and-death traumas of their own, Alice directed her energies toward the medical well-being of the ordinary citizens of the grand duchy. Hesse's healing arts were in a primitive state when Alice arrived in Darmstadt, not least were the problems of women in their birth confinements. She began to visit the homes of the humblest of the grand duke's subjects, often entering virtually unannounced, sometimes even unrecognized, and accompanied by no more than a lady-in-waiting. The princess wrote to her mother of her feelings about these activities: ". . . if one never sees poverty and always lives in that cold circle of Court people, one's good feelings dry up, and I feel the want of going about and doing the little good that is in my power." She added that "I am sure you will understand this." Based on the queen's views about the proper role of her daughters, it is unlikely that Victoria understood the smallest part of Alice's urge to go where princesses had rarely before ventured.

In the early spring of 1866, Louis and Alice finally took possession of the "palace" that would be their city home for the remainder of their married life. The unimaginatively named New Palace had been heavily subsidized by the British queen, who harbored strong feelings about the proper settings for her children. There were those who sarcastically described the building—which had run seriously overbudget—as a "Piccadilly mansion," a discordant architectural note out of place in the heavily Germanic cluster that made up central Darmstadt. The place had run through much of Alice and Louis's modest savings long before it was finished. Though the extravagance was controversial in the financially stretched grand duchy, as someone who regarded being royal as a normal condition Alice ignored the contrast between the opulence of her new home and the modest circumstances in which most Hessians lived. She filled the large, sunny rooms with portraits of her English family, hung amid furnishings that reflected more of Windsor than they did of Darmstadt. Far enough away from the Old Palace to give her a sense of independence from Louis's family, the New Palace soon became a sort of headquarters for the philanthropical and nursing pursuits that now filled much of her days.[5]

Much of 1866 proved traumatic for Alice, not only for the unnerving conflict with her mother and her family over Lenchen's marriage, but—of far greater consequence to her life in Darmstadt—because of the second of Bismarck's wars, one in which Hesse found itself opposing Prussia. The war would bring actual physical misery—that of the battlefield—virtually into the New Palace's drawing room.

While Alice was awaiting her third child, due that summer of 1866, Bismarck in Berlin was turning his skilled hand to the furthering of plans to make Prussia the controlling element in a new Germany, an entity that had never before been more than a geographical expression. As with his justification for the 1864 war over the duchies of Schleswig and Holstein, his design for this second conflict was built on a narrow and well-defined premise. Austria, which state the prime minister regarded as no longer fit for leadership of the German-speaking world, would see its intentions betrayed in its partnership with Prussia in participating in the latter's invasion of Schleswig and Holstein. Precipitating the war was the fact that Vienna was now calling for Berlin to hand over the joint Hapsburg-Hohenzollern administration of the province to the Augustenburg family (at this time Lenchen's about-to-be-inlaws). Bismarck refused, having long and hopefully suspected the Austrians would eventually tire of the arrangement. The prime minister gambled that he could turn Vienna's discomfiture into a *casus belli*, and took brilliant advantage of it by marching Prussian troops into Austrian-administered Holstein, at which provocation Austria predictably mobilized. The standoff quickly boiled over into war between the two German states. Hesse, along with much of the rest of South and Central Germany, took the Austrian side. Alice watched horrified as all Germany slid into what she, rightly, called "civil war." The war technically made her and her sister Vicky enemies.

As a major general, Louis commanded the Hessian cavalry brigade that was to oppose the Prussian forces under the command of his brother-in-law.[6] On their fourth wedding anniversary, Louis bade his wife farewell and left for the battlefield. Alice remained in a highly uneasy Darmstadt, expecting within days of her husband's departure the birth of her third child.

Determined to follow Louis to the war front after the baby was born, Alice sent the two older children—Victoria and Ella—to their grandmother in England. Her immediate postdelivery aim was to oversee the Hessian army's field hospitals, if she could arrange what would unquestionably be a unique and difficult undertaking. She sent Louis a copy of a letter from her friend Florence Nightingale, urging him to implement the British nurse's methods at the front. While she awaited her confinement Darmstadt's streets overflowed with soldiers, many of whom were marched off to war directly past the New Palace that she and Louis had occupied just three months earlier. So violent and chaotic was the atmosphere in the capital that rumors spread of a planned armed coup against the grand duke's throne.

Heavily pregnant and weighted down by the confining crinolined skirts of the day, Alice nonetheless undertook those war activities appropriate to her sex, principally making bandages from torn-up sheets and exerting pressure on the authorities to get the local hospitals ready for the expected casualties. Two days after Louis left, the clash that decided the war was fought in northern Bohemia at a place called Königgrätz (today's Sadowa). Austria would count on this one day 44,000 dead, injured, or taken prisoner, while Prussia lost less than a quarter as many. The latter's new "needle gun" turned the battlefield into an abattoir, with Austria's defeat consigning it to a new permanent role as, at best, a second-rank power. The German states that followed the Austrian flag could only wait to see what punishment Bismarck would mete out to them.

On July 11, Alice's baby was born, her third daughter entering the world just as Prussia's troops were on the verge of entering Darmstadt. The convalescing Alice begged Louis's uncle to accept Berlin's peace terms, though in so doing she incurred the enmity of the grand duke's brother, Alexander, who loathed the Prussians and cursed his nephew's wife for counseling surrender. But Alice realized that the German states would be forced to find some common ground after the war, even to the point of accepting Prussian hegemony.

Though her willingness to acquiesce to Prussia did not find universal sympathy in Darmstadt, Alice took the best possible view, approving the fact that Austria's removal from South German affairs would likely lead to a new and united German nation. Alice had, like Vicky, been forever predisposed to the union first heard expounded, literally, at their father's knee. Yet the behavior of Prussian troops in Darmstadt—where they would remain for six unpleasant weeks—still came as a shock. Alice learned what it was like to be among the defeated over whom victors preened and swaggered. Though civilians in the city suffered no violence, the Prussians nonetheless carried off whatever they could lay hands on and, for good measure, assessed Hesse-Darmstadt for 3 million florins in indemnity. What was left of Alice's dowry was spent in partial payment of this demand. Of critical damage to the Hessian economy, Berlin took over the grand duchy's railway, telegraph, and postal revenues. Alice wrote to her mother of these hardships, and the queen forwarded the letter to Vicky. The crown princess responded that she could do nothing to relieve the "painful and distressing position darling Alice is in," that position being "one of the unavoidable results of this dreadful war."

Still, it was fortunate for the grand duchy that its sovereign's sister was the Russian empress. Her husband, Tsar Alexander, helped persuade the Prussian king and Bismarck that Louis III should retain his throne. The fact that the Prussian crown prince was Alice's brother-in-law was also likely to have influenced Prussia's generosity. There was, however, a significant territorial loss which Hesse-Darmstadt would sustain when Hesse-Homburg in the north was permanently removed from the grand duchy to Prussian control. Though Alice undoubtedly did owe some of her country's mild treatment to her sister's influence, she was still furious when Vicky tactlessly visited Homburg soon after it became a part of Prussia.

In the years after the war, Alice's nursing mission became an obsession in her life, leaving the superficialities of a pampered and privileged princess at the outermost reaches of her existence. Every day she could be found routinely visiting hospital wards, where she tended the injured with a skill of compassion summoned from some inner wellspring. Staying in close touch by mail with Florence Nightingale, Alice received funds from wealthy Britons that were put to immediate use in improving the hospital facilities for the casualties of the Austrian war. The princess further established the new Women's Union in Darmstadt, an organization dedicated to training nursing assistants for wartime duties.

On September 12, 1866—Louis's birthday—Alice and her husband attended a ceremony they both hoped would dampen the horror of these difficult months. It was their third daughter's christening, and she was to be called Irene. Alice chose the name because it came from the Greek for peace.

With her three oldest daughters conjugally disposed of, Victoria turned to number four, the one she had long known would *never* be the crutch of her old age. Though Louise was the prettiest, the wittiest, and the best-dressed of the sisters, as well as by far the most artistically talented, she was—to her mother's everlasting vexation—also the most independent-minded of the five. All Victoria wanted was for Louise to be with her long enough to bridge the gap between Lenchen and Beatrice.

But with Lenchen married and spending more time with her husband than with her mother—despite her promise—Victoria had no illusions that Louise was going to take up very much of the slack while waiting for Beatrice to reach a useful age: "I can't speak *à coeur ouvert* to Louise (though she does her best) as she is not discreet, and is very apt to always take things in a different light to me." The monarch's complaint was a serious one for a woman who resented anyone taking a different light to her own views and partialities. But she had come to rely on her daughters for private needs in a way no servant high or low—Queen Victoria tended to regard everyone in her orbit as "servants"—could possibly be expected to fill, so Louise's peculiarities would have to be dealt with. Thus in 1866 it fell to her to serve her mother as best she could, at least until she herself got married and until Beatrice could finish growing up.

Louise's initial efforts at "service" were relatively friction-free, even though the queen plainly missed Lenchen's docility when she was faced with her fourth daughter's often impertinent and, so she believed, totally unnecessary rejoinders. Victoria couldn't help but regard her new helper as "very indiscreet" (her own words) when compared with her third daughter, who never for so much as a moment lost sight of the fact that her mother was also her sovereign. Yet so indispensable was a female child in seeing to the most intimate aspects of her life that the still largely hidden Victoria simply accepted whatever Louise could offer. One of the most important of the princess's new responsibilities, at least the one that would most inflate her own self-esteem, was serving as intermediary between her mother and her married siblings—duties that provided her with a first real taste of status in her supremely status-conscious family.

As would almost any girl of her station and circumstances, Louise desperately longed to partake of the fabulous social world in which she imagined her married brothers and sisters reveled without respite. Life with Queen Victoria may have represented the pinnacle of nineteenth-century British society, but for a teenager with an itch to escape the stifling and largely funereal pattern of life her mother maintained at the royal palaces, it usually translated into more grimness than joy. The queen for a long time even forbade Louise from accepting Bertie and Alix's repeated invitations to balls at the Waleses' London home, Marlborough House, only relenting on the eve of her daughter's seventeenth birthday. Even then she commanded that the princess not be partnered by anyone but a member of royalty.

Not only was Louise desperate to experience the pleasures she knew her rank could bring her, she had what was for a princess the misfortune of possessing an incontestable artistic talent, a faculty that sought expression beyond the limited opportunities at court. Albert's drawing and drafting skills had been nearly professional, and had reached that level without substantial training. His widow was an artist of remarkable expression and range, especially in the medium of watercolor. Victoria had admittedly been tutored by some of the best artists of the era, but regardless of her position or instruction no one could have brought out such talent had it been missing entirely. Of the couple's nine children, almost all appear to have received some share of whatever visual-artistic genes had gone into their parents' creative makeup: Vicky's and Alice's drawing talents far exceeded routine abilities, Beatrice possessed design skills, and all the boys except Bertie shared their sisters' good fortune to some degree. But in Louise such talents reached into the realm of mastery, and she would pursue her gifts far further than the other members of her family.

Her earliest drawing teachers were skilled court artists, men who had enjoined her to copy the things she routinely encountered amid the extraordinary beauty of her world: the grandeur of a Highland glen near Balmoral; Osborne's frosty lawns on a high autumn day; perhaps a copse of trees overhanging Windsor's flawlessly tended bridlepaths. Edward Corbould, the royal drawing master whom Albert had signed on to teach the royal children, became one of her closest companions, a man who later in life Louise would describe as "one of my *few true* friends that I have looked up to all my life and from whom I have . . . learnt much besides art." Corbould led Louise to draw what she saw around her, emphasizing that she use her imagination rather than simply mime technique. Her family and attendants grew accustomed to rarely seeing the princess's hand empty of its drawing pad and pencil. This endeavor gave the girl a shared passion with her artistic mother, and the mother a deeper understanding of the daughter. Victoria enjoyed the sketching forays on which she would lead her young daughter, the queen able to shake off for a little while the mantle of responsibility, the princess content to have found one domain in which she could begin to reach her mother's rank.

Yet as much as Victoria genuinely admired this daughter's skill and her determination to raise her gift to higher levels, a gift that some began to see most acutely in Louise's remarkable faculty for sculpture, one line remained uncrossable. As Louise grew older, the possibility of a professional standing in the art world—something she knew her mother would resist—began to loom in her mind.

The queen believed that the royal family stood above British society in all things, and that for any of its members to compete in the ordinary spheres of life was unfitting. Her sons were destined for military lives, as had been the male offspring of the nation's kings for countless generations; their positions would be in part honorary and—particularly in the case of the younger boys—in part the result of their own efforts. But daughters were destined for marriage. Thus, the unalterable fact of Louise's sex only strengthened the sovereign's resolve on this issue: daughters of the nineteenth-century upper classes, let alone princesses, simply did not pursue "careers." They pursued husbands, the indispensable adjunct to fulfillment.

Still, Victoria did not try to deny Louise her deepest desire, that of at least developing her abilities, and in this the princess would push the queen's indulgence to the absolute limit. Louise had sculpted a bust of her mother, the quality of which stunned its subject. While sitting for her daughter's work, Victoria listened to Louise's passionate pleas that she might raise her talents to respected heights. Possibly because she already knew that her daughter could never be the companion she coveted, her reluctance to letting Louise enter the unprotected world outside the court faded. In 1868, at the age of twenty, the princess begged for and received the permission of her mother to attend Kensington's National Art Training School.[7] This consent was a genuine stretch for Victoria, especially since sculpture was widely viewed in the nineteenth century as the least suitable art for women. (Vicky had dabbled in sculpture after her marriage, with her father's approval: Albert told his wife that "as an art it is even more attractive than painting.") And in 1868, the notion of a royal princess going off each morning to public classes in the heart of London was exotic; in fact, no monarch's daughter had ever before in English history been publicly educated at anything.

Because of her continuing responsibilities to her mother—Lenchen, constantly pregnant in the early years of her marriage, often wasn't available to attend the queen—Louise's attendance at the art school was necessarily erratic, and the princess was forced to restrict her coursework almost entirely to the sculpture classes. Still, with the 127 other enrollees she received genuine professional training and advice, and what she saw of the world beyond the palace gates made her yearn to see and do far more. As a bonus, she met people she would never have ordinarily encountered.

The National Art Training School was responsible for Louise coming in contact with the man who would exert the greatest influence on her artistic life. Joseph Edgar Boehm, a Hungarian born in Vienna, had been living in London for six years when the princess met him after starting classes at the National. Fourteen years older than Louise, married with a young family, the genesis of this sculptor's enormous popular success in Britain came from royal patronage, the wellspring of many an artist's prosperity. When Louise met him, the blue-eyed and curly-haired Sculptor-in-Ordinary to the queen was serving as an instructor at the school, and was preparing to undertake an enormous equestrian statue of the monarch, a work that would eventually gain fame as one of Windsor Great Park's most popular ornaments. Boehm's studio became a private haunt for the princess, as she fell under the artist's magnetism, her presence there lending luster to Boehm, his tutelage bestowing in turn a gravitas upon her.

Louise flourished into a hitherto unknown sense of accomplishment under her National training. A marble bust she made there of her brother Arthur was selected for exhibition at the Royal Academy. Probably an element of her august rank entered into the matter, but it is unlikely so prestigious a venue would have accepted just any piece. In truth, Louise never got ahead of the received taste of the period, personally rejecting the colossally talented work then coming from Auguste Rodin—she never went to Paris to see his work or that of the French Impressionists. Yet her sculpture would become ever more technically proficient, her works full of difficulties far beyond the abilities of the dilettante. The contemporary art historian Hilary Hunt-Lewis said that Louise's bust of her brother "infused life and flesh and blood to her marble"—high praise for any artist working in her medium.

Still, in her own eyes, and more importantly in the queen's eyes, Louise's principal duty was to marry, not because the succession was in any danger but because this was simply what was expected of her. Victoria accepted that the daughter would retain a prominent place in her life for art. Though the special circumstances relating to her *fifth* daughter would in Victoria's view dictate an entirely different outcome, it was time for her fourth daughter to find a husband.

Since the queen had no intention of losing Louise's assistance until Beatrice came of age, any husband must, as had Christian, agree to live nearby, thus eliminating any expectation that Louise might choose or be chosen by a reigning (or about-to-be-reigning) Continental prince. The queen's openly expressed edict put an end to the princess of Wales's hope that Louise might marry her brother Frederick, then Denmark's crown prince. Victoria's opposition to any more Danish matches was, in fact, equally founded on a desire not to rile Prussia unnecessarily, realizing that a second Dane in the family would be viewed in Berlin as provocatively excessive.

The queen's marriage concerns still left Louise much room in which to enjoy and broaden her new life. Coincidental with her signing on at the National had come a growing commitment by the princess to expanding the possibilities open to British women, especially those from the less privileged classes. In the mid-nineteenth century, females were looked upon essentially as chattel, organized women only just beginning to further the elevation of their rights. Sadly, the women of Britain and its empire were unable to look to their sovereign for support of independent legal rights or relief from their status as men's property. Victoria was, to the core, insensitive to the fact that her own range of freedoms in the kingdom was, for a woman, unique, that her female subjects might be less than content with the endless and relentless restrictions that limited their lives. The queen believed that women's aspirations for suffrage were misplaced, perhaps even wicked—she once remarked that a society lady advocating the vote for women "ought to get a good whipping." Raised in such an atmosphere at home, the wonder is that Louise ever came to think differently.

Training as a physician was a prominent undertaking from which females of the era were effectively barred, the common belief being that such an endeavor would rob a woman of her "purity" and thus render her undesirable as a wife. For women higher on the social ladder, those most likely to be able to afford a medical education, a further disincentive was the fact that the highest reaches of society seldom socialized with physicians, and a wealthy woman thus trained would practically guarantee herself disdain from her own class. Not only did Queen Victoria view the notion of women physicians with disgust, so—unsurprisingly—did most male physicians, who through their official journal, the *Lancet*, fulminated that women were "naturally" incapable of becoming physicians.

At the time Louise was matriculating at the National Art Training School, a pioneer woman doctor named Elizabeth Garrett was establishing a practice—with substantial difficulty—in London. Wanting to meet her, but knowing that the queen would be enraged if one of her daughters invited a female doctor to a royal residence, Louise instead went to Garrett's office. After what was for both women a pleasant and memorable visit, the princess asked the physician not to publicize the encounter lest Victoria learn of it. But her mother did find out, was predictably infuriated by such dabbling with the dangerous and unholy business of women's rights, and decided something had to be done to get Louise settled down.

Louise's unwed status was, in fact, beginning to raise questions beyond the circle of the court. Britain's public had started to speculate openly as to what might be wrong with a princess who appeared more every day to be becoming that symbol of misfortune in Victorian society, an old maid. Many ordinary Britons—read taxpayers—further couldn't understand why this beautiful and highly eligible woman should look to becoming a charge on her mother's purse. After all, Louise was all that her sisters weren't: tall enough that the amply proportioned Hanoverian bosom looked majestic rather than simply big; always exquisitely dressed as against the overfurbelowed fashions adopted by Vicky and Lenchen, or by Alice in her nurselike outfits; and inclined to gracious smiling rather than the grimacing that too often publicly distinguished the women of the royal family. Louise had, unmistakably, blossomed into a genuine beauty, her oval face gracefully framed by long and lovely brown hair, her stature poised beyond reproach. And thanks to her forays into the real world, she was an *interesting* woman. In consequence, many wanted to believe that if Queen Victoria only looked hard enough, she would quickly find a suitable prince to win this most exotic of her daughters.

So the enterprise began. And just as the ubiquitous prince of Orange had volunteered himself as possible consort to Victoria's three eldest daughters, so it would happen again with Louise. Feelers from Amsterdam suggested an interest in number four, but Victoria had by now flatly declared Prince Willem unacceptable for any of her daughters, continuing in her familiar comparison of the Dutch prince to her own eldest son. The Dutch queen, Sophia, was made sufficiently aware of Victoria's feelings to keep her son from making any more unnecessary trips to England.

The ever helpful Vicky did everything she could to further her own candidate for Louise. Inviting her sister to Berlin for a family get-together, she tried to pair Louise with the gigantically tall and wonderfully rich Prince Albrecht of Prussia, one of Fritz's cousins and a candidate of whom Vicky knew her mother would likely approve: of the thirteen eligible Protestant princes in the *Almanach de Gotha*, only Albrecht, or "Abbat," as he was called, did Vicky think would probably consent to live in England. On her visit to Berlin, Louise was stimulated by the electricity she generated on the dance floors of her sister's palaces, but nothing clicked with Abbat, the princess evidently uncharmed by the Prussian's Prussian airs. What was more, Albrecht let it be known he would *not* live in England. Victoria was disappointed, but, to her credit, would probably never have made an effort to marry her daughter off to someone the bride-to-be herself couldn't fancy. Indeed, the queen wrote to Vicky after Louise returned home: "Louise very properly said she could not and would not marry anyone she did not really like."

With no one immediately acceptable to Louise, a new and highly controversial concept began to take seed in Victoria's mind. If no eligible *foreign* prince presented himself, perhaps a *British* son-in-law might fill the bill. A nonroyal match for any of her children would unquestionably be novel, not to say extreme, but the more the monarch reflected on the notion, the more it seemed that such an outcome might be the right solution for Louise's unusual qualities. In the fall of 1869, both Victoria and the twenty-one-year-old Louise jointly decided that a home-grown, nonroyal husband would indeed be acceptable. Louise quickly conceded that she very much wanted to live in Britain and thereby remain a part of that nation's artistic life, a life she had tasted so pleasurably. Victoria could not know that this course would so affront the prince of Wales that he would threaten to withdraw from all further involvement in his mother's personal affairs.

What was so revolutionary about Louise's future, and what agitated Bertie so passionately, involved some very relevant issues. First was the fact that more than 350 years had passed since an English princess had married a subject of the sovereign, and such a union had now come to be considered politically impermissible. The last time it had happened was in 1515, when Henry VII's youngest daughter married the duke of Suffolk, though the duke was admittedly a great nobleman closely related to royalty. Even now Victoria held that the only possible home-grown husband for Louise would again be a limb off one of the nation's aristocratic family trees, and preferably a limb from a *titled* family tree.

Bertie's objections were not insignificant, nor were they based merely on caste snobbishness. In rational terms, royalty didn't marry their subjects because for a subject to enter the royal family would unavoidably lend, if not the reality, at least the appearance of unfair advantage—both political and social.[8] The lord chancellor wasn't even sure, when Victoria inquired, whether such a course was legally open to a daughter of the sovereign. A further difficulty lay elsewhere. Many of Britain's landed grandees considered their own social status equal to, if not exceeding, that of the royal family. Yet even the highest peer in the kingdom would on marriage to a royal princess be required to yield precedence to his wife, a prospect many aristocrats would just as soon avoid. Furthermore, to find a candidate willing to leave his own local responsibilities—likely significant, especially for the highest nobility—so that he and his wife might live in the queen's orbit would be notably difficult.

Whatever the difficulties, Victoria's mind was settled, and so began a well-orchestrated search through the kingdom for her fourth son-in-law. It started in July 1869. With personal wealth an unalterable prerequisite—her daughter had to be kept in the manner to which she had her entire life been thoroughly accustomed—it was presupposed that any financially embarrassed grandee would be ignored. Lord Lansdowne, one of those called to the queen's hospitality to be looked over, passed this first hurdle without difficulty. Unhappily, he failed in the area of eligibility. The marquess was about to become engaged, tidings said to have given Louise "really *quite a shock*" when revealed. The eligibility of subsequent candidates was more closely looked into.

John Douglas Sutherland Campbell, the marquess of Lorne, was twenty-five years old that summer. His father, to whom he was heir, was the eighth duke of Argyll, head of the great—some would say greatest—Highland clan of the Campbells. Called Ian in his youth, the young man was now known by all as Lorne, after the courtesy title he bore. On his father's death, Lorne would inherit the vast (though not especially fruitful) Argyll estates, including the great family seat, Inveraray Castle, a stone palace overlooking an especially beautiful corner of the Highlands whence the Campbells had sprung and prospered.

A Liberal member of Parliament at the time Princess Louise's search for a husband was getting underway, Lorne could have been a character from a Nordic saga. Of medium height, he had a handsome and uncomplicated face that still bore the flush of energetic youthfulness. But his most distinguished feature was a great mane of almost yellow hair, combed back in lofty bushiness worthy of a latter-day Samson. The least attractive physical attribute was a high-pitched voice, out of harmony with his arresting looks. His family had dealt magnificently in the history of Scotland, and his immediate predecessors, particularly his grandmother, Harriet, duchess of Sutherland, had stood at the nation's social height—she was, in fact, one of the queen's most intimate friends. After a mediocre university performance, Lorne's own extramural interests had begun to expand widely, from management of the family estates to the writing of competent poetry. As for his parliamentary life, he possessed little of the talent of a Lord Rosebery or a Lord Randolph Churchill, instead being marked in the House of Commons as a plodder. One biographer presented him as having the markings of an aesthete, though his feet perhaps were a bit too close to the ground and his head too aware of his responsibility for such a description.

Lorne's father, the duke of Argyll, met with the queen to discuss gingerly the subject of a possible liaison between their children; the proud nobleman tried to convince the monarch that the idea was not at present a good one. Argyll wanted his son to keep his future unencumbered, giving him a chance to experience more of the life his privileged position afforded. Nonetheless, he left Victoria with the impression that any decision on the matter would in the end be taken solely by his son, which she regarded as a hopeful sign.

When Louise was told of these proceedings, which had taken place almost entirely without her participation (she had met only briefly with Lorne), much to her mother's annoyance the princess signaled little interest. The monarch characterized her daughter as being "so very *difficile*," but Louise's attitude, while in large part shaped by a complete ignorance of the personality of the young man involved, was also influenced by Lenchen's warnings about the difficulties of marriage. Her older sister's position was likely to a degree self-serving, since she knew that if Louise left the fold for Scotland she herself would be much more frequently called up to duty by their mother, something Lenchen devoutly wished to avoid now that her own children were coming along at a healthy pace and she was perfectly happy at home with them at Cumberland Lodge, away from the oppressive duties of court. This left a somewhat flummoxed queen, struggling for the right words to tell Argyll that Louise wasn't yet ready for a commitment, that her daughter should be "a *little* older."

Victoria realized a more complete range of candidates would have to be paraded in front of her indecisive daughter. But events transpiring outside the sovereign's orbit would, in the end, bring Louise to settle on the Scottish nobleman.

6

Marriage and Death

In 1866, while her husband's soldiers were fighting Alice's husband's soldiers over Austria's role in the future of German affairs, Vicky was undergoing a life-and-death drama at home. With Fritz at the war front, she was alone as her son Sigismund lay dying. For all her position and rank, Sigi's illness was something against which the crown princess was just about powerless.

Vicky had been almost continuously pregnant in the seven years since Willy's birth in 1859. Though Charlotte had turned out physically perfect, already signs of the animosity that would spoil the relationship between mother and eldest daughter were becoming evident: the often unmercifully candid Vicky—a woman who rarely withheld rebukes of those she considered foolish, even her own children—criticized Charlotte in letters to Queen Victoria as "stupid" and "backward." The pretty but nervous and sullen girl sensed Vicky's disappointment from an early age, a realization that would eventually lead her to side with Willy in opposition first to her mother and, later, to both her parents.

Two years after Charlotte's arrival, Vicky's second son was born—the birth that had kept her from attending Alice's wedding.

Lamentably, Albert Wilhelm Heinrich[1]—Heinrich in public, Henry in the family—would, with his older brother and sister, complete the trio of children who would grow to deeply disappoint Vicky by what she viewed as their treachery—meaning primarily their outspoken opposition, political and social, to her and Fritz's views. As she had done with Charlotte, the crown princess also consigned Henry to the further reaches of her consideration, in large part because he, too, wasn't very smart, a condition the notably bright Vicky deplored. Although Queen Victoria had often been unforgiving of her own children's shortcomings, she was now making up for it with shrewd advice regarding her grandchildren. When Vicky wrote the queen complaining that "you do not know how much trouble we have had with Henry," her mother counseled patience and indulgence, advice she would offer wisely and consistently in the coming years.

Vicky's quick if sometimes feverish mind may have made her a natural catalyst around whom ideas and bright discourse were always welcome, but she was far from tolerant of her children's shortcomings and equally far from being a successful judge of juvenile needs. Tragically disappointed in Willy's laggardly development—the one child of hers whose future was critically important to the course by which Vicky set her bearings—and now deeming that Charlotte and Henry weren't going to turn out any better, her fourth child proved from the beginning an undiluted source of joy to the crown princess.

Sigi was born in September 1864, five months after the end of the war with Denmark. From the start, Vicky sensed a special closeness to this son, feelings that she claimed had been missing with the other children. Perhaps it was that she fancied he looked like his grandfather, Albert, or maybe it was just an infant's peculiar manner that appealed to a highly emotional mother. Whatever the cause, Vicky freely lavished her love on her third son, love that she would, in retrospect, better have shared out more equally with all her children.

Just as with Alice after the birth of Ella, the fact that Vicky decided to breast-feed Sigi generated an unpleasant row with her mother. The queen was always discomfited by the "disgusting details" of babies, and when she learned of the way her daughter fed Sigi, her reaction was astonishingly sharp. Referring to nursing as succumbing to the "animal side of our nature," Victoria suspected that Alice's decision had actually been the result of Vicky's influence: in a letter, the queen informed her second daughter that "it hurts me *deeply* that my *own 2* daughters should *set* at *defiance* the *advice* of a *Mother* of 9 *Children*. . . . *You* said you did it only for your health . . . & *because you* had *no social duties*. . . . Well Vicky has *none* of these excuses." The queen rationalized her anger on the grounds that as a busy princess with many social obligations, her eldest daughter simply hadn't the time to indulge this so-called whim. Though nursing an infant does require a fair amount of the mother's time, the crown princess's schedule could have been juggled. More to the point, Victoria simply considered the practice disgusting, all the more so for ladies of royal rank whose bodily functions had best remain entirely out of sight *and* mind.

Whatever her mother's criticisms, the crown princess increasingly found in Sigi a much-needed source of contentment, enabling her to forget Fritz's frequent absences, as well as the barbs directed at her from her husband's family. Convinced this son would be far more clever and intelligent than his older siblings, Vicky simply poured out her love.

In 1866, during the summer of the Austrian war, she was just recovering from having given birth again, prematurely this time; the child was another daughter, whom she called Victoria (later nicknamed "Moretta."). The crown princess was about to bid Fritz farewell on his departure to take command of the Prussian Second Army of nearly 120,000 men. Vicky looked forward to a rest, having gotten back on her feet too soon after her new daughter's delivery. Just before Fritz was to leave, the twenty-one-month-old Sigi suddenly grew feverish and restless, with what his mother assumed were teething pains. Not unduly worried, Fritz departed for the front according to plans. But almost immediately Sigi's illness took on serious overtones, the doctors now telling the crown princess that the baby had meningitis. The state of medicine being what it was in the 1860s, the outcome was virtually foreordained. In less than two weeks, Sigi was dead. Vicky was alone, without her husband to comfort her.

The world suddenly collapsed around her. The day after the boy died, the devastated crown princess wrote to Queen Victoria: "Your suffering child turns to you in her grief. . . . The hand of Providence is heavy upon me. I have to bear this awful trial alone without my Fritz." Though King William had granted his son leave to return home for the funeral, the crown prince refused it, making the painful decision that his presence was needed at a critical juncture in the war, and knowing that if his armies were attacked while he was absent, he could never justify having allowed personal grief to supersede military duty. Fritz's decision was painful to Vicky, who nonetheless bravely wrote her husband, "in you, of course, the soldier is uppermost."

Vicky's mother helped more than anyone to get her through the near-desperate grief that followed Sigi's death. Queen Victoria, who had turned herself into an astonishingly practiced mourner, ironically recognized that she had to cut Vicky off when her daughter threatened to go too far in her own tortured anguish. When the crown princess wrote that she would relinquish "house & home, future and all" if only she could have her son back, her mother told her, in effect, to get past it—that the loss of a child was nothing compared to the loss of a husband, which, of course, meant her own loss. She, Victoria reminded her daughter, still had her husband, whereas the queen of England did not.

By September, Vicky was finally coming out from under her anguish, and with the war over, her pride in Fritz's military victories was impossible to contain. She relinquished her mourning dresses (which would otherwise have been worn for a full year to mark Sigi's death) so she would look regal rather than tragic for the triumphant return of the Prussian Army into Berlin. For all Vicky's liberal sentiments and derision of Bismarck's hawkishness, the English daughter-in-law of Prussia's king took immense pride at what her adopted country had wrought, writing that "the beaming faces of our noble soldiers was [sic] touching to behold." The crown princess convinced herself that Prussia's present political leadership was only a temporary unpleasantness, one that would be remedied in the reign of the *next* king, who would yet rule a united Germany under Prussia's enlightened leadership and steadfast watchfulness.

In the six years following Sigi's death, Vicky had three more children: a fourth son, Waldemar, born in 1868, followed by two daughters—Sophie, born in 1870, and Margaret ("Mossy"), born two years later. While completing their family (they were to have eight children together), the darkest reality facing Vicky and Fritz continued to be the disastrous development of their eldest son. In his mother's view, Willy was fast becoming a laughable acolyte of Bismarck, increasingly bypassing his "liberal" parents in favor of a close relationship with his autocratic grandfather—a figure Willy considered worthy of Prussia's coming greatness. The young prince listened to his mother's continual praise of Fritz's ideals and, as quickly as she finished, put it out of his mind. Not yet in his teens in the 1860s, he had already begun to reject his father as his principal authority figure, understanding little more than that his father disagreed with Bismarck's policies, policies that to Willy's way of thinking were making Prussia evermore respected throughout Europe.

While the royal family's internal relationships were unraveling, Bismarck was laying the ground for the final transformation of Prussia into the Continent's preeminent power. In 1870 and 1871, the prime minister's policies bore their mature fruit. The Franco-Prussian War was Bismarck's masterstroke, and though largely the Machiavellian result of Bismarck's need for an excuse to realize the last elements of Germany's conversion into a unified state, it would never have happened had it not been for the blockhead who sat on the French throne.

Nephew to the great Napoleon, but possessing not the palest shadow of his uncle's abilities, Emperor Napoleon III cared more than anything about thwarting the creation of a politically unified Germany. The emperor (a title he assumed after a few years as merely "president") had just suffered an embarrassing debacle in the New World. The Hapsburg prince he had sponsored as French-controlled monarch and then abandoned had been driven from the

Mexican throne by peasants possessed by the stunning temerity to shoot not only a Hapsburg, but the younger brother of the man who ruled Austria's jigsaw puzzle empire. Putting that tawdry and tragic fiasco behind him, Napoleon III now had to face a worrisomely united Italy forming on France's southeastern flank. But the French emperor's biggest problem at the moment was one that threatened the soul of French foreign policy: it looked very much as if a politically unified German state was about to come into existence on the country's relatively exposed eastern flank, under a Prussian despot who declared, in effect, that the best way to rule was by blood and iron.

Well aware of Napoleon III's alarm, Bismarck devised a stunningly brilliant scheme that would play on France's anxieties and then cripple that nation from becoming a future threat to Prusso-German interests. Judging that, in any conflict between Berlin and Paris, the remaining independent South German states would quickly come to his own country's side, the Prussian prime minister could reasonably look forward to the opportunity finally to create a united Germany, bereft of Austrian interference, which had been his goal ever since Schleswig and Holstein had been invaded six years earlier. What opened France to this design was Napoleon III's conviction that if his French armies could win a war—any kind of war—his subjects would forget how badly their emperor and his government had been mismanaging the decaying French state. Granted, France was still possessed a substantial military potency—at least on paper. But Napoleon III badly overestimated his military strength, while at the same time just as badly underestimated how lethal the Prussian Army had become since the passing of his uncle's era five and a half decades earlier. Yet in the absence of any other likely target, he chose, disastrously, Prussia against whom to throw his legions. The fuse that actually lit the war involved his belief that the Spanish throne was to be offered to a prince of Hohenzollern-Sigmaringen (a branch of the Prussian ruling family), which would threaten France with encirclement by Prussia or its interests. History has it that, to provoke a crisis, Bismarck "doctored" a telegram that made it seem as though Napoleon III was impugning the Prussian king's honor. The fact was that the French were more than ready to initiate hostilities, and on July 14, much to Bismarck's joy, France declared war on Prussia.

The German armies united under Prussia's leadership easily and quickly crushed the badly outclassed French Army, mowed down in its thousands by the new Prussian needle machine guns. Napoleon could find no allies, Bismarck having taken careful steps to ensure France's diplomatic isolation, guaranteeing that the war did not become a general European conflict; furthermore, Napoleon III's domestic record had been so shabby for so many years that every other European power now had good reasons (or, at least, good rationalizations) to look the other way when German battalions marched with merciless efficiency through the cities and towns of eastern France. (This time, Hesse-Darmstadt fought on Prussia's side, much to both Vicky and Alice's relief.) The French government capitulated mere weeks into the war, after a dreadful humiliation at the decisive Battle of Sedan. Only Paris itself held out, its besieged citizens eventually reduced to eating their domestic pets; the capital would require a Prussian bombardment to bring it to its knees. (Vicky showed her sympathy for the city's humiliation by banning all luxuries from her own table throughout the siege, a symbolic gesture that Bismarck gleefully held up to ridicule.) Napoleon III and his throne were finished (after a short imprisonment at German hands, the ex-emperor would die in exile in England in 1873), though Empress Eugénie displayed enormous courage in facing down hostile mobs as she fled alone to England. Bismarck was now positioned to create the German empire that would be in large part simply an expanded Prussia.[2]

Having defeated Napoleon III and dictated peace terms to the French, Bismarck's next battle turned out to be with King William. It had seemed beyond question that, in a united Germany composed of a rainbow coalition of kings, sovereign princes, and reigning dukes, Prussia's monarch should occupy the imperial throne. But the Hohenzollern king insisted for his part that the situation was something like a major being offered the rank of "acting lieutenant colonel," and petulantly rejected a new crown whose authority was on offer from the North German Parliament, calculating that being the sovereign of a state forged in the blood of his forebears meant infinitely more than election to emperor of Bismarck's geopolitical melange. In a memorable but idiotic phrase, the increasingly eccentric monarch vowed he had no desire to "trade the splendid crown of Prussia for a crown of filth."

Initially, Bismarck (who was to be the first "chancellor"[3] of the new state) feared that his efforts at creating a unified Germany might have been in vain: not only was his king resisting the upgrade, but of the four princely states still outside the 1866 Confederation, only one—Baden, ruled by William's son-in-law—endorsed the Prussian prime minister's plan. Fritz, however, agreed wholeheartedly with Bismarck that Prussia should be the nucleus of a unified Germany, and for what it was worth he was backed enthusiastically by Vicky. The crown prince urged his father to reconsider, pointing out that ruling the new empire meant not giving up Prussia but *expanding* it. Bismarck's designs finally prevailed with the remaining independent monarchs when they were promised indemnities and a range of privileges within the new nation. Meanwhile, William was further nettled at his prime minister's proposition that his title would be "German Emperor" rather than "Emperor of Germany." Bismarck simply wished to avid the geographical connotations, but William thought the variant implied diminished status for himself.

In the end William acquiesced—*after* the offer came from the German princes in place of the North German parliamentarians. Bismarck set January 18, 1871, for the ceremony of formally declaring the creation of the German empire. It was to be held in the Hall of Mirrors at the Palace of Versailles, the location itself a final insult for the defeated French monarch. On a dais at the end of the glittering chamber, surrounded by the great and noble of his new patrimony, King William of Prussia became the first *Kaiser* in a united Germany. His son, the committed nationalist of the new order, stood before him, beaming with pride at the accomplishments of the house from which he had sprung and which he would one day head. William, remaining in character, still did little to hide his disdain for what was happening. And as for Bismarck, the new imperial chancellor betrayed no emotions anyone could fathom, though he must have been proud that he had made sure German liberalism would always be overpowered by the retention of the traditional elites in the new empire. Though Bismarck[4] would sometimes play to the bourgeois chorus, the government he had created was a dangerously militaristic authoritarian state, led by an unrepresentative and thus undemocratic government.

The twelve-year-old son of Vicky and Fritz was fully aware of his unique destiny by the time of the Franco-Prussian War and his grandfather's promotion, and the machinations behind these monumental events would play an immeasurably important role in shaping that destiny. If he surmised that he was little respected by his parents, he knew he would one day command the respect of his nation, a nation now much inflated through Bismarck's brilliantly ruthless efforts. With each passing day, Willy would move farther away from the crown prince and princess's influence, gravitating inexorably to that of his grandfather—and that of his grandfather's chief minister.

During the same eventful days in 1871 when Vicky was finally being reunited with her returning hero husband, Louise and Lorne were married. In a placid atmosphere strikingly different from the pandemonium sweeping Vicky's world, Louise entered one of the oldest and most prominent families in her mother's kingdom.

Whereas Victoria's fourth daughter had been allowed to spend the early weeks of 1870 in a relatively unhurried assessment of the small pool of potential spouses, Lorne had been left in a position in which his future had now been attached to hers until one or the other decided to definitively sever the connection. In the meantime, he could not pursue another possible wife. Though this was beginning to make the queen uncomfortably guilty toward the Campbell family, she continued to page through her well-used *Burke's Guide to the Peerage* in hope she might stumble on some eligible nobleman who had so far escaped her notice. The queen's efforts indeed led to several peers being paraded before Louise; but when the daughter still couldn't make up her mind—only the "quiet and gentleman-like and agreeable" Lord Cowper seemed to interest her at all—Victoria realized Lorne would have to be informed. The undecided Louise, aware that the issue was the most important in her life, officially replied that Lorne should be told that he was free of any obligation to her.

Though Louise and Lorne reverted to the *status quo ante*, the princess's thoughts continued to return to him, and she began to realize that in many ways marriage to the romantic-looking Scotsman might be the best she could expect. The catalyst who finally brought the pair together turned out to be her mother's longtime bête-noire, Prime Minister William Gladstone. When the queen relented to Louise's pleas to be allowed to gain more social exposure, Victoria permitted her daughter to accept an invitation to one of the Gladstones' famous breakfast parties held at Carlton House Terrace. There by chance she met Lorne, for the first time away from her mother's orbit. In the chic atmosphere of London's highest society—a milieu notably different from the airless and courtly formality of Windsor—the princess found that she was entranced by the marquis's sophisticated appeal.

Though the queen continued to display still more candidates at Balmoral, the magic of the meeting at the Gladstones' led a reinvigorated Lorne to ask Louise to marry him. She accepted, and as though it had been expected all along, her mother and his parents agreed to the engagement. Victoria expressed some concern over Lorne's financial situation, his income a meager £4,000 a year, but the expectation of ten times that much on his eventual accession to the Argyll title satisfied her.

Romantic love is unlikely to have had very much to do with the engagement. Though Louise and Lorne probably found each other physically attractive, what followed proceeded more from a sense that each could live harmoniously and contentedly with the other. Upper-class Victorians feared an overabundance of passion, believing it only complicated matters and, more dangerously, led to thoughts of unrealistic liaisons between persons of unequal social station. What was important for the principals—especially in this case—was that they were convinced of mutual compatibility.

While the Franco-Prussian War raged, Louise and Lorne, their parents, siblings, and households undertook the endless details for what amounted to a semistate wedding. Since the engagement raised important questions of precedence, especially in the minds of Continental royalty, Victoria considered it important to explain to Queen Augusta in Berlin just how it came to be that one of her own daughters was marrying one of her subjects: "I know that such a marriage is at first bound to cause sensation and surprise in Germany . . ." Presumably Victoria's substantial understatement was inadvertent, though she knew Fritz's family found Louise's proposed union bizarre. But the monarch didn't want Vicky to be embarrassed among her in-laws, and tried to put the best face on circumstances by explaining that "the Princes of small German houses, without fortune, are very unpopular here" (evidently Augusta was expected to find Victoria's candor instructive rather than insulting), and went on to clarify to Fritz's mother how the British royal marriage law "does not forbid, as many believe, marriage with a subject."[5]

In the end, it wasn't the House of Hohenzollern whence the bitterest gale would come to discompose Victoria's normally placid home. Though Louise and the queen expected Vicky and Alice's opposition to marriage with a subject—both understood that in Germany the union would inevitably be seen as hopelessly unsuitable—it was the reaction from Marlborough House that proved most censorious. The princess of Wales coolly but civilly wrote to Louise that "whatever may happen," she hoped they would remain friends; but the prince of Wales remained fiercely opposed to what he strongly believed was a *mésalliance*. Bertie's objection was not only that Lorne was not royal: because Lorne's family were prominent Liberals and Lorne himself sat in the House of Commons as a supporter of Gladstone, the crown was being degraded to the level of party politics.

It is likely, however, that Bertie's most fundamental objection to his sister's marriage purely concerned Lorne's rank, a complaint (as we've seen) founded on what were at the time rational grounds. In fact, all sorts of problems *would* inevitably have to be sorted out: Lorne's precedence, the unedifying specter of Louise and her spouse being distantly separated at official functions, the Argylls' deep involvement with banking and commerce (which might generate conflicts of interest, not to mention smacking of actually *working* for a living), even whether Louise herself might have to give up her own royal status.

As to the last, the queen wrote her son that "Louise remains what she is and her husband keeps his rank only being treated in the family as a relation when we are together." Victoria additionally surmised that Lorne would "infuse new and healthy blood" into the royal family, a genetic concern the sovereign wasn't squeamish about raising. Although Bertie's vehemence in objecting to the marriage unquestionably shook the princess, still the bride-to-be wasn't overawed by his challenge. Louise would instead suffer her brother's opposition to strengthen her own resolve to make the marriage work, without detriment either to Lorne and his career or to the monarchy. But the prince wouldn't easily give up on this particular point, constantly warning her about the social problems she would face. In an October 1870 letter, he wrote his sister asking her not to "think me unkind, dearest Louise, for adhering to my position . . . I can only trust that these numerous difficulties of position etc. which have come before me, may never give you cause to regret the step you have taken. I always liked Lorne—but his position will require tact and discretion which cleverer men than him would find difficult to maintain." In the end, it would take a long time for Bertie's feelings about Lorne to mellow.

Yet another source of objection remained: the surprising public derision over the marriage. As the 1870s opened, Queen Victoria's reputation had fallen to a seriously low point over the public's view of the way she was carrying out her obligations as queen. As a result of her virtual agoraphobia since Albert's death, Victoria had for nearly a decade now refused to be looked upon by almost any of her ordinary subjects, with even greater aversion to appearing before "society." Her few public forays were always arranged so as to keep her person half-hidden, dressed as somberly as she could possibly contrive, and *never* in anything so celebratory as robes or regalia. All of this countered national expectations of how the head of state should comport herself, which led the British taxpayer to feel he wasn't getting value for his money. In short, the public was widely disappointed in their sovereign, so much so that an expanding body of republicans had been agitating to do away with the monarchy and replace it with something more to their liking, presumably a presidential-style republic.

In this unexpectedly tense atmosphere, the queen once more was forced to submit to Parliament—just as she had with each of her adult children—to provide for the maintenance of her offsprings' sumptuous standards of living. For her sons, this had involved state allowances on leaving home, and for the girls, dowries on marriage. Though hitherto the requests had been granted by her Commons without untoward fuss, Victoria's reluctance to play the queen that the public wanted worried her. Their irritation might be reflected in a withholding of Louise's chit.

To complicate matters, Prince Arthur was coming of age at the same time Louise was getting married, so the queen had put in a supplication for £15,000 annually for life for her third son, which would overlap Louise's dowry request of £30,000 together with a stipend of £6,000 each year for life. This, it might be remembered, was when one-hundredth of either sum was more than all but a minority of her subjects could expect to earn in a lifetime. The queen nonetheless considered the figures in question modest, her frame of reference being, of course, exceptional.

Victoria took careful note of the national opposition to providing public funds to enrich her daughter. But she remained determined that the throne would not be embarrassed, and headed off opposition at the pass, as it were, by agreeing to personally open Parliament—a task the sovereign had virtually foresworn since her bereavement but one she knew would play well to a public that didn't appreciate how hard she worked. At the ceremony, Louise pointedly stood beside her mother on the steps of the throne. The ploy didn't appreciably stanch the sovereign's sinking popularity, but the mollified House of Commons approved the princess's money, after Gladstone made an eloquent case for the crown.[6] An anonymously written pamphlet appeared to wide distribution, in which the whole affair was held up to public ridicule. *The Fight at St. Stephen's, Otherwise Dame Britain's School, Over a Wedding Present* caught with a brilliance no organized opposition could have conveyed the hypocrisy of the enormously rich monarch come to the public trough.

The wedding was set for March 21, 1871, at Windsor. Most ordinary Britons finally seemed happy enough about the match, the queen still the repository of a vast reserve of loyal good feelings and her daughter never, of course, having done anything personally to sour public opinion. At a time when royal events provided an appreciable measure of the public's entertainment, Louise and Lorne's coming nuptials were looked forward to with a kind of national proprietary joy. The princess was popularly termed "The Maiden All for Lorne," and a London perfumer even concocted a new scent for the occasion called "Love-Lorne."

The one shadow over Louise's big day was the sorry spectacle of her mother's old friend Napoleon III limping into England on the eve of the wedding, this French symbol of political malfeasance an uncomfortable reminder of the queen's flagging touch with her own subjects. Bertie, though, demonstrated good grace by agreeing to stand beside his sister as she wed her Scottish nobleman.

For the wedding morning—three days after the bride's twenty-first birthday—an unclouded sun shone over Berkshire, and the royal town with its ancient castle was jammed with sightseers and well-wishers. The ceremony was performed in St. George's Chapel. In that ancient site, surrounded by members of her own and her bridegroom's families—the groom's male kinsmen in Campbell green and kilts, Lorne in the dress of the Royal Argyllshire Artillery Volunteers, Bertie regal in the uniform of his mother's Hussars, the queen in black but nonetheless smiling broadly—the lace-draped and multidiamonded Louise entered into holy matrimony according to the instructions of the officiating bishop of London. Victoria formally gave the bride away, refusing to relinquish this usually male task to Bertie on the premise that she was merely substituting for the missing prince consort. The old duke of Cambridge, who cordially disliked the queen and who in turn was cordially disliked by the same, pronounced that "the bride and bridegroom behaved uncommonly well."

Lenchen likely viewed Louise's departure with some uneasiness. With three of her sisters gone, and Beatrice still four years from leaving her schoolroom, Victoria's middle daughter knew she could expect a steady stream of summonses for help from her mother. Though Christian had, as promised, thoroughly established himself as an English gentleman, he and Lenchen had worked hard to make a life away from court. The queen magnanimously gave the couple Frogmore House at Windsor as their first home, the small palace that had been the duchess of Kent's residence during the long twilight after her daughter's accession. Later, the Christians would move to nearby Cumberland House, located in the same vast parkland; the latter was still close to Lenchen's mother, but not so near that a visit to her didn't require some substantial planning.

If the Christians' marriage wasn't particularly consequential in a historical context, it nonetheless had brought both husband and wife a settled contentment. Lenchen felt secure in the heart of the English countryside as she watched her more brilliant sisters in Germany struggling with their responsibilities and often difficult families. The queen had even provided Christian with a sort of job, though it was really nothing more than a sinecure to help fill his leisure-filled days: as "Ranger" of Windsor Castle's surrounding parkland, the easygoing German enjoyed a respectable position, even though the monarch saw to it that her son-in-law was denied any part in the estate's shooting arrangements, a chore she preferred to keep under her own personal control. Occasionally Victoria summoned Christian to read to her, the prince performing dutifully for the mother-in-law who had saved him from a life without purpose in Germany only to give him about the same in England.

In 1867, Prince and Princess Christian, as the couple was officially styled, first became parents. Christian Victor—always called
"Christle" in the family—was born in his grandmother's main home,
Windsor Castle, a year after his parents' marriage. When Vicky first
saw a photo of her new nephew, she was bewildered by what she assumed was some kind of a "dribbling-bib" around his neck, and decided the innovation must be something German, from Christian's
side; she wrote her mother that the device had to belong to the
"swaddling clothes . . . and the rest of the antediluvian apparatus
the poor little Germans are stuffed into . . . which always shocks
my English principles."

After two years, Christle was joined by a brother, whom Lenchen
named Albert, a name Victoria wanted as many of her grandchildren as possible to bear, in either its male or female form. Born in
the airy Georgian elegance of Frogmore House, the boy was destined one day to inherit the duchy of Schleswig-Holstein. Albert
had given his mother some difficulties on his delivery; the queen
wrote Vicky to explain Lenchen's complaining as "partly (unfortunate) habit, and her not having been very well, from one thing or
another." The monarch added that her middle daughter was "inclined to coddle herself (and Christian too) and to give way in
everything. . . . So, pray for Lenchen's sake, don't write to her to be
careful etc. for between her and Christian, who is so nervous, the
fear is all the other way." After nine births of her own, Victoria was
unsympathetic to any complaints her daughters had about their
pregnancies, though she was still willing and indeed anxious to help
at the deliveries.

The two sons were followed by two girls: in 1870, Princess Helena Victoria—officially nicknamed "Thora," but less kindly referred
to as "Snipe" in the family circle, betokening her long face and severe features—and, two years later, Marie Louise, who was destined
for one of the most bizarre and unfortunate marriages of all forty of
Victoria's grandchildren. Marie Louise's birth evidently took a toll
on Helena: two weeks after the event, the queen wrote Vicky to inform her that "Lenchen is 26 today. She looks much older."[7]

Of Victoria's daughters, indeed probably of all her children, it was Vicky whom the queen came closest to appreciating as an individual. But it was Beatrice whom she regarded as her greatest treasure. Except for a coming episode that deeply aggrieved the sovereign, Victoria's youngest child would always return her love most completely and, perhaps of greatest importance to the monarch, the least critically.

The beginnings of Beatrice's adult life came when she was nearing fourteen, Louise's departure having left her sisterless for the first time. Beatrice had always lived in the shadow of older female siblings who took precedence in her unique family circumstances whenever the queen depended on a daughter's services. Yet the royal family all knew and had long accepted the life that was in store for Beatrice: the queen did not hide her view that she considered herself a church and her youngest daughter the nun whose mission it was to serve that church. None of her children would have dared suggest to Victoria that Beatrice might covet a life—a husband, children, a home—of her own, such as the sovereign herself had so treasured. And for many years, it looked as if Beatrice would accept this scenario without question, would in fact consider such a calling the highest honor she could receive, and one to which no other person could possibly aspire.

Several months after Louise's marriage, Victoria met with the first major physical illness of her life. While at Balmoral in the late summer of 1871, the fifty-two-year-old monarch was diagnosed as having both rheumatic gout and an axillary abscess. The abscess eventually required surgery, which was performed under a small dose of chloroform, mercifully lessening the ordeal. Alice, who happened to be visiting from Germany, once again became her mother's bedside nurse during the crisis, for which the queen wrote of her gratitude: "Dear Alice was in and out constantly, and very affectionate and kind. . . ." But Victoria was sicker than the public was informed, and the aftermath lasted for two months. It was during this recovery period that Beatrice first became an important support to her mother, helping her with many of the duties that never lessened regardless of the sovereign's state of health.

After the queen's health returned, her family was thrown into a new crisis. In late autumn, Bertie developed typhoid while staying at Sandringham, the lavish new country house that he and Alix had built in Norfolk. At the time, typhoid was considered a likely death sentence, and when the news arrived at Balmoral, where his mother and Beatrice were staying, a sense of mortal peril enveloped the house. On December 8, Bertie's doctors wired Victoria's private secretary begging the monarch to come to Sandringham as soon as possible, the physicians clearly believing that the prince of Wales was close to death. So near to the Terrible Fourteenth on which her husband had died, Victoria was stricken with fear that the tenth anniversary of that day foreshadowed a repeat disaster for the family.

When the queen arrived at Sandringham accompanied by her two youngest children, she found Alice at Bertie's bedside, just as this daughter had sat by after her own surgery a few weeks earlier and, chillingly, for the prince consort exactly ten years before. Two days after Victoria's arrival, Sir William Jenner, the attending physician, informed the monarch that her son and heir was in fact on the verge of death, news that sent Victoria racing to the sickroom still in her dressing gown. Bertie was clinging to little more than a thread of life. Alice, despairing as well as dead tired, murmured to her mother that "there can be no hope." But at midnight, when the 13th turned into the 14th, the terror-stricken queen, now constantly at Bertie's bedside, was stunned as her son suddenly looked at her in a rush of recognition. He breathed, "It's Mama—it's so kind of you to come," the illness having miraculously broken. In the new day, Victoria, undeniably thankful and relieved, took Beatrice out on a quiet ride around the cold, flat Norfolk countryside.

In 1871, anybody's recovery from advanced typhoid seemed a genuinely divine act. And it occurred to many that the queen was, if not exactly old, then certainly vulnerable to the illnesses that swept off so many in an age whose medicine we now classify as virtually primitive. Bertie's heir, Prince Albert Victor, was only seven years old. Had both the queen and the prince of Wales died, the nation would have been subjected to a regency—most likely under the princess of Wales—until Albert Victor's eighteenth birthday. The prospect of an underage monarch was not a popular one, and it was the avoidance of this scenario that may have contributed most significantly to the national mood of unfeigned thanksgiving for the prince's recovery. Whatever other elements went into the phenomenon, the specter of republicanism vanished like the sun on a spent day. Bertie's growing record of debauchery, a catalogue of misdeeds especially embarrassing to his mother and his wife, was forgiven overnight by the public. Also forgiven was the queen's decade as a recluse. More important, Victoria seemed to sense this support, and thereafter conducted herself less like a hermit and more like the socially connected sovereign her nation expected. The transformation represented an astonishing and historic crossroads in the chronicle of this monarch's reign.

It is difficult to comprehend how the queen kept her youngest daughter's head from being turned by the succession of splendid weddings of her siblings. Beatrice wasn't allowed to go to St. Petersburg for the marriage of her brother Affie to the tsar's daughter in 1874—Victoria thought of the Russian court class as virtual libertines and wanted none of their influence to rub off on her youngest daughter—but the later celebrations held at Osborne represented a fairly lavish substitute for the real thing. To mark the occasion, the queen bestowed the Victoria and Albert Order on Beatrice, giving the girl something to help elevate her a little closer to all the grand guests her mother invited to the festivities.

After Affie's wedding, the queen resumed matchmaking—this time for Arthur, the son Victoria was always purported to love the most of any of her four boys. She raised Arthur to the title of duke of Connaught to increase his marriage prospects (her sons were routinely granted royal dukedoms on attaining anything resembling manhood), but the search still went on for a long time. Eventually, a proper and comely Prussian princess named Louise was found for Arthur, and the pair would marry in 1879.

Beatrice formed special relationships with the ever-growing swarm of nephews and nieces produced by her siblings' marriages. So much younger was she than what a child normally thinks of as an "aunt" (she was, for example, only a year and a half older than Vicky's son, Willy) that Beatrice was regarded by many of them as more of a playmate or contemporary. Though Victoria gave her youngest daughter wide social latitude within the family, she carefully kept the maturing young woman from experiencing any substantial life beyond the privileged confines of the palaces, and in consequence Beatrice remained extraordinarily shy and immature, unable to communicate on any informed basis with those outside the royal circle. The princess seemed committed to life as the queen's secretary, while her mother carefully saw to it that she was given little chance to see what might lie on the other side of the desk.

When Beatrice was sixteen, she had in fact experienced something like a mild shock of romance. While Victoria comforted the distraught empress Eugénie after the exiled French emperor's death that year, Beatrice sat one day talking with her son, Louis Napoleon, called the Prince Imperial. The prince had grown into a remarkably handsome, well-spoken young man who was already attracting favorable notice from influential Britons, not least the commander in chief of the British army and the queen's cousin, the duke of Cambridge. The episode could have led to nothing, though. Even if Victoria's plans for her youngest daughter had been alterable, marriage between a daughter of the sovereign and a prince who might, so it was conjured, try someday to recapture his father's throne amounted to political dynamite. In 1873, Beatrice hadn't the first clue how to respond to romantic overtures, had they even been offered, and it's likely the relatively sophisticated Prince Napoleon understood this. In the event, the young man would die six years later, impaled by eighteen spears thrown by Zulu warriors during a military expedition to southern Africa.

Occasionally, a token would be thrown to Beatrice by the queen, to satisfy her daughter's curiosity and desire to be esteemed without too much loosening the velvet reins that bound her. Starting in

1874, Beatrice was permitted conversation with the prime minister during his routine audiences with the sovereign. The sparkling and erudite Disraeli must have especially thrilled the adolescent girl with the sympathetic attention he paid her, always expressing his great pleasure to see the queen's daughter wearing the bee-shaped pin he had given her. But pleasurable as such discourse must have been, controlled conversations with an elderly statesman couldn't substitute for seeing young people her own age, visitors who might show her what life *could* be for someone of her rank and station.

While Beatrice struggled with emotional starvation, one of her older sisters found herself visited by poverty of another kind. Though Alice and Louis's increasingly urgent financial difficulties never meant that their family had to be troubled about the food on their table or keeping a roof over their heads, she and her husband and children had never been able to live on anything like the scale Alice had known in her life as the daughter of the queen of England. Alice had come to Hesse with a £30,000 dowry, but that princely amount had been almost totally depleted, first in building the New Palace, and later in paying off the penalty Hesse was assessed by Prussia for taking the wrong side in the Austrian war. As for any wealth Louis might inherit, access to the small Hessian treasury would have to wait until he succeeded to the grand duchy's throne.

Though her inability to live as financially a carefree life as her sister galled, one of the most irritating outcomes of this relative penury was that Alice simply couldn't afford to come to England as much as her mother wanted—or, after her mother tired of having her presence at all, as often as she herself wanted. Even had Louis not been constrained by his duties in Darmstadt, particularly the military commitments that made up the bulk of his employment, the expenses of travel on a princely scale would have been beyond the couple's purse: no royal family of the era could conceive of travel without a battalion of servants and courtiers, the bedding and feeding and transport of which retinue required deeper pockets than Louis and Alice possessed. And though Queen Victoria was indisputably rich, she was not always either generous or particularly welcoming when it came to hosting her children and their entourages on their visits to England.

So far as Alice was concerned, the situation led to a circular animosity: the begging letters Alice sent to the queen ("if in your kindness, you could see your way . . .") had by the early 1870s rapidly become a source of irritation to Victoria, whose wounded and disingenuous tones of self-poverty in her replies served to cement an angry rift between the two women into near estrangement. That Alice had often and tactlessly urged her mother to appear more in public, advice the queen viewed as near treason (though Alice of course saw it as sound political counsel), only added to the queen's pique. Also annoying to Victoria was the perception that Alice spent too much time and energy trying to cheer everybody up when she did come back to England. Victoria didn't want cheering up, but was instead content in her morbidity, especially in the funereal quiet of her palaces that came of her insistence that everybody speak in little, low voices. All that appalled Alice—and Alice's being appalled appalled her mother.

This sniping went on throughout the decade, well into the years when Victoria had begun to appear more often before the British public. When Alice returned to Germany, the comparative poverty of life in Darmstadt—plain dinners, made-over clothes for the children—kept her in a simmer at her mother's tightfistedness and seeming lack of understanding of the couple's straitened situation. Trips to Berlin to visit Vicky only caused the princess to regret even more the relative poverty of her life. Further, her mother tried to get her own sisters to avoid seeing her more than was absolutely necessary, the queen evidently convinced that her daughter's mischief was contagious.

Alice's troubles began to widen far beyond the mere lack of money. Most notably, relations between the princess and her husband had been deteriorating for a long time, Alice disappointed with Louis's inability or unwillingness to engage her intellectually, Louis irked at his wife's preoccupation with the "projects" and "causes" she had spiritedly taken up in Darmstadt. The Princess Alice Society for Women's Training and Industry, dedicated to educating women, and the Princess Alice Women's Guild in which nurses were trained, had become substantial organizations. The latter came into its own on the outset of the Franco-Prussian War, when the organization took over the administration and staffing of three military hospitals in Darmstadt. In Louis's view, though, they seemed to be consuming his wife at his expense.

Not surprisingly for a woman so sensitive to caregiving, Alice's attitudes ran far ahead of the late nineteenth-century norms by which such things were measured. The princess courageously spoke out for public funding for her nursing institutions, maintaining that while both orphans and nursing patients should, insofar as possible, be cared for privately, the public treasury should also help pay for such private undertakings. While at first funding did come primarily through private donations and was augmented by the groundbreaking bazaars she sponsored, the grand ducal treasury began in 1869 to allocate public monies for the causes Alice promoted and sponsored. The Hessian social innovations of the 1870s in nursing and child care would become the principal memorial to Alice's life, a life that is still remembered in Darmstadt today.

The princess had continued to bear children at a regular pace: after Victoria, Ella, and Irene came the first son, Ernst Louis, in 1868, followed by Frederick William in 1870. Even during her years of active motherhood, Alice still continued to build a local reputation for nursing that almost put her on a level with the esteem that enlightened Britons held for her heroine, Florence Nightingale. Her own institution—the Alice Hospital—treated the city's indigent sick without charge, and at the height of the Franco-Prussian War more than a thousand wounded French soldier-prisoners were cared for in beds set up in her New Palace garden, the work consuming the princess, who passed days on end with little rest. At the war's conclusion the exhausted princess begged her mother to be allowed to come with her children to Balmoral—"the smallest corner is enough for us"—even though she knew the queen now resented any unscheduled dislocation of her own intricate and carefully protected schedule. Nonetheless, Victoria unselfishly bid her daughter come to the Highland castle.

It was during this two-week visit to Scotland that Alice helped her mother recuperate from her axillary abscess operation. From the queen's bedside at Balmoral, Alice and her children had moved on to join Bertie and Alix at Sandringham on their autumn shooting houseparty, and here the princess's nursing skills had been further employed in caring for Bertie in his bout with typhoid, the prince's survival likely due in large part to the exhaustive and professional care given him by his sister. The princess of Wales forthrightly recognized her sister-in-law's skill and commitment, and in effect permitted Alice to take charge of the house. Yet, though Alix praised Alice for her commitment to Bertie's care, others in the royal circle resented—or were daunted by—Alice for having stepped into a role princesses weren't expected to fill. Even the queen didn't want Alice overcredited with Bertie's recovery, especially at the expense of the more important princess of Wales. Alice wrote to Louis from Sandringham saying she would have to go soon, "and of course Mama would be pleased to be rid of me." This rancor weighed heavily on a daughter whose admiration for her mother far outweighed any resentment of her own.

A peripheral source of Victoria's disenchantment with Alice turned on her daughter's outspokenness on gynecological matters and eagerness to extract as much information as possible on the subject from her married sisters, information Alice hoped to put to use in her nursing work in Darmstadt. Louise received a letter from the queen just after returning from a honeymoon visit she and Lorne paid Alice in Darmstadt: "I would rather you had not met her so soon, for I know her *curiosity* and what is *worse* and what I hardly like to say of my own daughter—and I know her *indelicacy* and coarseness . . . (she was as nice and refined as any of you and has learnt all of this from the *family there* [Hesse]). . . . When she came over in '69 and saw Lenchen again and asked her *such things*, that Christian was shocked. . . ." As has been noted, Victoria abhorred matters of the body, and highly resented anyone—especially her daughters—who didn't share that discomfort.

While Alice's yearning to provide relief for the unfortunate of Darmstadt grew ever deeper, Louis remained the indulgent soldier-prince, largely involved with his fellow officers in the planning of military exercises. When Alice reproved him for what she regarded as his purposelessness, Louis freely admitted what his wife viewed as his faults, though he pleaded for understanding. But as her marriage now provided less satisfaction, and with sick headaches and exhaustion her routine condition, Alice turned to another source to help her contend with the malaise and metaphysical questions that preoccupied her.

The German theologian David Friedrich Strauss was in his early sixties when Alice met him in Darmstadt just before the Franco-Prussian War, and she soon came to admire his writings. The princess provided him with an introduction to Vicky when he went on to Berlin, though as it turned out he wouldn't be much admired in the less welcoming atmosphere of a capital whose society was little interested in theological musings; nevertheless, the crown princess admired Strauss for stripping history "of all earlier and later embellishments." Strauss's famous 1835 *Life of Jesus* questioned the historical accuracy of the Bible because of its later accretions, a view then verging on heresy in culturally orthodox Germany. Upon returning to Darmstadt, where he hoped he might find more fertile ground, Alice saw to it that the theologian was regularly invited to the New Palace. When a siege of the deadly scarlet fever kept visitors away from the New Palace, she asked Strauss to come and read to her privately in the evening—fairly daring visits that continued for two weeks. Then she permitted Strauss personally to dedicate a series of lectures to her, in effect granting her public, official imprimatur on his "excessive" views.

Empress Augusta, Vicky's mother-in-law, got wind of Alice's role in promoting Strauss and immediately labeled the Hessian princess a "complete atheist." The charge was unfair. Strauss pleaded in his work that the Bible couldn't be considered a literal interpretation of God's word, and that to maintain such views would only diminish the appeal and thus the future of Christianity, a conclusion in which Alice found personal resonance. She had come to feel that

Victorian intellectual society, for the sake of its own interests in defending the status quo, had turned God into a creature that would be unrecognizable to the early Christians. Though Louis remained the loving and lovable husband, he was intellectually unequipped to explore these matters with her, and it was Strauss who most satisfyingly helped Alice to understand a difficult world.

At the same time she was being vilified by the German empress, Alice was giving birth to a future empress of far greater consequence to the world than Augusta. On June 6, 1872, her fourth daughter was born. Alice and Louis named the baby Alix—after Alice herself, but Germanized in light of the difficulty Alice knew her husband's countrymen experienced in trying to pronounce her English name. Following the nearly universal practice for babies born in Queen Victoria's huge family, this one too was given a nickname, in fact, *two* nicknames: Alix would be known until her murder as Tsarina Alexandra forty-six years later as both "Alicky" and "Sunny."

Disaster struck the family the year after Alix's birth. As Vicky had lost Sigi seven years earlier, so now Alice suffered a similar horror. Wilhelm Frederick, whom she called "Frittie," was three years old in 1873, a strikingly good-looking boy with white-gold hair and an open face; his grandmother Victoria affectionately described him as "a very pretty winsome child." He had only shortly before been confirmed a hemophiliac, when unstoppable bleeding over three days from a cut on his ear left no doubt as to the illness and to the realization that his mother was a carrier of the disease. Alice and Louis had been badly shaken on learning of Frittie's condition, but believed that if the boy were well protected there would be no immediate cause to fear for his life; the view echoed that which Victoria and Albert had adopted in regard to their own son and Frittie's uncle, Prince Leopold.

Frittie was his mother's favorite, an adorable little boy doted upon by Alice far more than her four daughters and her older son, Ernie. The young prince repaid his mother's love in remarkable measure, and he became Alice's foremost diversion from the frenzied aftermath of the Franco-Prussian War and from the family pressure resulting from her involvement with Strauss. In March 1873, Frittie's wound appeared far enough recovered that Alice felt safe in leaving on a long-planned visit to Italy, where she was to be received in Rome by Pope Pius IX. Having returned to Darmstadt in May, rested from peaceful trips to Florence and Sorrento, the princess felt largely free from the worries that had accumulated since Louis had first gone off to war in 1866.

On May 28, Alice's entire family spent the afternoon in the hills outside the city. Everyone was particularly carefree, with Frittie clambering gaily after his parents and siblings. The boy's four-year-old brother Ernie would remember for the rest of his life how Frittie that day gave him a bunch of lilies-of-the-valley that the younger boy had picked. This lovely spring day was perhaps the last truly unblemished day of Princess Alice's life.

Early the following morning, Louis left the New Palace for an appointment, with his wife lying in bed later than was her usual practice. Alice's bedroom was located on an interior angle of the palace, and from it one could look out the window at the sitting room around the corner. Ernie and Frittie had joined their mother, and were playing together on the floor. Ernie left to go to the sitting room, and Frittie, wanting to keep an eye on his brother, jumped onto a chair near an open window so he could see through to where Ernie had gone. The younger boy leaned too far out the window, and either lost his balance or the chair tipped under his weight. He fell, about twenty feet, to the stone terrace below.

Frittie lay deathly still on the stones, his full weight heavily resting on a twisted arm. When servants rushed to pick him up, the child was unconscious, though there was no visible bleeding. Doctors suspected a skull fracture, but found none. All too aware of his hemophilia, they knew that internal uncontrolled bleeding into the brain could well prove more dangerous than a fracture. Though Frittie regained consciousness, he remained absolutely quiet. His stunned and tormented mother refused to leave his bedside for even a moment. Louis was called home immediately, and a telegram was sent to Queen Victoria letting her know that her grandson was injured, likely seriously.

The end wasn't long in coming. There was massing effusion of blood into the brain tissues, bleeding that wouldn't stop because the child's hemophilia kept the blood from coagulating normally. Alice's beloved Frittie died the afternoon of the day he fell. It was a calamity from which Alice would never recover. After Frittie died, she turned the window from which he had fallen into a stained-glass memorial, with the words "Not lost, but gone before" worked into the pattern.

Prince Leopold (who was also Frittie's godfather), the family member who because of his own hemophilia most likely understood Frittie's special torment, wrote Alice after the boy's death: "I know too well what it is to suffer as he would have suffered, and the great trials of not being able to enjoy life or to know what happiness is. . . . I cannot help saying to myself that it is perhaps well that the dear child has been spared all the trials and possibly miseries of a life of ill health like mine." The letter may have been overly candid for his sister to read at a time she was blaming herself for "allowing" Frittie to fall, but Leopold—who adored his elder sister—unquestionably meant the condolences as the most tender compassion he could offer.

Though Victoria was not aware of the full circumstances of Frittie's accident, she nonetheless reproached Alice in a letter to Vicky four days afterwards: "I think it is merciful that no unhappy nurse or other person was to blame as that would have added to the misery. But I think little children, unless you are doing nothing and can be constantly watching them, should never be left without a person to watch them."

The queen refused to treat her grieving daughter gently. When Alice's brother, Affie, became engaged to the daughter of the Russian tsar Alexander II, Victoria wanted the young bride-to-be to come to England so she could be properly inspected. The tsar thought differently, and enlisted Alice (his wife's niece) to persuade the British monarch to herself come to the Continent for any inspection she wished to carry out. Alice should have known better than to try to influence her mother in this way. She received a letter from England that left little question of what the queen thought about her daughter's views on the matter: ". . . I do *not* think, dear Child, that you should tell me who have been nearly 20 *years longer* on the throne than the Emperor of Russia & am the Doyenne of Sovereigns . . . *what I ought to do.* I think I know *that.* The proposal received . . . was one of the *coolest* things I ever heard. . . ." This was received in Darmstadt just two months after Frittie's death.

Alice was to have one more child. In May 1874, just after she turned thirty-one, the princess gave birth to her fifth daughter, Mary Victoria Feodora Leopoldine, who would be called May. Strauss had died three months earlier, but his death affected Alice less than it might have had Frittie lived. With her son's loss, the princess's views resumed a more orthodox course. Alice left behind the intellectual musings that had drawn her to the theologian. Unfortunately, neither of the deaths of those near to her drew her closer to Louis. She would write of her marital disappointments to her husband: "Every little emotional upset, for instance over your being cross, is a strain on my nerves." Louis hadn't been able to help Alice much with her grieving at Frittie's loss: "The wound . . . is not yet healed. . . . I sometimes need to talk about it. . . . But I don't do it with you—I know it hurts you." Had the couple been able to share their feelings more fully with each other, these last years might not have been filled for Alice with an almost unmitigated melancholia.

During the late 1870s, she carried on with her "works." The Darmstadt Women's Day under her sponsorship dealt with how to improve women's lives, although the event drew a predictable snort from Queen Victoria, who thought women were doing perfectly well without any liberal meddling in their condition. Alice also underwrote fund-raising for her medical and charitable efforts, laying a strong foundation for such activities in Hesse-Darmstadt that carries over to the present day.

As hard as she worked outside the New Palace to try to bury her demons, her relationship with Louis continued to deteriorate. Alice began to sense that time was running out in which to put things right. In October 1876, while visiting Balmoral, the princess wrote her husband a letter that seemed to release pent-up frustrations:

I longed for a real companion, for apart from that life had nothing to offer *me* in Darmstadt. I could have been quite happy and contented living in a cottage, if I had been able to share my intellectual interests, and intellectual aspirations with a husband whose strong, protective love would have guided me around the rocks. . . . So naturally I am bitterly disappointed with myself when I look back, and see that in spite of great ambitions, good intentions, and real effort, my hopes have nevertheless been completely shipwrecked. . . .

Obviously, Victorian correspondence wasn't always written with its meaning obscured between polite lines. Alice's remarkable letter to her husband is a confirmation of that truth. Alice went on to reproach both herself and her husband: ". . . but we never meet each other—we have developed separately—away from each other, and that is why I feel that true companionship is an impossibility for us—because our thoughts will never meet." Alice had undeniably found Louis a good and caring father for her children, but just as clearly she had not met a man who was (as Fritz was for Vicky) the overriding passion of her life. Alice ended her remarkable confession with the observation: "I love you too so very much, my darling husband, [and] that is why it is so sad to feel that our life is nevertheless so incomplete—and sometimes so difficult." She would not, she assured him, "blame [him] for this—I *never* think that, *never*. . . ."[8]

With their marriage on shakier ground than ever, Alice and Louis soon had to face their elevation to sovereigns of their small state. Though Hesse-Darmstadt had been formally subsumed into the German empire, it still retained a legal independent status within the larger entity. Berlin now made the major decisions, particularly those regarding military and diplomatic issues; but the grand duke retained lesser domestic matters under his control, ass well as the ceremonial role to play at home. In March 1877, Louis became heir presumptive to the throne when his father, Prince Charles (the grand duke's brother), died. Louis's direct apprenticeship as heir was short: three months later, Grand Duke Louis III died, and Alice's husband became, at thirty-nine, the sovereign Louis IV. As the grand duchess, Alice was now called *Landesmutter*—"Mother of the Country."

Regardless of little Hesse's diminished status, Alice's new duties almost overwhelmed her. Writing to her mother, she admitted that "I am so dreading everything, and above all the responsibility of being the first in everything. . . ." As Louis himself struggled to fill his new and much more visible role, Alice lent him encouragement in every way she could. Even when she left Darmstadt to get needed rest at a French resort, she sent frequent letters of encouragement to a husband elevated beyond his true capabilities.

As grand duchess, Alice took important advantage of her new authority in Darmstadt. She decided to tackle what she called the "intolerant interfering people" who stood between her and the social goals she meant to accomplish. She judged that Louis could not be the helpmeet she wanted, frankly writing to him that he would "shake off anything serious or unpleasant like a poodle shaking off the water when it comes out of the sea." The new sovereign must have become aware that he was losing his wife when she wrote in the same letter that "natures like yours are the happiest in *themselves*, but are not made to help, comfort and advise others, nor to share *with* others the heat of life's noon-day or the cool of the evening, with insight, understanding and sympathy. . . ." Alice would still try to love her Louis as best she could, but their souls seemed no longer to be bound together.

During the remaining months of 1877, life passed relatively smoothly for Alice. Determined to continue improving social conditions in Darmstadt, she rushed about extinguishing little fires as though preternaturally aware that her clock was winding down. As *Landesmutter*, more demands had now begun to impose on her time and energy, and she wrote her mother that "it is more than my strength can stand in the long run." Little nettles that inevitably come with greater rank and visibility began to sting, such as a rumor that Alice had been somehow unkind to the dowager grand duchess—Louis's aunt—which troubled her greatly. At the end of the year, she complained to Louis of a hurtful letter from her mother, one "so unfair it makes me cry with anger. . . . I wish I were dead and it probably will not be too long before I give Mama that pleasure."[9]

Alice spent one more summer in England, at Eastbourne on the coast in Sussex. The queen, who apparently realized that Alice was in serious need of rest, paid for her daughter's and grandchildren's vacation; Louis accompanied them during the holiday's first days, but soon was forced to return to business in Darmstadt. Typically, Alice spent much of her seaside days inspecting the town's charities and hospitals. A local minister who met her at a charity bazaar was struck by how much "our Princess Alice . . . had lost her English pronunciation of English."[10] Alice ended her holiday with a short stay at Osborne, the last visit to a scene from her childhood.

Returning to Darmstadt in late 1878, she lived normally at the New Palace—until the afternoon of November 5. In the early darkness of the South German autumn evening, just after the dishes had been cleared away from the family's tea, Victoria—Alice's eldest daughter[11]—complained to her mother of a stiff neck. The grand duchess thought it might be the mumps. But on the next morning, the fifteen-year-old princess was diagnosed with diphtheria, a highly infectious disease that Alice's nursing experience had given her good reason to fear. After Victoria had started to pass the threshold of greatest danger, her younger sister Alix came down with the illness. May, Irene, and Ernie quickly caught it also. Louis, too, was pulled in by the pervasive bacteria scourging the New Palace. In the 1870s, treatment of diphtheria was rudimentary and often futile.

What could be done was to send away any uninfected family member. This was exactly what Alice did with Ella, the one daughter so far to escape the infection, who was packed off to her grandmother Charles's palace. By November 15, young May's symptoms had become extremely alarming, the membrane in her mouth growing dangerously close to blocking off her breath. Just after going to bed that night, the doctors awakened the grand duchess with the news that May was critically ill. By the time Alice threw a wrap around herself and rushed to her youngest daughter's bedside, it was too late. May had choked to death. The recipient of so much of the love left in Alice's heart after Frittie's death, little May's passing nearly killed Alice. In a telegram to the queen, she simply said, "the pain is beyond words."

For two weeks, Alice tried to keep word of the death from the other children. Irene had just come off the danger list. Ernie remained the sickest, Alice almost certain she was going to lose this last of her sons. At the beginning of December, with the boy finally seemingly past the worst of the danger, the young prince begged his mother to know what had happened to his beloved little sister. Alice was heartbroken at the pain on her son's face when she had to tell him that May was gone. Herself still well, a miracle in the face of the diphtheria she had nursed for nearly a month, Alice would now break the cardinal rule of keeping away from any physical contact with the disease's victims. She bent over to kiss and comfort her tormented son. It was for her family and for Hesse a dreadful mistake.

On the evening of December 7, Alice herself finally became sick, the doctors quickly diagnosing diphtheria. Louis notified Queen Victoria, who immediately dispatched Sir William Jenner, her own doctor, to her daughter's bedside. Despite everything, on Friday the 13th the grand duke was told that there was no hope, that his wife was dying. The next morning—just after 8:30 A.M. on Saturday, December 14, exactly seventeen years since the horrible day in 1861 when a much younger Princess Alice watched her father die in Windsor—she murmured two words: "Dear Papa." Princess Alice, the Grand Duchess Louis IV, exhaled her final breath.

Prime Minister Disraeli, as earl of Beaconsfield, expressed in a memorial speech to the House of Lords one of the most touching tributes to Princess Alice's gentle memory:

> My Lords, there is something wonderfully piteous in the immediate cause of her death. The physicians who permitted her to watch over her suffering family enjoined her under no circumstances whatever to be tempted into an embrace. Her admirable self-restraint guarded her through the crisis of this terrible complaint in safety. She remembered and ob-

served the injunctions of her physicians. But it became her lot to break to her little son the death of his youngest sister, to whom he was devotedly attached. The boy was so overcome with misery that the agitated mother clasped him in her arms, and thus she received the kiss of death. My Lords, I hardly know an incident more pathetic.

7

Tragedy Again, and Leave-taking

With the horrendous shock of Alice's death, Queen Victoria was jolted into a reappraisal of what this daughter had meant to her. In a torrent of grief, she wrote Vicky of her agony: "My precious child who stood by me and upheld me seventeen years ago on the same day taken, and by such an awful fearful disease. . . . She had darling Papa's nature, and much of his self-sacrificing character and fearless and entire devotion to duty!" The bitterness and animosity she had shown Alice, the anger at this daughter's progressive views and her willingness to thwart her mother's wishes, would appear to have fallen away. It would be a stretch, however, to surmise that Victoria regretted any of the settled partialities that had led to her alienation from Alice.

Simultaneously, Vicky was pouring out her own grief in a thirty-nine-page letter to Victoria: "Darling Alice—is she really gone—so good and dear, charming and lovely—so necessary to her husband and children, so widely beloved, so much admired. I can not realise it—it is too awful, too cruel, too terrible." Vicky deeply mourned the sister to whom she was closest—in age, in the liberality of their political and social views, in their marriages to German princes and life in closely comparable cultures so different from that in which they had grown up.

Painfully, her in-laws had forbidden Vicky and her family from going to Darmstadt for the funeral, Fritz's father afraid—not unreasonably so in light of the medical realities of the age—that it would be too risky for his son to get anywhere near the Hessian contagion. Neither Vicky nor Fritz could foresee that the same nightmarish disease that had destroyed so much in Darmstadt would soon turn their own homelife into horror, and Vicky's day into a long and nearly unlivable night.

Although for Prussia the war with France had come to a glorious conclusion, in its wake Vicky's and Fritz's lives lurched even more precipitously in what the crown princess called the "humbug" world of her father-in-law's newly elevated court. Her refusal to bend even slightly to the court's received sensibilities—a rebuff in which Fritz usually concurred and joined—was mortally jeopardizing her influence in the world to which she was joined by marriage.

Even where Vicky could have accommodated herself to Fritz's family's wishes without any injury to her beliefs, she would not do so. Empress Augusta expected princesses in the House of Hohenzollern to follow her lead in the capital's turbulent social life, and it was especially important to her that her daughter-in-law, a woman destined to become empress herself, do so. But Vicky hated what she considered the superficial and purposeless round of teas and balls and court receptions, gatherings at which her mother-in-law reigned in a variety of ludicrous wigs and overdecorated gowns. Though a little forbearance in these essentially nonpolitical areas might have gone a long way toward making Vicky's life less stressful and less extraneous, the crown princess resisted bending to any degree that would satisfy the empress.

In the more consequential realm of politics, Vicky was seen by the court and royal family as an unseemly force behind Fritz's quarrels with his father over Bismarck's increasingly authoritarian and reactionary tactics. Offensive as the imperial chancellor's actions were to the crown prince and princess, his accomplishments were proving remarkably successful in turning Prussian Germany into the strongest economic engine the Continent had ever seen—a consequence, paradoxically, that both Fritz and Vicky viewed with great pride. Cursing a lamentable chancellor but savoring Bismarck's results, the crown princess could only fantasize of a time when the present kaiser's reign would be over: William I was seventy-five at the end of the war with France, and Vicky understandably calculated that it couldn't be many more years before she and Fritz would ascend to the throne and realize their own agenda for the new and vastly expanded Germany. High on the list of the crown princess's changes was the condition and treatment of German women. For females to be permitted to work in the national bureaucracies and to attend universities as equals of men were desires coveted long and ardently by Vicky, and advances she believed her husband would support as emperor.

To make the couple's lives even more difficult, Fritz had become nearly as much the object of Bismarck's contempt as Vicky. Whereas the crown princess's mischief was immaterial to Bismarck's agenda, her husband would soon enough succeed William I, and the chancellor knew Fritz would thus be in a position to dismiss any minister, especially one who so strongly disagreed with his views on the desirability of a true constitutional parliament. Though not the democrat some historians have imagined him to be, Fritz wanted to take Germany in the direction of British constitutional practices, albeit under a far stronger monarchy than in his mother-in-law's kingdom. The new German empire had been laid close to the old Prussian mold: the monarch's theoretical power was, if not quite absolute, then close to it.[1] But as Emperor William was sinking into greater eccentricity (and possibly senility) every year, so his dependence on his chancellor was growing commensurately. That chancellor, or chief minister, was little constrained in many of the most important areas of government, even if the parliamentary majority were of his party, which was in any case unlikely. Bismarck as the absolutist so scorned Parliament that no party worthy of its legitimacy or independence could be said truly to represent this uniquely powerful titan. Frightened at the thought of Fritz as his emperor, Bismarck ever more disparaged the crown prince for being as he reckoned (with a degree of justice) a man too far under his wife's influence and out of sympathy with Prussian military aims—the latter an irony in light of Fritz's hawkishness in the three wars that earned Prussia its control over a unified Germany.

As Willy increasingly sensed this situation, it pushed him yet further away from his parents' influence. To make matters even worse, Vicky's disappointment in Willy was something she made not the slightest effort to hide, at least not from her English family. Writing as candidly to her mother as her mother did to her, she cruelly sized up her son as "not possessed of brilliant abilities, nor of any strength of character or talents. . . ." Though her assessment wasn't strictly accurate—Willy was not unintelligent, but instead simply unable to focus on any single subject for the time it takes to become truly knowledgeable in the matter—it represented her profound opinion and poisoned any prospect of a happy relationship with her eldest son. Aggravating this alienation had been the vicious and unnecessary influence of Willy's tutor, George Hinzpeter. The teacher, a Calvinist zealot bereft of the slightest degree of kindness or warmth, despised the crown prince and princess's political views and never missed an opportunity to disparage the boy's parents to his pupil. Sadly, Vicky had long been aware of the tutor's opinion of herself and her husband, and knew that he was helping to turn her son against them. Yet, hard as it is to comprehend, she allowed the situation to continue until Willy was eighteen, inexplicably assessing Hinzpeter as "a *great* great blessing for Willy."

In fact, on both physical and educational fronts, Willy had long been making substantial progress. To overcome the limitations imposed by his paralyzed arm, special eating implements had been made for him: an apparatus that allowed the prince to eat without the humiliation of having to have his food cut up into pieces by one of his parents or by a servant. The boy mastered a near-normal seat on horseback, the result of concentrated efforts and a great deal of trial and error. By his teen years, Willy showed genuine if modest talents in anything that had to do with military science, a worthy subject in which to excel given a future as head of his nation's armed forces. In 1873, at fourteen, Willy would pass the examination that allowed him into a *gymnasium*, or academic high school.

To the young second heir to the imperial crown, the real-life consequences of Prussia's actions were unimaginable. Bismarck could, for the young Prince William, do no wrong. Though Vicky and Fritz tried to steer their son away from this unbecoming hero worship, for Willy it was his parents who seemed pallid next to Bismarck's brilliance. What was more, the boy transferred much of his immediate familial love to his grandfather, Emperor William, and his more distant hero worship to his English grandmother, whom Willy imagined to actually rule her kingdom and far-flung empire. The triumvirate of emperor, queen, and chancellor had by the mid-1870s become Willy's pantheon.

During these years, Vicky's children clearly chose up sides as though rival teams were being formed. Princess Charlotte, having turned into a young snipe whose behavior as a teenager increasingly distressed and alienated her mother, sided with Willy and her German grandparents. Her brother Henry went the same route. In truth, Vicky was likely largely responsible for driving these two children from her influence and from her affections. If the crown princess's open disdain of the pair in letters to Queen Victoria mirrored the way she communicated with them at home, the brother and sister must have been easily pushed into the more receptive arms of the emperor and empress, grandparents who indulged the children. From Vicky to the queen in 1874: "Beatrice was only a little older at Osborne than Charlotte is now [the latter was fourteen], yet she was quite formed—so were Alice—Lenchen—Louise and I. . . . Charlotte is in everything—health, looks and understanding like a child of ten! I suppose it belongs to the family here!" In 1875: "Charlotte's figure is alas! not quiet straight—one shoulder and one hip a little higher than the other. (I supposed inherited from the Empress who has that defect. . . .)" In 1877: "I have painted a very large still life which I have given to Charlotte and Bernard [Charlotte's fiancé] for their future dining room! I fear I am naughty enough to wish it were yours and not theirs because they understand nothing whatever about it. . . ." And in 1877 to her mother: "She [Charlotte] has grown very stout; now and then her figure reminds me of what Lenchen's was—only much much shorter!" (Vicky was at this time notably stout herself.) More followed: ". . . she has an immense bust and arms—a long waist and neck, and looks like a big person when she is sitting—and when she gets up she has no legs almost. Unfortunately she is most ungraceful when she moves and walks, sticks out her elbows and trundles about. . . . She has alas her Papa's hands and feet for which a young girl is most unfortunate." Vicky's antipathy toward her daughter is almost palpable in these words, and it is difficult to imagine that Charlotte could have grown up not sensing it.

As for Henry, Vicky's comments to her mother were, if anything, even less kind. In 1872: "To my horror Henry will get a uniform on his birthday as he is ten years old. His poor ugly face will look worse than ever. . . ." Two years later: "Henry is awfully backward in everything, and does not grow—is hopelessly lazy—dull and idle about his lessons—but such a good-natured boy—everybody likes him though he is dreadfully provoking to teach from being so desperately slow." Two more years later: "He gives a great deal of trouble, and his character is so weak. . . ." Still, the occasional letter allowed as how her three older children weren't entirely impossible: "Willy is loud and rough, Charlotte is very troublesome and Henry most provoking at times—but really they are very dear and nice—and I am very proud of them."

Though it was the common practice between Queen Victoria and her children to speak of other family members—especially their own offspring—as "ugly," this did not necessarily imply ill will on the part of the writer. In some cases this sort of candor was simply the family's way, though it is hard to reconcile Vicky's desire that her mother approve of her grandchildren with the sorts of things she wrote about them.

But the comments on character and learning difficulties were far more serious, and if they reached the children, surely harmful. It isn't known to what degree Vicky make such feelings apparent to her offspring, but in view of the continuing estrangement between their mother and Willy, Charlotte, and Henry, the three eldest likely sensed her disappointment. Yet the crown princess was not intentionally cruel to her children in deed; and compared to the run of upper-class Prussian mothers, she spent an inordinate amount of time with them. Her second daughter, Victoria (known as Moretta in the family), later gave her great credit in this regard: ". . . she never neglected her children. Every moment that she could spare away from the various duties . . . was spent with us." The pity is that such unusual physical attention could not be translated into imparting—to the three eldest at least—a sense of genuine pride in them. The gulf between her outward attention to the children and the outcome was vast and is one of the great enigmas of Vicky's life.

Hannah Pakula, biographer of Queen Victoria's eldest daughter, revealed letters from Willy to his mother that suggest an unstable personality far predating his own years as emperor. Writing to his mother from Kassel, where his parents sent him for schooling to get him away from the influences of the court, Willy drafted what seem to be subliminal love letters. In amazing detail, he describes to the crown princess dreams in which she appears to be the object of his desires: "I have again dreamt about you, this time I was alone with you in your library, when you stretched forth your arms & pulled me lower to your chair . . . I instantly seized your hand & kissed it; then you gave me a warm embrace & putting your right arm around my neck and got up & walked about the room with me . . . I dreamt about what we will do in reality when we are alone in your rooms without any witnesses . . . this dream is *alone* for *you* to know." As Pakula notes, Vicky intelligently treated these fantasies (which continued until Willy turned seventeen) lightly in her answering letters, trying to direct her son's passion toward his Hessian cousins.

Just after their son's eighteenth birthday, in 1877, Vicky and Fritz sent Willy to the University of Bonn. Both parents fervently hoped some of that institution's accumulated centuries of academic merit might rub off on the future emperor. The experience would instead prove a disappointment for both parents and son. Willy's intelligence simply could not be brought to bear on anything to the point that the subject was comprehended beyond its surface. The prince did, characteristically, find more than enough time to join the most aristocratic of the university's famous fraternities, the Borussia Society, so called for the Latin name for Prussia. Fritz had belonged to Borussia in his own schooldays, though Willy's affiliation would actually be a degree less than that of a full member, the intent to keep him clear of the dueling that was the chief public mark of these exclusive societies.

It pleased Vicky that while her son was at university, Willy would regularly visit Darmstadt to spend weekends with his aunt Alice and uncle Louis. During one of these visits he thought he fell in love with his cousin Ella, a passion that was not returned—the princess had already been affianced to Grand Duke Serge of Russia. In any case, Ella didn't find Willy an object of romantic appeal; nor did any of her sisters regard their loud Berlin cousin as particularly welcome company. Having been rejected by the amazingly beautiful Ella— far the most physically attractive of any of Queen Victoria's granddaughters—Willy evidently decided he wasn't going to let rejection happen again. Instead, he soon settled on one of the least prepossessing of the Continent's Protestant princesses. Princess Augusta of Schleswig-Holstein, called "Dona," shared some of Queen Victoria's genes, having been the granddaughter of the British monarch's half sister Feodore. Unfortunately, another grandmother was a mere countess, a stumbling block that the enormously rank-conscious Hohenzollern court was going to have some difficulty swallowing.

While Willy was spending the last months of 1878 courting Dona, the deaths in the Hessian grand ducal family ended the year in a tragic vein for all his maternal relatives. Willy's mother mourned as much as any of the family, but the crown princess was able to retain one cheerful corner in a heart too often occupied with political aggravations, filial disappointments, and family catastrophes. The three youngest daughters—Moretta, Sophie, and Mossy[2]—were an undiluted pleasure for Vicky, and she adored them for the love they gave her, which stood in such sharp contrast to the difficulties from

the three oldest. But her son Waldemar's breezy exuberance papered over the never-quite-healed wound that had been left in the
wake of Sigi's death twelve years earlier. As an added balm to Vicky,
the boy seemed to her to have some of the qualities of her late father, and she was convinced Waldy would grow up, like Albert, into
a great and useful man.

Nearing his eleventh birthday at the beginning of 1879, Waldy
delighted his entire family with his loving and extroverted personality. Vicky enjoyed teaching this bright and receptive son herself; in
a letter to the queen, the crown princess reported: "Waldy learns so
well, and is such a nice boy to teach, with such a good memory. He
is by far the most gifted of the boys . . . he has such an open, hon-
est nature . . . I trust he will make a real man someday, if he is
spared." A born prankster, his tumultuous behavior was treasured
by both parents, and even his oldest brother, Willy, felt a special pro-
tectiveness toward Waldy.

In the first weeks of 1879, Vicky was just getting back on her feet
after the shock of Alice's death. One more aggravation was Willy's
seeming indifference to his aunt's death, though such unconcern
might have been triggered by memories of her daughter Ella's lack
of interest in his romantic overtures. But at the end of March a new
disaster was about to strike the Neues Palais. Vicky sent a short note
to Windsor on the 24th: "One line to say that Waldemar has the
diphtheria. . . . You can imagine, dear Mama, that I feel anxious."

Vicky's anxiety would in the following days rapidly escalate into
hysteria, and it was all Fritz could do to calm his wife. Even Willy
seemed to sense another tragedy rushing toward his family as the
twenty-year-old eldest son kept an all-night vigil in the Friedens-
kirche for his sick young brother. Vicky tried desperately to put on
a mask of coolness in the face of a disease that had just swept
through her sister's family, writing matter-of-factly to her mother
that "I gargle, & put on a mackintosh over my clothes while I am
with the dear child."

Waldy's struggle was horrible. His mother described his inflamed
tonsils as "large as a walnut," adding that he was unable to swallow,
or indeed fully to close his mouth. Even with his mother's unremit-

ting care—washing the boy with hot vinegar and water and constantly changing his soaked linens—the doctors could not save the young prince. The end came only three days after the first signs of the disease had been diagnosed. Early in the morning of March 27, unable to breathe through the diphtheria membrane, Waldy died. Within hours, the crown princess described to her mother the emotions she felt: "With trembling hands I write these few lines . . . how great and how bitter this agony is words cannot say! My beloved darling, my sweet Waldy, the dearest nicest and most promising of my boys is gone."

When many years later Willy, as emperor, wrote his memoirs, he said of this period: "The grief of my parents for the loss of this splendid son was unbearable; our pain deep and cruel beyond words." As for Vicky, her husband said she was "never the same woman again."

The years had been passing considerably less turbulently for Louise. For the first time in her life, the newlywed princess was genuinely free to experience life without the often-overwhelming penumbra of the queen shadowing her every action. Not that Victoria hadn't tried to remain firmly attached. In March 1871, two days into the first stage of Louise and Lorne's honeymoon, spent at Claremont House near Windsor, Victoria visited the couple to see how her daughter was getting on with a new husband and married life. Though the call could be viewed as motherly and solicitous, to the newlyweds' irritation the sovereign tried to stop the second part of the planned honeymoon, a much-anticipated tour of the Continent. Since chaotic conditions in much of Europe over the just-ended Franco-Prussian War would probably mean that Louise wouldn't receive the courtesies due a daughter of the British sovereign, this was not an unreasonable objection. But Lorne firmly rejected the maternal interference, and wanting a chance to get to know a wife who was still a virtual stranger to him, told his mother-in-law they meant to proceed as planned, regardless of the difficulties. The prince of Wales cordially saw the newlyweds off at Charing

A Victorian montage: all eleven members of the family, artificially assembled in an 1859 group photo. Left to right: Helena, Vicky, Bertie, Arthur, Prince Albert, Beatrice, Queen Victoria, Louise, Affie, Leopold, Alice.

Queen Victoria at Windsor Castle exactly one month before Albert's death. The resemblance between the queen and her eldest daughter is striking.

Vicky with Willy and Charlotte, 1860.

At this point in her young married life, Vicky's matronliness was already
well established.

After her widowhood began in 1888, this costume represented Vicky's habitual dress. Like her mother after the prince consort's death, the dowager empress never again wore colors.

Family group photo taken at Schloss Friedrichshof on Queen Victoria's birthday, 1900.
Wilhelm II is seated at center on the steps. Empress Frederick stands third from right.

Alice at the time of her 1862 marriage. The severe hairstyle was highly fashionable during this period.

Prince Louis shortly after marriage to Princess Alice. It's clear why the queen's daughter was initially attracted to the young Hessian.

Princess Alice in her middle years. She was rarely photographed with any but a melancholy expression on her face.

Helena (on the left) and Alice flanking their mother, the latter dressed (as she always would be after December 14, 1861) in deepest mourning for Albert. Photo taken at Balmoral in 1863.

Helena, the shyest and plainest of Victoria and Albert's daughters.

Helena's daughter, Marie Louise, after leaving her husband, Aribert.

Louise, the future Duchess of Argyll, in a tartan skirt.

Hulton Getty\Tony Stone Images

The widowed Louise, Duchess of Argyll, lending a royal smile to a Highland trooper.

Beatrice the bride, July 23, 1885. She was the only daughter allowed by her mother to wear Victoria's own wedding veil. The diamond cross nearly outshone the décolletage.

The widowed Beatrice in the Edwardian years.

Cross Station on April 3, Bertie by this time having apparently reconciled himself to this commoner brother-in-law.

The idyllic days of her European honeymoon would be remembered by Louise as one of the happiest times of her life. Though the queen had mean-spiritedly demanded that the Lornes' visit in Darmstadt with Alice be of short duration—Victoria suspected, rightly as it turned out, that Alice would raise indelicate gynecological matters with her younger sister, a discussion their mother believed would jeopardize Louise's innocence—the other, sunnier parts of the journey were nearly perfect. From the windows of their Florence hotel, both husband and wife sketched the serried rooftops of the city. By using the incognito of Lord and Lady Sundridge (one of the duke's secondary titles), they kept to a minimum the obligatory calls on foreign royalty expected of Louise in her capacity as a British princess. The new bride loved the anonymity she thought the stratagem was providing and tended to become annoyed when her true identity was discovered.

On returning to London, the Lornes' first obligation was to find a town home into which to settle in something approaching royal state. While they were looking, the couple stayed at what was, in effect, the Campbell family's private London clubhouse. Argyll Lodge was a rambling mansion set in a pasture just north of Kensington High Street, the area still in the 1870s a village. It was connected to Westminister by a turnpike passing through the open fields that gave the western side of the capital a countrified appearance. The lodge, bordering on Holland Park, had been purchased by Lorne's father some twenty years earlier. The place was a virtual paradise, its gracious chestnut trees shading verdant lawns, the only imposition on privacy the faint hum of carriages as they progressed along the nearby High Street. With Campbells dropping in whenever they were in London, Louise was able at last to achieve a degree of intimacy with her husband's exuberant family. The clan included in-laws and cousins and siblings from the nation's nobility: Argylls and Sutherlands and Westminsters, Leinsters, Northumberlands, Blantyres, and Carlisles, all names redolent of the exploits in Britain's history books. Louise couldn't reign as mistress of this house—her mother-in-law, the duchess, claimed that distinction by right—but she loved Argyll Lodge and would have been happy to live there permanently, chatelaine or not. Indeed, the mansion would often serve Louise and Lorne as a city refuge, until a few years later when a Campbell family feud caused Lorne to vow never to set foot in it again.

Probably the most overwhelming event in Louise's early married life was her introduction to Inveraray Castle, the seat of the Argyll dukedom, principal home of the Campbell family, and, on Lorne's inheritance of his birthright, her future residence. Inveraray is a vast granite pile, heavily romantic, with battle-ready turrets emphasizing its awe-inspiring bearings and a monumental tower projecting over the central block. Set in a depression backed by Argyllshire's brooding green hills, the Campbell residence was one of the most dramatic of the grand mansions of Scotland. Its upkeep, unfortunately, was slowly driving Lorne's father bankrupt.

On the day in August 1871 when Louise was first welcomed to the castle, nearly the entire surrounding district turned out to see the queen's daughter come home with their chief's son. With pipers playing "The Campbells Are Comin'," the sky dropping a steady rain, and winds howling through the nearby lochs and glens, all honor was directed at the radiantly beautiful young bride. These first days at her in-laws' home passed in a haze of parties and receptions and balls, climaxed by a huge regatta that was marred only by a typically frightful Highland summer storm. A tenantry ball for 710 people brought the visit to a close, on a day on which the sun had finally shone through the mist and Louise first saw the castle in all the fullness of its summer beauty.

On returning to London, the couple again joined the uncompleted task of finding their own city home. Eventually, Louise leased a five-story townhouse in Belgravia's Grosvenor Crescent. Then a relatively new area, Belgravia had been purpose-built as an enclave of wealth, with huge stone mansions lining still-immaculate streets. When the new houses were filled up with their millionaire owners, many of whom were titled, the area became, after nearby (and still more expensive) Mayfair, the most fashionable neighborhood in the capital. The owner and lessor of the Lornes' townhouse was the duke of Westminster, one of Lorne's many uncles. The couple planned to keep the imposing mansion only long enough to find something they wanted to buy, Lorne knowing full well that the rental was beyond his financial means—the fabulously wealthy Westminster was not giving it to his nephew at any kind of a discount. But the young husband believed he had to ensconce Louise in a physical setting of which her mother would approve. As it happened, the princess often found herself absent from London, since the queen constantly begged her daughter to give her assistance, demands to which the new marchioness obligingly acceded.

In her early married days, Louise would find that her status as a princess abruptly ran up against her hunger to relish life as at least an independent woman—independent, of course, only insofar as any woman could achieve that status in mid-Victorian England. Marrying outside her ultra-restricted caste into the only slightly wider realm of upper-class peers and commoners had given Louise the best chance of any of her sisters to break the palace bonds. Vicky and Alice, for all their intellectual or social undertakings, remained largely creatures of what they had been born into, and Lenchen, basically afraid of the world, found comfort in her mother's gilded orbit. Though it was impossible for Louise completely to shed the load of being the monarch's daughter, she would make the best job—the best of any of her family—of enjoying the lifestyle of her mother's ordinary subjects, albeit rich ones.

In these years, the queen tried on more than one occasion to get her son-in-law to accept a dukedom (in a letter from Victoria to Louise: ". . . if I *approved* of Lorne *marrying* MY *Daughter*, he *ought* to have rank as her husband"), a status she felt would clothe him in a more acceptable dignity as the monarch's son-in-law, as well as providing his and Louise's children with appropriate position and titles. Lorne just as consistently refused, principally on the grounds that he didn't want to leave the House of Commons, believed his own anticipated title of duke of Argyll was perfectly adequate, no matter how long he would have to wait for it, and that he didn't wish to do disservice to his own father or the Argyll inheritance by ending that title (which his acceptance of the queen's offer would have unavoidably entailed).

Two overriding issues shadowed the Lornes' lives in the first years of their marriage. The first was their inability to conceive a child. Though questions would eventually be raised about Lorne's sexual orientation, evidence from Louise's writings suggests that the couple did engage in physical marital relations. Louise wanted the Argyll succession to be passed down through her own son, and her lack of success in becoming pregnant—in Victorian days the woman was invariably held accountable in such instances—was troubling to her. Lorne, to his credit, apparently never blamed Louise for their lack of a child, treating the fact with understanding sympathy. In the summer of 1873, she went to Germany for medicinal baths designed to improve her prospects of conception, and her mother even had the most senior royal physician, Sir William Jenner, advise the princess on the subject. For the first dozen years of marriage, Louise continued to take the Continental waters, and European spas such as Marienbad and Homburg regularly saw the princess on her summer attempts at a "cure." The actual cause of her childlessness may, in fact, have been her teenage bout with meningitis.

Vicky also fretted about Louise's lack of children, wondering in a letter to Louise when "a host of small Campbells" might be available to keep their various cousins company. When later complimenting her daughter on a new country house she had taken, Vicky commented not very tactfully how much nicer it would be if there were a "few little fair heads looking out of the windows." Their mother helpfully told Louise to "be careful in your diet and in *not* omitting aperient medicines. . . ." The queen also weighed in with the view that no children were preferable to "wicked" ones. Leopold tactlessly wrote his congratulations to Louise when her sister-in-law (the wife of Lord Archie Campbell, Lorne's younger brother) had a son, with the inane observation that the birth was of a "possible future (*I hope not*) Duke. . . ."

Nearly as troubling, albeit of less dynastic significance, was

Lorne's perpetual shortness of funds. Though he would someday inherit one of the kingdom's great noble patrimonies, that patrimony was not by the second half of the nineteenth century nearly as cash-rich as it had once been. Nor was Lorne's father particularly generous, mostly because he didn't have too much to be generous with; he had a half dozen daughters for whom he must provide suitable dowries, but also his Scottish sense of thrift kept the Argyll purse fairly tightly closed. Lorne was finding that Grosvenor Crescent was turning out to be enormously expensive in spite of Louise's earnest economies, such as her decision to paper rather than paint the walls of the vast, high-ceilinged reception rooms that overlooked Belgrave Square.

The queen, aware of the Lornes' financial difficulties, ultimately came through for her daughter and son-in-law when in 1873 she offered the couple an apartment in Kensington Palace. Lying in an untidy mass at the west end of the Kensington Gardens–Hyde Park complex, in the mid-nineteenth century the area was just becoming a part of developed West London. The palace had long been a state residence; the monarch alone decided who could live in its many flats—some cramped, some palatial. Victoria herself had been born at Kensington Palace in 1819, and the place held enormous nostalgia for her. The large but grimy and rundown apartments Victoria had in mind for her daughter had been the duchess of Inverness's home, but would require many thousands of pounds (of public money) to be made suitable for the sovereign's daughter. It took nearly two years before Louise and Lorne were able to move into their new home; but in March 1875, the princess gave her mother a tour of the almost-finished residence. Victoria's reaction in her diary was poignant: "Though quite unfinished, when I went in and saw the well-known look out, the doors etc. where I spent 16 years of my life everything came back again so vividly to my mind!" The queen's only slight regret was that her daughter would not be living in the actual rooms she herself had once occupied.

With an affordable city residence now secured, the Lornes' attention moved to finding a relatively inexpensive house in the country. Though Louise loved Inveraray, understandably she would never feel completely at ease in a house in which her father-in-law reigned as duke. Argyll had lent them a country place, called Macharioch, near Inveraray, but the remote estate was inconvenient; what was more, Lorne's family continued to use it as a gathering point for their yachting trips and Louise thus lacked privacy there. The couple finally bought a country house of their own called Dornden, near Tunbridge Wells in Kent, south of the capital. The property was smallish (at least in terms of a duke's residence, especially a duke married to a royal princess) but possessed extraordinary charm: the ivy-covered house was set on 170 of Kent's lushest acres, land studded with orchards and even a lake on which floated its own little island. The queen, typically, worried that Louise might be "molested" by importunate locals crowding near enough to the house to get a peek at a princess. Of the cost— £30,000—the princess came up with £15,000 from her dowry, Lorne borrowing the remainder from his father.

Louise now began to widen her social circle to a degree her mother could never have been able to understand. The princess took up interests that would have been unthinkable had she been living under the queen's roof, not the least a passionate pursuit of fly-fishing while in the North—an endeavor then considered saucy for women. More important, in London the princess ventured far outside society's rigidly circumscribed pale. Among the most important enterprises for Louise was the Ladies' Work Society, an organization she herself founded and underwrote. One of the many hidden evils inherent in Victorian society was the treatment accorded to women of the middle and upper middle classes who had fallen into poverty. If unable to find jobs as governesses, or the other very few avenues of employment open to them, such women were unwilling to enter domestic service, a realm of the working classes. In the Ladies' Work Society they learned crafts—needlework, embroidery, repairing of items of fine art—that enabled many to earn modest but livable wages. The society set up a shop in highly respectable Sloane Square, where the results of their at-home work were displayed and sold. And its founder was inevitably its best customer.

Another of Louise's undertakings was the sponsorship of an "Educational Parliament" out of which arose the Girls' Public School Day Company, in which middle-class parents were given enough financial assistance to see that their daughters could be educated. From an initial facility in Chelsea, by the turn of the century the venture would grow to thirty-two more schools, providing secondary education to more than seven thousand students. As patroness, Louise lent the invaluable cachet of her name to the organization, and for over fifty years gave generously of her time at school openings and fund-raisers. That the recipients of both these ventures were exclusively middle-class sounds discriminatory to modern sensibilities, but accurately reflects the customary Victorian practice of dealing with and maintaining class divisions as they existed. Even these seemingly tepid efforts met with heated, sometimes vehement, opposition. Louise's relative by marriage, the duchess of Northumberland, protested that "schools for women are in themselves, in their very nature, bad, and to be avoided as much as possible." For many Englishmen—and women—educated females seemed to present a threat to men, something that was to be avoided at whatever cost. The nation's monarch might have been chief spokesperson for this view.

Though Lorne was sympathetic to his wife's activities to a degree unusual in the aristocratic classes, he was still a husband who regarded his wife as in need of constant protection and monitoring. He would not, for example, allow Louise to speak in public, even at one of the organizations which she sponsored; instead, Lorne would read the speeches his wife wrote, as she sat decorous but silent on the platform.

Such efforts held little attraction for the Scot. Lorne had been captured since youth by the beauty and stateliness of poetry, and it was in the literary arts, not politics or diplomacy, that he made what he regarded as his greatest mark. In the late summer of 1875, Lorne prepared the final proof corrections on his first book of poetry, *Guido and Lita—A Tale of the Riviera*, a narrative poem that was published by Macmillan. Lorne recounted the medieval struggle between Christians and Muslims as representatives of good and evil, with a young hero, Guido, who eventually wins fair Lita as his bride. This sort of piece maintained a certain following in the Victorian era, though Lorne at first considered that a pseudonym might be appropriate. At any rate, Macmillan was only too glad to publish the work, possibly stimulated by the author's status as the queen's son-in-law, then as now a connection carrying inestimable prestige. Over three thousand copies were sold; American and Canadian counterparts followed upon the British edition. Reviewers snidely agreed the work was "old-fashioned."

Lorne's next effort was a rewriting of the Psalms, another Victorian-era endeavor long since faded away. *The Books of Psalms, Literally Rendered into Verse* was published in 1877, and had in part been prompted by Louise's criticism of the "dull way in which some of the grand old Psalms were put into verse." If her referent was the King James Version of the Bible, what made these words so "grand" was precisely the way they were rendered. Nevertheless, Lorne embarked on a heroic effort to improve upon them. The most famous psalm, the Twenty-Third, originally "The Lord is my shepherd; I shall not want/He maketh me to lie down in green pastures," was transformed into: "My Shepherd is the Lord, and I shall never want or fear/To streams of comfort he me leads . . ." Though Lorne by no means disgraced himself, the critical consensus was that it was foolhardy to change something that was already just about perfect.

While Lorne was occupied by writing and his lackluster career in the House of Commons—as a Liberal, he had been lucky to survive a landslide in the 1874 elections, when Scottish Conservative seats rose from seven to nineteen—what made Louise happiest was her involvement with an artistic and literary fraternity. Its membership included some of Britain's greatest nineteenth-century artists, men such as Fredrick Leighton and John Millais, who in their day were nonetheless ostracized by the conventional arts community for what was, in effect, their unaccountable abandonment of Victorian banality. Fortunately for Louise, her status as Lorne's wife allowed her something approaching normal social access to these talented giants, an entree that would have been difficult for her as an unmarried princess except in the role of royal patron. Conversely, some of London's most controversial artists were by the fact of her royal status lent a respectability they might otherwise have waited years to acquire. Louise even got the prince of Wales to take some slight notice of their work, Bertie informing his sister that he was "looking forward" to seeing the pictures of her modern friends.

In the autumn of 1877, a fire at Inveraray brought calamity to the Campbell family. The blaze erupted while Louise and Lorne were visiting the duke and duchess. Early on a stormy and bitterly cold October morning, a fisherman tying down his boat in the violent squall looked up from the loch at flames bursting from the castle tower. A signal was quickly passed to the castellans, awakening the family and servants. As the duchess had recently suffered a stroke, she was unable to move on her own. The princess got the elderly woman into a coat, and she and Lorne half-carried and half-walked the dazed duchess out of the furiously blazing castle, just missing the ceiling that came crashing down into the main hall. When told that two of his female relatives were unaccounted for, Lorne ran back in through the fire, ignoring his father's order to stay put. Lorne made it to the women, and got them and himself out through a side door. A human bucket chain up from the loch to the castle succeeded in extinguishing the fire before the building was destroyed, but it seemed for dreadful moments as though Inveraray Castle was about to be lost entirely.

For Lorne's ailing mother, the disaster greatly taxed what was left of her strength. While dining at Carlton House Terrace in London the following May, the duchess of Argyll collapsed next to her dinner partner, William Gladstone. Lorne and Louise were just up the street at Marlborough House, dining with Bertie and Alix, when they were urgently summoned to the Gladstones. The princess found her mother-in-law lying on a mattress in the mansion's study, Mrs. Gladstone doing her best to nurse her. Doctors diagnosed a brain hemorrhage. The Duchess died within hours.

In 1878, Louise's and Lorne's lives changed in a way that would lead to more trials as well as triumphs for both of them when the prime minister, Benjamin Disraeli, offered Lorne the governor generalship of the Dominion of Canada, one of Britain's great viceroy-

alties. Lorne as a Liberal was, of course, a member of the party opposing Disraeli's Conservatives. But the top gubernatorial posts in
the empire were conferred almost exclusively on peers or about-to-
be peers. Lorne, as the queen's son-in-law, would carry inestimable
value as Victoria's representative in Canada, with Louise's stature as
a royal princess an added cachet. Disraeli believed they would serve
as a focus of loyalty among the inhabitants of a vast but still disjointed dominion. The prime minister's colonial secretary, Sir
Michael Hicks Beach, regarded Lorne as a potent symbol of imperial harmony, an asset that appealed strongly to an ardently imperi-
alistic prime minister.

Canada's governors general in that time routinely found themselves deeply involved in politics, a notable difference from the essentially social figurehead role that would later dominate their
office. In theory, the official bodily represented the queen in
Canada. As such, Lorne would be the highest-ranking person in the
country, in effect, head of state, with the more politically powerful
Canadian prime minister in second position as the head of government. In diplomatic terms, he would stand as surrogate for the
British government, specifically the Foreign Office, and was a kind
of two-way ambassador between Canada and Britain. Like the
monarch in the United Kingdom, he would be constitutionally responsible for ministerial succession were a government to resign or
be defeated at the polls, though in reality he was constrained to appoint as prime minister whichever political leader commanded a
majority in the Canadian Parliament. In addition to these broad duties, which left limited leeway for independent action on the in-
cumbent's part, Lorne would be unofficially expected to settle any
number of administrative and diplomatic problems arising between
London and Ottawa. Finally—and the role in which Louise was regarded as a tremendous boon—Lorne and his wife would stand indisputably at the peak of Canadian society, where the governor
general's wife was every bit as important as her husband.

Disraeli had, of course, broached the proposed appointment to
the queen before Lorne himself was officially sounded out. Though
Victoria was not enthusiastic at the thought of sending her daugh-

ter half a world away, she realized the "fine, independent position" would likely reflect well on Louise, and that the still-young Lorne's prestige in both the nation and the family would, assuming he succeeded in the post, take a giant leap upward. The queen may also have thought that Lorne and Louise might have a better chance to put the problems of their troublesome social status out of mind—in Ottawa, as governor general, Lorne would for the first time take precedence over his wife. Thus, with the sovereign's only slightly hedged approval, Disraeli formally tendered the post to the thirty-two-year-old Liberal MP whose parliamentary career had looked to be petering out due to Lorne's own lack of commitment.

There was never any doubt that Lorne himself would be over-joyed at the prospect of going off to Canada for the five-year appointment. A lover of travel and adventure, he knew his membership in the House was going nowhere; with his party out of office he stood no chance of a ministry in the foreseeable future, and was too young and inexperienced to expect one anyway. His writing career stalled by a lack of public interest, Lorne likely regarded the immensity of Canada as prime material with which to revitalize his creative juices. Furthermore, he hoped the appointment might lead to Ireland's Lord Lieutenantship, or even to the most prestigious imperial post of all: the viceroyalty of India. The only downside he could see was the possibility that Louise might not be very anxious to leave her home and its securities to sail off to the relative barbarities of Ottawa.

As it happened, Louise was thrilled at the prospect of such an adventure, at least in the beginning, though after more reflective deliberation it would begin to niggle at her. The princess knew she would miss her family as well as her newfound pleasures in London's glamorous literary world. And there was the matter of Arthur's planned marriage to Prussia's Princess Louise—an event only a few months off and one she didn't want to miss. Leopold might have a deadly bleeding emergency at any time. She could expect no social peers in the very rough world that Canada still represented. Finally, Canada was *extremely* cold. This point wasn't simply a matter of comfort: the facial neuralgia she had long suffered would be intensified in the Canadian winters, when protracted bitter plunges in temperature might prove physically unendurable.

In the end, though, it came down to duty, the concept her mother had instilled in her over a lifetime. The knowledge that her husband desperately wanted to take the appointment, and with it the honor of representing the queen, overcame Louise's doubts. Lorne formally accepted at the end of July 1878. After working out such details as their departure date and his salary, the couple began the considerable chore of packing for life in a new world. Bertie made a last effort to persuade his brother-in-law to accept the queens' proffered dukedom, which Lorne persisted in declining, even though he would be leaving the House of Commons and no longer had as much reason to defer the peerage.

Sensitive to Lorne's inexperience, the queen sent the new governor general a kind and typically deft letter with advice she hoped would serve him well during his first days in his new post. "What I would principally wish to advise and impress on you, is to be very cautious and do nothing in a hurry—not to be rash—or *act* on the spur of the moment. But always to *reflect* well, and delay any answer or action for a day or two . . . when one pauses and waits for a day and a night, one calms down and is able to take a different and more impartial view of things." There were times when Victoria's commonsensical wisdom shone through with crystal clarity. Additionally, she was aware of how big were the shoes her son-in-law and daughter would be stepping into: " . . . Lord Dufferin [the current governor general] with the best intentions has not made it easier for either of you, by making people expect so very much."

A series of emotional family leave-takings followed, and Lorne resigned his Argyllshire parliamentary seat, passing it over to his brother Colin (who would, fortunately, hold on to it for the Liberals in the by-election held to decide Lorne's permanent replacement). On November 14, 1878, adorned with the newly minted insignia of a Knight Grand Cross of the Order of St. Michael and St. George, given him by the queen in honor of his imperial appointment, the new pro-consul and his wife sailed out of Liverpool Harbor on the Allan Line steamer *Sarmatian*, which Lorne insisted was good enough in spite of the queen's view that her daughter should arrive in Canada on a warship of the Royal Navy.

A few days before their departure, Louise had received a letter from Alice. Her sister wanted Lorne to look into an immigration case for her, apparently of a woman who wished to meet the new governor general when she arrived in Canada; Alice said she would be "*very* useful if you would both lend your attention. . . ." Her letter closed with best wishes for a safe passage as "there have been such storms." One month to the day after the *Sarmatian*'s departure, Alice would succumb to diphtheria.

While the lives of her sisters were being agitated by death, displacement, and distress over troublesome offspring, Lenchen's placid existence generally flowed through the royal family like a languid stream in summer: few eddies, no sharp currents, little chance of flooding. Lenchen and her Christian got along splendidly, perhaps because neither was exciting enough to give the other any kind of trouble; more likely because they were simply well suited to each other.

Since leaving Frogmore House, the couple had made their home at Cumberland Lodge (when in London they economized by staying in Buckingham Palace's Belgian Suite), a mansion buried in a wooded copse of Windsor Great Park, just beyond the far end of the Long Walk. Historically used as the residence of the Ranger of the Park—the position the queen bestowed on Christian after his entry into the family—the nucleus of the house was already two centuries old when they took it over. One of its occupants had been Sarah Churchill, the first duchess of Marlborough, who was made Ranger by her great and good friend, Queen Anne. Sarah was reputed to have preferred life at the lodge to the luxuries of her far more commodious residence at Blenheim, a preference that may have been based on the proximity to her sovereign. A later resident was King George II's son, the duke of Cumberland, famous to posterity as the Butcher of Culloden and for having a flower called after him: the

Sweet William. James Wyatt, the architect of Windsor under William IV, remodeled the west side of Cumberland Lodge in the Gothic style. Largely rebuilt after a fire in 1869, the mansion was to remain Lenchen's country home until her death in 1923.[3]

When misfortune touched the couple in the 1870s, it was in the horror that so many parents had to face in an era in which medicine was still more fallible than not. Prince Frederick Harald, born at the Christians' home at Cumberland Lodge in 1876, died eight days later; after another year, Lenchen delivered a stillborn infant, a second shock from which she only slowly recovered. To honor these two ill-fated grandchildren, the queen asked Louise to commission a statue created in the monarch's name. Her daughter chose Aimée-Jules Dalou (it isn't known why Louise didn't put herself forward as the sculptor), who designed an angel paired with small children, the princes supervising the work as Dalou brought Lenchen's babies to sculpted life in his Chelsea studio.

Happily, Lenchen and her husband were blessed with four other growing children to keep them occupied, a matter of importance to the largely unemployed Christian, who had not much else with which to fill his hours. In fact, Victoria was displaying increasing irritation at her inert son-in-law, herself a woman who believed that an idle mind was an idle mind. Writing at her desk while on holiday at Osborne (Victoria kept working wherever she was in residence, holiday or not), she spied Christian through her study window, loitering in the garden and evidently at loose ends. She instantly dashed off a message for him to the effect that he had best find something constructive to attend to.

His torpor should have come as no surprise to Victoria. Since marriage, both wife and husband met only one real need: to help the queen with her paperwork—particularly involving the family—until Beatrice could fully step into the role. This situation left Christian little else to do other than his part in the making of babies. Even that often irritated the monarch, for whom the thought of her daughter's satisfying conjugal life served as a painful reminder of what she herself had lost in 1861. The Christians would remain physically near enough to the sovereign to serve as tempting choices for court duty, which the queen reckoned they were being well paid to tender.

The queen's annoyance at her son-in-law sometimes extended to Lenchen as well. Writing to Vicky, the monarch observed that while Beatrice hadn't yet got as "touchy" as her siblings, her middle daughter *was* proving a worry: "That [touchiness] has increased with poor Lenchen (partly from health and partly from Christian's inordinate spoiling and the absence of all actual troubles and du- ties) to a degree that it makes it very difficult to live with her. But pray keep this to yourself and say nothing to anyone about it—but it grieves me to see it and to see what poor health she has. She won't either do anything to get better and says she don't care if she is ill or well!" The nature of Lenchen's indisposition is unknown.

A year after her stillborn baby was delivered, Lenchen again had to face deep grief, this time at the news of Alice's death. Though Alice had been one of her two sisters who stood in bitter opposition to her marriage, Lenchen came to understand that her antagonism hadn't been personal, but rather only represented her view that the union was arranged strictly as an accommodation to their mother's wishes. When it became clear that the younger woman herself des- perately wanted to marry and get out of the suffocating atmosphere of the court, it was Alice who helped convince Bertie to drop his own bitter fight against the Schleswig-Holstein family connection. In the event, Lenchen lovingly commemorated Alice's memory when she wrote a foreword to a published edition of the late grand duchess's letters to Queen Victoria; the second edition of the book was given the title *Memoir of Princess Alice by Her Sister, Princess Christian.*

Greatly loved by their parents and spoiled on frequent visits with the queen, the Christians' two sons and two daughters passed golden childhoods virtually untouched by the horrors of industrial- age Britain. Prince Christian's lack of employment meant that his children regarded his full-time presence as normal. He taught the four children his native German tongue, and like most of Victoria's grandchildren, they became fluent in this language used nearly as much as English in the British royal family. Family life in town and country was one of perpetual pleasantness, at least while the children were small. Each homelier than the next, they grew up playing with the offspring of their grandmother's household officials and those of the far more humble estate workers. Christian Victor, the oldest, was groomed for the army on the basis that there wasn't much else that a peripherally royal young man could aspire to; if, in fact, he had leaned in any other direction, it would have been thought decidedly odd. Christle, as he was called at home, became the first member of the royal family to go to school (rather than being educated by a tutor at home), in his case Wellington College, which he entered in 1881. Bertie had rejected his mother's advice to send his own sons to Wellington, and the queen was happy that Lenchen's boy would go to the school the prince consort had many years before helped to establish.

Two years younger than Christle, Albert was foreordained to inherit the dukedom of Schleswig-Holstein-Sonderburg-Augustenburg on his childless cousin's death. Unlike his elder brother, young Albert seems to have hated the thought of being a soldier; yet he would one day be required to serve in the Prussian Army, a military establishment that made its British counterpart seem democratic in comparison.

The girls' upbringing wasn't much more remarkable than that of their brothers. They had their own personal French maid—these *were* the queen's granddaughters—but both Helena Victoria and Marie Louise were taught to take care of their rooms and their appearance themselves. Their clothes were about as unprincesslike as the circumstances of their lives would permit: severe blue-serge dresses were standard, though both changed into more formal frocks for dinner. In addition to their father's German lessons, the princesses were taught French by their governesses (which they had to speak to their maids), and a Madame de Goncourt came to the lodge twice weekly to tutor them in literature and history. Like all their female cousins, both girls were instructed in the graces required of women of their rank: how to sit and walk gracefully, how to converse easily with people, how to look engrossed when one was really bored witless. Lenchen made sure, too, that her children were grounded in the realities of British medical and welfare work; she herself would become one of the founding members of the nation's Red Cross during the Franco-Prussian War. Marie Louise got practical training in this field, and many years later Lenchen's daughter would recall, as a six-year-old, rolling bandages for wounded soldiers of the Russo-Turkish War of 1877–78.

In the spring of 1878, when she turned twenty-one, Beatrice was—legally, at least—an adult. Now that her sisters were all grown up and living with their husbands away from the queen, she had finally blossomed into womanhood. But though she stood a head taller than her mother, unfortunately her mind had been left a long ways behind her prematurely matronly body, and almost entirely unformed. With the queen again undertaking a measure of the ceremonial tasks expected of her—during Disraeli's years as prime minister she actually willingly opened Parliament—Beatrice graduated fully into the role of physical supporter and helpmeet (as well as intimate secretary) to the sovereign, and became Victoria's most visible daughter to the British public.

Increasingly, the queen became obsessed with the idea of keeping her "baby" unmarried, convinced that forbidding any mention of marriage or young men would keep her daughter safely at her side. When Beatrice was at the queen's table (the usual case as the girl had, of course, no independent status of her own), conversation among family and guests was often ludicrously constrained. Everyone in the queen's orbit was warned to stay clear of any talk of matrimony or anything even remotely connected with the topic, and when someone did mention the unmentionable, an icy royal stare quickly put a pall over the rest of the meal. Later, the person would receive a curt after-dinner note instructing him or her not to repeat the error. Though these tactics couldn't have done Beatrice's emotional and mental development much good, neither were they in the long run successful. Aware of the hothouse treatment she was receiving, the princess clung to her dignity by doing her utmost to serve the sovereign well in a job that was not, after all, unimportant given who her mother was.

Though Victoria remained unwavering about her right to claim Beatrice's life to the service of her own, she was not ungenerous in her regard for her youngest daughter. In a letter to Vicky, she wrote candidly: ". . . I hope and trust [Beatrice] will never leave me while I live . . . I do not intend she should ever go out as her sisters did (which was a mistake). . . ." (When she wrote these words, the ever hypochondriacal Victoria probably did not think she would live long enough to see her youngest child reach middle age.) In another letter to the crown princess, the queen professed that she "never saw so amiable, gentle, and thoroughly contented a child as she [Beatrice] is. She has the sweetest temper imaginable and is very useful and handy and is unselfish and kind to everyone. . . ." Aside from the fact that the sovereign might have been talking about a new parlormaid, her views of what constituted "contented" would soon come to sharp odds with those of her "child."

After Alice's death, Victoria came up with one of her most bizarre family schemes. She reasoned—perhaps in a weak moment—that if Beatrice married Alice's widower, Louis, a man she considered incapable of raising his children to adulthood by himself, her late daughter's son and four daughters could then come and live in England with Beatrice as their stepmother. This would keep her private secretary at home, and provide the queen herself with the happy task of looking out for four highly eligible granddaughters and eventually marrying them off. If Louis himself were happy, well, that would prove a nice bonus. Victoria apparently didn't think of Hesse-Darmstadt as very important, certainly not important enough to require a full-time grand duke in residence.

Had Louis and Beatrice developed any romantic feeling for each other, and there is no evidence that they did, there remained one unavoidable hitch in the queen's program. In England, marriage between a sister- and brother-in-law was illegal. Victoria, though, viewed this proposed union as a solution to a number of problems and she further believed the legal barrier was something Parliament could fix. To that end, the queen instructed her prime minister to get busy. The prince of Wales agreed with his mother that Beatrice's marrying Louis would be a good idea, and presented a petition in favor of an enabling bill. The Commons approved it; but when it came up in the Lords, a body much under the influence of the bishops, all of whom opposed such change in the law, the bill was killed. In her journal, the queen pronounced Parliament's obstinacy "incredible!"[4]

8

Canada and Scandals

Lorne could have had few illusions that it was his talent to which he owed his new post. A decade as a nearly mute backbencher in the House of Commons was in itself scant qualification, especially when his seat had been a personal sinecure entirely anticipating his future lairdship. Realizing that he faced a big job in repaying Disraeli's generosity, he was additionally daunted by the knowledge that he would have to fill his immediate predecessor's extraordinarily large shoes.

Frederick Temple Hamilton Temple Blackwood, fifth baron and first earl of Dufferin and second earl of Ava,[1] had achieved a notable success in the Canadian appointment he had filled since 1872 with much panache and even greater accomplishment. For six years, Lord Dufferin had enthusiastically promoted all things Canadian, particularly and most importantly a united Canada within a strong British empire, an arrangement he regarded as likely to bring the greatest good to the vast but still largely unformed dominion. Having turned the post of governor general from one of attending to odds and ends into one in which he was Canada's "social arbiter and political referee,"[2] he had served the people with skill and imagination and they very much regretted his imminent departure.[3] Lady

Dufferin would be missed keenly as well, the countess having impressed on the capital city of Ottawa more social graces than it could have hitherto imagined. Rideau Hall, the couple's official residence, had become in some ways more important than the legislative chambers on Parliament Hill. All in all, Lorne and Louise would find themselves taking over roles already finely etched in the Canadian political scene by exemplary predecessors.

In fairness, Lorne was not coming without gifts of his own. Though not a skilled politician, he had made himself an able and enthusiastic writer, and would soon put his literary talent to the service and credit of Canada. Further, he was young and energetic, eager to learn everything about his North American realm, and after his appointment became a dedicated student of all that Dufferin could impart to him. In a series of highly detailed letters, the earl set out his own experiences, as well as the requirements his successor would be expected to master. Frankly and tacitly acknowledged, Lorne's chief asset at the beginning would be his wife, his intimate connection to the living symbol of the British empire. Though neither Lorne nor Louise would be able to match the Dufferins' brilliance—Lady Dufferin had been fully her husband's equal in popularity—they were bringing to the post the tantalizing and, in the late nineteenth century, invaluable magic of being royal.

In place of the warship on which the queen wanted to send her daughter to the shores of the New World with pomp and in appropriate state (as well as the greatest possible security), Louise and Lorne made what was, even in 1878, a grueling voyage on the steamer *Sarmatian*. Specially designed for conversion to military use should need arise, the *Sarmatian*'s power and speed would be useful if a rumored Irish Fenian attack against the couple on the high seas were carried out. It wasn't terrorists who were to make the trip a misery, but instead the November storms lashing the Atlantic. For the ten days of the crossing, the passengers were rocked almost continually by roaring gales, and even during calm weather the captain would be all but blinded by thick fogs. Though a series of cabins had been turned into a luxurious suite befitting a princess and a marquess—Louise and Lorne each had a bedroom, sitting room, and bathroom, with appropriately scaled-down arrangements for their fourteen staff members and servants—the only joy in the crossing was the contemplation of its being over. Lorne, evidently a fair sailor, sketched seagulls throughout a good part of the journey; but Louise stayed miserably in her cabin. Though her berth had been specially rigged out to remain tolerably steady in rough seas, the contrivance did little to mitigate her discomfort.

The exhilaration of arrival was immediately tainted by family tragedy. Louise's brother Alfred, whose warship, the *Black Prince*, was sailing in Canadian waters, appeared at the dock to greet her. Affie bore the sad news that their young niece May had died of diphtheria in Darmstadt. Further anxiety was caused by the absence of the dominion's prime minister to meet the new governor general. The real power in Canada, and the man who could more than anyone else make or break Lorne, Prime Minister Sir John A. Macdonald, had come down from Ottawa on the train, but having gotten too drunk during the ride decided for the time being to remain out of sight.

Enjoying an already outsized reputation, Sir John possessed as well an outsized personality—one that Lorne would find himself occasionally bumping into as his term progressed. The sixty-three-year-old Scottish-born lawyer and leader of Canada's Conservative Party was, aside from being a two-fisted drinker and a master politician, by far the best known Canadian of the era. When in 1867 Upper Canada and Lower Canada merged into the new Confederation, Macdonald became the new nation's first prime minister, receiving a knighthood at the time. For the four years before Lorne's arrival he had been out of office, a situation partly caused by bribery charges lodged against his government in the building of the transcontinental railroad. But weeks before the *Sarmatian* docked in Halifax Harbor, Macdonald's Conservatives had been voted back into office with a stunning majority of seventy-eight parliamentary seats. He told the Canadian people, "a British subject I was born," and swore to them, "a British subject I will die," a sentiment Lorne would greatly appreciate. Lord Rosebery would later say of Macdonald that he had "grasped the central idea that the British Empire is the greatest secular agency for good now known to mankind . . . and strove that Canada should live under it." In 1878, Lorne and Macdonald seemed a good pairing, and a good omen for the furthering of Canadian loyalty to the mother country.

When they left for the capital, the Lornes were greeted rapturously all the way from Halifax to Ottawa, with knots of people at every stop singing disjointed versions of "The Campbells Are Comin'" and journalists outdoing one another in the overwrought prose believed necessary to describe a genuine princess. The good weather the couple had enjoyed since Halifax unhappily broke in Montreal, and they completed the last leg—into the capital itself—through a miserably sleety rain storm that presaged the approaching winter. One thing that raised their arrival a notch above the other stops was that Macdonald finally sobered up enough to greet his new superior at Ottawa's train station. Louise, presumably exhausted, decided to pass up attending the twelve official speeches later addressed to her husband in the Senate Chamber.

Life in Canada was clearly going to be very much less grand than anything the princess had ever known. The godawful coldness of the place was something that Lady Dufferin had never been able to get used to, though her husband professed that he had quite liked it. In winter, temperatures considerably below zero degrees Fahrenheit were common, resulting in journeys negotiated by horse-drawn sleigh over the frozen ruts that defined rough streets. Ottawa stood on a cluster of hillocks whose height averaged a few dozen feet above the Ottawa River, a stream that during the summer conveniently connected Montreal via regular steamers. Overlooking the river was the principal (many would have said the only) architectural splendor of the town, a Gothic pile of three huge and unquestionably impressive structures that represented the Confederation's capitol buildings.

Ottawa itself lay in Ontario, while directly across the river spread the much smaller and low-lying Hull, Quebec; the juxtaposition of the two provinces and the rivalry between far larger Montreal and

Toronto had been the principal reasons this inconvenient site was chosen in 1858 by Louise's mother as Canada's capital, following the same kind of political rationale that had made Washington, D.C., the American capital when New York or Philadelphia would have seemed better suited.

The city was cut into two sections by the Rideau Canal: a mainly English-occupied Upper Town to the east of the canal, and the predominately French Lower Town to the west. The fashionable Sandy Hill on the east was the site of Louise and Lorne's official home-to-be: the official governor general's house, the mansion—by local standards—called Rideau Hall. Named for the canal, which in turn had been named for the small stream the canal was built to bypass, the kernel of the house that became Canada's First Residence was built in 1838 by a Scotsman in what he thought would suggest a Regency style. By the time the Lornes arrived four decades later, the eleven-room kernel had almost been lost in various accretions, primarily from a large addition built in 1865 to make the place worthy to serve as the residence of Lord Monck, the first governor general of confederated Canada. The Dufferins added their own bits in the 1870s, notably a ballroom that became the scene of the capital's choicest social extravaganzas. The thrifty Dufferins also had a tented-over tennis court built, one that could be converted into a banquet room when the need arose. By the time the Lornes moved in, Rideau Hall was the sort of place that, transported to a London suburb such as Wimbledon, might have been home to a successful wholesale grocer.

The first days of Lorne and Louise's life in Ottawa passed in an agony of suspense awaiting word from Darmstadt on Alice's family's condition. A week after they arrived in the capital, a telegram informed the Lornes that Alice herself had come down with diphtheria. Louise was understandably wracked by apprehension, able to do nothing but anxiously await word from England. The dreaded telegram came a few days later, Lorne breaking the news to his wife as gently as he possibly could. So distantly separated from her family, unable even to think of returning to Europe for the funeral,

Louise's early weeks of life in Canada were horribly overshadowed by this family tragedy.

On recovering her equilibrium, the princess determined to make the best of what she found in Ottawa. Her first job was to elevate what she called "the hideous Rideau"—sophisticated Ottawans tended to drop the word "Hall"—to something approaching the level she was used to. At the outset, she ordered that foresters clear a path through the villa's heavily wooded grounds so she could have a view from the house through to the Ottawa River and across to Quebec (the prospect is still called Princess' Vista). She herself painted dainty arboreal scenes on a number of doors and walls in the house; one, a rendering of a blossoming crabapple tree on a paneled boudoir door, has been preserved.[4] Her own studio, filled with the implements of a dedicated painter, soon was hung with her workmanlike renderings of Canadian life in the capital. A boudoir, its walls papered in peacock blue, had dozens of portraits and photographs of her family scattered over the walls and on every surface. Lorne was happy enough with the mansion, writing to his father that "we are settling down in this big and comfortable House, which I tell Louise is much superior to Kensington, for the walls are thick, the rooms are lathed and plastered (which they are not at Kensington) and there is an abundant supply of heat and light." He was clearly and admirably intent on making the best of what was presented to him. In time, even Louise would develop a contented fondness for the place's coziness and idiosyncrasies.

Though she feared the cold because of her health problems, Louise soon discovered that winter life in Ottawa held substantial pleasures, at least for the pampered wife of the governor general. Daylight hours, during which the temperature sometimes dipped to twenty degrees below zero, were filled with sledding and sleighing parties and lots of skating, with Louise inevitably wrapped up in massive sealskin furs, her face all but concealed under what she called her "cloud"—a great white woolen muffler draped over her hat to protect the ears. Her greatest joy was skimming over the icy crust of the snow in marvelous horse-drawn sleighs, the bells on the animals jingling musically while the occupants burrowed snugly under bear and buffalo skins. And if she wasn't buzzing along in her sleigh, Louise was tramping the mile between Rideau Hall and the town center over the crude but scenic road that connected them.

Finding glamour in the Lornes' royal connection, the Canadian press almost inevitably treated the couple's private life more freely than had been the case with prior governors general and their families. Lorne was reported not to get on particularly well with Macdonald, while it was likewise held that Louise didn't get along much better with Lady Macdonald. As for the first charge, the prime minister considered himself—rightly—the power in the country, and resented even a minor attempt by a British newcomer, governor general or no, to dictate Canadian affairs. Soon after Lorne's arrival, a delicate matter having to do with a provincial lieutenant governor's appointment—which Lorne proceeded to resolve without Macdonald being fully involved—created a brief tension between the two men. Lorne decided, wisely, that thereafter he would act only on proper ministerial advice.

Many of the "problems" Louise was said to have had with the prime minister's wife were invented by a press eager to sell newspapers. It was said the older woman resented that Louise outranked her, not just constitutionally through Lorne's post but by virtue of princesshood. Especially within the socially unsophisticated atmosphere of a rambunctious Canada, some friction between the two might perhaps have been inevitable, given the unique circumstances of a strong-willed wife of the country's leading politician coming up against the daughter of the superseding empire's sovereign. A reported instance of Lady Macdonald's pique involved an evening at the opera when Louise stood to acknowledge the audience's tribute, only to look around to see Lady Macdonald on her feet as well in response to the applause. In truth, the princess had insisted that the prime minister's wife stand with her so they could both receive the audience's applause. Lady Macdonald was horrified at the reports of trouble between herself and Louise, and Louise for her part was anxious to consign such rumors to the oblivion she thought they deserved.

An advantage the Lornes would both have over their predecessors was their joint fluency in French, which enabled husband and wife to make inroads into the French-Canadian community in a way no governor general or his wife had ever done before. Louise would be very much the benefactor of these "other" Canadians, Francophones being as a group far more cultured in the arts she herself loved than were their English-speaking counterparts.

Though Canadian life brought its own undeniable delights, after nearly a year in Ottawa the homesick Louise told Lorne that she wanted to go back to England to visit her family, and in October 1879 the princess reboarded the *Sarmatian* at Quebec City. Her first stay was at Osborne with her mother; then she moved on to see Bertie and Alix at Sandringham, before rejoining the queen at Windsor. A journey to Scotland took her to Lorne's family at Inveraray, and she rounded out this series of visits with a brief call on Lenchen and Christian at Cumberland Lodge.

Many Canadians naturally wondered why she had to go home after "only" a year in their country. To some degree, the princess's return had been made in response to Fenian threats to her and Lorne's lives in Ottawa, the same sort of threat all members of Victoria's family faced constantly as Irish republicans fought to rid their island of Britain's control. But rumors soon spread across the dominion to the effect that her marriage was in trouble or that the princess had been mortally insulted by Macdonald, who had supposedly "taken a liberty" with her a year earlier after getting drunk at a state ball. More scurrilous gossip had her mentally ill; the worst stories of all portrayed Louise as pregnant with a baby fathered by someone other than Lorne, an American newspaper the creator of this last and most ridiculous tale. London's *Reynolds Newspaper* picked the story up, solemnly informing its readers that Louise would be bringing a "little stranger" back to Canada. None of this represented anything more than unjust gossipmongering—with the possible exception of the stories of trouble between husband and wife.

Four months after having departed, Louise returned to Ottawa. According to the duke of Cambridge—the queen's cousin and a relatively reliable reporter of family affairs—the princess went back with a "very heavy heart." Heavy heart or not, Louise tried to get back into the capital's social flurry of balls and skating parties and late suppers at Rideau Hall. Though she still stunned Canadians with the bejeweled splendor of her appearance—a typical favorite evening toilette would find her in black velvet, with a royal ransom in diamonds and emeralds cascading down her generous decollatage—Louise now seemed to bear an otherworldly reserve that many took for hauteur. One observer that season wrote that "although most likeable, [she is] without our Crown Princess's [presumably meaning the princess of Wales] charm of manner." The likelihood was that at this time Louise realized her marriage was beginning to come undone.

Whatever the pleasures Lorne and Louise had found in each other, physical passion seems not to have been one of them. She missed out on the kind of sexual joy and passionate love that Vicky had enjoyed in her marriage, the tender love of Lenchen and Christian, even the sweetness that Alice and Louis bore for each other in an otherwise often-unfulfilled relationship. An explanation offered by many historians and biographers is that Lorne was homosexual.

During Lorne's lifetime, it would have been difficult for a homosexual to live what in modern terms would be called an open "gay" life. For someone of Lorne's class, visibility, and family connections, it would have been virtually impossible. Homosexual contacts were difficult enough to keep secret, assuming one wished to keep them secret. Lorne's young uncle (his mother's brother) and lifelong friend, Lord Ronald Gower, did live a comparatively open, if still illegal, homosexual life. But Gower was a highly unusual exception. Being homosexual wasn't something that was publicly discussed, if for no other reason than that same-sex sexual contacts were against the law and often heavily punished, as was famously the case for Oscar Wilde.

Neither Lorne's close friendship with his uncle, nor a marriage in which the physical relationship with his wife had according to some sources ended soon after the honeymoon, necessarily indicate that Lorne was homosexual. But they suggest it; and homosexuality would also account for how his later years came to be lived. Nonetheless, Louise's preeminent biographer, Jehanne Wake, dismisses the possibility, partly on the basis of old Scottish rumors that Lorne had, like his father, sired a number of young Scots out of wedlock. Since Lorne himself never commented on his sexual orientation, whether he was homosexual or not simply isn't known to history. What is fairly certain to Louise's biographers, though, is that by 1880, when the princess sailed back to Canada, her marriage had become one of companionship only.

Eleven days after her return, Louise suffered an accident that was vastly to change her own and Lorne's lives, especially as it bore on their Canadian experience. It was St. Valentine's Day, a time of year that was for Ottawa typically cold and snowy. The couple left Rideau Hall by sleigh, on their way to the Houses of Parliament where they would hold a "Drawing Room," the first social event of the just-opened 1880 season. They had been joined in the sleigh by Lorne's aide-de-camp, Colonel John McNeill, and Louise's lady-in-waiting, Mrs. Eva Langham. Two other sleighs filled with the governor general's party preceded them down the icy driveway. Upon leaving the residence's grounds to turn onto the main road leading into the city center, the Lornes' horses began to jerk sharply on their leads, and quickly went out of the coachman's control. Rounding the turn into the road, the unruly animals cornered too sharply, and the sleigh veered abruptly, overturning onto a bank of snow. The driver and footman were thrown out, but the horses sprang forward, startled, pulling the now-overturned sled behind.

Louise had been pitched headfirst against one of the iron rods supporting the roof, Lorne thrown over his wife. Mrs. Langham's head skidded just above the ground, saved from the road and broken glass only because Louise was managing to hold it up with her free hand, and Colonel McNeill in turn held up the princess's head. The entire scene transpired in an eerie near silence, only the braying horses breaking the bitterly cold night's calm. When the rushing carriage began to overtake the two vehicles ahead of it, whose occupants had until now been unaware of the accident, one of Lorne's aides jumped out and managed to subdue the horses. The overturned sleigh had been pulled about a thousand feet. As quickly as possible, the four injured people were taken back to Rideau Hall.

In the aftermath, Lorne's staff deliberately downplayed the seriousness of the misadventure, especially the extent of the princess's injuries. The governor general's aides believed that that would be less worrying to the queen (who would soon enough find out that the accident had been a very close call for Louise, and who would upbraid Lorne for not having reported its true gravity in the first place). But to achieve that end, Canada itself was badly misled. In fact, Louise had been seriously injured, both physically and emotionally. Her head was badly jolted, resulting in frequent and excruciating headaches long afterward. For a woman who had since infancy been cocooned from real life and its dangers, the shock badly depressed her, and only an ingrained determination kept her from withdrawing from public life altogether—a social maneuver that might in similar circumstances have been taken by many Victorian women of her class. As it was, Lorne put a virtual end to the winter social season in view of his wife's impairments, a turn of events whose effect was to direct public opinion sharply against the princess.

Whether or not the accident was to blame, immediately afterwards Louise's marriage dipped into a sharp spiral from which it never truly recovered. During that spring of 1880, Leopold arrived in Ottawa for a visit with his favorite sister. Since both knew the hemophiliac prince's trip had been allowed only over the strenuous objection of their mother (for whom his absence meant not only unforeseeable health dangers but also the temporary loss of a man who had become one of her most intimate political aides), Louise determined to show her beloved brother the best time she could. Without Lorne, the siblings began a trip to the United States, a substantial effort for Louise in the face of her own still-shaky health. Visiting Niagara Falls and Chicago, the pair saw themselves referred to in American newspaper headlines as "Vic's Chicks": the humor of this completely failed the queen when she was sent a copy of the article, though Victoria did express amazement at the American infatuation with her children. Lorne showed less equanimity than his mother-in-law, and was irritated by the breeziness of the American reporting on his wife and Leopold: in a letter to his father, he protested that "the vulgarity of the Yankee press about them surpasses belief."

After ten days of travel and a further month of fishing at the governor general's summer lodge on the Cascapedia River in Canada, Louise arrived at a fateful decision: she didn't want to go back to Lorne and Ottawa, and concluded she would return to England with her brother. A convenient excuse presented itself. Leopold had overdone the fishing, which injured his legs. His condition provided a plausible reason for Louise to go home: to nurse her brother on board ship. Though Lorne made no objections, he would soon find that much of Canada had come to wonder whether Louise's departure was the result of a failing marriage or his wife's dislike of Canada—or perhaps both.

While Louise was attempting to come to terms with a marriage no longer fulfilling to her, her sister Vicky in Berlin was contending with marital difficulties too—in her case over what was to become the most consequential union of any of her children. Willy was about to get married to the only woman, Vicky hoped, who might moderate some of the twenty-one-year-old prince's increasingly bizarre behavior. Showing ever more copious signs of psychological instability—intense braggadocio, a restless and inappropriately oafish manner among nearly everyone with whom he came in contact, an inability to concentrate on anything for any length of time except the building of his theatrical and enormously expensive uniform collection—Willy had become a serious and ineradicable worry to his parents.

After Waldy's death, Vicky's mental condition had come dangerously close to a breakdown, her state at the beginning of the 1880s much as her mother's had been in the aftermath of Albert's passing. One significant difference in their circumstances was that the German crown princess did not have an entire family, court, and nation willing to tolerate and indulge her behavior. Showing newfound wisdom on the subject, Queen Victoria warned her daughter that she must quickly come to terms with both her loss and the increasingly difficult circumstances of her life—or else risk losing whatever influence was to come her way when Fritz inherited the throne. Fortunately, Vicky possessed a core of steel, even if it was often difficult to reach, and she eventually found herself able again to cope with her trials. *Un*fortunately, the need to enshrine her dead son's memory led her even more pointedly to belittle her two surviving sons, comparing them unfavorably to what Waldy would have become had he lived. Badly afflicted by the blows hammering her, Vicky was sadly uncharitable when her daughter Charlotte's first baby made her at thirty-eight a grandmother, feeling less happiness than anger because this disappointing daughter had brought a baby into the world so soon after her beloved Waldy was taken out of it.

Whatever the reasons that caused Willy to decide to marry Princess Augusta Victoria of Schleswig-Holstein-Sonderburg-Augustenburg, physical beauty couldn't have been very prominent. But Dona, as the utterly unexceptional princess was called by her family, possessed an appearance of robust fecundity that appealed to a dynastically minded future emperor. Not only was the young woman sturdy, she was wonderfully stupid, a quality of inestimable merit to Willy, given his dislike of being upstaged. Dona for her part was clearly thrilled to have been chosen by Willy and thereby given the destiny to propagate the Continent's most formidable dynasty.

Vicky and Fritz seemed little more than lukewarm about their son's choice of a wife. Aside from Dona's ordinariness, there remained the troubling fact that the girl's grandmother had been a mere countess, something that Fritz especially had difficulty coming to terms with. Yet when it seemed evident that Willy was really in love with his princess, his parents laid aside any misgivings; and Vicky, with her usual full-steam-ahead style, undertook to lobby the emperor on her view that Dona represented excellent value as future empress material. Obtaining the sovereign's permission was not, however, a shoo-in, as she found out when William referred the matter to Bismarck to investigate. The chancellor, always happy to thwart Vicky in any way he could, delighted in keeping the crown prince and princess dangling over the matter of Dona's provenance. Bismarck reminded the emperor that Dona's father, the duke of Augustenburg, might still be up to some of the same political mischief that had made him a Prussian enemy in the Prussian-Danish War of 1864; at the time, the king's chief minister had famously called the duke the "idiot of Holstein." But this "idiot" had been a good friend to Fritz and Vicky, that friendship weighing heavily on their siding with Dona as a daughter-in-law. When the duke suddenly died in the middle of the chancellor's investigation, much of Bismarck's dudgeon went with him, and Emperor William finally gave his formal sanction for his grandson to go ahead with the marriage. Willy dutifully wrote his father to thank him for his efforts.

Vicky told her mother that she was relieved the parrying with Bismarck was over, but nonetheless couldn't hide a certain disappointment that the match was not going to be "brilliant" in the view of the German people, who had been hoping for someone clearly more alluring than Dona as their future empress—though how Vicky deduced what the German people were hoping for is difficult to know. Still, even Willy's sister Charlotte derided her sister-in-law-to-be, telling her father that the people—Charlotte probably meant her own elevated court circles—were "turning up their noses" at Willy's choice. Nonetheless, now that the matter was decided, the old emperor received Dona with a kindness and graciousness that he generally showed to everyone except his own son and daughter-in-law. And Vicky was secretly pleased that Willy had chosen someone who went against the grain of the Prussian society she had come to hate, writing that it did Willy "great credit" to overcome the opposition in taking Dona as his wife.

Sadly, Vicky's pleasure with Willy's choice would not last long. Dona soon came to understand and resent that she could never equal her future mother-in-law's extraordinary intelligence. Likewise, Vicky would shortly tire of the younger woman's striking dullness. But the crown princess would try hard to gain Dona's affections, even while an impenetrable barrier was steadily being erected—misunderstanding by misunderstanding and insult by insult—between the two. Dona would prove to be one of the most heartbreaking disappointments of all the many Vicky would endure in Germany. Yet, ironically, she was just about the perfect wife for Willy, who would have had trouble finding another eligible princess anywhere near so willing and suited to pampering his moods and piques and pomposities. Furthermore, Dona would never see herself as her husband's equal; it had, after all, been Vicky's attempt to stand as an equal with Fritz a generation earlier that had been perhaps her greatest offense to the sensibilities of the Prussian court, and Dona either comprehended this by herself or was quickly apprised of the gravity of the point.

On the day before the winter wedding, Dona had been transported to the royal palace in Berlin in a carriage drawn by eight horses, and would long remember how the bitter cold felt as she swayed back and forth in the huge contraption dressed in a bareshouldered court gown. As her fiancé rode behind, dressed as Captain of the Bodyguard, a flight of white doves flew by, released from a cage atop the Brandenburg Gate.

The next day—Sunday, February 2, 1881—the couple was married, the twenty-two-year-old bridegroom's grandfather having just promoted him to the command of the First Regiment of the Foot Guards, Willy's first real authority. The twenty-three-year-old bride looked uncharacteristically luminous as she gazed in adoration at her new husband. Much of royal Europe had gathered for the ceremony in the Royal Palace; the prince of Wales was his sister's special guest, though Bertie's attendance was not warmly welcomed by Willy, who had already developed a jealousy-driven loathing for his supremely sophisticated uncle. Vicky wrote to her mother that Dona "looked charming and everyone was taken with her sweetness and grace." The queen was informed that the bride wore "light blue and gold brocade, with pink and white China asters, and her pearls and your beautiful pendant around her neck." Vicky's only complaint was of the tiara she herself wore for the six and a half hours of the enormously complex and tedious ceremony, remarking that it "pressed my head a great deal."

Vicky and Fritz were to be crushingly disappointed in their hope that marriage would domesticate Willy. They found themselves almost completely marginalized: with a simperingly doting wife, Willy became the entire creature of his grandfather and the first minister. The prince's now-independent social life moved from any parental supervision to the center of the court regiments' undivided and worshipful attention. Since the old emperor showed no signs of expiring any time soon (Vicky facetiously wrote her mother that Emperor William's age must have been "put down wrong" in the *Almanach de Gotha*), it began to seem frighteningly possible that Fritz's reign would represent little more than a mere bridge between two thoroughly Prussian Williams. Vicky sensed that her son's eventual reign would undo anything her husband might accomplish, and would in fact be the antithesis of all that Prince Albert had hoped for in her own marriage to Fritz.

Back home in England, Louise first passed a few days with her mother in Osborne, but then decided to go immediately to the Continent to recuperate at greater privacy and leisure from whatever had been so troublesome in Canada. Her discontent with a faltering marriage had translated into an overwhelming desire to get away not only from Lorne but from her mother's orbit as well. Traveling incognito as Lady Sundridge, the camouflage she had used on her honeymoon, Louise found herself on this journey with as much freedom as she had ever known. She spent the greater part of her days sketching and painting, and the evenings relaxing with the small party of friends who had accompanied her.

When in October she returned from the Continent to England, both her mother's court and the governor general's office in Ottawa expected an imminent announcement as to precisely when she planned to return to her wifely duties as Canada's first lady. Yet weeks passed without any word from the princess about rejoining her husband, and gossip ran rife on both sides of the Atlantic. Louise's protestations that she was still recuperating from her sleigh injuries were devalued by the original reports Lorne's aides had released as to that incident's lack of seriousness, and were then further weakened by the good time Louise was clearly seen to have had in Europe. Indeed, she plunged now into London's avant-garde art scene with an enthusiasm she hadn't felt since her days in art school. Word inevitably began to spread that she might never return to Canada and her waiting husband.

The queen acted very much as a party to her daughter's prolonged absence. With Louise conspicuously in Europe instead of Canada, the sovereign could not have been unaware that the chances were that all was not well in the Lornes' marriage. Victoria wrote her son-in-law at Christmas that Louise still wasn't looking well: "She suffers so much from her head, and any fatigue or excitement brings it on. . . . We must hope that time and continued quiet will restore her shattered nerves." But other reports on Louise conflicted with this. Some, like that from Lucy Cavendish, did suggest that she was doing poorly, while others saw things in another light. Disraeli commented on Louise's evident high spirits, noting too that she had "never looked prettier." At all events, her flurry of social engagements acted as a tonic, and Victoria was unquestionably aware that Louise was anything but quiet in her present life away from Lorne.

When by spring 1881 Canadians still had no indication that their governor general's wife planned to return to their country, Louise's good name began to attract serious imputations. The worst of the gossip was that the princess hated Canada and its people—a tale that obviously fed off the early malicious and untrue reports on Louise's relations with the Macdonalds—or that her marriage was finished, both cases long whispered but now openly put out as fact. Strangely, Lorne seemed to make no great effort to get his wife to return to Canada, accepting the queen's observations about Louise's weak state of health. Lorne was, to be sure, still concerned about the Fenian threat, particularly as the queen's daughter was a far more attractive target than himself. But royalty was expected to accept such risks with sanguine doughtiness, and he understood that her absence was injuring the dignity of his office in the estimation of the Canadian people. Louise, too, fully realized that her prolonged absence was raising embarrassing questions. She wrote Lorne that she wanted to return in the summer to help him with a tour of Manitoba he was planning; but still, oddly, it was the husband who insisted she remain in England for the sake of her "health."

Lorne undertook the trip without Louise, extending his travels to cover the Northwest Territories, the first time any Canadian governor general had visited that largely unexplored region. While traveling across the dominion, Lorne officially named the brand-new capital of Manitoba for his mother-in-law, and the tiny spot on the vast prairie would henceforth be called "Regina" (the name "Victoria" had already been taken by a new and even more remote settlement on the Pacific Coast). The honor couldn't have meant much to the queen, whose name already conspicuously dotted the globe; the next geographical location Lorne got to name would be a signal distinction not for his mother-in-law but for his wife. The province beyond Saskatchewan might be known to us today as "Louiseland" were it not that the hybrid sounded so strange that Lorne instead chose "Alberta," his wife's second name.

More than mere ceremonial flag-waving, his trip embraced two important national issues: the rationalization of a speedy completion to the transcontinental railroad, and the resolution of a boundary dispute between Manitoba and Ontario. Also of critical concern were issues dealing with Canada's Indians. Lorne was aware that the aspirations of white settlers would soon run unavoidably into the legitimate claims of native Canadians, possibly resulting in tragedy for both groups. He drafted suggestions for Macdonald's government on ways to avoid such an outcome, principally through Indian education and restricted allocation of acreage to newcomers who were, fairly or not to the indigenous people, turning disparate lands into a united nation.

On Lorne's return to Ottawa at the end of his strenuous journey, the first personal news to greet him was from the queen, writing to say she didn't want her daughter to leave for Canada with winter coming on. Knowing that he had to make some public relations gesture to show that he and the princess planned to continue as husband and wife, Lorne decided his best move would be to go to England.

The relationship kept Canadians in thrall that autumn. Louise publicly met her husband's ship at Liverpool, helping to stymie rumors of personal animosity between the couple, their dockside embrace reported in intimate detail in the Canadian press. The reunion did seem happy enough, with the Lornes embarking on a series of family visits—to both his family and hers. They even stopped by the Gladstones' at Hawarden Castle in North Wales, an event that couldn't have been received with much favor by a queen who intensely disliked her former prime minister. However, the fact was that Louise contrived to pass most of Lorne's two-month stay in the company of others, and very little of it alone with her husband.

Whether or not the princess was feigning poor health for her husband's benefit, upon seeing his wife Lorne was convinced that she was still too poorly to return with him to Canada. According to her doctors, her symptoms seemed to relate to the meningitis she had suffered many years earlier. When, in January 1882, Lorne reboarded his ship to return to Ottawa, his sister and brother-in-law to accompany him (the former would deputize for Louise during the oncoming winter social season), he announced it would be better for the princess to stay behind in England, evidently judging that whatever criticism might arise in Canada was preferable to her returning an invalid. Though the queen had earlier written Lorne that Louise was "so afraid that people in Canada will think she is not doing her duty," she believed her daughter wholly justified in worrying about her health: ". . . it was *in doing her duty* that she met with her dreadful accident and . . . she would be of no use to you if she returned quite weak and broke down again." How much Victoria understood of the intimate state of the Lornes' relationship is unknown, but she may have been to some degree dissembling in order to keep Louise from returning to an increasingly intolerable marital situation.

By now, Louise must have been close to admitting that to stay away indefinitely from Canada was tantamount to marital separation, regardless of any other rationale that might account for her absence. But still she wavered, determined to remain in Europe long enough to see her brother Leopold marry Princess Helena of

Waldeck-Pyrmont (planned for the end of April), a wedding that many in Victoria's family thought could never occur because of the groom-to-be's dangerously fragile health. That spring Louise brought her new mother-in-law to meet the queen, the widowed duke of Argyll having recently married Mrs. Amelia Anson in a union that would on Lorne's next return to England lead to deep strains within the Campbell family.

In May 1882, with Lorne's sister presiding over Rideau Hall as its provisional hostess, Oscar Wilde visited Ottawa during his year-long lecture tour of North America. Fully expecting to be honored by an invitation to the governor general's residence—Wilde was a close friend of Lorne's uncle, Lord Ronald Gower—the world-famous English writer and playwright nonetheless freely and not very respectfully expressed to Canadian reporters his disappointment about what he viewed as their nation's lack of artistic sophistication. Further, he commented ungraciously on their first lady, saying that Princess Louise "was such an admirer of art . . . [but] had not accomplished more." For reasons that are not entirely clear, Wilde was not invited to Rideau Hall; nor did Lorne attend the writer's lecture or in any way acknowledge Wilde's presence in Ottawa. Whether the governor general acted as he did from lack of interest in a writer not especially admired by members of his own class, or from offense at the visitor's criticism of Louise, or from reluctance to meet because Wilde's generally acknowledged homosexuality could fuel local tittle-tattle about his own sexual makeup, Lorne's actions toward his famous countryman were widely noted and commented upon.

Knowing she couldn't dawdle any longer if she wanted her own reputation to remain reparable, Louise finally returned to Rideau Hall that same spring. Again she traveled on the *Sarmatian*, a ship she had grown to know well and whose steerage section she visited on the first day at sea to assess the treatment its humble passengers were receiving. Her arrival ended an avoidance of Canada for nearly two years. Recent Fenian attacks had the queen especially nervous about Louise's safety, and she gave orders to her ministers that everything possible should be done to ensure her daughter's security. In fact, American-based Fenians operating out of New York City were rumored to be planning to kidnap Louise. Macdonald warned the governor general to take the danger seriously: in a letter to Lorne, the prime minister reported that "these demons will stop at no atrocity, and I don't think any risk should be run." Louise asked that Victoria not be told about the warning so as to spare her mother unnecessary worry. On her landing at Quebec City, Louise and Lorne decided to spend the summer at the Citadel, the governor general's official summer residence and as secure a haven from Fenian threats as they could have found anywhere in Canada.

In spite of the danger, the couple resumed a relatively normal life, so normal that they set off together at the end of the summer on an excursion across the United States—an undertaking staggeringly susceptible to terrorist depredations. The official object of the trip was to visit the Canadian Far West, which in 1882 could only be reached from eastern Canada by rail by crossing the United States. From Ottawa they went first to Niagara Falls, the premiere tourist attraction in the entire western hemisphere. A two-week train journey then carried the couple through what was extremely hazardous Indian territory in America's Wild West, a long way from any protective embrace the British government might have been able to provide. They arrived in San Francisco in mid-September, where they roamed about almost as free as any other tourists of the era, experiencing a Chinatown dinner infused with the fragrance of smoke drifting from opium pipes, a ferry trip around the bay, and a luxurious sojourn in the astonishing splendors of the Palace Hotel. But unlike other tourists, the couple attracted attention everywhere they went, Lorne taking a backseat to a wife who was not only the daughter of the queen of England but the first honest-to-God princess ever to visit California. Not surprisingly, Louise was lionized by every society matron in the rough San Francisco of the 1880s.

Politics reentered their lives when, just before boarding a British warship to be taken to nearly primordial British Columbia, the captain reported a threat that the ship would be blown up as soon as Louise and Lorne set foot on deck. No bomb was found, but the threat was a nasty reminder that every step of their trip was attended by danger from the Fenians.

The couple's presence in British Columbia turned out to be a triumph. For three months the Lornes lent their prestige to this still-ignored corner of the Canadian dominion, giving the capital city of Victoria its first ever taste of royalty. Louise did all she could to impart her own cachet to the province, whether it was by covering herself with diamonds at formal evening Drawing Rooms or democratically mixing with all classes of British Columbians in as informal a manner as she could manage from her limited experience at such public encounters. One official said he thought Louise ought to become queen of Vancouver Island, a view forwarded apparently only half in jest. While Louise lent a fairytale sparkle to the visit, Lorne worked hard to convince the local leaders that a transcontinental Canadian railroad would be built soon. It was this prospect that had led British Columbia to join the dominion, and its absence to date was causing mutinous rumblings. For three weeks, he traveled about the province alone reassuring the locals while Louise remained in Victoria.

In December, the Lornes retraced their journey east. They first stayed several weeks at Monterey's opulent Del Monte Hotel, then headed for Los Angeles and Santa Barbara, the pace leisurely because Lorne wasn't required to be back in Ottawa until Parliament reopened in February 1883. The long train trip eastward across the continent was this time accompanied by a detachment of U.S. troopers lent by President Chester Arthur against the composite danger of Indians, outlaws, and Fenians. But instead of returning to the cold of frozen Ottawa with her husband, Louise then went to Bermuda, where she remained for three months, apparently perfectly happy with her own company. Officially Ottawa was told that "on the advice of a London physician and by the express command of Her Majesty," the first lady's health was simply too delicate to subject herself to the rigors of a Canadian winter. When she at long last came back to Ottawa in April, almost three years had passed since she had been in the city whose initial pleasures had become so disagreeable for her.

Louise would not have much time remaining to serve as unofficial queen of Canada. Lorne decided to resign his post a year earlier than the normal five-year span of a governor general's term. It isn't known if his decision was taken because he feared that if he stayed any longer in Canada, he would never want to return to Britain—as he disingenuously protested—or because he thought his marriage might be saved if he and Louise returned home at this time. Lorne had, in fact, come to love Canada deeply, leaving as his legacy the Royal Canadian Academy and the Royal Society, foundations on which art and scholarship in the dominion would grow to formidable proportions in the years ahead. His own writings about Canada would reflect a genuine admiration for the huge land that he, more than any of his predecessors, had come to know at firsthand. Yet he probably knew Louise couldn't stand another year in the cold without her family and friends to cushion the disaffection that had come between them.

As for Louise herself, she surely knew that her rejection of her husband and her duties as the dominion's first lady were likely responsible for Lorne's determination to go home. In October 1883, for the last time—neither would ever return to Canada—the couple boarded a steamer, the *Sardinian,* for the journey back to England. In spite of her tendency to flee, Louise expressed tearful regret at leaving a country that she, like her husband, had come to admire deeply and at the loss of a nearly unfettered freedom she had never known before and would never know again.

On March 24, 1884, only months after the Lornes returned to England, the royal family suffered a devastating shock. Prince Leopold died in Cannes, after having sustained a fall on his hotel staircase. Cerebral bleeding had set in and doctors could not stop the subsequent fatal hemorrhage. The sovereign's youngest son had been close to his sisters Louise and Beatrice, and his death after a lifetime of agony from hemophilia grieved these two sisters with a special anguish.

Leopold's relationship with his mother had differed from that of any of his brothers, the prince having become a skillful (though not official) private secretary to the queen in 1877. He had been given a key to the box holding the Foreign Office papers, something Victoria never once considered for her heir, the prince of Wales. Leopold had evolved into a trusted intermediary between the monarch and her ministers, gaining the confidence of many of the leading politicians of the era. Created duke of Albany in 1881, a year later he had married Princess Helena of Waldeck, a sister of the Dutch queen. Their first child, Princess Alice (later countess of Athlone and sister-in-law to Queen Mary), became the last survivor of Queen Victoria's forty grandchildren and died as recently as 1981. Helena was pregnant with Leopold's second child, Prince Charles, at the time of her husband's death.

In a letter to Vicky, Queen Victoria expressed deep sorrow but an acquiescence in the inevitability of Leopold's early death: "For him we must not repine; his young life was a succession of trials and sufferings though he was happy in his marriage. And there was such a restless longing for what he could not have. . . ." Would that the monarch had brought a tenth part of such wise acceptance to the loss of her husband twenty-three years earlier.

When Alice died, Britain's queen had all but adopted her beloved Hessian grandchildren, concerned that their inadequate father wouldn't be able to provide a sound home for his offspring. Victoria was keen that the four girls especially should be protected—at least until they all found husbands and were settled into lives of their own.

Her namesake, Princess Victoria, twenty-one years old in 1884, was not only the eldest but also the stateliest of Alice and Louis's children. This plain but sturdy princess inherited many of her mother's traits, especially the grand duchess's sense that the privileged members of the class into which she was born owed special care over those less fortunate than themselves. Not a few of Princess Victoria's cousins found such solicitude either tiresome or bizarre, or both.

Her fiancé, Prince Louis, the eldest and handsomest of the Battenberg brothers and young Victoria's first cousin, was an officer in the Royal Navy, a calling in which he immersed himself with both passion and enormous pride. Queen Victoria had been pleased when her Hessian grandchildren's cousin had joined her navy, and even more pleased that her namesake granddaughter's suitor now considered himself far more a British naval officer than a German prince. Despite all of Louis's merits, a large part of the princess's extended family disapproved of the engagement. The problem was his rank—or, more to the point, the lack of it.

Like Princess Victoria and her three comely younger sisters, so too Louis of Battenberg possessed three handsome younger brothers. This quartet of princes were the sons of Prince Alexander of Hesse, Alice's uncle-in-law who had a generation earlier made the morganatic marriage to his *unebenbürtige* countess, Julie Hauke. In consequence, the sons of the union possessed no rights of succession to the Hessian-Darmstadt throne and were disbarred from inheriting their father's titles, though their mother had been created princess of Battenberg in Hesse-Darmstadt, and the sons had all assumed this maternal title.

Where some of her British relatives believed that Princess Victoria should have felt obligated to remain in Darmstadt to care for her motherless siblings and preoccupied father, the Prussians simply held young Louis of insufficient status to marry a German princess—even though the girls were themselves merely "serene" rather than "royal" highnesses.[5] Louis's membership in the Royal Navy politically aggravated the Hohenzollerns, and the unalterable reality of his mother's low origins was anathema to Prussian sensibilities. But in spite of such opposition, Victoria and Louis were determined to marry. The bride's British grandmother's blessing to the match immensely supported their resolve.

The wedding, set for April 1884, would be one of the outstanding royal events of the year. Though her son Leopold's death in March might have been expected to keep her at home, Queen Victoria decided it wouldn't stop her from being at her revered granddaughter's side. The monarch traveled to Darmstadt accompanied by Beatrice, who with Leopold's passing had now settled into the role of indispensable aide to her mother in spite of what remained near-crippling shyness. Though the occasion was expected by its participants to represent nothing more significant than a family celebration, in the middle of the festivities the father of the bride-to-be shook the family with a scandal that required the full measure of Queen Victoria's awe-inspiring talents to overcome.

Though Alice and Louis's marriage had not been without its deep difficulties, the grand duke had loved his wife profoundly and now missed her painfully. But in the six years since her death he had come to feel desperately in need of a replacement, and to those ends had recently been mesmerized by a thirty-year-old Polish woman named Alexandrine von Kolemine. The lady was the daughter of the count of Hutten-Czapsky, and was thus of aristocratic though not royal birth. Now divorced from a Russian diplomat, Madame Kolemine was described by the Paris correspondent of London's *Daily News* as "one of the most beautiful and highly-accomplished women of her time." Others, less generous, called her "depraved" and "scheming." Whatever the case, when on arrival in Darmstadt Queen Victoria was informed of Madame Kolemine's close liaison with her son-in-law, she found the whole affair unthinkable, a *mésalliance* that could bring Louis and his family nothing but the gravest embarrassment. And when gossip reached her that a second wedding—one legally joining Louis and Madame Kolemine—was to take place while she was in the city, she was horrified. Bertie, also in Darmstadt, had heard these same rumors and knew well what kind of explosion to expect from his mother if they proved to be accurate.

Louis himself appeared in the best of spirits when he greeted the queen at the station. Though his daughter's wedding was the pre-eminent event in what turned out to be the largest family gathering in Darmstadt in years, Louis had planned a string of lesser celebrations to make the reunion as happy and memorable as possible. But the grand duke knew when he so fondly greeted his mother-in-law that one unannounced ceremony was going to rock the family to its core.

In fact, the entire gathering became a jumble of interfamilial machinations. In the first place, Vicky was beset by the fact that the bridegroom's most immediate younger brother, Prince Alexander of Battenberg—"Sandro" in the nickname-crazy family—had his eye on her own daughter, who was also named Victoria. Her in-laws and eldest son virulently opposed this union, regardless of the fact that the young woman professed desperate love for Sandro. The German emperor and empress were also upset that the bride's sister, Ella, had fallen in love with the Russian grand duke Serge. This was the same Ella who had thrown over Willy as though his future as a German emperor wouldn't be of substantial benefit to Hesse. In fact, Ella's engagement to Serge would be announced to the gathered royalties by her father just before his eldest daughter's nuptials.

Despite all these concerns, the wedding in Darmstadt was relatively happy and gay, Grand Duke Louis beaming throughout with pride at the royal collection gracing his little capital. But all this happiness and gaiety suddenly became very much subdued when, on the evening of the very day that the young couple said their vows in the palace's Marble Chamber, the bride's father retired to a less grand room in the palace and there married his divorcée in a clandestine little ceremony that was a threadbare simulation of the main event a few hours earlier. Though there was no question of Madame Kolemine becoming the new grand duchess of Hesse-Darmstadt, Louis must have known that his actions were, by the overarching rules of nineteenth-century European royal conduct, scandalous. He also must have been truly besotted to think that making Kolemine even his morganatic wife was going to be easy.

Though a pathetic effort was exerted to keep what he had done a secret—why Louis would have even thought about an attempt at confidentiality beggars understanding—just three days passed before the entire assemblage of royals and semiroyals were talking of nothing else. Vicky found out and told Bertie, who went bravely to his mother to be the bearer of the astonishing tidings. While word rippled outward into a messy skein of near hysterics (on hearing of it Empress Augusta ordered Fritz and Vicky to return to Berlin immediately, apparently fearful their continued presence in Darmstadt might taint the Hohenzollern dynasty), Queen Victoria as the family matriarch told Bertie to tell Madame Kolemine that there could be no possibility that the marriage she had just entered into with the grand duke would stand. It was to be annulled, on Victoria's authority. Though the English monarch was not the arbiter of Hessian law, the new bride caved in to the prince of Wales's practiced persuasiveness. Louis was not, by the way, asked for *his* acquiescence, that being expected. Victoria told her ambassador in Berlin, Lord Ampthill, to do whatever was legally necessary to complete the voiding of the union.

Within weeks she received assurances from her former German secretary, Hermann Sahl, that in German law the marriage simply never took place. Victoria thereafter described her son-in-law as having been "entrapped" by a "depraved" and "scheming" woman. Bertie put his own postmortem on the affair by smugly but correctly noting that "we are a very strong family when we all agree." Louis's happiness or lack of happiness had no bearing on the matter: by his interrelationship with European royalty—especially that of Britain—certain behavior was expected, certain behavior proscribed. He had crossed the line at his own peril, and lost. That he waited until his mother-in-law came to Darmstadt to replace her own daughter with an inappropriate woman is, in the end, inexplicable. As for Madame Kolemine, she got a lump-sum payment of a half-million marks from the grand duke and the title of Baroness Romrod, and later married a Russian diplomat.

If Louis's stunt hadn't been enough to turn what was to have been a happy family gathering into a near nightmare, the British monarch was soon going to find another shocking revelation awaiting her. Beatrice, who had come to Darmstadt mostly to attend to her mother's needs, was over the course of the festivities attending to her own needs by falling in love herself.

The queen's youngest child had just turned twenty-seven, and it appeared she would become an old maid—literally, so her mother hoped. Victoria was frankly buoyed by the knowledge that her youngest daughter's experience of men was as close as possible to nil. Since Beatrice already had become, in the kindest word, matronly, the queen simply assumed her daughter was past any thought of a married life. With an enormous Hanoverian bust kept that way by a healthy appetite, bereft of any one attractive feature or even a sparkle to give substance to her light blue eyes, Beatrice looked far more like a girls' school headmistress than she did a maiden princess. Her family was certain that, like a nun, she was happy with her lot and had no desire to marry, and, furthermore, thought serving her illustrious mother the highest calling imaginable. Some people even assumed that the imperious cast on her often-sour face and lifting of her rapidly doubling chin when a man so much as looked at her meant that she must be frigid.

What Beatrice found in Darmstadt would totally change these dour and sad realities. What she found was, in fact, the bridegroom's younger brother. The first moment she saw him, she was smitten. Prince Henry of Battenberg—"Liko"—was, apart from his sex, as physically different from Beatrice as possible. Athletic and muscular, darkly handsome, with more than a suggestion of Balkan smokiness in his physiognomy, small where Beatrice seemed big, he manifested himself like a Renaissance sculpture among the overfed and underendowed royals who had gathered for Victoria of Hesse's wedding. Unlike Beatrice, who was so shy that she could barely talk, Liko, like all the Battenberg brothers, was brashly charming and possessed the manners of a king. Though not as bright as his older brothers Louis and Sandro, Liko was still a dazzler who had already broken many hearts.

A year and a half younger than Beatrice, this member of what was widely known as Europe's handsomest family (the four boys had a sister who was as lovely as they were handsome) was at the time of the Darmstadt weddings an officer in the Prussian Household Cavalry, the famous eagle-helmeted *Garde du Corps*. While he was stationed in Potsdam, his life was essentially one long carouse punctuated by occasional martial duties in the premiere military body in Germany. It is difficult to think exactly what it was that attracted Liko to Beatrice, unless it was the fact that her mother was queen of England.

When the British delegation to Darmstadt prepared to return

home, Beatrice murmured touching good-byes to the new prince she had come to know during her niece's wedding, and determined that she would soon see him again. Weighed down by the awareness of the future that the queen had slated for her, she still couldn't have gauged just how bitterly her mother would resist a liaison with Liko. Her life so far free of any significant romantic turmoil, Beatrice was unprepared for her coming trial.

Upon returning to Windsor, Beatrice bluntly told her mother she had fallen in love with Prince Henry of Battenberg. This didn't surprise an astonishingly observant and informed monarch, who knew pretty much everything going on in her far-flung family. But the declaration implied that Beatrice and Liko had engaged in serious conversations in Darmstadt, her daughter's talk of marriage denoting some assurance on Liko's part that he indeed wished to become her husband. If Beatrice imagined her mother might be pleased at the prospect of a fifth son-in-law, the princess had seriously misjudged the situation. Victoria was furious at the impertinence, believing her daughter understood—or *should* have understood—that her life was destined to be one solely of golden servitude. Even had the queen been willing to accept another son-in-law, she was certain that Liko himself would insist on remaining in the Prussian *Garde du Corps*, and thus take his bride away to Berlin. When Beatrice refused to abjure Liko, the queen simply stopped speaking to her until she came to her senses and gave up any notion of marriage with him—or anyone else.

It isn't likely that Beatrice was actually stunned by her mother's intransigence. Surprised, maybe; stunned, no. The princess had, after all, been kept from men almost as though she were a vestal virgin. Though she had not since puberty been alone with a man, even a brother, Beatrice still regarded marriage as a natural state, something her sisters had, after all, been allowed. Even Lenchen, whom Victoria would have kept as her unmarried secretary if that daughter had been so amenable, had been permitted to marry. The fact was, Beatrice thought she deserved a husband, just as her mother had herself deserved one, and she wasn't going to give in on this first real standoff with Victoria.

Within a month of their return from Darmstadt, the dispute between mother and daughter had settled into an ugly impasse. The queen wrote to her eldest child warning her not to discuss with Beatrice Vicky's own daughter Victoria being in love with the second Battenberg brother. She informed the crown princess that "we (Beatrice and I) are very sad! And for me pleasure has for ever died out of my life." Meanwhile, a bellicose series of notes passed back and forth between the sovereign and Beatrice because each refused to open her mouth to the other. Beatrice still came to the queen's table to eat, but perfect silence was maintained as neither spoke to the other, instead shoving their notes across the table if there was something the other needed to know. This went on for six months.

One of Beatrice's biographers—David Duff—observed that the queen even cut out virtually all mention of her youngest daughter in her famous journal, with the exception of a single postcript during the half year of the Battenberg Battle.[6] For a long time, she was absolutely determined not to lose Beatrice's services, so armed was she with almost biblical certainty that a mother had the right to retain her youngest daughter's usefulness to death itself.

But eventually Victoria evidently sensed that she might, after all, lose the war. Beatrice was, at the end of the day, an adult, and could simply have left home to start a life with Liko. Not that any such outcome was likely, given the nature of Beatrice's loyalty to her mother, but it was possible. As Duff pointed out, the queen's extreme behavior might simply have been her way to make sure that, when a compromise was reached, she would be in the strongest possible position to set the terms. As for Beatrice, she was probably desperate to regain her former closeness to the woman who represented the sun around which her world revolved.

The stalemate ended in December 1884. The family, appalled at the situation, suggested to the sovereign that her behavior toward Beatrice had reached a level that could only be described as bizarre. Bertie and Louis of Hesse—the latter now back in his mother-in-law's good graces—were the principal bearers of this consensus. The queen decided the moment was right to give in, and Beatrice was sent for.

The only nonnegotiable demands Victoria made were that, if Beatrice wished to marry Liko, she would still remain in her (the queen's) service and that Liko would leave the Prussian Army, the latter something his brother Louis had already convinced him would be necessary in order to marry Beatrice. The couple would not have residences of their own (the dispensation Lenchen had received), either in London or in the country. They would live at Windsor Castle, Balmoral Castle, and Osborne House—under the queen's roof and at her constant call. If Liko agreed to these conditions, then he could marry Beatrice. If he didn't, he couldn't. If Beatrice wanted to negotiate further, the Great Silence would continue.

Beatrice turned out to be more than amenable. Liko, too, jumped at the offer. He was a semi-impoverished, semiroyal princeling who might not succeed in the Prussian Army, a man who knew his brother Sandro was hated by the present and future German emperors, either of whom might well take out his wrath on Liko. His prospects if he remained in Germany seemed very limited. But if he accepted Queen Victoria's terms, he would suddenly be at the right hand of the most consequential monarch in the world, living in luxury at a string of palaces and, not incidentally, likely see his stock rise mightily in royal circles. Victoria might even promote *him* to royal highness. There had been precedents after all, such as Louis of Hesse on his marriage to Alice.

At Christmas 1884, Liko came over to England to be broken like a young pony and, so one guesses, to propose formally to Beatrice. He stayed at Osborne's Kent House with his brother Louis and new sister-in-law Victoria, who was expecting a baby. Two days before Christmas, all the available Battenbergs were asked to dinner with the queen, where Liko received permission from his future mother-in-law to "speak" to Beatrice. Happily, during these days Liko was making a very good impression on Queen Victoria, who was won over by the young man's charm and the air of youth and virility he brought to her home. Chances are she was wondering why such a fuss had been raised over all this in the first place, so swiftly and artlessly had he seemed to become a part of her family. On December

30, she wrote to Vicky about the path her youngest daughter had chosen: "[Lenchen] has told you of the pain it has caused me that my darling Beatrice should wish (which she never did till she had lost her dear brother [Leopold]) to marry, as I hate marriages especially of my daughters, but as I like Liko very much and as they are both so very devoted to each other, and she remains always with me, I cannot refuse my consent."

The sovereign continued her letters in this vein to her eldest child for several days. Though she professed that "Liko has won my heart," she nevertheless continued to regret Beatrice "leaving" her. Although no such leave-taking would actually take place given the conditions regarding housing, she made it clear in her journals that, once a child was married, his or her primary allegiance inevitably transferred to the spouse. Victoria believed she inhabited a pinnacle that none of her subjects could either share or even fully understand. Though her advisers, counselors, aides, and secretaries represented a theoretically almost infinite phalanx of subordinates, it seems that the monarch only fully trusted a female member of her own family, someone of her own blood, to assist her in her most private social intercourse. If the fifth and last of her daughters married—of her sons, she only ever allowed Leopold participation in any significant part of her private affairs—there was, in her view, no one left whose entire existence would be wholly dedicated to her well-being.

But Victoria very often displayed profound commonsense where she came up against a wall, and it was in Beatrice's unshakable determination to marry that she made the most of the situation. She would, after all, retain Beatrice physically. She also very much liked and was amused by her daughter's future husband, and judged that there would be no surprises that might alter this state of affairs. Wedding plans proceeded from these understandings.

One prospect Victoria couldn't control but fervently hoped would not arise was the specter of little Battenbergs tearing around her palaces. She plainly didn't want Beatrice to get pregnant, writing Vicky of the impending marriage, "I hope and pray that there may be no *results*! That would aggravate everything and besides make me terribly anxious." She was happy that Beatrice and Liko refrained from "kissing, etc.," perhaps judging that this might portend an infertile marriage. Vicky and Fritz's behavior in this regard in 1858 had apparently annoyed her, intelligence she passed along to her eldest daughter. In fact, the queen was not pleased with Fritz just at the moment, regarding as gross impertinence his comment about Liko "not being of the blood," which she thought was "a little like [discussing] animals." The queen rightly held Liko's only slightly twisted parentage as of no great importance, if for no other reason than Beatrice's distant remove from any chance of inheriting the throne.

However, almost all the Hohenzollerns loathed the very idea of the Battenbergs getting above themselves. Willy and Dona and Henry, joined by the emperor and empress, were all openly critical of Beatrice marrying Liko, their vehemence increased by the romance simmering between Sandro and Victoria (Moretta). The British monarch dismissed the criticisms, assuring Vicky that Liko and Beatrice would never dream of going to Berlin, where they might "hurt Fritz's dignity." But Fritz's objections stung his mother-in-law, who already believed the Hohenzollern concern for "rank, etc." had become irrational. For all his "liberal" ideals, Fritz was often as stiff as a Spanish infante where it came to courtly prerogatives, and he was "frantic" at the idea of Liko being made a royal highness and receiving the Garter from Victoria. He even sent the duke of Connaught a memorandum outlining the difficulties with precedence Liko would experience whenever he came to Germany.

The weeks remaining until Beatrice's wedding sped by, with her mother in a state about what Liko would do to her "baby" on their wedding night. "I count the months, weeks and days," she said in a letter to Vicky, "that she is still my own sweet, unspoilt, innocent lily and child. That thought—that agonising thought which I always felt, and which I often wonder any mother can bear of giving up your own child, from whom all has been so carefully kept and guarded— to a stranger to do unto her as he likes is to me the most torturing thought in the world . . . we must trust in a higher power." The idea that sex was going to be something enjoyable for any of her daughters was evidently inconceivable. The only good sex was that which Victoria had enjoyed with the incomparable Albert.

Unhappily, the intended bride, protected though she was, heard the criticisms of her marriage from far and near. The Hohenzollerns were the nastiest, partly understandable because of the standoff between the crown princess and the rest of her father-in-law's court over the Sandro-Moretta brouhaha; but snipes came from Russia as well, again principally over Sandro, who, as reigning prince of Bulgaria, was thwarting Russian plans to control that country. Republican French comment, too, was often spiteful, largely because of the lowly origins of Liko's mother. Hardest to take, even local views were far from universally favorable, the British public generally having hoped that the queen's youngest daughter would follow Louise's lead and marry some homegrown grandee. Liko was described in the penny press as a "German pauper," one who would represent a continuing drain on the national exchequer.

The wedding was planned for Whippingham Church, Osborne's little parish chapel that the bride's father had helped to design. An air of festive exhilaration swept the Isle of Wight, its inhabitants proud that this would be the first time a monarch's daughter was to be married in anything so simple as a local parish church. In truth, the reason the queen chose the little chapel for Beatrice's wedding was precisely because it was so small—the smaller the church, the fewer people who could be invited. Victoria hated crowds of any kind at her homes, especially at Osborne, where she considered herself as much off-duty from affairs of state as she could ever be. Much was made of the fact that no members of the German ruling dynasties were invited except for Louis of Hesse, who was a first cousin to the bridegroom and the brother-in-law of the bride. Vicky asked if she could come, but her mother told her she couldn't be invited because Liko's brother Sandro would be there, and the German crown princess shouldn't be seen socially with a man her father-in-law's government was in the process of vilifying.

Though the chapel could hold only a handful, certain people *had* to be invited, and therefore plans were made for outdoor seats to be erected on the path leading to the church door. Even with these additional accommodations, Victoria refused to send an invitation to her nemesis Gladstone (she fatuously referred to him in letters to Vicky as "Merry Pebble"), a man who had known and been fond of Beatrice since her birth. The snub caused widespread public comment, and the former prime minister (his government had been defeated just a month before the wedding) was understood to be deeply upset at the queen's apparent scorn.

On the morning of July 23, 1885, a warm and cloudless day gracing the island off England's southern coast, Beatrice was trussed into her skin-tight wedding dress, over which she wore a lace tunic that had belonged to Henry VIII's first wife, Catherine of Aragon. So great was Beatrice's love of lace—the Tudor queen's overskirt was one of her most treasured possessions—that her mother bestowed on her the signal distinction of being allowed to wear her own Honiton lace veil. Victoria regarded this as one of her most precious possessions, and Beatrice was the only one of her daughters so honored. Liko actually looked considerably more soigné than his bride. Above thigh-high black riding boots were white suede breeches as tight as was his bride's wedding dress. A white tunic, the uniform of the Prussian *Garde du Corps*, was adorned with the brand-new insignia of the Garter (as Fritz had feared, the queen evidently believed her sons-in-law should be Garter knights, though Lorne remained only a Thistle knight), bestowed the day before by the queen in a private ceremony. The princess of Wales, evidently taken by her new brother-in-law's beauty, referred to him as "Beatrice's Lohengrin."

After a two-day honeymoon at Quarr Abbey, only six miles from the Osborne estate, Liko began to find out what his bargain with the British royal family would really amount to. The couple came right back to the queen's residence to take up their married life, he alone stealing a day to go up to London to get his naturalization attended to. Though they would be styled "Their Royal Highnesses Prince and Princess Henry of Battenberg," Beatrice would always take precedence over her husband. On the Continent, his new status as a royal highness—also conferred by the queen—wouldn't be recognized, instead reverting to serene highness. Even so, Victoria was annoyed to learn that Fritz had written to her son Arthur asking him to try to stop her raising Liko to his postmarital status.

At least Beatrice had a job. Trained from girlhood to serve her mother, the princess's days would be filled with work that, if often tedious, carried with it an undeniable importance. Her husband would have nothing of the kind; the comparison between himself and his brothers Louis—an up and coming Royal Navy officer—and Sandro—an on-again, off-again ruler of Bulgaria—was difficult for him. Whereas Prince Christian had at least been allowed to make a private home for himself and Lenchen, Liko's bargain denied him even this degree of independence. He would live in Queen Victoria's luxurious homes, estates where her word was law, her presence at every moment palpable, and his own amusements or interests restricted to such as he might invent. He also carried the realization that even the roof over his and Beatrice's heads was entirely dependent on the queen's life: at her demise, neither could continue to live in the principal royal residences, which would become Bertie's homes by right of inheritance. For the next ten years, Liko essentially vegetated and fathered children.

The queen's fifth son-in-law negotiated through his new life with a gingerness that might have stood him well in the diplomatic service. Aware that the queen was coming to regard him with a tenderness she afforded few men, Liko began to test the strictures that made life at the Victorian court famously tedious. And he broached to the monarch what was, aside from William Gladstone, perhaps her best-known bête noire.

Reviling tobacco in any of its forms, Queen Victoria absolutely forbade its use in all her homes, or anywhere near her wherever she was. Unfortunately, Prince Christian was an addicted smoker, and his hours spent in his mother-in-law's orbit were an agony of nicotine deprivation. When the queen heard that Christian blew smoke up the chimney in his room in order to get an occasional fix during his and Lenchen's stays, she decided she might as well give this son-in-law, as well as his fellow smokers, some better place to satiate their habit. Consequently, she assigned them a cubbyhole in a distant part of Windsor Castle, which they had to reach by crossing open courtyards in all weathers.

Liko, also an addicted smoker, decided to try to make life for the royal family's smokers more pleasant. Using his charm, and banking on the queen's sympathy, he managed to talk her into assigning a larger, less inconveniently located chamber as the designated smoking venue. The new room was furnished with comfortable furniture and a billiards table, very different to the first stone-bare chamber. The queen did direct that smoking be allowed only after eleven in the evening, but for sons-in-law Liko and Christian her agreement remained a capital victory.

Just as the queen feared, Beatrice became pregnant soon after the wedding, though this first pregnancy sadly ended in a miscarriage. Dr. James Reid, the principal royal physician, bluntly noted the occasion in his diary: ". . . at home all day with the Princess—at 6:00 P.M. removed contents of uterus." Though the queen tried to cut her daughter's convalescence short—Victoria correctly believed that long bedrest did more harm than good—Dr. Reid managed to convince his most important client that Beatrice should refrain from any tiring outings for a reasonable period.

Quickly pregnant again, Beatrice bore at Windsor a strong and healthy son, who arrived almost exactly a year after the miscarriage. The boy was named Alexander, after his uncle, Prince Alexander of Battenberg. The princess had been "taken ill," in the standard language of the time, during the early evening of November 22, 1886, and Reid immediately sent for the queen's obstetrician, who delivered the baby after a relatively speedy labor.[7] Queen Victoria sat by the bedside through most of Beatrice's labor, and when she took the infant from the midwife-nurse, became the first member of the family to hold the new prince. It was the monarch's thirty-seventh grandchild, but one who would give her pleasure as few of the others had. Beatrice's baby would live under the queen's own roof, and when Alexander—"Drino" in the family—was joined by two more brothers and a sister, a large part of the agony of the quarter-century-long travail of her widowhood would be lifted.

9

German Horrors

After Willy's marriage, Vicky's political difficulties went into something approaching free fall. The immediate cause was the volatile love affair between her daughter and Prince Alexander of Battenberg. Like many of Europe's problems, it was born in the geopolitical quicksand of the Balkans, and further nurtured by an animosity on Bismarck's part toward Vicky that had settled into a deep and near-unchecked loathing. Hard on the ordeal of this calamity would come the greatest disaster of her life.

The breakup of the Ottoman empire was one of the longest-running stories of the nineteenth century, as well as one of its most mesmerizing. The Sublime Porte—the name popularly used to designate the sultans' government—could do little more than watch as bits of power and territories were slowly torn away from its long-enfeebled grasp. One such chink was an area, inhabited by the Bulgars, that had been under Ottoman Turkish dominion for five hundred years but that had been partially freed from the sultan's control by the 1878 Treaty of Berlin. The treaty provided that the northern Bulgar lands, to be called Bulgaria, would be headed by a sovereign prince. Except for the payment of a tribute, it would be independent of Constantinople—a formula designed for Turkey to yield to political reality while saving the Ottomans' face over their loss. Importantly, the southern Bulgar area, known as Eastern Rumelia and virtually in Constantinople's backyard, wasn't to become part of the new principality, but to remain under the direct control of the Porte. The jury-rigged arrangement was to have disastrous consequences for Bulgaria's attempt at transition from Eastern despotism to something approaching Western modernity.

Since the newly instituted Bulgaria consisted largely of Orthodox Catholics, and its language and Cyrillic orthography further tied it to Russia, Tsar Alexander II considered the country to be within Russia's sphere of influence. He was thus allowed by the powers to select Bulgaria's inaugural prince, a prince who would clearly understand that the principal shots would be called from St. Petersburg. The tsar actively and unsurprisingly supported the eventual joining of both parts of the Bulgar lands, which would involve wresting Eastern Rumelia from the Ottomans and tacking it onto northern Bulgaria.

Because Sandro, young Prince Alexander of Battenberg, was the tsar's nephew (the tsarina was the sister of the prince's father) and a highly regarded officer in his uncle's army, and was trusted by the Russian monarch, he seemed a perfect and perfectly compliant choice to reign in Sofia, the Bulgarian capital. Even Great Britain, Russia's most powerful antagonist, did not object to a Battenberg becoming prince of Bulgaria—the young man was not only not Russian but enjoyed the advantage of being closely related to Queen Victoria's family. Britain did at first object to Bulgaria's desire to get the Ottomans out of Eastern Rumelia, however, believing the province provided the Turks with a natural defense line against foreign (read Russian) invaders.

When Sandro arrived in Sofia in 1879 to take up his duties as reigning prince, he quickly found that his job would call for an almost unachievable balancing act. The Russians, to whom he owed his position as their puppet ruler *in situ,* wanted Bulgaria and its ruler to be dominated wholly by Russia's political ends. The Bulgarians, on the other hand, wanted genuine independence and the immediate takeover of Eastern Rumelia—or what they held to be southern Bulgaria. Before long, Sandro showed signs of favoring the Bulgars to whom he had, after all, pledged his solemn allegiance on taking up their throne. In the meantime, Russia got a new tsar, Alexander III, who was far less apt to put up with any deviation by Sandro than had been his father, Alexander II. The new monarch decided Russian influence in Bulgaria was under threat from Sandro's pro-Bulgar notions, and set about getting rid of his cousin, whom the caste-conscious Alexander hated as a parvenu, cousin or not. The coup staged by Alexander's agents against Sandro failed; but Russia's displeasure with how things were going in Bulgaria aroused Bismarck for having riled the tsar, who was Germany's valuable ally.

Badly injuring Sandro's standing with both Berlin and St. Petersburg was the fact that he had the bad luck to have gotten himself involved with Fritz and Vicky's daughter Victoria—Moretta to her family. The princess was a wild, not-quite-balanced tomboy who looked half-Tartar and possessed, unfortunately, some of the same eccentricity as her eldest brother. When in 1879 Sandro paid a courtesy call on the crown prince and princess of Prussia, the thirteen-year-old girl instantly fell into a kind of hero-worship adulation of the tall and strikingly handsome new prince of Bulgaria. Sandro's later visits to the Neues Palais would result in a budding love affair, though it isn't likely that Sandro regarded Moretta with quite the same passionate adoration that she felt for him.

By 1885, Sandro and the nineteen-year-old princess privately pledged to marry, and the strangely matched pair became affianced in all but name. Vicky approved heartily of her prospective son-in-law; but Fritz, far more conscious than his wife of how blue one's blood had to be to marry a Hohenzollern, knew that Sandro came up far short of the requirement. But if Fritz harbored relatively mild objections—he already considered the two Battenbergs in his wife's family (Louis with Victoria of Hesse and Liko with Beatrice) more than enough—his parents, his three eldest children, and his father's chancellor greeted the proposed engagement as though the young princess were to be coupled with a snake charmer.

Had Vicky been capable of judging the depth of Bismarck's opposition, she might have reconsidered what was to be a long, futile, and destructive support for the marital alliance, support that was fatally damaging to what was left of her own and her husband's political standing. Bismarck's objections stemmed from a combination of factors: first, reasoned political antagonism—by this time Sandro was anathema to Russia, and the chancellor had no wish to antagonize the tsar or to involve Germany in the stew of Balkan affairs—and second, a reluctance to allow further British influence in the Balkans. The status-conscious chancellor also was personally offended by what he held to be an uneven match. Vicky found his attitude preposterous. As she saw it, if the queen of England would welcome two of Sandro's brothers into her own family, what right had Bismarck to hold Sandro unworthy of marrying a Hohenzollern princess?

But the chancellor was easily able to win over that part of Fritz's family already antagonistic to Sandro on dynastic grounds. Most important, the emperor refused to listen to Vicky or Moretta's entreaties; and Willy, along with Charlotte and Henry, eagerly backed up their grandfather's animosity to the almost-engagement—Bismarck's reminder that Sandro's mother had been a "mere" countess was, for Willy, like throwing gasoline on the fire. Unfortunately, Willy's view as future emperor had to be listened to with a degree of seriousness, a factor that literally sickened Vicky. When she talked Fritz into foolishly helping her support the match, the damage the crown prince did himself was significant. Because of his stance, Fritz would soon become a virtual nonentity in his father's and Bismarck's views, both of whom would begin to put Willy forward in a way that suggested there would never be any significant reign between those of William I and William II.

As with nearly all important matters in her life, Vicky was highly influenced by her mother in this self-destructive championing of Sandro. The queen obviously now considered the Hohenzollerns' attitudes about the Battenbergs particularly abhorrent, and sharply criticized Willy and Dona's snub of her youngest daughter when Beatrice and Liko visited Potsdam on their honeymoon: ". . . extraordinary impertinence . . . poor little insignificant Princess [Dona] raised entirely by your kindness to the position she is in." She reminded Vicky that Lord Granville had remarked "that if the Queen of England thinks a person good enough for her daughter, what have other people got to say?" Bismarck believed the English queen's favoring of Sandro had as much to do with politics as with prickly family pride; that the prince's continued leadership of Bulgaria "would make a permanent estrangement between ourselves and Russia."

By mid-1885, shortly after the wedding of Beatrice and Liko at which Sandro had been an honored guest, the Bulgarian debacle played itself out. It did so in a Balkan melodrama that ended in discredit for just about everyone involved.

When the Eastern Rumelian Bulgars revolted against Ottoman control, seeking union with the rest of Bulgaria with Sandro as their ruler, the demand enraged Tsar Alexander III, whose personal loathing for his cousin had reached astonishing levels. Meanwhile, the newly enlarged Bulgar state was viewed as a mortal threat by its Serbian neighbor to the west, whose King Milan began an invasion in the sanguine expectation of wiping Bulgaria off the map. Much to Milan's astonishment, under Sandro's expert military leadership the Bulgars trounced the Serbs, bringing about an even larger Bulgaria that was recognized by the powers. Enraged at these events, Alexander bribed or otherwise managed to convince a group of disgruntled Bulgarian officers to attempt another coup. This one was, so it seemed, successful. Sandro (along with his visiting younger brother Francis) was kidnapped by the conspirators, beaten rather badly, and put on a boat to be sent up the Danube into what was expected to be permanent exile. But it wasn't over yet.

As in a Lehár operetta, loyalists at home managed to overturn the coup, and immediately invited Sandro back to his throne. Urged by Queen Victoria and the German crown princess to go back to Sofia, Sandro foolishly returned to a country where menace was etched into the very earth. Had he and Moretta been allowed to marry, he might have been a success: with a wife at his side he would likely have been strengthened, and thus sustained for whatever lay ahead. But so long as Bismarck opposed the marriage, there wasn't the slightest chance that Moretta was going to be joining him. Nor could Moretta's English grandmother be of much help: Prime Minister Salisbury sympathized with Sandro's plight, but had no thought of sending British soldiers to bail out the young Battenberg.

Sandro's spirits were finally worn down. In September 1886, he left Bulgaria, a place he would never see again.[1] Sadly, even after the prince gave up his throne, Bismarck remained adamantly opposed to his marriage into the House of Hohenzollern, for what he thought now was the justifiable reason that the prince might be tempted into returning to Sofia someday to reclaim it. But Bismarck had other reasons as well to keep the Battenberg out of the imperial family: he was informed through his own sources that Fritz favored Sandro as governor of German-annexed Alsace-Lorraine, and perhaps even as German chancellor one day—advancements Fritz would be in a position to effect upon his accession. Whispering this intelligence into the present emperor's ear, it wasn't hard for Bismarck to keep William and Augusta on his side while further discrediting Fritz in his parents' estimation.

The other wounded party in the romance threatened to kill herself, and generally declined to bear her disappointment with much dignity. Though Moretta's hopes would not be extinguished for a few more years, she *would* eventually marry another, with some degree of happiness. But Vicky for her part would never recover from her single-minded advocacy of something that could not be. And she had squandered whatever resources might have ameliorated the pain of the next—and greatest—trial of her life.

Just after New Year's in 1887, Fritz began to be bothered by hoarseness, at first dismissing it as merely a holdover from a Christmas cold. But the problem wouldn't go away, and while delivering a speech to commemorate his father's ninetieth birthday in late

March, the crown prince found he wasn't able to clear his usually distinct voice. Knowing her husband had long been susceptible to throat problems,[2] Vicky counseled him to wear an overcoat in Berlin's bitter cold. But her father-in-law considered that a sign of unmanliness, and Fritz, now eager to please the emperor by acquiescing to even his most fatuous notions, refused to contravene William's wishes. Within days, the hoarseness settled into what was assumed in the family to be merely a bad throat infection. The doctors sent the prince to bed for two weeks to try to shake the ailment.

For years subject to depression—his father's almost bizarre long-livedness had Fritz nearly convinced that his turn on the throne would come too late to implement his own agenda—mandatory bedrest left him even more deeply melancholic than usual. The sense of optimism that had kept the crown prince buoyant during his difficulties with the emperor and the chancellor was now abandoning him, despite Vicky's constant and sometimes extravagant attempts to cheer her husband. His voice had almost disappeared, making every utterance by midwinter a wheezing croak that badly frightened Vicky. In March the couple consulted with Dr. Karl Gerhardt, a University of Berlin throat specialist; though not a laryngologist, the physician was well known and respected among the capital's laryngological experts. On examination, Gerhardt saw what he described as a small but unidentifiable growth on Fritz's left vocal cord. Gerhardt tried to cauterize it with a red-hot platinum wire snare, but it reemerged despite his efforts.[3]

Suspecting cancer, Gerhardt asked Dr. Ernst von Bergmann, a well-known surgeon, to examine the crown prince. Bergmann agreed with his colleague that cancer was the probable cause of the growth, and together they advised Vicky and Fritz that an immediate operation to remove the tumor was the surest way to save the prince's life. Four other doctors present at the consultation agreed. The physicians knew that, if the tumor were indeed malignant, it would grow and spread cancer cells throughout the body. The consensus was that Bergmann should perform a laryngectomy, or throat incision, to remove the growth. In 1887 this procedure was extremely dangerous, the mortality rate on Bergmann's seven similar previous cases not very promising: most of the patients had died within eighteen months of surgery. Even if he survived the operation, Fritz would almost certainly lose his ability to speak—an almost unimaginable consequence for a future emperor. In the meantime, the doctors continued to cauterize his throat with the platinum snare, still hoping to burn the mass out; he went through thirteen such agonizing sessions. These "treatments" left him exhausted and depressed, his throat in agony for hours afterward.

Both Vicky and Fritz were, naturally, horrified by what clearly had become a serious medical crisis. The crown princess tried to keep the worst of the doctors' reports from her husband, including delaying the news that they had agreed upon an operation. At this point, Bismarck entered what would in an ordinary case have been a private family matter. Furious that so important a person as the nation's crown prince—heir to an emperor who clearly didn't have much longer to live himself—wasn't aware of the decisions being made on his behalf, the chancellor demanded that the laryngectomy, scheduled for May 22, be halted until another, wholly independent opinion could be obtained. Bismarck wanted the best non-German throat specialist available, a man with an international reputation—the manipulative chancellor's possible motivation being that, should the worst happen, German medicine alone couldn't be blamed for the outcome. Bismarck did, though, have good reason to be concerned: if a laryngectomy were performed, the patient stood only a small chance of surviving the operation.

Introducing a foreign doctor was almost guaranteed to provoke a tense and possibly harmful rivalry among the physicians already involved in the case. Though it might seem that the chancellor would have welcomed seeing Fritz removed from the succession, Bismarck knew he could control him as emperor. Fritz had already made clear he would need Bismarck to help him govern, at least during the early months of his reign. A youthful, impetuous, and quite possibly uncontrollable Emperor William II would be a loose cannon. The chancellor reasonably feared that Willy wouldn't hesitate to do whatever an emperor had the constitutional power to do, irrespective of the consequences.

Morell Mackenzie, a famous and successful throat specialist with offices in Harley Street, whose textbook, *Manual of Disease of the Throat and Nose,* was used in German medical schools, was chosen to come to Berlin. Vicky was ecstatic, of course, both that the operation had been put off until Mackenzie had his own chance to weigh in and because the doctor involved was one of her own, a matter of great concern to a woman who had remained essentially English in her deepest views. Fortunately, no one told Vicky Sir William Jenner's opinion of Mackenzie. Jenner, one of Queen Victoria's personal physicians, called him "greedy and grasping about money," and said he "tries to make profit out of his attendance." The royal physician did admit, however, that Mackenzie was "very clever . . . about throats." Though the queen knew of these views, her only concern was that the best man be sent to Fritz, and she was satisfied that Mackenzie was that man.

Mackenzie was impressed by his patient—both for his exalted position and for the genuine warmth with which Fritz received him. The doctor knew his reputation was riding on the outcome of the case. After examining the crown prince, he unhesitatingly ruled out cancer as the cause of the vocal cord growth, diagnosing instead a "wart or a papilloma." There is no reason to suspect that his opinion was guided by what he thought the patient wanted to hear, even though Mackenzie would develop something approaching friendship with Vicky and Fritz. Yet it would not be surprising if he was guided by extreme conservatism and the wish to avoid a surgical procedure of whose dangers he was all too aware. To verify his initial assessment, Mackenzie sent a sample of Fritz's affected tissue (a growth he described as "about the size of a split pea") to Dr. Rudolf Virchow, then held to be the world's greatest living authority on cells. Virchow found nothing in it that confirmed cancer, but hedged by saying that the sample sent to him was "too superficial for a proper diagnosis."

At this point, the course of treatment developed into virtually a pitched battle between the Scottish doctor and the German team, of whom Mackenzie was openly and undiplomatically contemptuous for their lack of specific knowledge of laryngology. For their part, the Germans accused Mackenzie of damaging Fritz's unaffected vocal cord, which led to the Scot throwing back charges of professional jealousy by the Germans. The xenophobic German press inevitably got wind of the bickering and, not unexpectedly, excoriated the foreign physician. Yet even when a larger sample of affected tissue was removed for Virchow's analysis, the pathologist persisted in his view that the abnormality was not a malignant growth. Some historians suggest that because Virchow was a friend of the crown prince and princess, he was overly cautious in an effort to spare their feelings. But there is no historical evidence that Virchow weighted his professional view against cancer merely to placate the patient.

During these horrifying days at the Neues Palais, one happy family celebration temporarily took Fritz and Vicky's minds off their ominous future. Their second son, Henry, had fallen in love. The young woman was his own first cousin, Princess Irene of Hesse, Alice and Louis's third and least exceptional daughter. Though neither the crown prince nor the crown princess was enthusiastic about the idea of royal marriages between first cousins, both held Alice's daughters to be models of sensible young womanhood. As for their views of the difficult Henry, a strong wife could be what he needed to escape the overwhelming orbit of Willy's own minicourt. Vicky still hoped that Henry might turn out to be a more loving son than Willy, considering that when he was alone for a few days with her and Fritz, his elder brother's-inspired braggadocio lessened notably.

With rumors running frenziedly through Berlin over the crown prince's health, Vicky and Fritz decided to leave for England. The principal reason was that Mackenzie wanted to be able to treat his patient using his own familiar facilities. The Germans just as much wanted to absolve themselves of responsibility, leaving the Scotsman to take the blame for what they believed by this time was going to be a tragic outcome. Vicky was still doing her best to keep some of the worst from her husband—the doctors affirmed that the tumor was continuing to grow—in hope that a respite might in itself ease her husband's suffering and even help to cure him. Vicky also wanted desperately to be in England, in the company of her husband, for the Jubilee ceremonies that were to mark Queen Victoria's fifty years as monarch. Using the pad and pencil that had by now become his sole means of communicating, Fritz agreed to his wife's desires, and the couple duly departed for England in mid-June.

Even this attempt on Vicky's part to lift the spirits of her depressed and pain-wracked husband was almost destroyed by the latest outbreak of their eldest son's increasingly brazen hubris. Willy decided *he* should be the Hohenzollern at his grandmother's Jubilee. Judging his father too ill to go to London, the younger man had at the end of May obtained his grandfather's permission to represent the German crown at the English celebrations. Presenting this as a fait accompli to his mother, Willy wrote Queen Victoria that he alone was coming, at the "Emperor's orders." Vicky was enraged by what she rightly considered her son's gross disrespect to his father, and Queen Victoria was equally disgusted with Willy's presumption, almost matching her anger with the whole German imperial family over its behavior in the Battenberg affair. Furthermore, the queen wanted no part of her grandson at the celebration, judging that Willy would treat Liko—his uncle by marriage—badly and thus upset Beatrice. Yet Vicky, evidently in the pursuit of something like family accord, repeatedly assured her mother that Willy meant no harm by his behavior. The future emperor did not repay his mother's efforts, instead continuing to bombard his English grandmother with letters urging that she withdraw her invitation to his sick father.

Vicky was wise enough in this instance—a rarity by this time in her troubled life—not to insist that Willy stay away, only that she and Fritz be present as the ranking Hohenzollern representatives. Desperate to get her husband away from the horrors at home, she believed that the difficulties of the trip would be outweighed by the psychological good it would do Fritz to be seen at the Jubilee in the roles of the queen's senior son-in-law and successor to the German crown. The British monarch agreed. Emperor William gave in, and allowed his son to go. Fritz's German doctors secretly hoped that the trip would do him in.

When Fritz and Vicky arrived in London, they became part of one of the most colossal celebrations of the Victorian era. The nation had been unable to stage a "Silver" Jubilee because of Prince Albert's death the year before it would have taken place, so the anniversary of Victoria's fifty years on the throne now became an excuse for Britain to go wild.[4] This national party was a chance, as many touchingly believed, to make the queen happy again after twenty-six years of mordant widowhood. By 1887 most of her countrymen truly adulated their monarch, convinced that she was responsible for the fact that the United Kingdom was the greatest imperial power and industrial workshop the planet had ever known. The fête would be one of the watershed events of the nineteenth century, the peak of Britain's confidence in itself, in its monarch, and in its glorious destiny.

The leading actors in the Jubilee drama were, naturally, the queen's own relatives and descendants, the vast cast of occupants of the Continent's thrones and Britain's own extended royal family. Related to nearly every royal house in Europe, Victoria had long since become the acknowledged doyenne of monarchies, the model to which every ruler aspired, or the woman every ruler at least admired. Yet ever self-pitying, she wrote in her diary her belief that she was alone amid the endless pomp and crowds and adulation; and she still reminded all who would listen of the loss she had suffered in Albert's death. Driving to Westminster Abbey on Jubilee Day—June 21, 1887—she was surrounded by dozens of relatives, guarded by thousands of marching troops, and thronged by hundreds of thousands of cheering spectators. In the place of highest honor beside her, Vicky and the slowly dying Fritz basked in the luminous rays of this queen-empress's glory. Willy, playing very much a subordinate role, remembered the thrill of the occasion four decades later: "That day gave us all an overwhelming impression of the power and extent of the British Empire." It is a pity that the impression was too soon forgotten by the queen's proud grandson

Vicky, who together with the princess of Wales rode with the queen on the short trip from Buckingham Palace to Westminster Abbey, was enormously proud of Fritz. That day he was spectacularly arrayed in the all-white uniform of the Pomeranian Cuirassiers, a shining eagle-crested helmet on his head, his field marshal's baton firmly gripped in a still-strong right hand. Most important to the British onlookers, the Garter star that had been given him by his mother-in-law glinted brightly in the June light. Mounted on a white charger, he had turned himself into the vision of some mythical prince guarding a fairy queen. Lorne said that he looked like "one of the legendary heroes embodied in the creations of Wagner." Towering above all others in the queen's orbit, Fritz drew loud applause as he passed by, many Londoners aware that he was seriously ill and had made an enormous physical effort to honor their sovereign by his presence.

At the climax of the commemorative service at the abbey, all the aristocracy slowly progressed toward the queen seated on her coronation chair, and there paid their respects. As Victoria stepped down from the throne at the ceremony's conclusion, she gathered Fritz into her arms for a long moment, embracing him as she made manifest her own respect, love, and tacit understanding of the terrible torture he was enduring. If sheer self-fortitude could have made him well, his illness would have surely disappeared. But the illness was inescapably real, and what energy he expended on this occasion represented the last great physical exertion of Fritz's life.

After two days' rest at Buckingham Palace, a relatively refreshed crown prince noted that his throat felt a bit better, and even the constant swelling beside his Adam's apple had gone down a bit. In the days following the celebrations, Fritz was driven daily to Mackenzie's offices in Harley Street, where the physician inserted snares down his throat to cut out as much of the growth as possible. The tissue was again sent to Virchow, who still could find no positive proof that it was cancerous.[5] Though the patient rallied away from the contentiousness of Berlin's doctors and in the gentle ministrations of his wife's care, the growth was not eradicated even by Mackenzie's formidable exertions. From London, Vicky and Fritz traveled down to Osborne, where bright sunny weather improved the crown prince's spirits, as did seashore excursions with his wife's nieces and nephews. Queen Marie of Romania, the daughter of Vicky's brother Affie and at the time a little girl, remembered her playful yet imposing uncle many years later: "He was jolly and yet somehow one felt he was condescending." Likely, the illness draining his life away could never have been far from his mind.

After a restful spell at Balmoral, where much to the queen's joy some of her son-in-law's voice had even returned, Vicky and Fritz decided against returning to Berlin, knowing winter was not far off. Instead, they went to Toblach, a health resort in the Austrian Tyrol, where Fritz would be situated relatively close to Germany in case of his father's death. Though the crown prince was urged to return to Berlin—it was generally acknowledged that William I was rapidly nearing the end of his protracted life—the couple ignored criticism from home; when Toblach's winter began to set in, Vicky moved on to warmer Venice, then to Baveno on Lake Maggiore, and finally to San Remo, on the Italian Riviera. The world's press quickly converged on the seaside resort, desperate to report on a royal heir who might or might not survive his ailing father to become emperor himself. Some of the German press blamed Vicky personally, not only for supposedly dragooning her husband, but for relying on foreign doctors instead of their good German counterparts. In Berlin, the debate over the prince's treatment had turned essentially into a dispute between a liberal minority who supported the royal couple and the conservative majority who believed Fritz had become his English wife's victim.

In November, at San Remo, in a private mansion called the Villa Zirio, the diagnosis of Fritz's cancer was finally revealed to him. Dr. Mackenzie bore the tidings. After finding more swelling on Fritz's throat, the physician was himself finally persuaded that a malignant tumor was the cause. When he was told, Fritz meekly responded that he had "lately been fearing something of this sort." The doctor gave his patient two choices: to submit to surgery in an attempt to cut out the cancer, which offered very little hope of success; or else to let the disease run its course, only performing a tracheostomy so Fritz could breath more easily. The crown prince decided on the latter course, understanding now that it was far too late for any hope of a cure; he formally wrote out his assent—"I do not wish to have surgery, but I would accept tracheostomy if necessary." Vicky, too, had made it clear that she opposed any kind of surgery other than the palliative tracheostomy. When the couple was finally alone, Fritz fell exhausted into Vicky's arms, both husband and wife in tears.

Now came yet another nightmare, mired in the peculiar politics of Bismarckian Germany. The crown princess's conservative opponents, who were legion, began to agitate for Fritz's actual removal from the line of succession. Basically Willy's allies, their leader was Herbert von Bismarck, the chancellor's son, who had all his father's vituperativeness but none of his brilliance. Spreading word that Vicky intended to rule for her husband should Fritz survive his father, the younger Bismarck's charge found resonance throughout Germany. Judging that the crown princess's liberal tendencies would put the nation's security at risk should she control an incapacitated emperor, the chancellor demanded and got written consent from Emperor William that, in effect, politically disinherited the crown prince by allowing Willy to act as his grandfather's deputy should the monarch become incapacitated. The chancellor also threatened upon William's death to make Willy regent should Fritz remain in his present state of incapacitation. Willy was overjoyed. Fritz had not been consulted in any of this and was deeply aggrieved when he learned of it, especially at hearing that his eldest son had been actively urging Bismarck to take these decisions, although the order probably can be said to have made a kind of political sense while Fritz remained out of Germany. But the manner in which it was achieved was an ominous indication of Fritz's dwindling authority and Willy's gathering arrogance and importance.

During these weeks, elements of the German press kept up a steady drumbeat of calumny against the crown princess and what it characterized as her meddling and self-serving behavior during her husband's illness. Many of the comments, which deeply distressed Vicky as she faced the papers at her breakfast table every morning, suggested that rather than do what was best for Germany—which was to allow Fritz to withdraw from the succession—she was interested only in his succession to the throne so she herself could control Germany. Some ascribed her motives to power lust, others to a wish to bend German policy to England's will, while still others believed she was interested in making sure she inherited an emperor's fortune rather than a crown prince's comparatively paltry assets. The British ambassador, Sir Edward Malet, tried to get Herbert von Bismarck to have corrected a particularly meretricious story in the *Norddeutsche Allgemeine Zeitung.* But Malet was ignored, and the press continued in its anti-British strain. With inexorable menace, this course of events was gradually sowing a national mind-set that would within a generation reap a catastrophe of unimaginable proportions.

Still half-deluding herself as to the desperate nature of her husband's condition, Vicky continued to hold out hope for Fritz's restoration. Every time he had a comparatively good day, or Mackenzie reported some minor improvement in his color or ability to breathe, she took the tidings as though full recovery was just around the corner, and remained adamant that this was no time to jeopardize what hope existed by an unwise move. (In justice to Vicky's frame of mind, the doctors themselves were at this time telling her husband that he could conceivably live as much as two more years.) The political urgency of his return to Berlin was hidden from him by his wife, for whom his health was the sole issue.

Just after the turn of 1888, Fritz became almost totally unable to breathe, and the tracheostomy that Mackenzie had spoken of could no longer be postponed. A large steel cannula was inserted into a surgical opening in the crown prince's throat, and it was through this cumbersome and painful tube that he would until his death obtain the air necessary to life. Although the procedure lessened the panic that comes of impending asphyxiation, soon the metal itself began to irritate the raw tissue and had to be frequently removed for cleaning. Vicky did what she could to help by constantly renewing the ice bandages made up for his throat. Even Henry and Charlotte, who came to San Remo when the operation was performed, seemed distressed at the misery their mother felt. Back in Berlin, Willy had in the meantime with typical loutishness styled himself "Deputy Emperor."

When, in early March 1888, Bismarck absolutely demanded the heir's return to the capital in view of the emperor's imminent death, Vicky finally accepted that her husband had to return. Writing to her mother, she rationalized that "Fritz must be there to assume the responsibilities of his position." Time ran out for ninety-one-year-old Kaiser William I on the morning of March 9. Tragically for German history, this survivor of the eighteenth century had simply lived too long. Mortally ill, Fritz was finally Kaiser Frederick III.[6] The first act of the new monarch's reign carried out in San Remo had been to bestow on Vicky the Order of the Black Eagle, the highest honor a sovereign could give. When Willy's friends heard of this controversial act, they professed disgust that a Prussian king should so honor a mere woman.

The morning after William's death, the imperial party left a warm and cloudless San Remo to arrive next evening in a bitterly cold Berlin. Instead of going to their own palace on Unter den Linden, Fritz and Vicky decided to occupy the Charlottenburg Palace, located in the capital's less congested west end. Its principal advantage was that it was surrounded by spacious grounds—as Vicky put it, "so the people cannot look in at the windows." She wrote a note to her mother saying she would miss her younger daughters, though, who returned to the Crown Prince's Palace. She added that, since all their things were there, "this [Charlottenburg] is more or less an encampment."

Never, even now, a woman to let well enough alone, Vicky prevailed on her husband for his official sanction to allow Moretta and Sandro to marry. Fritz very likely understood the stupidity of reopening what had become a touchstone of Prussia's conservatives, but at this point he evidently felt he could deny Vicky nothing—a point he had made clear when, immediately after his succession, he thanked his doctors for "having made me live long enough to recompense the valiant courage of my wife" by allowing her to become an empress. It would have been unlikely he could now deny her something of such importance to her personal happiness, even if it were something she should have long ago put to rest.

While Vicky was expending precious political capital on this cause, Sandro, unbeknownst to the imperial family, had lost interest in Moretta. After forfeiting the Bulgarian throne, he was refused a commission in the German Army; consequently without a job, he went to Darmstadt to live near the family that welcomed his presence. In the meantime, Moretta fell out of his thoughts, even though she continued to profess her love for him when writing from Berlin. In fact, while in Darmstadt, Sandro had met an opera singer named Johanna Loisinger with whom he had formed a romantic relationship that appeared to be leading toward marriage. Vicky should have known, or, at least, could have learned of it. She also should have realized that, with or without his father's sanction, Willy, when he all too soon would inherit the crown, would never approve of the marriage he had fought so hard against. Her son had let it be known unequivocally that for Moretta to marry Sandro would precipitate his sister's disinheritance from the imperial family.

Against all reason, Vicky stubbornly pressed the matter. Bismarck was furious when his new sovereign informed him that he was about to give Sandro not only a military command but the prestigious order called the *Pour le Mérite*—as well as his permission for the Battenberg prince to marry Moretta. The chancellor virtually ordered Fritz to rescind the latter decision, justifying his anger by insisting that such a marriage would dangerously threaten Germany's relationship with the tsar, who now loathed Sandro with a frightening intensity. Fritz submitted, in spite of a tearful scene played out by his wife.

As it happened, Bismarck's true reason for refusing to countenance the marriage had little to do with Russia and much to do with his relationship with Fritz's heir. He knew that Willy hated the idea of what he considered a low marriage between his sister and a Battenberg. So, to keep in his master-to-be's good graces, Bismarck simply continued to block the union and to make sure the new crown prince knew who had done him the favor. Vicky, almost mad with frustration over how her own and Fritz's lives had turned out, saw the issue as a make-or-break struggle with forces intent on destroying her husband's reign, family, and reputation. All she achieved was her eldest son's hatred—an enmity whose depth and ferociousness she would soon plumb for herself.

Bismarck trumped Vicky in the end over the matter. He finally told her that if she would agree to a postponement of the match, he himself would agree to the couple's eventual marriage, and would see to it as well that Moretta and her two younger sisters were provided with dowries from the vast estate of William I, money to which Fritz had not yet gained full access. Vicky assented, believing the arrangement would solve many problems. What she didn't know was that the chancellor had no intention of carrying out his promise, either in this reign or the next.

Meanwhile, Queen Victoria's sources in Darmstadt informed her of the opera singer's significance. She immediately wrote Vicky, urging that any thought of marriage between Moretta and Sandro be put out of her head unless she had the "perfect acquiescence" of Willy, warning her daughter that anything contravening the young heir's wishes would "never do," though she did not enlighten her daughter as to Sandro's relationship with Johanna Loisinger. Close to derangement over Fritz's failing health, desperate to do whatever was necessary to ensure Moretta's happiness, Vicky ignored the advice and continued to hope her mother would help influence the Germans eventually to allow the marriage, as Bismarck had promised.

Victoria decided to go to Berlin to see her dying son-in-law for what she fully expected would be a last visit. Bismarck didn't want her anywhere near the city—afraid of the British queen's influence over her daughter and Fritz, he threatened to resign if she came. Ignoring Bismarck's threats, which had been forwarded to her by her ambassador in Berlin, Victoria arrived on April 25 (the queen was returning to England after a holiday in Italy) accompanied by Beatrice and Liko. Vicky's hope was, of course, that her mother would demand that Moretta be allowed to marry Sandro. But Victoria now knew the time had passed for any such outcome, and she had no intention of allowing her own government and nation to be calumniated in Germany by openly advocating the union. When she did meet with Bismarck in a famous forty-five-minute confrontation at Charlottenburg the day after her arrival, the nervous chancellor expected to be badgered by the tiny but powerful monarch. Instead, he found a woman whose political acumen seemed to him to equal that of any king. She mentioned neither Moretta nor Sandro. She only asked that Bismarck "stand by poor Vicky." For her discretion and good judgment, the chancellor would call the queen a "jolly little body" with whom he could "do business."

When Victoria talked with her daughter about Moretta and Sandro, she convinced Vicky that the Battenberg marriage was impossible, and finally revealed the underlying reason why Moretta could not, even in the face of Willy's threats, marry Sandro: he simply no longer wanted to marry *her*. Had Moretta not been supplanted by a serious rival, Victoria might have ignored the political ramifications of the affair and come to her granddaughter's aid. But in the end, the odds were too heavily stacked against the match.

In the midst of the dismantling of Moretta's hopes, her brother Henry was married to their cousin Irene, the daughter of Princess Alice. Sadly, the wedding on May 24, 1888, at Charlottenburg Palace recalled much of the gloom a quarter century earlier when the bride's mother had married Louis in the dining room at Osborne. Though neither Sandro (Irene's uncle and cousin) nor his father, Prince Alexander of Hesse, were invited, the Battenberg family was represented by Irene's sister, Victoria, and Victoria's husband, Prince Louis of Battenberg. To honor Henry, Fritz was able with difficulty to get into one of his elaborate full-dress uniforms. Leaning heavily on a cane, he entered the palace chapel looking pale and thin, but otherwise dignified and in command of his faculties. Conservative critics sniped that the empress had only managed to get her husband through the ceremony by plying him with wine and stimulants, a view seemingly confirmed when after the service some of the guests saw Fritz being wheeled away in a chair. But his own determination, combined with the resolve not to upset his son's wedding, enabled him to endure throughout without once coughing, even though the horrible sound of air hissing through his cannula could not be hidden from the guests. Field Marshal von Moltke, once Fritz's chief military aide, said that though he had seen many brave men, "none [were as] brave as the Emperor has shown himself today." Few present realized that, a week before the wedding, Dr. Mackenzie had discovered conclusive evidence that their monarch's laryngeal cancer had spread to his lymph system glands, by which route it was now coursing through his body.

Shortly after the wedding, Fritz decided to move from Charlottenburg back to his beloved Neues Palais. He knew the end was almost upon him, and he wanted it to arrive in the place that was for him home. On June 1, he and Vicky boarded the royal steamer *Alexandra* to be carried along the Spree and the Havel and the superb lakes that connected them to Potsdam. The cruise ended at the palace they had both loved more than any other residence throughout their married life. The journey was to be Fritz's last.

Whatever potential strength he could summon at this time came down to the one substantive liberal act of his reign for which the emperor was to be personally responsible. Interior Minister Robert von Puttkamer was an arch-reactionary whom Fritz found particularly objectionable. The bureaucrat had recently ousted a number of Liberal officials from his ministry, and then further angered the emperor by blatantly gerrymandering Prussian electoral districts to help ensure the election of Conservative members. Fritz's potent imperial reprimand forced the minister's resignation. Unfortunately, the causes of the dismissal—Puttkamer's reactionary practices—were by no means themselves suppressed, an outcome that badly disappointed Liberals who had hoped for more from a new emperor supposedly sympathetic to their views.

Unbeknownst to Fritz, Bismarck had, ironically, both wanted and permitted Puttkamer's cashiering, to be rid of a man he trusted little and regarded as future trouble for himself. However, the chancellor made sure that the nation saw the affair as a liberally inspired act by the new emperor, and as such Fritz was vilified by the right wing. Bismarck even abetted the rumor that it had actually been the empress who was responsible for having forced her husband's hand. Two days after Puttkamer left office, the chancellor hosted a lavish soirée with the ousted minister as the guest of honor.[7] Despite the duplicity, both Fritz and Vicky regarded Puttkamer's removal as a moral victory, a small step toward political justice in Germany.

Though in the few months of her husband's reign Vicky was maligned nearly universally by the center-to-right component of the nation's press, as well as by the entire Conservative political establishment, the empress strove desperately to make her husband's last days at the Neues Palais as gentle and sweet as possible. Fritz had commanded that the palace's name be changed to *Friedrichskron* to mark forever its association with himself and his wife. These final two weeks in his beloved home were passed calmly, the splendor that had been created by Hohenzollern kings securely sheltering the tormented family. The vast royal park in what has rightly been called the Versailles of Germany reached its peak of beauty that early summer. Fritz's chamber had been specially chosen so he could step outside into the gardens on days when he had a little extra strength, or look out of the window to see the trees and flowers when he was too unwell to leave his bed. With every passing day, his agony ratcheted upward until he could barely endure the pain, and even those who considered themselves Vicky's enemies were starting to hope the gallant emperor would be delivered from his trial. For her, the time passed in a blur of fear and grief and fussing over her husband. "I feel so like a wreck," she wrote, "a sinking ship, so wounded and struck down, so sore of heart, as if I were bleeding from a thousand wounds. . . . Even my memory seems to fail me, and at times I can remember nothing but the pain."

Two days before Emperor Frederick's life ended, his chancellor paid a last visit to Friedrichskron. Vicky took Bismarck into her husband's ground-floor sickroom. The June sun was flooding the chamber in an unreachable reflection of the beauty outside. Too weak to do more than move his arms, Fritz gathered in his own hands those of his beloved wife and the man who had been his enemy for so many years. He pressed them together, and in so doing silently implored Bismarck with an unmistakable plea in his eyes to see to his empress's welfare when he was gone. The chancellor murmured, "I will take care of her." Vicky likely didn't believe the words. She saw no sadness or sympathy on the politician's face as he left the imperial presence, only a look telling her that Prince Bismarck had been the victor in the great struggle over Germany's future.

An hour before noon on June 15, 1888, Fritz died. He was fifty-six.[8] His reign had lasted ninety-nine days, hardly a blip in the militaristic history of the House of Hohenzollern. Willy and Dona, Charlotte and her husband, and Fritz's three youngest daughters were all on hand at the end, the crown prince having arrived only a few minutes before his father's last breath. Though Vicky would have given much to spend those last few moments with her husband alone, court protocol wouldn't permit such a normal human desire. All she could do was dip a sponge into a bowl of white wine and wet her husband's parched lips. Just before the end, Vicky asked Fritz if he was tired, his response the words "very, very" forming on his lips. He tried to write a last message—"Victoria, me, the children . . ."—but the pen fell from his failing fingers before he could complete it.

Immediately after his final breath, the drained Vicky went to a withered laurel crown hanging on the bedroom wall. She had given it to him seventeen years earlier as a symbol of victory on his return home from the war with France. The widow, now haggard and with hair turned noticeably grayer just in the last several weeks, placed it on his body. She fetched his cavalry saber and laid it beside the wreath. Then she knelt beside the bed and buried her face in the sheets still warm from her husband's body. She neither cried nor wailed, but only seemed stunned by what she had lost. For the dowager empress, a new and almost equally formidable trial was about to begin.

Within moments of Frederick III's death, the seeds Vicky had sown in her relationship with her son—now Emperor William II—began to uproot her already shattered life. Willy ordered a detachment of his own Hussars (in whose uniform he himself was dressed) to surround the palace, permitting no one to enter or leave the building that he had already resolved to return to its former name. Having gone into the garden to cut some roses to place on her dead husband's body, Vicky was shocked to see helmeted soldiers forming a cordon around what was clearly no longer her home. One of the officers came up to her and led her back into the house, explaining he was only acting on his master's orders.

Soldiers had already begun ransacking the palace, searching for any of Fritz's and Vicky's papers they could lay hands on, though they wouldn't likely have been able to differentiate between a treaty and a laundry list. An officer ripped open Frederick III's desk drawers, strewing papers all over the study. Willy himself looted his mother's room in his desperate search for evidence to incriminate his parents. Fortunately, the most private and personal of Fritz's papers had already been safely removed to Windsor, having been taken when the couple went to England for the Jubilee; the remainder were just sent the day before via the British ambassador in Berlin. Willy soon discovered this, which increased his fury at the mother he had so long scorned. Nonetheless, a general officer made a second rifling through Fritz's desk, positive there was a secret drawer that would contain certain proof of the late emperor's collusion in "liberal plots" or God knows what mischief. The raid turned up no state secrets, only personal correspondence whose contents undoubtedly told unpleasant things about Willy's own behavior over many years.

Compared to the golden panoply of William I's funeral three months earlier, the service for Fritz seemed almost an afterthought in its lack of ceremony. Having specifically commanded that his own body not lie in state, Fritz was taken to the palace's Jasper Salon. Though Willy knew his mother was adamantly opposed to an autopsy, he had ordered one performed anyway, as though there might have been some question as to what killed the emperor. Fritz's three youngest daughters were allowed a last look at their father's face. Vicky then gazed at her beloved husband for long minutes, after which the coffin lid was screwed down. Though she did not attend the funeral—Vicky couldn't bear the prying eyes of the public, and left the palace the night before the services—she saw to it that Fritz's coffin was, as he had wished, placed next to Waldy's in the small mausoleum in the palace grounds. In her diary entry of June 15, the day her husband died, Vicky wondered, "why does pain not kill immediately?"

The principal joy of Queen Victoria's existence had meanwhile become the young family that Beatrice and Liko had brought into her homes. Following Alexander's birth in 1886, Beatrice had had another child, this time a girl, born on October 24, 1887. Beatrice was at Balmoral when she gave birth to Victoria, thus making her the first royal child to be born in Scotland in almost three hundred years. Victoria Eugenia Julia Ena would for the rest of her long and extraordinarily eventful life be known simply as Ena, from the ancient Gaelic, bestowed in honor of her birthplace.[9]

The two children were, for their English grandmother, a gift of enormous significance. Though they chased through the palaces like little steam engines, often accompanied by one or more posses of available cousins, the queen ignored their lack of discipline, behavior that had been so rigorously proscribed for her own children. The "Battenberg kids"—the not very deferential designation given them by her household and staff—were allowed to storm in on the sovereign in circumstances always before held rigorously off-limits to young and spirited voices. She was even contented that she no longer commanded first priority over Beatrice's time, realizing that her grandchildren's needs ranked highest with their mother. Perhaps Victoria had simply grown heartily sick of the funereal regime she herself had decreed in what she considered respect to the prince consort's memory. Whatever the reason, for the first time since almost anyone could remember, the head of the family actually seemed happy.

Beatrice, slow where Vicky was brilliant and simple where her eldest sister was complex, inhabited her own limited but peaceful plane with a sense of well-being. She had her beautiful husband, two beautiful children, and an undisturbed life in beautiful palaces. Her work was reading to her mother, or transcribing personal family correspondence, or taking little messages to her mother's servants—a generic class ranging from prime ministers to scullery maids, and all pretty much of a single genus to the British monarch.

Beatrice found herself the recipient of much national admiration for the devotion she showed her mother. Victoria's own popularity had in recent years been on a steep rise now that she showed herself far more often; and her always-at-hand youngest daughter (usually with Liko at her side) was becoming a demisymbol of a reinvigorated monarchy. Women's magazines took to portraying Beatrice as the perfect mother, her little family giving the queen happiness the older woman apparently hadn't know for years, her husband graciously fulfilling the role of steadfast consort to the princess and esquire to his august mother-in-law. Beatrice's domestic interests became grist for the press, and songwriters wrote songs with the princess as their inspiration: the fetching "Beatrice Waltz," a bridal march named after her; and a toe-tapper called "The Royal British Rose Bud." Most appreciated by the queen was the fact that not so much as the merest breath of scandal had ever been attached to her youngest daughter's name.

Beatrice shone with particular luster during the year-long Jubilee celebrations. Though only sixty-eight at the time, Queen Victoria's stamina was sharply limited by the fact that her physical exertions had long consisted in the main of talking and writing, with only a modicum of very slow walking to tone badly underused muscles. Thus it was Beatrice's job to see that the many celebrations, and especially the events of Jubilee Day itself, were paced so as not to overtax the sovereign. Because of unalterable protocol, Beatrice had to be placed in her usual low order of precedence, which meant below her siblings and siblings-in-law. But ways were craftily found to keep her close at hand to Victoria. In the state drive from Buckingham Palace, the queen rode with Vicky and Alix, but Beatrice was just behind with Lenchen and Louise and Affie's wife. When they finally returned home from the abbey, Beatrice got her nearly fainting mother up to her room for a rest before they both had to face the state dinner that evening.

Worry over Fritz's decline had weighed on the days following the Jubilee. When they were at Osborne or Balmoral, Beatrice did all that she could to help Vicky keep the stricken emperor as comfortable as possible. Beatrice was expecting Ena during that summer, and the absurd corsets that even pregnant women of her class were supposed to wear often caused her to feel faint herself. Ena's birth at Balmoral in October was especially difficult for the princess, though the news that it made the estate tenants wildly happy seemed to lift her tired spirits.

Queen Victoria was desolated by the loss of her son-in-law. Though there had been unpleasant spots in their relationship—most especially Fritz's animosity toward the Battenbergs—over the long run theirs had been an enormously loving and mutually supportive association. On the day Fritz died, she wrote to her daughter that he "was so kind to me always. . . . I see him always before me with those beautiful, loving blue eyes." Most of all, Victoria had been deeply grateful for the gentle kindness and sympathy her son-in-law had shown when Albert died, and always remembered it when some nettlesome act on Fritz's part threatened rancor between the two.

In the same year of Fritz's passing, Liko also endured a family loss. His father, Prince Alexander of Hesse, died on December 15, 1888. When Alexander's approaching death was obvious, Beatrice went through terrors that her father-in-law would die on the Terrible Fourteenth, a repeat of the day on which not only her own father but also her sister Alice had died. That Alexander lived until the 15th provided psychic comfort for Beatrice, though it is unlikely to have much eased Liko's grief. After the funeral in Darmstadt, the Battenbergs returned to Osborne, the traditional Christmas haven for the family. There Vicky joined the saddened gathering, a great consolation for her that she didn't have to spend her first Christmas without Fritz anywhere near Willy and Dona. At New Year's 1889, the queen honored Liko by appointing him governor and captain general of the Isle of Wight as well as governor of Carisbrooke Castle, the island's preeminent historic site.

In May 1889, Beatrice and Liko had their third child, a second son whom they named Leopold, for Beatrice's brother. The name was tragically appropriate. Unknown to anyone, Beatrice was, like her sister Alice, a carrier of the hemophilia gene, and it was with this son that it became evident. Because Louise had been the closest of all the sisters to Leopold, Beatrice asked her to stand as godmother at the baby's christening.

Beatrice spent part of 1890 working on a project for herself rather than for her mother, a translation into English of Emil Kraus's *The Adventures of Count George Albert of Erbach;* the book was published later that year. After her thirty-third birthday, spent in Aix-les-Bains, she and Liko and her mother passed through Darmstadt to visit their Hesse relations. Willy and Dona were in the area and stopped for the reunion. Beatrice was worried that her nephew might snub Liko, since his comments on her husband's parentage when they married had bordered on the obscene. But the new emperor remained on his best behavior, and though he privately thought the attribute of royal highness given Liko by Queen Victoria was ridiculous, there was at least nothing less than outward cordiality between the two men.

Ready to deliver her fourth (and last) child by the autumn of 1891, Beatrice went to Balmoral, producing another Scottish birth in the family. As with Ena's birth, the arrival of the new Prince Maurice of Battenberg, Victoria's fortieth (and last) grandchild, was the occasion for widespread rejoicing in Scotland, the Scots feeling closer to the throne by virtue of a second royal birth in their kingdom. Sadly, Maurice too inherited hemophilia.

With four grandchildren living under her own roof, Victoria's metamorphosis from sour and reclusive widow into happy and contented materfamilias reached its conclusion. At seventy-two, the monarch was still young enough to cavort with the youngsters she loved best of any in the world, not yet the almost immobile invalid she would become in the later 1890s. Staff and servants saw extraordinary sights: the queen making handkerchief mice, which she would move up and down her body, while the young Battenbergs screamed in delight at the old lady everybody else had to treat like a diety; "Gangan" surrounded by the children at breakfast, or at tea, where her favorite golden table implements bewitched the young eyes. The sovereign proudly looked on as Beatrice's children played with their Connaught cousins, Arthur's offspring, who spent nearly as much time with their grandmother as did Beatrice's tribe. With the nurseries directly overhead from her own rooms in all of her residences, even when the children were out of sight they could often be heard banging around on wooden floors, a disturbance that once would have been unimaginable. The only real brake on the royal youngsters' existence was the special care that had to be accorded the two younger boys for their hemophilia.

The darkening cloud over this idyllic existence was Liko's lack of anything to do. Watching as his elder brother Louis rose steadily in the Royal Navy must have galled a still-young man who had once enjoyed his own budding career in the German Army. He spent more time with his children than his wife did, the latter busy most of the day with her mother and not particularly maternal in any case. Like his late father-in-law, Liko assumed responsibility for his children's education, supervising their classroom as each left the nursery to go under the teaching of, first, nannies, and later, full-fledged professional tutors. On a few occasions each year, he managed to get away on sailing holidays, his mother-in-law not objecting in deference to what she realized was a trying situation for any man. Indeed, the stresses caused by a busily employed wife and a prominently unbusy husband were leading Beatrice's marriage to start to fray around the edges.

Lenchen's marriage, meanwhile, showed every sign of progressing smoothly along the path it had taken since 1866. Prince Christian didn't appear to be burdened by any of the wanderlust or sense of nonproductivity beginning to bedevil Liko. He was perfectly happy to putter in his garden or answer his mother-in-law's call to come read to her or work on whatever it was he worked on in his capacity as governor of Windsor Castle. The Christians' relationship reflected the placidity, if not the passion, that had for so long characterized Vicky's union with her beloved Fritz.

Just after Christmas 1891, Christian went out for a day's shooting with the duke of Connaught. Possibly having confused his white-bearded brother-in-law for a low-flying waterfowl, Arthur lost control of his aim and shot out one of Christian's eyes, damaging the other. The queen's eye specialist, Dr. George Lawson, decided that the worse-injured eye was beyond saving, and therefore enucleated the damaged orb. Queen Victoria's permission to operate had to be obtained, so Dr. James Reid went to tell her what had happened. The sovereign was provoked at the thought of her son-in-law not having both eyeballs in his head, and told Reid she didn't see why such a procedure was necessary, implying, according to Reid, that Lawson "wished to do it for our own brutal pleasure."

Christian made the best of the wreckage. The prince gradually collected an impressive assortment of artificial glass eyeballs, done up in a variety of tints. The effect of occasionally mismatched eyes must have made for startled guests at the Christians' home. An artfully "bloodshot" model was used for days when he was feeling a little worse for wear from the prior evening's entertainment.

In 1888, Moretta threatened to kill herself when she couldn't marry Sandro, but learning of the Darmstadt opera singer later stunned her back into her right mind—there were, after all, worse fates than being an on-the-market princess. She finally met and chose Prince Adolf of Schaumburg-Lippe, of whom everyone approved, especially Willy and Bismarck. The whole Schleswig-Holstein family gathered in Berlin in 1890 for the marriage.

It was at Moretta's wedding in Berlin's Royal Palace that the Christians' younger daughter, Marie Louise, met a tall and handsome—if somewhat saturnine—prince from the fairytale principality of Anhalt-Dessau, located deep in the Harz Mountains, whose capital was the fairytale town of Dessau. The prince's name was Aribert, he was a cavalry officer in the army, and Marie Louise found him charming. She was instantly smitten. According to her recollection of the evening, "he paid me a good deal of attention which both flattered and bewildered me."

During the time Marie Louise was first beholding Aribert, her cousin Willy—now emperor and host of the gathering—came round to the rooms where her family were staying, to look in and see that their comforts were being attended to. On one such pop-in, he told his aunt Lenchen that Prince Ferdinand of Romania would shortly come to Berlin for a semistate visit, and while there, the none-too-appealing prince planned to propose marriage to her daughter—the same Marie Louise who had just been so dazzled by young Aribert. He had evidently spotted the princess on one of her endless perambulations around the Continent's spas and thought she looked like a suitable future queen for the Romanians. But Marie was, in her words, already *"sous le charme"* of Aribert, and wanted nothing to do with Ferdinand. The princess bluntly told her mother, "No, nothing doing" (her exact words), and the princess duly became engaged to Aribert. Ferdinand would later marry another of her cousins, Marie of Edinburgh, who would one day play the exotic role of Queen Marie of Romania to an admiring world.

Aribert took his bride-to-be to Dessau, where she was shown around the charming but sleepy little town like a war trophy. She took to Aribert's mother, and thought her fiancé's father a "dear, kindly, but not very intelligent old gentleman"; the old man did, however, own thirty-six castles in the tiny duchy.

The Anhalt family was brought over to the bride's home at Cumberland Lodge for the wedding. Willy and Dona came too, the emperor interested in anyone marrying into one of the toy German courts under Hohenzollern dominion. Queen Victoria dominated the proceedings, as she was prone to do at any family gathering she chose to grace with her presence.

Part of the honeymoon was spent in Bayreuth, where Cosima Wagner, widow of the famous composer, took a shine to the new Princess Aribert. Marie Louise herself later wrote that she didn't really understand Frau Wagner's interest in her, though it might have been connected to the fact that the young bride was a granddaughter of Queen Victoria. As it happened, the two women grew close, Frau Wagner often traveling to Dessau to grace its little opera house, Marie Louise grateful to the older woman for helping further her musical education.

The bride found life in Dessau virtually medieval, at least as compared with how things had been done in England. Given her own apartments at the top of the picturesque town castle, Marie Louise soon discovered that etiquette in Anhalt made Windsor's rules seem almost lax. Even if she wanted to bid a good morning to her sister-in-law, who lived at the other end of the corridor, Marie Louise was forced to send a footman to inquire whether it would be convenient to come by with her greetings. The princess was allowed to go nowhere alone in the town, not even to her other sister-in-law's home, a walk of only a few minutes. Instead, she was required to order a carriage and be guarded by a proper lady-in-waiting. Dinnertime was at 4:00 P.M., and the meal generally centered on an enormous bowl of cold meat that was cut up into thick slices. Ladies drank tea, gentlemen beer.

Fortunately for Marie Louise, she and her husband would not actually live full time in any of Dessau's thirty-six schlosses. Aribert maintained a home in Berlin on the Tempelhofer Ufer, whence the prince could go off daily to attend to his military duties in the Germany Army. He served in the First Dragoon Guards, of which his wife's grandmother stood as colonel in chief, the sort of honorary position military contingents offered to royal ladies, even, as in this case, *foreign* royal ladies. But Marie Louise was merely the wife of a lowly major, and as such often found herself entertaining at tea other wives she would never have met as a royal princess.

One of the pleasures of her life in Berlin was nearness to her aunt Vicky, who since Fritz's death styled herself Empress Frederick. Though Vicky totally adopted the panoply of upper-class mourning symbols for the rest of her life, including black dresses and a widow's cap, her social recovery had far outpaced that of her mother upon the prince consort's death. At her Berlin home, Vicky established a cultural salon that attracted the most distinguished and talented men not only from Germany but from all of Europe.

Such behavior, however, tended to confirm negative family attitudes toward her: for a member of the Hohenzollern family to invite artists, writers, and professors to her home was horrifying to many of Fritz's relatives and Willy's courtiers, and further evidence to them of her despicable Englishness.

But for Marie Louise, the chance to exercise her mind at her aunt's palace in Unter den Linden came as a godsend. Her union with Aribert had quickly proven a sham. For Aribert, the marriage had been strictly one of convenience; from the time the couple settled in Berlin, it was clear even to a princess who had been closely sheltered that her husband had no physical interest whatever in her. In her memoirs, she wrote that "as time went on, I became increasingly aware that my husband and I were drifting farther and farther apart. I had no share in his life. . . ." Meeting only at meals, and then but rarely, the two could pass many days without seeing each other at all. The deeply depressed Marie Louise had to get away. Her brother Christian had just been killed in the Boer War, and she decided she had to escape her life with Aribert, at least temporarily. In 1900, without her husband's permission, she went off on a trip to the United States and Canada, evidently in hopes she might somehow collect the strength to go on with her existence in Germany.

After a private visit with President McKinley at the White House (these things were normal for royal persons), Marie Louise went on to Canada to stay with Lord and Lady Minto, successors to her aunt Louise and uncle Lorne at Rideau Hall in Ottawa. In the last stages of preparing for a trip across the continent—her bags had already been put aboard the train—she found Lord Minto at her door with a cable from her father-in-law in Germany. The message peremptorily ordered her to return to Anhalt immediately. An hour later, Lord Minto again came to her room, this time with a cable from London. This second telegram was from her grandmother: "Tell my granddaughter to come home to me. V.R."

Marie Louise returned home—not to her husband's home, but Cumberland Lodge at Windsor. There the reasons for the two summonses were revealed. A letter from Prince Aribert to Prince Christian was shown to the princess, who couldn't have been entirely surprised at its contents. Aribert wrote, in effect, that his wife had deserted her marital duties, and he therefore demanded that the marriage be proclaimed null and void, as if it had never been contracted, never mind the nine years they had been married. Since his father represented the supreme law in Anhalt, his father could so order, bringing among other scurrilous charges the justification that his daughter-in-law hadn't presented his son with children, evidently ipso facto proof in Anhalt of a marriage's invalidity.

Though deeply wounded by the episode, for the rest of her life Marie Louise would always consider herself a married woman. The immediate cause of her in-laws' disgraceful conduct was that Aribert had been caught with another man, which his wife was evidently not apprised of at the time. Both sets of parents knew, however. Aribert's father acted shamefully in placing blame for the marriage's failure on his daughter-in-law; the Christians acquiesced to avoid their daughter's being caught up in what at the time would have been a monumental scandal. As for the injured party, Marie Louise eventually settled down with her unmarried sister, Helena Victoria, with whom she spent the last long years of her life in perfect contentment. Marie Louise would be the only one of the Christians' four children to marry.

While her daughter was undergoing the ordeal of an unhappy and artificial marriage, Lenchen herself was in the grip of a drug habit that was threatening to destroy her health. Claiming unspecified illness, Dr. Reid, the queen's physician, diagnosed the princess with "imaginary ailments"—probably meaning psychological problems—and in keeping with the practices of the day prescribed laudanum and opium. The first drug was an alcoholic tincture of opium, which is to say a relatively small amount of opium dissolved in pure alcohol. Prescribing it freely and perfectly legally for a wide range of ailments, contemporary medicine was unaware it could cause disabling dependency. The effect on Lenchen was, according to Reid's understatement, "rather queer."

By 1894, her daughter's behavior was beginning to cause the

queen "grave concern." Prince Christian begged Dr. Reid to try somehow to get his wife to break off her use of laudanum and opium. In consequence, when the princess demanded that Reid supply her with more, he decided the best course was to cut her off, cold turkey, so to speak. For awhile Lenchen complained about having become "almost blind," but Reid told her her eyes were perfectly all right and whatever complaints she had were the result of nerves "shattered" by the misused drugs. The physician gave her a spirit lotion to rub into her eyes, which was nothing more than a placebo to tide her over until the laudanum cravings disappeared on their own accord. As it happened, Lenchen grew inordinately fond of the spirit lotion and got some for her mother to use on holidays.

10

End of an Era

Upon returning to Britain, Louise and Lorne found the familiar and cozy world of the Campbell clan conspicuously changed. During their absence in Canada, Lorne's widowered father had taken a second wife. "One of the pleasantest people in the wide world is the little Mrs. Anson," was how Lorne's sister Mary had described her in a letter to Rideau Hall. But a new chatelaine having taken his beloved mother's place at Inveraray Castle was an unpleasant—and untenable—shock to the duke's heir.

"Little Mrs. Anson" was not some Scottish farmer's wife, despite the sentiment the family appellative implied. A niece of the earl of Dudley and daughter of the bishop of St. Alban's, Amelia—"Mimi"—Anson came from the same rarefied world as her new husband, but was twenty three years younger than the fifty-eight-year-old duke on their marriage, and only a year older than Lorne. Since the first duchess's death and his eldest son's absence in North America, Lorne's father had been badly stricken with loneliness, and the charming Mrs. Anson's entry into his life in 1881 had proven a tonic to his spirits. But as future lord of the Argyll patriarchy, Lorne considered the memory of his mother virtually sacred

271

and his father's remarriage a betrayal of that memory. Louise agreed that her father-in-law's remarriage only three years after Duchess Elizabeth's death was troublesome—she too had been genuinely fond of Lorne's mother—but was stunned at her husband's startling vow that he would never again return to his family's homes.

Louise made a pointed effort to get to know her new mother-in-law, and soon found Duchess Mimi a charming woman, much deserving of the great marriage she had entered into. Using the powers of gentle persuasion, Louise was eventually successful in bringing her husband to accept another woman in his father's life, even if the oddly unbending Lorne continued to regard the second duchess as an unworthy replacement for his dead mother.

Since Louise and her husband were uncomfortable using Argyll Lodge now that the reigning duchess was no longer Lorne's own mother, Kensington Palace was their only immediate option as a London residence. Getting its apartments back into shape was the princess's first objective in her early days back from Canada. She was eager to remodel the sumptuous rooms—which had been closed up for nearly five years—to make them fit again for occupation.

The couple's return to London did little to ease the strains plaguing their marriage. Now often depressed, Louise didn't even seek the company of her family to alleviate her cheerlessness. Lorne at least was preoccupied with his hopes of gaining another office, specifically one of the great imperial prizes Victorian Britain bestowed on its titled grandees. Both the lord lieutenantship of Ireland and the viceroyalty of India came vacant in the mid-1880s, and he considered himself a prime candidate for either post, preferably the latter: in India he would be virtual emperor over hundreds of millions of his mother-in-law's subjects.

Lorne had been such a near-unqualified success as governor general in the limited role his position had demanded that for the rest of his life he would be asked to serve as a spokesman in Britain for Canada's interests. George Stephens, president of the Canadian Pacific Railway, hailed him as "a good and true Canadian," a description that found few dissenters. Now with copious time on his hands,

Lorne turned to producing a body of literary work on his adopted nation, books that achieved high critical success on both sides of the Atlantic. His *Canadian Pictures*, written as a kind of guide for British emigrants to North America, was, together with Lady Dufferin's memoirs, the most popular travel volume on Canada published before World War I.

Still, an appointment to Dublin proved politically impossible for the government, even with the prince of Wales's enthusiastic backing. One difficulty was that during Lorne's tenure in Ottawa, the Canadian Parliament had passed resolutions calling for Irish Home Rule, or limited local government; and, despite Lorne's own well-known views opposing Home Rule, Whitehall held that Lorne's association with the resolutions disqualified him as overlord in its most contentious dependency. Lorne believed that what progress Ireland had made in its rocky road to the late nineteenth century, it had achieved only because of Britain's patronage and occupation of the island. Thousands of Britons agreed, believing that Home Rule would inevitably lead to Irish independence and thus the breakup of the United Kingdom. The concept of dominion status for Ireland—in which the Irish would see to their internal affairs through their own separate parliament while Britain remained responsible for their foreign affairs—was for the United Kingdom a matter of overriding national public interest. Even in the Lorne family, a deep rift existed over the issue: where Lorne opposed Home Rule, Louise endorsed it, believing the "Other Place," as Ireland was often called, should be treated more like the semi-independent Canada. Furthermore, Lorne's father had quit his ministerial post over an Irish issue on which he could not agree with the government, making any Campbell a politically shaky choice for Dublin. A final consideration was that the post required a rich man, which Lorne would not be until he succeeded to his father's title: maintaining the degree of pomp required in the empire's most visible pro-consular posts generally involved expenditures that barred all but the richest from being considered for them.

In the end, it was probably Queen Victoria who conclusively vetoed Ireland for her son-in-law. The monarch simply could not allow her daughter to be placed in Fenian danger, a risk that would have stalked Louise every minute of her life in Dublin. And it would not have been possible for Lorne to go without his wife; after the Canadian separations, such a scenario would have been scandalous. Though his mother-in-law continued to try pressing a new peerage on Lorne, Lorne (and, more to the point, his father) continued to refuse such a gift, holding out for the day when he himself would be duke of Argyll. In justice to Lorne, his father didn't then seem as hardy as he would in fact turn out to be.

Meanwhile, the viceroyalty in Calcutta—the most glittering imperial jewel of all—also beckoned. Lord Granville, the foreign minister, believed that to have the empress of India's daughter sitting beside the viceroy would be almost like having an empress in India—"an immense effect," he characterized it. But Gladstone considered there were men better fitted for the subcontinent, and decided upon Lord Dufferin, Lorne's predecessor in Ottawa. Queen Victoria had also legislated against Lorne on the same grounds as Dublin: she wanted Louise at home and out of harm's way, and she didn't want to risk the embarrassment of her son-in-law going without his wife. (Had Gladstone been determined on Lorne, he would, of course, have received the post, regardless of Victoria's wishes.) In the end, all the prime minister would offer was the largely ceremonial job of Lord High Commissioner to the General Assembly of the Church of Scotland, which Lorne declined in his resolve to keep clear of Scottish political policies, particularly his own controversial support for Scotland's disestablishment.

Lorne sought work for himself by running for the Commons. But instead of trying to regain Argyllshire, the constituency he had held before Ottawa (and the seat his brother Colin had contested and won when the Lornes left for Canada), he ran as a Liberal from Hampstead. To his embarrassment, he was decisively defeated by the Conservative candidate in what was a national sweep against Gladstone and his Irish policy, and found himself still unemployed. Since Gladstone had sponsored the extraordinarily controversial issue of Home Rule for Ireland, the imperially minded marquess decided to leave the Liberal Party to help form the Liberal Unionists, a party whose whole being was founded on opposition to Gladstone's Irish proposal.

The family misfortune of Leopold's sudden death in March 1884 came at the time when Lorne's political future was being juggled between the monarch, the prime minister, and the voters. The news of her brother was broken to Louise by Lorne, and the princess immediately left for Windsor. She and her mother soon joined Leopold's wife at nearby Claremont where, fortuitously preoccupied by pregnancy, the duchess got through her loss without the sort of nervous breakdown to which royal widows were almost expected to give themselves over. For Louise, who described Leopold as "the joy and object of a lifetime," the death was one of the most painful tragedies of her life.[1] Months after her brother's death she still hadn't gotten past the shock, and friends remarked on how sallow her face seemed. The added bitterness of seeing Leo's wife already mother of one child and expecting a second jolted the thirty-six-year-old princess into increased absorption with her own childlessness. Sadder yet, Leopold had been a confidant of Lorne as well as of Louise. On his death, the couple lost an important mutual connection, a brother and brother-in-law whose company would be cruelly missed by both as one of the strongest bits of glue holding their marriage together.

The thirteen years of her life with Lorne now began to seem to Louise a hopeless waste, the relationship irreparably frayed beyond its early dreams of shared destiny. Physical love had gone, and without children as a bond, even her sense of allegiance for a man she had once respected enormously was ebbing away. Divorce was not a possibility, even if Louise had wished it; neither was formal separation a realistic option for her as both the queen's daughter and the duke of Argyll's daughter-in-law. Like many couples of their era and class, their one course was to maintain the facade of a marriage, living under the same roof in their palatial suite of apartments at Kensington Palace and joining each other at just enough social occasions to keep tongues stilled (though by the mid-1870s, Louise had been spending increasing amounts of time alone at the palace while Lorne took care of estate affairs at Inveraray). The state of their marriage had not yet gone so far beyond amicable under-standing that they couldn't at least live as close friends. Lorne still professed his own kind of love for Louise, an affection surely con-sisting of at least respect and shared memories. Louise herself never hated her husband and probably did not even dislike him. Instead, she had simply lost any truly deep feeling for him as the years passed, a loss that produced understandable sexual frustration for her. What was needed to make their relationship workable was some kind of occupation for Lorne as he awaited his eventual hereditary advancement.

But a "suitable" position was not to be found. A governorship of New South Wales was proffered, but represented, in Lorne's view, a demotion from Ottawa; what was more, Louise refused to go to Australia, then thought about as far away as we consider the moon today. When the ambassadorship in Berlin became open, a brief pro-Lorne lobby sprang up; but after the queen heard from Vicky on the suggestion, she quickly put an end to any speculation that her son-in-law could serve in a country of which his sister-in-law was a very controversial crown princess.

Louise's depression deepened; even her long-standing interests in the arts and artists—and extensive public duties, which she carried out in spite of her dislike of being stared at—didn't suffice to take her mind off her frustrations. Additional worries from the Campbell side of the family distressed both the Lornes. His youngest brother—Colin, the successor to his old seat in the House of Commons—had made a mess of a low marriage and become the hub of a scandalous divorce proceeding, involving his wife's charges of venereal disease and adultery, and his own counteroffensive of claims of noncon-summation and adultery. It was not an edifying state of affairs, es-pecially with the family's royal connection at hazard. Colin's behavior was, in fact, so dreadful that the otherwise quick-to-for-give princess never received her brother-in-law again.

During the Jubilee celebrations in 1887, Louise finally managed to bring her expert skills in sculpture to national prominence. As a tribute to their queen, the women of Kensington Borough commis-sioned the princess to create a statue of her mother to stand in the public park fronting Kensington Palace. Carved in the studio in her walled garden, and destined to be placed at the head of the Broad Walk, the piece was completed in 1893 after six years in the making. For its unveiling, Victoria came with Beatrice and Liko. Once the sun had reemerged after a violent downpour, she gave from her carriage what was described as a "very nice address," pointing out that the new statue had been "so admirably designed and executed by my daughter." The white Carrara marble tribute became an enormously popular success, a seated representation of the nineteen-year-old queen in her coronation robes, her right hand holding a scepter over the vista down the greensward. It was the first public monument in London to have been sculpted by a woman.

Lorne was, alas, often still at loose ends compared with his wife. His books on Canada had been his one great burst of creativity, but when the spirit fled he took a long time to find something to replace it. Gallingly, he was usually seen as an adjunct to Louise on her busy schedule of appearances representing her mother. His topple from high position as one of the nation's pro-consuls to a sort of consort-in-waiting caused Louise at least as much pain as it did him. Distancing herself from Lorne's lack of ambition and diminished performance, she began to look outside marriage for her own fulfillment.

The single most important human element in her life remained her mother, whose vastly increased popularity with the British public after the Jubilee had rubbed off on most of the family. The queen expected her daughter to come to her every Christmas, an expectation Louise unhesitatingly obeyed; if Lorne wished to be at Inveraray during one of these periods, he went without his wife, his presence little missed by Victoria's other children, who in any event continued to regard the Scotsman as somehow alien. Louise passed lengthy periods at Windsor, Osborne, and Balmoral, where her sharp wit and native intelligence were regarded by the queen's household as fresh air injected into the stuffy interstices of court life. For her part, Louise kept current on the national and imperial political affairs as well as the cultural life of the era. Though most conversation at court—especially that from ladies—was restricted to weather, food, and children, Louise was always expected to break this mold. And she generally did, to her mother's frequent annoyance and her mother's courtiers' more frequent delight.

Sometimes Louise carried her enthusiasms too far, doing her reputation with the household officers more harm than good. Her attempts at political involvement occasionally ended in embarrassment: one time she inappropriately lobbied for the recall of a supposedly disagreeable British consul general in Zanzibar, based on the counsel of a single member of her husband's former staff in Ottawa. As her restlessness over her life with Lorne increased, Louise's tongue began to wag unbecomingly, leading to a reputation for spitefulness among some in her family and the court.

Concerned with her son-in-law's continued lack of employment, Victoria had offered Lorne a small bone when, in 1892, she appointed him governor and constable of Windsor Castle, a sinecure involving little real work, but one that Lorne would magnify by writing a history of what is generally acknowledged to be the seat of the British monarchy. The queen had tacitly admitted the ceremonial nature of the post by telling Lorne that "the slight duties can I am sure be made of more importance even than they are now." Ceremonial or not, the post paid about £12,000 a year—a sum one newspaper described as "given for doing nothing whatever." When Lorne was unsuccessful later that year in another run for Parliament, the queen again stepped in by making him a privy councillor. The Campbell family was itself honored by the sovereign with the conferring of a United Kingdom dukedom on Lorne's father, allowing the old Scot to sit in the House of Lords as a duke instead of by his former highest U.K. title as Baron Sundridge.

In the mid-nineties, Louise became involved in a family feud that created a division between herself and Beatrice. According to Dr. James Reid, who recounted the incident in his diaries, Beatrice's husband had initiated some kind of advances toward Louise, which the latter said she rebuffed. Some sources argue that Louise was the aggressive party in what couldn't have been more than a trifle in the psychologically overheated atmosphere that characterized Victoria's homes.

Whatever the full extent of Liko and Louise's feelings toward each other, the relationship was important to the princess, who wrote that he was "almost the greatest friend I had. . . ." The fact was that both Louise and Liko sometimes found themselves bored witless in serving attendance on the queen, and the pair discovered in each other a quality that helped them get through the monotonous days and immaculate nights of Victoria's court.

But the trifle turned to tragedy when Liko decided he couldn't stand his aimless life any more as it was. He talked his mother-in-law into letting him go off to Africa to participate in the Ashanti expedition, wherein Britain tried to get an African ruler to give up his traffic in slaves and predilection to cannibalism. By ill luck, Liko came down with a nasty jungle fever, and was sent back to England to recover. He died on the way home. The ship's captain had the prince's body put into a barrel of rum to keep it intact for the remainder of the voyage (Liko's intestines were removed and put overboard).

Now Louise's friendship with him apparently produced real wounds. Probably no family row would have occurred if she hadn't let her mouth get ahead of her brain when Liko's death was reported while the family was at Osborne. Sadly, his overwrought sister-in-law let his equally overwrought wife know that she was Liko's "confidante & Beatrice nothing to him." It was a stupid and careless thing for one sister to tell another under the circumstances and, understandably, for a time it badly strained relations between Louise and Beatrice. The latter was mollified when her sister began work on the altar screen that Queen Victoria commissioned in Liko's memory for Whippingham Chapel. Obviously sorry for having hurt Beatrice, Louise joined her younger sister in France, where the widow had gone to mourn away from her mother's overpowering presence.

Meanwhile, Lorne still had no luck getting back into the House of Commons, and decided instead to concentrate on what he *could* do, which was to write. Magazine articles had proved their usefulness by keeping his name before the literate public. Although his first big book after the Canada series of the late 1870s, his biography of Lord Palmerston, published in 1892 to tepid critical acclaim, earned a respectable commercial status. By virtue of his appointment to that eponymous position, Lorne published *The Governor's Guide to Windsor Castle*, which he himself illustrated and which sold well. Novels and works of nonfiction, most today completely unknown, followed these two books. Their primary utility seemed to have been to fill his days and allow his wife to fill hers alone.

Through sheer persistence, Lorne finally regained a seat in the House of Commons in the July 1895 elections, becoming the member for South Manchester. When he came to understand that his literary talents weren't going to pay many bills or dazzle many critics, his writing took a U-turn in 1897 and he put together an opera. *Diarmid* was staged at Covent Garden, Lorne's lyrics accompanied by Hamish MacCunn's music. A few performances in London were followed by a few more in the provinces, and climaxed in a staging before Queen Victoria in Balmoral—after which the opera disappeared.

Weakened by asthma attacks, Lorne's stepmother, Duchess Mimi, had died in 1894 after having slowly gained acceptance in the Campbell family. The family sanguinely expected the septuagenarian widower to end his days in the company of his children— and wifeless. But the duke had different ideas. Shortly after Mimi's death, Argyll took a third wife, the former Ina McNeill, a one-time member of Queen Victoria's household staff who had served as an Extra Woman of the Bedchamber and reader to the queen. The dislike the entire Campbell family felt for her was fully reciprocated by Duchess Ina, who ran what the family came to call the "Court of St. Ina." Louise carefully kept her distance from her third mother-in-law. At this time, Lorne virtually severed all ties with his father in disgust at what he considered a *really* unforgivable affront to the memory of his own mother.

The Lornes no longer even visited Inveraray because of the new duchess's overbearing presence. Instead, they took possession of another residence, a Highland palace where they would work out a kind of marital serenity they hadn't known since the years before Canada. Rosneath Castle had been a subsidiary Campbell home since the sixth duke built it, and was especially beloved by Lorne's father; it was to this romantic Italianate chateau that the duke brought his new bride on their honeymoon in the 1840s. The place had been empty or rented since Duchess Elizabeth's death in 1878. Sited at the end of a narrow peninsula dividing Gareloch from the wilder Loch Long—the family said life there was like "living in a luxurious ship" because of the waters that nearly surrounded the site—its beauty was overwhelming: colonnaded facades on both sides, two floors of graceful rooms, and a spectacular round library under the high circular central tower, all of which appealed greatly to Louise's penchant for gracious living. But the castle had been a drain on generations of Campbell finances, Lorne's father having even once tried unsuccessfully to sell the place. In 1895, his heir came up with the money—£170,000—to buy it outright, Louise's dowry funds making up for her husband's own cash shortfall.

Knowing her aged father-in-law was unlikely to live much longer, the prospect of Inveraray Castle coming to her husband in his patrimony gave Louise pause; in fact, she was far from sure they would be able to keep up both of these fabulous Scottish castles once Lorne assumed sole responsibility as ninth duke. Throughout the late 1890s, the Lornes rented out Rosneath during the summer months to pay for the improvements they were making. While there were tenants in their new Scottish home,[2] Lorne and Louise themselves were put up at the bucolic Ferry Inn, which became famous for their patronage and the fact that the princess herself had painted its outdoor sign.

But Louise undertook Rosneath's rehabilitation in a manner befitting Queen Victoria's daughter. She hired a brilliant young architect, Edwin Lutyens, to help her. Lutyens would later gain international fame as one of the foremost architects of the early twentieth century, best known for the transformation of New Delhi into the showplace capital of British India. The architect would also develop such a close working relationship with the princess that his own fiancée became jealous, though he allayed her suspicions by telling her that as much as he enjoyed Louise's company and her patronage, "real friendship was impossible with a Royalty."

One more stir over a political appointment gave Lorne hope for a continued diplomatic career. Though Louise had already vetoed the idea of her husband in Australia, the notion was raised again by the colonial secretary, Joseph Chamberlain, early in 1900. It was Louise who vetoed it, both out of an abhorrence for the lengthy sea journey out and back, and the unsettling thought of Lorne alone as her principal company.

Louis of Hesse, rather like the old duke of Argyll, was having a hard time without the comfort of a loving wife. The disoriented widower had been a long time getting over his liaison with Madame Kolemine. All but banished from the Prussian and Russian courts for his bizarre act of *lèse majesté*, it was only at his mother-in-law's homes in England that he could now feel at all welcome among people of his own rank. As for his Hessian subjects, Louis understood it would be nearly impossible to replace Alice in their affections, his late wife having become at the end of her life a kind of local saint. Some of his hopes for help were focused on his sister-in-law, Vicky, whose slander at Prussian hands—along with that of her husband's memory and record—bewildered Louis, who had always been fond of his wife's eldest sister. He showed many kindnesses to Vicky, and the German dowager empress would remember for the rest of her life the support the Hessian grand duke gave her in the difficult early days of her widowhood. She wrote her mother that it was "only Louis . . . who *understood* and who could share many of my feelings and fears." Sadly, he would outlive Fritz by just four years.

Though the Kolemine entanglement had taken much of the life out of him, Louis remained duty-bound to see that his younger daughters got themselves happily and comfortably wed. Just as important, he would also have to supervise his son Ernie to make sure the boy married a fitting future grand duchess of Hesse-Darmstadt to provide for the succession to this little chip of the German empire.

To see to it that Louis got his children off to fitting matrimonial starts in their lives, their English grandmother made frequent trips to Darmstadt to ensure that the memory of her daughter wasn't again besmirched. In fact, from the time Alice died, Queen Victoria superintended nearly every important aspect of her Hessian descendants' lives, most especially their education. Their annual trips to their grandmother's homes became as important for the monarch as they were for the children, Victoria's way of keeping the spirit of Princess Alice alive.

Alice's eldest child, Victoria, had been wed to her Battenberg prince in 1884, with the enthusiastic blessings of Queen Victoria. As Prince and Princess Louis of Battenberg, the couple would produce a family that came to include a queen of Sweden, as well as the man who would become the most honored British soldier of World War II: Lord Louis Mountbatten.[3] In the years when her own younger sisters began to marry, Victoria and her husband lived at Sennicotts, their country house near Chichester, the prince rising at a regular pace in the Royal Navy.

The second Hesse daughter would see a life vastly different from that of her older sister. Elizabeth—Ella—was the young woman who had once been hotly pursued by her first cousin, Vicky and Fritz's son, Willy. If the future emperor hadn't been such a bully on his visits to Darmstadt, or if he had requested rather than ordered, or if he had kept his voice toned down to a less offensive level, Ella might have been able to see through to the few admirable traits in his otherwise deplorable personality. Queen Victoria especially had favored a match between these two of her grandchildren, hoping that Ella's calm maturity might have a soothing effect on Vicky's jackrabbity son. On the other hand, Willy's paternal grandmother, Empress Augusta, reviled the prospect of the second heir to the Prussian throne marrying a Hessian, a family for which her contempt was unremitting. In any event, Willy was never a serious contender for Ella. Before he had even approached her in any romantic way, the girl had fallen in love with Russia, where her aunt was empress, and where on childhood visits to the imperial court she was treated to all the unending splendor and color the tsar's riches could, in a flash of an imperial command, conjure up. It was not surprising that Ella would fall in love with a Russian cousin, as well.

Unlike Willy, this cousin was related through her father's side (he was her father's first cousin). The Grand Duke Sergei Alexandrovitch of Russia was the fifth son of Emperor Alexander II and Empress Marie, and thus the brother of Tsar Alexander III, as well as the brother-in-law of the princess of Wales, the sister of Alexander III's wife. As thin and trim as a Russian birch tree, strikingly handsome (as opposed to the extraordinary bull-like ugliness of his elder brother, Alexander), Sergei—in the family always called Serge, with the English pronunciation—burned with hatred for the anarchical murderers of his father, Tsar Alexander II.[4] His Hessian cousin was utterly smitten by this strange young man, and their 1888 wedding echoed all the glory of Russia, of its monarchy, and of the Russian Orthodox Church. (A Lutheran service was also held in respect for the bride's religion, which Louis had refused to let his daughter change.) Sadly, this young man would turn into one of the least likable members of the European royal fraternity. In their married life, Serge would treat Ella as a precious chattel, a Russian grand duchess imprisoned in golden palaces and beholden to the onerous etiquette of the richest court in the world. The couple would have no children.

Though not required to convert to Russian Orthodoxy because her husband was not in direct line of succession to the throne, Ella nevertheless eventually adopted the faith that seemed at first glance so much at odds with her native German Lutheranism. The move met with little approval from Ella's family, most of whom believed she took the step only under pressure from her husband. In fact, the conversion reflected Ella's growing religious mysticism—beliefs that would take an extraordinary turn after her husband's assassination at the hands of adherents to the same movement responsible for the murder of his father.

Alice and Louis's next two children made very different marriages. In the presence of her dying uncle, Emperor Frederick, Irene wed her first cousin, Prince Henry of Prussia. Thereafter playfully called "The Very Amiables" in the family, the marriage would prove contented and long-lived, the couple happily growing close to Henry's mother in the thirteen years between their wedding and Vicky's death. One tragic shadow over the lives of these two grandchildren of Queen Victoria was the fact that Irene was a carrier of hemophilia, which would kill two of her three sons.

Irene's brother Ernie was homosexual. His sexual orientation was hard enough for a royal person in nineteenth-century Europe, but for an heir to a throne—even the insignificant throne of Hesse-Darmstadt—it made life very complicated indeed. In 1892, when Ernie was twenty-three, his father died, and the untested young man inherited the grand ducal throne. At the urging of his English grandmother, who believed a wife was what Ernie needed to make him into a proper ruler of his little grand duchy, he soon married, another cousin-marriage like those of his three older sisters. Ernie's bride was actually a first cousin on both his mother's and his father's side. Queen Victoria had chosen Victoria Melita of Edinburgh, Uncle Affie and Aunt Marie's daughter, and Ernie had dutifully complied. In 1895, Victoria Melita—"Ducky" in the family—gave Ernie one child, a daughter ineligible to inherit the "Salic" (meaning only males can inherit) Hessian-Darmstadt throne. The partners were wholly mismatched, conflict between them growing more intense every day. Understandably disillusioned, Ernie's wife would write of her husband that "no boy was safe [from him], from the stable hands to the kitchen help, he slept quite openly with them all." Because he had no physical interest in her, Ducky sought out someone else who did, and thus Grand Duke Cyril of Russia, another of her first cousins, became her lover.

Since Queen Victoria wouldn't countenance a divorce between two people whose union she had personally arranged, Ernie and Ducky would wait until their grandmother's death to end their marriage. When the couple did finally go their separate ways, Ducky and Cyril were married. For dynastic purposes Ernie, too, remarried, to Princess Eleonore of Solms-Hohensolms-Lich, who managed to provide her husband with two healthy offspring, George and Louis.

Of all Victoria's grandchildren, it was the youngest surviving child of Alice and Louis who would, aside from her cousin Willy, have by far the greatest impact on the world. Until her mother's death, Princess Alix had been, by all accounts, a sweet, good-natured, and sunny child. But then she grew dark and moody, given to introspection and, eventually, religious superstition. Alix's shyness became so crippling that visitors to Darmstadt sometimes took the little princess's tied tongue for arrogance. Stunningly beautiful as a teenager, Alix could have had her pick of almost any of Europe's eligible princes. But it was while visiting Russia as a member of Ella's wedding party that she met the young man who would still be the sole love of her life three decades later, when both would die horrifically at precisely the same moment.

Only twelve when she met the tsarevitch Nicholas, Alix was even then enchanted by the slim and fair-haired sixteen-year-old heir to the Russian throne. When she next visited Russia with Ella, it was Nicky who monopolized her days. Though her Russophobic English grandmother would attempt to pair her with Bertie's eldest son, Albert Victor (Alix's first cousin)—a match at the time expected by the monarch to make Alix the eventual queen of England—the young Hessian princess was already resolutely determined on Nicky.

Alix faced an enormous personal obstacle to a marriage to the tsarevitch. Unlike her equally Russia-besotted sister, Ella, who could marry Serge without having first to change her faith, this was not possible for Alix. Nicky was the direct heir to the Romanov throne, and as such his wife would have to share his Orthodox religion. Alix was, unfortunately, almost mystically engrossed in German Protestantism. When Ella told her that she herself was determined to convert to Orthodoxy, the revelation became a big step in inspiring Alix to do the same thing so she might marry Nicky.

When, in 1894, the tsarevitch came to Coburg for Ernie's wedding to Ducky, he decided to make his move. Aware that to accept the young Russian's proposal of marriage would necessitate a change of religion, the still-hesitant Alix at first refused. But the otherwise impassive Nicky was nothing if not determined. The very day after Ernie and Ducky were married, the overwhelmed princess finally agreed to become both Russian Orthodox and wife of the heir to the Russian throne. Just as Queen Victoria, the preeminent guest at the festivities, was finishing her breakfast, Ella burst in on her grandmother with the dramatic announcement that "Alix and Nicky are to be engaged."

The wedding was planned for the spring of 1895, but the death of Nicky's father changed all the elaborate arrangements, including sufficient time for Alix to become literate in the Russian language. Alix had just joined her future husband at the imperial summer palace of Livadia in the Crimea when Tsar Alexander III died on November 1, 1894. His widow Minnie, the princess of Wales's sister, became the dowager empress; and her son Nicky the new tsar, Nicholas II. The morning after her fiancé's accession, Alix was received into the Orthodox faith and at the same time given the new name of Alexandra Feodorovna. The imperial family decided the wedding should follow the late tsar's funeral within the week. Like her mother's wedding at Osborne in 1862, Alix's was far more funereal in tone than joyous. All that saved it from complete gloom was the depth of the young bride and groom's love for each other.

During the years when Alice's children were marrying their cousins and producing a multitude of little second cousins, Vicky had moved from the hurricane's eye to near oblivion. Though she had been wounded by Fritz's illness and Willy's uncivil behavior, until June 1888 she at least had a loving and sympathetic husband to share her distress and lighten her sometimes intolerable burden. After his death, Vicky was left to face her martyrdom stripped of that unfaltering support.

With her widowhood, her difficulties centered, inevitably, on the new emperor. Such was the exquisite release Willy experienced in succeeding his father to the throne that he took vainglory to new heights. To the horror of his mother and English grandmother, he jettisoned the standard symbols of mourning that were obligatory for a son in so visible a role, notably refusing to refrain from travel for pleasure. One a grander scale, in his eagerness to test his new powers, Willy made the most disastrous mistake of his early reign only two years after coming to the throne: to free himself of a chancellor he knew regarded him as immature and impetuous, in 1890 Willy dismissed Otto von Bismarck, the only man who thoroughly understood how to control Germany's complex array of interwoven alliances that he himself had created.

The dowager empress faced a bewildering lineup of new tribulations. High on Vicky's list of priorities was finding a home that, in her widowhood, she could call her own, one from which she couldn't be evicted. A few hundred yards from the ostentatious Royal Palace which she and Fritz had wholly ignored during her husband's ninety-nine-day reign, her central Berlin residence remained the Crown Prince's Palace on Unter den Linden. It was a spacious and imposing structure, full of stately chambers overlooking Berlin's most fashionable street. For social reasons, the widow was expected to keep the Linden palace going—her presence was required in the capital for at least a few weeks every winter social season—and it provided a base from which periodically to check in on her many Berlin charities. But Vicky disliked it, both for its nearness to the throngs on the Linden and for its associations with her in-laws. What was more, the palace would someday be required by her grandson, the new crown prince, though for the time being six-year-old William—"Little Willy"—still required little more than a nursery.

Hers and Fritz's real home had been the Neues Palais, at Potsdam. But the new monarch considered the mammoth Rococo confection the perfect setting for his own majesty, and had without the slightest compunction ordered his mother to leave as soon as he acceded to the throne. Vicky's anger was genuine, though Willy's eviction was not out of character and probably came as little surprise to her. He gave her until the end of 1888 to vacate her home of nearly three decades, but she in fact left sooner, within weeks of Fritz's death. She asked her son if she might have Frederick the Great's famous and beautiful Sans Souci, a palace whose loveliness might have done much to help soothe her grief. But Willy refused, explaining that the place was needed as a state guest house for visiting royalty. He did say that she could have the Villa Liegnitz—one of the smallest dwellings in the Potsdam Royal Park, and an offer that to a dowager empress amounted to an affront, even causing his grandmother to express surprise at his impudence. At any rate, Willy soon decided even this modest villa was needed as a shelter for his gentleman attendants during their rotas on service.

While Vicky endured Willy's lack of generosity, the horrifying circumstances surrounding Fritz's death resurfaced, with accusations against the dead emperor's British doctors and against Vicky for alleged meddling in her husband's course of treatment. Dr. Bergmann, the German physician displaced by Dr. Mackenzie, blamed the dowager empress for allowing the late emperor to be placed in "inexpert hands." Mackenzie shot back his reply in a controversial book called *The Fatal Illness of Frederick the Noble*. Though the book achieved considerable commercial success, Mackenzie's reputation suffered badly, and he died in disgrace three years after it was published. Willy gloated over the attacks on his mother and her national doctors, while Bismarck gloated over everybody's discomfiture. Vicky could do little other than remain silent though she poured out her feelings in the letters she sent to her mother, in which she decried her ungrateful son.

Beyond the controversy surrounding Fritz's illness, a rumor rippled through Germany that the widow had married her court chamberlain (an officer who was, in effect, the manager of her home), Count Seckendorff. Even while Fritz was still being nursed in the Austrian Tyrol the year before his death, gossip had already begun to spread that Vicky and Seckendorff were lovers. Count Radolinski, who acted as Bismarck's fifth columnist in the crown prince's household, had been the one responsible for disseminating this malevolent nonsense. Described by one of Vicky's biographers as "dry as dust," Seckendorff was a man of incontestable moral probity and served as a crutch on whom the hard-tried dowager empress often leaned; he nonetheless represented a useful target for Vicky's enemies. In point of fact, Vicky's views on remarriage for herself—or for *any* widow—were rigid and widely known: she was against it; just as her mother had been guided by the passion she had felt for a beloved husband. Furthermore, the idea of a princess royal of England and dowager empress of the Germans marrying outside the royal caste would have seemed preposterous to Vicky.

Compounding the problems caused by Willy's overt hostility was the fact that Vicky wasn't, by royal standards, particularly rich. Fritz simply hadn't been sovereign long enough to provide a fortune for her. The principal of an emperor's financial inheritance being considered inalienable from his throne, whatever capital Fritz had received during the ninety-nine days of his reign was not his long enough to earn any substantial interest before it had to be passed, in toto, to his successor. Willy, of course, hadn't the slightest notion of relieving his mother's relative indigence, most certainly not to the point of giving her any of what was now *his* money. As a widow, Vicky would possess less than one-sixth of the capital her mother-in-law Augusta had had as the previous dowager empress.

Happily, an unexpected, timely, and generous bequest from a recently deceased friend, the wealthy duchess of Galliera, soon resolved Vicky's difficulties in a way that turned out almost miraculous. In 1889, with the Galliera money, she bought 350 acres in the Taunus Hills, a tranquil little range that cuts through the Hessian countryside just north of Frankfurt. The property lay outside the charming town of Kronberg, within an easy train ride of almost anywhere Vicky might want to go, especially nearby Darmstadt, where she would be able to visit Alice's children. Her newly acquired estate had a small villa sitting on it, one that Vicky ordered torn down. Under the direction of the Berlin architect Ernst Ihne, she replaced it with a home in which she would spend the remainder of her life. Every detail in its construction would be completed only after the architect obtained her counsel and agreement.

In its sixteenth-century character, Vicky's house winningly fused the architecture of her English heritage with the local area's traditional half-timber Rhenish style. She lined the walls of every room with paintings of her family: Charlotte in Renaissance costume, as a fresh and virginal girl, far from the hardened woman her eldest daughter had become by the 1890s; Henry as a young midshipman, unmistakably Charlotte's brother in the eyes and attitude; Mossy as a little girl in court costume; and, most remarkable of all, her own simple charcoal sketch of Fritz, with gay, happy, living eyes, so different from the usual somber representations of the martyr emperor. A big self-portrait of Vicky showed the dowager empress in widow's weeds, her habitual costume after June 1888. The room closest to her heart was the magnificent library, its shelves filled with virtually every book that contained any mention of her husband; its only flaw was that the room turned out to be too small for her own vast collection, and more than two-thirds of her books had to be shelved or stored elsewhere. Vicky's love for her new home can be surmised by the fact that she dedicated it to her late husband. The name she chose—suggested by her daughter, Moretta—was *Friedrichshof*, "Frederick's Court." Over its main portal she had carved in prominent letters the legend: *Frederici Memoriae*—"To the memory of Frederick."

Throughout the estate, Vicky strove to secure Fritz's spirit in her life with him, to surround and immerse herself with all that had been her husband's. In this she was immensely successful. Peace would invariably come upon her the moment she arrived at the Kronberg station: the ride up to the castle soothed her whatever the season, but especially so in winter, when the snow-covered surroundings seemed a bewitching wonderland. Vicky made her house gloriously comfortable. It was described by relatives as a reflection not of the cold and austere grandeur of the palaces and castles in which all the Hohenzollerns lived, but instead of the dowager empress's own innate charm.

Beyond matters related to her homes, Vicky's life was now less complicated than when Fritz had been alive. Her political involvement in German affairs was so sparse as to be nearly nonexistent. Instead, it was her family that filled her days. The greatest joy in Vicky's life was seeing to her younger daughters' happiness, especially the fostering of contented marriages. Enormously fond of her grandchildren, for whom she had a great and natural affinity, she was sickened that Willy and Dona were keeping their sons away from her. The new empress made it clear that her mother-in-law's influence on the young princes could be little other than malign, just as it had been, in Dona's estimation, on Vicky's own children. The always prickly relationship between Vicky and Dona grew icier by the day in the early years after Fritz's death, Dona's open contempt for Willy's mother wholeheartedly supported and actively abetted by the emperor. When she gave birth to her seventh (and last) child, Victoria Louise, Dona cruelly made sure that Vicky understood that *she* was not the Victoria for whom her only daughter was named.

Charlotte, Vicky's own firstborn, remained a disappointment to her mother in almost every way imaginable—in personality and looks and in a lifestyle the dowager empress considered "fast." Yet Vicky's eldest daughter did please her in one important way. Charlotte's own daughter, Feo, destined to be an only child, often visited Friedrichshof, her mother only too happy to leave the girl (who had been Queen Victoria's first great-grandchild) while she and Bernhard went off on their many holiday trips. Henry and Irene sometimes left their hemophiliac son with Vicky as well, but—unlike Charlotte—they did so more out of affection for her than to use Friedrichshof as a convenient nursery.

Vicky's three younger daughters became her primary concern in her later years. Moretta's future with Alexander of Battenberg had come to a dramatic halt when Sandro morganatically married his opera singer mistress in Darmstadt. The disavowed princess's mother and maternal grandmother, two of Europe's most practiced matchmakers, began to scour the *Almanach de Gotha* to find a mate for a girl rapidly assuming the attributes of old maid. The most successful candidate they turned up was Sandro's complete opposite. The Battenberg prince was dashing and handsome and ambitious; Prince Adolf of Schaumburg-Lippe was awkward and homely and sedentary, as well as badly educated—he considered book reading "wasted time." Willy, however, approved of Adolf as a brother-in-law, what with his being a good and loyal German and safely apolitical, and Moretta duly married her replacement prince at the end of 1890. The couple lived in the Schaumburg Palace, Adolf's family seat in Bonn,[5] and tried without success to have children. This greatly saddened Vicky, who nonetheless most wisely counseled the unhappy Moretta, telling her that "life is a long sequence of sacrifices, trials and difficulties and one rarely gets what one wants." Her daughter no doubt realized these words arose from her mother's need to cope with her own tragic experience.

Sophie was the shyest of Vicky's children as well as her favorite, although this princess's marriage would make for an explosively charged relationship with her eldest brother. At first, Willy expressed benign pleasure when Sophie became engaged to Prince Constantine of Greece, known as "Tino," who as duke of Sparta was crown prince and heir to his father, King George I of the Hellenes (brother of Bertie's wife, Alexandra, and of Marie, the dowager empress of Russia). Vicky regarded Sophie's choice as uncertain, not because she disliked the good-natured if somewhat slow Tino, but because, compared to Western Europe, Greece was primitive and immature in its government, its royal family apt someday to find itself in the line of political fire.

The match sparked serious problems with her powerful brother when Sophie decided to convert to Greek Orthodoxy, the state religion and the faith of which her future father-in-law was constitutionally head. When Dona first heard of Sophie's intentions, she peremptorily summoned the girl to the palace and asked if the "rumor" were true. When Sophie admitted it was, Dona shot back that "we shall never agree to that. If you have no feeling about yourself, William, as head of the church and of your family, will speak to you. . . . You will end up in hell." William was not, of course, head of Sophie's "family"—his sister was herself the crown princess of a sovereign state, and had every right to do as she pleased in the matter of her personal religious beliefs.

Willy nonetheless barged ahead like an offended bishop. Appearing at his mother's home the next day, he told the dowager empress that, if Sophie proceeded with her plans, he intended to "forbid her the country"—that is, prevent her from setting foot anywhere in

Germany. It should be born in mind that this ultimatum was addressed as much to the future king of Greece—his brother-in-law—as it was to his own sister. What was more, Willy wrote to his English grandmother explaining that the argument had led to his pregnant wife delivering two weeks early, and that, if his new son died, it would be Sophie who had "murdered it." Despite her brother's objections, Sophie joined the Greek Church the following Easter, and Willy did indeed banish his sister from Germany.

At Christmas 1889, Vicky wrote a moving letter to Sophie, trying to convey to her daughter something of the emptiness her life had become: "This is Xmas Eve, I can hardly believe it, and the struggle hard to be a little cheerful. I long for beloved Papa, for my Waldy, my home and for you, my own Sophie. And the bitter, bitter change in my existence comes upon me with all its force, and all its cruel and sacred recollections of the happy past, gone never to return." Most distressing to the dowager empress were thoughts of what was going on that very night at the Neues Palais, the home she and Fritz loved so deeply and where every Christmas they had been so especially happy:

> I dare not think of Friedrichskron tonight [she ignored Willy
> having spitefully returned the original name to the palace],
> all lit up and full of gay people, and we, whose home it was,
> driven out and banished by the angel of death; and the
> rooms where so many bitter tears were shed and such hours
> of agony gone through [presumably her husband's death at
> the palace] now ringing with laughter and merriment. The
> thought drives me mad. . . . Oh my Sophie! May you never
> know what it is to grieve as I grieve, and suffer as I do, it is
> too terrible.

Sophie would learn soon enough.

Vicky maintained a loving relationship with this daughter through a long and remarkable correspondence between Germany and Athens, one that lasted from Sophie's marriage in 1889 to Vicky's death in 1901. (The letters were published in Great Britain in 1955 through the offices of Sophie's daughter, Helen, who married King Carol of Romania and became that country's queen.) Sophie's own life in Greece would end badly. Tino died shortly after being forced from the Greek throne for a second time in 1922. The government in Athens refused to allow his body to be returned home for burial, and he was instead interred in the Russian Orthodox church in Florence, where Sophie spent the last years of her life, outliving her husband by a decade.

Vicky's youngest surviving child, Margaret (Mossy), who as an adult closely resembled her long-dead aunt Alice, made a happy if not a dynastically important marriage. After Ella went off with Serge of Russia, Queen Victoria looked on this cheerful and well-adjusted granddaughter as an ideal wife for her tragically wayward Wales grandson, Prince Albert Victor. Mossy, fortunately for herself, passed on the chance to be queen of England. Later, Victoria came to the opinion that the princess shouldn't marry at all, but instead remain with Vicky as she herself had expected Beatrice to stay with her. Even after it became obvious that Vicky wouldn't stand in Mossy's path to marriage, the queen persisted, telling her daughter that Mossy should be made to stay home instead of making a life of her own. Vicky wisely demurred against her mother's advice to exert any such influence.

When Mossy married the cultivated and well-rounded Prince Frederick Charles of Hesse—called "Fischy"—on what would have been her parents' own silver anniversary, the attractive young princess entered into a happy and prodigiously fecund relationship. She and her husband ultimately produced six sons, including two sets of twins. Convinced that the sister of the German emperor should not marry a "minor" prince, especially one whom he judged "too thin and too solemn," Willy threatened to veto the match, but eventually relented, graciously telling his sister she could go ahead because "she was so unimportant" herself. Fischy would become Vicky's favorite son-in-law, the dowager empress grateful for his warm and friendly sense of humor.

When Finland won its independence from Russia in 1917 after the Bolshevik revolution, the nation's new parliament elected Frederick Charles to be Finland's first king, which of course meant that Mossy would be its queen. Though technically he reigned as monarch for two months, Fischy relinquished the honor, explaining that he wanted the Finns to await the results of the Versailles peace negotiations before making such an important decision. The Finns decided on a republic, their brief flirtation with monarchy quickly forgotten as kings and emperors were being unseated all over Europe.

In the spring of 1894, Vicky finally moved permanently into the just completed Friedrichshof. Away from the court intrigues of Berlin and Potsdam, in a supremely comfortable home and, importantly for her own peace of mind, one that she owned outright, Vicky finally relaxed a bit and began ignoring the worst of the indignities directed at her by Willy and Dona and Charlotte. Ironically, when these perpetrators of her unhappiness saw that their intended victim no longer railed so violently at the very sight of them, they began at last to pay her a measure of the respect each had withheld for so long. Occasionally Willy even became magnanimous, as when he bought for his mother a small chunk of land that encroached on the otherwise perfect privacy of her Taunus wonderland.

She in turn had diplomatically invited her eldest son to be her first official guest at Friedrichshof, which she knew would flatter him. He quickly accepted, and her palace was thus christened with the presence of the nation's emperor. Friedrichshof became a mecca for Vicky's huge extended family and far-ranging circle of friends and admirers. Lenchen was an especially welcome guest, Vicky understanding her younger sister's laudanum problem and helping her to overcome it in the peace and beauty the castle afforded. Dona began to bring her children to see their grandmother, though only when she would be present lest young minds come under the influence of Vicky's cosmopolitan and un-German ways. The whole course of family feelings now running in a smoother direction, Willy even made up with his Greek Orthodox sister Sophie in 1894, when he again "allowed her the country."

Back in England, the time approached to commemorate sixty years having passed since Queen Victoria succeeded to the throne. The rites planned for the spring of 1897 to mark the anniversary—the much-anticipated Diamond Jubilee—would be the nation's most lavish festivities since the 1887 Jubilee, and maybe even the most spectacular splurge in British history. The ostensible purpose was to give national thanksgiving for Victoria's longevity, a matter of wild pride in the years since the monarch had begun to reenter the nation's social life. To a larger degree, though, the event was an overdue salute to and recognition of Britain's unparalleled economic progress, remarkably achieved in the absence of any pan-European war. Even more fundamentally, the Diamond Jubilee represented a tribute to imperialism, to Britain's self-chosen mission to civilize the uncivilized world in its own likeness.

At home, a few naysayers objected to this national ethos: the Liberals, who wanted to give Ireland some hand in shaping its own destiny; the socialists, who wanted the working classes to live a better, less brutish life; those few who were beginning to worry about Britain's course in southern Africa. Former prime minister William Gladstone even hoped the queen might celebrate her Jubilee by abdicating. But public opinion strongly supported the view that the nation had reached the pinnacle of what mankind could fairly achieve, with only a bit of fine-tuning here and there left undone. Victoria agreed, believing wholeheartedly that she herself had had a great deal to do with Britain's gravitas in the world's affairs, and it all made her very proud.

She took added pride in having recently celebrated another milestone in her remarkable reign. On September 23, 1896, she had become the longest-reigning monarch in British history, passing the span served by her grandfather George III, his reign marred for two decades by both his own incapacitation and his regent son's incompetency. Symbolically and physically, Victoria's unbroken presence in her nation's life seemed to bring her an increasing sense of indispensability as her tenure on the throne continued.

On Wednesday, June 23, 1897,[6] the queen was transported by state landau to the front steps of St. Paul's Cathedral, there to be the focal point of a Thanksgiving Service and a celebratory *Te Deum*. Accompanying her were her daughter-in-law, the princess of Wales, and her daughter Lenchen, the two facing her in the carriage. (Vicky was transported in a separate carriage since her rank as an empress kept her from traveling with her back to the horses.) Now seventy-eight, the queen didn't actually enter this great mother church of the empire, her inability to get up the front steps forcing her to stay in the landau. When Grand Duchess Augusta of Strelitz heard that her distant cousin had remained in the carriage, she was aghast: "No . . . after 60 years reign to thank God in the Street!!!"

Victoria was overwhelmed by the reception given her by the million cheering people lining the streets of London that day: "No one ever, I believe, has met with such an ovation as was given me . . . every face seemed to be filled with joy." She found herself deeply moved by a popular demonstration such as she had rejected for so many years after Albert's death. And her family rejoiced in the occasion. Vicky wrote to Sophie in Athens that "when the bells pealed out from the dark old Cathedral, and the cheers rang out again, and the sun shone on all the glitter of the escort and carriages, it was as fine a sight as you could wish to see."

In the autumn of 1898, Vicky, an expert horsewoman, was taking a routine afternoon ride through the fields near Friedrichshof, accompanied by Mossy and her lord chamberlain's wife, when her horse shied at the unexpected commotion of a threshing machine. The dowager empress's riding habit caught on the saddle's pommel and she was thrown. She fell forward, her head and shoulders landing on the ground almost directly under the horse's hooves. She professed more embarrassment than injury. Making as little as possible of the incident, she scoffed that "I have been riding for fifty years, and in that time it is possible for an accident to occur." However, she admitted the results were "extremely painful": one hand was badly sprained, her back painfully wrenched, and she had to go to bed to fight a fever. She was also more badly frightened by the accident than she admitted.

Within a few days, her pain had sharply increased, and the doctors diagnosed lumbago in the back. But when they examined her more extensively, something far more serious was found: the dowager empress had breast cancer. Understandably stunned upon hearing this, Vicky nonetheless courageously insisted on carrying out her schedule. Always a physically active woman, sometimes to the point of obsessiveness, she went to the Breslau wedding of her granddaughter Feodora—Charlotte and Bernhard's only child. But the effort badly worsened her distress, as did another trip soon thereafter to her mother at Balmoral. While she was in Scotland, a British doctor confirmed the German doctors' diagnosis, and Vicky was told that the carcinoma was "far too advanced" to any longer be curable by surgery. The dowager empress told only her mother, her brother Bertie, and her sister Beatrice.

On New Year's Day, 1900, Queen Victoria made her usual diary entry, a task she had seen to virtually every day since her eighteenth birthday. In the two and a half years since the celebrations of her Diamond Jubilee, the queen had suffered the demise of many relatives—most recently her twenty-one-year-old grandson, Alfred,[7] the duke of Edinburgh's son (the duke himself would within the year be dead)—as well as of many old friends, which left her at eighty ever more bereft of contemporaries. That day she wrote with particular feeling of Lenchen's son Christian Victor, who was off in South Africa fighting in the Boer War, praying God that "dear Christle will be spared" from the horrors he was facing in that faraway conflict. Her wish was not to be granted.

Though Beatrice was a full-time secretary to her mother, Lenchen and Christian had stayed physically close to the monarch in the decades since their marriage. Following the queen from one royal residence to the next, Lenchen was always depended upon to accomplish diligently many of the near-endless little tasks that Beatrice was too busy to see to. Though their daughter, Marie Louise, was at this time still living her sad life as Aribert of Anhalt's wife as best she could, the other daughter, Helena Victoria, remained a spinster, doing for her mother basically what Beatrice was doing for hers. The Christians' younger son, Albert, had gone off to Germany like his cousins Alfred of Edinburgh and Charles Edward of Albany. While there in training to take over the Schleswig-Holstein-Sonderburg-Augustenburg dukedom, he accepted a commission as a serving officer in the German Army over which his cousin Willy reigned as commander in chief.

Thirty-three-year-old Christian Victor—Christle—had decided to make an English life for himself, specifically as a full-time army officer, and was now earning his superiors' praise in the 60th King's Royal Rifles. Already he had fought under Kitchener in the Sudan, and had served with Prince Henry of Battenberg, his uncle by marriage, in the same Ashanti expedition that had been Liko's undoing. In South Africa in October 1900, while preparing to return to England, he came down with malaria only three weeks before he was to board ship.

On October 25, Lord Roberts, the commander in chief in South Africa, wired the queen that her grandson was "seriously ill but there are no complications and he has the best of nurses and doctors." Five days later, a wire from Pretoria informed Lenchen and Christian that their son was dead. Helena Victoria broke the news to his grandmother. This new shock to the queen, on the heels of Affie's death from cancer three months earlier, was a blow from which she never really recovered. Lenchen seemed to stand the news of her son's death better than did her weakening mother, Victoria writing Vicky that "poor dear Lenchen bears up wonderfully." But the monarch also added: "poor Christian [has] terribly aged."

In the year of Affie's and Christle's deaths, Lorne and Louise faced a death in the Campbell family—one that finally raised Lorne to the inheritance he had waited fifty-five years to receive. Yet now that the dukedom was upon him, he threatened to throw it away. The cause of the bitter family row was, not surprisingly, his stepmother, Ina.

His father's third marriage had, Lorne believed, far transgressed the bounds of propriety, not only because he thought no one could or should replace his mother, but because he held Ina infinitely below the social threshold required of a duchess of Argyll, or of much of anything else for that matter. When he learned that his father had named Ina his literary executor, Lorne's fury was nearly unbridled. Angered enough by his father's second marriage to have threatened estrangement from the family, since Ina's appearance Lorne had carried out the threat to near completion. It was only on Louise's insistence that he joined the princess in stiffly greeting her father-in-law on birthdays. The Lornes never once set foot in Inveraray Castle in Ina's day, their sole Scottish residence being Rosneath Castle.

By March 1900, the health of the seventy-six-year-old duke had declined to a dangerous state. Still Lorne refused to see his father, and even Louise was unable to budge him from his obstinate stand; his nephew Niall wrote that "Uncle Ian [Lorne] absolutely refuses to set foot in the house as long as Duchess Ina is in it." Likely in the clutches of senility or even Alzheimer's disease, the duke's mental condition was described in the family as "absolutely insane," with manifestations that gave Lorne further rationalization for staying away. Victoria was distressed at her son-in-law's behavior, warning that if Lorne didn't change his attitude, "he would never forgive himself hereafter," and hoping that, if he wouldn't listen to anyone else, he would at least take seriously her motherly (and queenly) advice. She wrote to Lorne listing the reasons he should see his father, even though she diplomatically admitted that he had been "monstrously treated"—whether she was referring to the old duke's temerity in ignoring his son's wishes regarding his last two marriages or to Ina's eccentric behavior isn't clear. But Victoria nonetheless thought Lorne's intransigence both "unfilial and unChristian." His written reply, to the woman he had hitherto called his "second mother," was so bitter that Louise simply wouldn't allow her husband to address the queen so rudely, and tore up his intended letter. Lorne, undeterred, told Louise that she wasn't to go anywhere near Inveraray as long as Ina remained there.

Staying at Clachan, the Rosneath dower house, Lorne was sufficiently aware of his father's impending death that he ordered a variety of coffins so he could pick out something appropriate and of the right size. When word got out about the coffins, Lorne's stock in the family was further lowered since he was so widely known to have refused to visit his dying father. The family dispute was turning into a genuine scandal—*nobody* treated their father in such a way—and even Louise's embarrassed family was becoming annoyed with her for her inability to bring her husband to his senses.

At an impasse which now even the queen could not break, Lorne made an astonishing announcement to his family: he was absolutely not going to accept the title of duke of Argyll on his father's death. Convinced that Duchess Ina had "contaminated" and "degraded" the name, he wanted Victoria to give him some other title. Aside from the obvious lunacy of the idea, his declaration infuriated his brother-in-law Bertie, who feared that if all this were made public, Lorne would become a national laughingstock. Sensitive to ridicule, Bertie recommended that his brother-in-law simply "bury the hatchet," adding: "I sincerely hope that he will not think of calling himself in the future anything else than the fine historic title to which he must succeed." Finally, in desperation to abide by her family's wishes, the nearly frantic Louise told her husband that if he continued to refuse to visit his father's deathbed, she intended to separate from him.

Before she had to act on the threat, the eighth duke of Argyll solved the problem by dying, and in the early hours of April 24, 1900, Lorne[8] ascended to the ninth dukedom of Argyll, his wife becoming the new duchess. His seemingly kind comment upon the eighth duke's death belied his conduct over the preceding month: "The last weeks of my father's illness were full of suffering; it is a relief to know he is at rest from pain." But Ina was going to see to it that the family's pain didn't stop. Lorne was his father's executor;

but the dead duke had designated that Ina be in charge of the funeral. Though the old man had wanted to be buried next to his first wife, Lorne's mother Elizabeth, Ina had no intention of allowing such a thing. She refused to set a date for the funeral until Lorne agreed to bury his father at a place of *her* choosing and where *she* could someday lie next to the remains. She thought Westminster Abbey would be nice, specifically the Henry VII Chapel. Louise wrote her mother asking her to try to get Ina to stop any thought of such an absurdity, to which the queen immediately agreed. Meanwhile, Lorne had his stepmother informed that, unless she set a date for the funeral—a funeral in which her husband would be buried next to the *first* duchess—he would physically eject her from Inveraray, presumably onto the bare soil of Scotland. Lorne was so irate that Louise thought he might even attempt to abduct his father's body from Inveraray and bury it himself in the ground next to his mother.

Though the "infamous Hellcat"—one of the many unkind names Ina bore in the family—kept threatening rearguard action, including having her husband's heart cut out so she would have something of him to bury beside her on her own death, Queen Victoria finally weighed in with an ultimatum that Ina immediately end all further fantasies and serve up the body forthwith. The funeral was held at last at Inveraray's parish church, with only one of the old duke's daughters accompanying Ina to the service. Louise awaited the party at Kilmun churchyard, where the coffin was to be interred, doing her best to stay out of Ina's sight. When the widowed duchess found that her successor was in the church, she left immediately. Scotland had rarely witnessed such mummery.

Though badly disgruntled, Lorne was now in possession of one of the finest inheritances in Scotland. In addition to his principal title, upon his father's death he had also become Earl Campbell and Cowal, viscount of Lochow and Glenisla, Baron Inveraray and Mull and Morvern and Tivy, and possessed yet half a dozen more baronies. By virtue of his inheritance he became a member of Parliament's upper though far weaker chamber, the House of Lords. In addition to the peerage, he had acquired the titles of Hereditary

Master of the Royal Household in Scotland and Admiral of the Western Coasts and Isles, Keeper of the Great Seal of Scotland, and Lord-Lieutenant of Argyllshire. Perhaps of greatest importance to Lorne was his headship of the Clan Campbell and thus of his own, immediate family. He was still, however, outranked to a very considerable degree by his wife.

With these changes, Lorne and Louise found their housing situation technically improved but financially worsened. Inveraray Castle, now Lorne's by inheritance, had been rebuilt after the 1877 fire, with treasures accumulated from generations of Campbell collecting decorating its lavish salons and halls. Many of those possessions were museum-quality rarities, such as the glorious French and Flemish tapestries that adorned the walls. But the Highland castle required a fortune to maintain, and the income from the marginal agricultural lands that comprised the Argyll estate was found to be barely sufficient. Though Inveraray, the greatest treasure associated with Lorne's dukedom, was mammothly expensive, Rosneath—still the Lornes' private home—was as much a castle as Inveraray and became an intolerable strain on his pocketbook. And by the recent enactment of the inheritance tax law, within three months of Lorne's accession, the courts ruled that he owed £46,000 to the Exchequer as a result of acquiring his father's property. The amount was, in 1900 terms, staggering.

There was no question of selling either Inveraray—for centuries the clan seat—or Rosneath, family and clan pride legislating against the loss of either of these estates. Though the valuable Argyll Lodge in Kensington was sold (the land on which it sat had, by the late nineteenth century, become enormously valuable), the Lornes only just managed to stay in the black, principally by economizing. Inveraray was rented out, as was Rosneath when they did not occupy it themselves; and Louise's dowry income and her £6,000 parliamentary annuity became the main source of the Argyll family finances. Life would henceforth be lived almost entirely at Kensington Palace, which became the couple's primary home.

In January 1901, down at Osborne House the emblem of the nine-teenth century was dying. Bowed by the war raging between her troops and the Boer farmers in South Africa, by the heart-wounding deaths in her family—especially the recent crushing loss of Affie—and by a body that would not respond to a still-alert mind, perhaps the greatest agony Victoria had to bear was the thought that she might have to survive her own firstborn daughter's death. Most tragic of all the burdens for these two great women was the fact that, though they were united in suffering, they would not be able to see each other during their final illnesses.

Another blow to the queen's fast-diminishing well-being was the death on Christmas Day 1900 of her lady-in-waiting of many years, Jane, Lady Churchill. What might thereafter have rallied Victoria would have been to see her armies victorious on the distant South African veldt and the return home of what was left of her badly decimated legions. Lord Roberts, the retiring commander in chief in Africa, brought his sovereign at least some good news in the first days of the new year, news of military successes that the rapidly sinking queen received with undisguised pleasure. Roberts's happy tidings were the last she was fully conscious of. On January 18, she began a final decline that prompted her doctors to call the members of the royal family to gather at Osborne around their matriarch's deathbed.

On the morning of the 22nd, Sir James Reid noted changes in the queen's breathing—tracheal rales, crackling noises made in the windpipes—that told him his patient was going to die very soon. The three daughters who were at Osborne at the center of the death drama—Lenchen, Louise, and Beatrice—had made heroic ef-forts to keep their nephew Willy out of their mother's bedroom, even out of the house if they could. Knowing the queen's eldest grandchild's obnoxious behavior could bring on illness even in a well person, they were rightly concerned that it very likely might hasten her end. But Dr. Reid promised the emperor that if he pos-sibly could, he would get Willy in to see Victoria one last time: the two leaders of Europe's greatest powers should, Reid thought, have a chance to exchange last words, despite the misgivings of the family. Having obtained the prince of Wales's permission, Willy was taken by Reid into his grandmother's bedroom, and left there alone with her on what proved to be her last afternoon.

Though no miracle of diplomacy or statecraft passed between the two monarchs, Willy was overcome by the five minutes he had with the woman who had given her name to an era and who had, despite many reasons not to, given him her love all his life. All that the queen could whisper to Reid after the visit was: "The Emperor is very kind." A few hours later, at six-thirty on that Tuesday evening, her head held up a bit by Willy's strong right arm (her grandson was, like the rest of the family, allowed back in when the end was believed to be imminent), Victoria died. The end came gently, with little pain. The cause was a mix of debilitating health problems—strokes, physical deterioration, starvation from inability to eat, exhaustion from sleeplessness—all of which essentially added up to death from old age. It was as if this tiny, eighty-one-year-old woman had been keeping the twentieth century at bay. With her passing, England could finally get on with a new age.

Vicky had been informed of every shift in her mother's condition, the agony of her own ravaged body worsened by the realization that the lifelong anchor of her life was about to disappear. Her mother had been all kindness to Vicky since the disclosure of Vicky's diagnosis of cancer, the queen making sure the daughter always knew she was welcome at her old British homes. For a while after the diagnosis, Vicky had continued to feel well, other than the odd spell of dizziness that might strike at any hour. She even told her lord chamberlain that she planned to last until her seventieth birthday, an age at which she judged that "every person has lived her life." (She was then fifty-nine.) Above all, Vicky had not wanted Willy to know of the cancer, and was successful in keeping it from him until the signs of mortal illness became all too apparent on her haggard face and bowed body. It was her chamberlain who counseled her to get yet another physician's opinion to add to those of the German and British doctors she had already consulted—urging that, if the findings were again positive for cancer, she should tell *all* her children. Though the inevitable reconfirmation in the spring of 1899 did not lessen Vicky's determination to keep the nature and seriousness of her condition from the public, she conceded that her children, including the emperor, had to be informed. Very soon thereafter, all were told—excepting only Charlotte, whose near-life-long animosity obviously still wounded her mother.

Vicky spent her sixtieth birthday in November 1900 on her back. She had already been confined to her bed for more than a month, the cancer pitilessly spreading into her other organs. Most noticeable to visitors was the dowager empress's weight loss, the flesh on her arms and legs having withered away to near nothing, her face all too clearly divulging the pain that even carefully rationed morphine wasn't able to defeat. It became usual for uncontrollable screams to echo through Friedrichshof from a woman whose whole life had, ironically, been a study in physical control. The only medicine that seemed to genuinely please or help Vicky was her family—especially the grandchildren who gambolled through their grandmama's castle as though it were their best and most treasured playground.

The pain became a constant chord running through Vicky's whole existence. A spasm would come about every second hour or so, each lasting many long minutes. Her screams would summon the doctors, but inadequate relief came from their injections, which brought perhaps a quarter of an hour's release, if that. A physician moved into Friedrichshof so as to be available at any moment of the day or night. But still the doctors' well-intentioned promises that "the pain will soon wear off" went unfulfilled. Vicky wrote to Sophie that she wished for nothing so much as that "I were safe in my grave. . . ." Tried beyond endurance, she admitted to her daughter that "my courage is quite exhausted." At sixty, she looked like a wizened woman far beyond six decades, strangely now like her mother because of a face swollen to the roundness that had characterized the British sovereign.

When Victoria had asked Willy for permission to send over her own English doctor, the emperor refused, basing his disapproval on the grounds that "it would create a most deplorable feeling here. . . ." The memory of the Mackenzie disaster clearly weighed more on his mind than did his mother's suffering. Word of her daughter's distress had so unsettled the queen that Beatrice and Lenchen stopped reading Vicky's graphic letters to her in case the news were to prove more than she could bear.

At the end of 1900, Vicky again wrote to Sophie of her trial, expressing better than any biographer the depth to which illness had overtaken her:

> I have been in bed *six weeks* today. We have passed from summer to autumn, almost winter without my perceiving it. Of course I have plenty of time to think and think, and my thoughts are *not* cheerful. My legs are shrunken and fallen away to nothing, a mere skeleton. The agony is as bad as ever, the nights are a torture. In 24 hours I do not get 2 hours sleep. The pain is too frequent, too violent, like ever so many razors driven into my back. The tears and groans all night long drive me utterly mad. I often think I should put an end to myself if only I could. Oh, I cannot bear it any longer! Pity me! I do not think anyone can suffer much more.

Vicky's gravest blow came in January 1901: the news that her mother had died. Many Germans had been pleased to hear that their emperor's wife was at the dowager empress's bedside when the tidings were broken—her youngest daughter Mossy was the one to actually transmit the news—despite the still-widespread public animosity felt for *die Engländerin*. All Vicky could murmur was: "I wish I were dead, too." Her sympathetic staff had wished some way was possible to keep the news from their mistress, so sure were they that it would kill her. Vicky later expressed the depth of her anguish in writing: "Oh, how can pen write it, my sweet darling beloved Mama; the best of mothers and greatest of Queens, our centre and help and support—all seems a blank, a terrible awful dream. Realise it one cannot." The moment Moretta returned from England after

Victoria's funeral, Vicky begged her to recount each detail of what had transpired.

Removed from any direct effects of the queen's passing, many Germans still feared Victoria's death might well portend political disaster. Victoria's strong German ties—her mother and husband were German, her children married Germans, her grandchildren sat on German thrones—had forged a link between London and Berlin that seemed to guarantee that the growing malice between the two nations could be kept under control. Though it wasn't universally understood in Germany that the British head of state didn't possess the same political weight as did their kaiser, it was clear that England's new king was far less connected to either their nation or its interests than his mother had been.

A few weeks after Queen Victoria's funeral, Bertie—now King Edward VII—went to Friedrichshof to see his sister. So ill was Vicky from the spreading cancer that one courtier described her as looking "as though she had just been taken off the rack after undergoing torture"—and he knew this visit would be his last. Accompanying him was his personal physician, Sir Francis Laking. Bertie hoped Laking might be able to have Vicky's morphine dosages increased; but the doctor's presence infuriated both the emperor and the German doctors, who believed, with a logic that beggars understanding, that more morphine would shorten the dowager empress's life.

Another member of Bertie's traveling party was Frederick Ponsonby, his equerry, who happened to be Fritz's godson. It was to Ponsonby that Vicky entrusted her letters (they would fill two large suitcases) to be taken from the house and carried under the aegis of the British royal party back to Windsor for safekeeping. The memory of what had happened to her husband's papers on his death was still painfully fresh in her mind, and she was desperate that it not be repeated. She knew that if her son found out what she and Ponsonby were up to, he would instantly move to prevent the documents going out of his control—no matter her wishes or her brother's rank. On March 1, the morning of the English party's departure, Ponsonby showed up in the main hall at Friedrichshof with the two satchels among his own baggage, one marked CHINA WITH CARE, the other BOOKS WITH CARE. Under the protective screen of the king of England, the precious archives left Germany for England, where they remain to this day.[9]

When Bertie left Friedrichshof and returned to England, a long parade of Vicky's relatives replaced the king at her bedside. England's new queen, Alexandra, came in March for a visit—one filled with long talks that were marred only by Vicky's weakness and Alix's increasing deafness. Vicky's spirits were again lifted a bit when both Beatrice and Lenchen came to stay. Sophie and Tino arrived from Athens, Moretta and Adolf from Bonn, Mossy and Fischy from Kassel, Henry and Irene from Kiel. Those who had children brought them. Willy lent his presence to Friedrichshof twice in his mother's final months, at the end of April and again in mid-July. Dona visited, too, but Vicky clearly did not want her daughter-in-law around to taint days she wished to be filled with the family members she genuinely loved.

Just before Sophie's arrival in June, Vicky had sent this far-off daughter a report on her condition: "I have been terribly bad these last few days. The attacks of pain so violent, the struggle for breath so dreadful, when in bed or lying down, most distressing. . . . I manage to struggle through the day, I know not how. . . ." Still, she kept giving Sophie advice on how to be a good and useful queen to the Greeks, sending recommendations for everything from washing down the streets of Athens with seawater to the more subtle counsel that she "not be an idle spectator of what is going on" in the young nation over which this daughter and her husband would one day reign.

With the end obviously approaching—the sentries outside Friedrichshof asked to be moved so they wouldn't hear the screaming coming from Vicky's bedroom—Willy decided it was all right to go off on his annual summer cruise in the North Sea, which he did in the middle of July. He gave excuses, mainly that his mother seemed sufficiently mentally alert to last until his planned return.

To the end, Vicky's doctors carried on with their program to give her just enough morphine to ease the pain for a few minutes at a time, and then no more until the schedule allowed. She found the strength to dictate to her chamberlain what she wanted done after her death: no autopsy, no embalming, no photographs, no lying-in-state at Friedrichshof. She asked for a closed coffin at a service to be held in the Kronberg town church; and she wanted but a short prayer, and no sermon. Vicky also commanded that Friedrichshof itself go to her youngest daughter, Mossy, and that its contents—the lovingly collected treasures and trivia that had contented her since Fritz's death thirteen years earlier—be divided among her children. A gift was left for every employee and servant, and for many of the multitude who had been close to her or kind to her. Everything was neatly and tidily taken care of, just as one would have expected of this most orderly of women.

On Vicky's last full day, the Berlin papers finally stopped printing that her condition was "quite satisfactory," admitting instead that "the strength of the illustrious patient is fading fast." Willy had been notified of his mother's decline, and was scurrying home in a dash to reach Friedrichshof before the end. He arrived only thirty-six hours before she died. The three younger daughters took turns in the vigil at their mother's bedside. When Mossy and Sophie went outside to the garden for a short breath of air, it was Willy who was with the empress Frederick when she took her last breath, though she had been unconscious for hours and did not know he was there. It was early in the evening of August 5, 1901.

Vicky had been right to send her papers to England with Frederick Ponsonby. Before the warmth had gone out of her body, Willy set his Prussian cavalry searching every cavity and cubbyhole of Friedrichshof in a vain attempt to find the letters he suspected would show the world just how he had treated the woman who brought him into the world.

11

After Years

Her husband and now her mother dead, her children approaching adulthood, Beatrice sensed the familiar underpinnings of life were being swept from under her. The greater part of her adult lifetime had been spent working as Victoria's unofficial private secretary and she had grown accustomed to feeling generally useful. Though her services had consisted mainly in reading to her mother and writing personal letters for her, in seeing to minor family chores and crises for which the sovereign had no time, and in making sure the queen was properly attended to and never overextended, Beatrice had been in the most intimate private employ of the ruler of the largest empire and most powerful nation on earth. When that ruler died, so did Beatrice's significance.

Reduced to mere princesshood, she was too junior in the remaining royal family to count for much of anything, even as an ornament. She had too many times angered Bertie, now Edward VII, for being the bearer of disagreeable messages from their mother, or for being privy to matters of which he, as heir to the throne, had been left out. There was, though, one great contribution she might make to the new monarchy, and that would be a brilliant match for her only daughter. Though Beatrice never intended it so, that marriage would in fact turn out to be one of the most consequential of any of the unions of Queen Victoria's scores of descendants.

The loss of Liko had been a bitter blow for Beatrice. Though strains between the partners had surfaced when he went off to Africa in 1895, their relationship had provided Beatrice with the accoutrements of domesticity that counterbalanced her job at the queen's elbow. She had undoubtedly understood Liko's growing sense of futility and uselessness, his feelings of inadequacy when contrasted to his brother Louis's stunning headway in the Royal Navy. But there had been almost nothing Beatrice could do at court to promote wider responsibilities for her husband. He had freely made his promises on marriage—promises that had bound him to a regimen of amusing a sovereign mother-in-law for the rest of her life.

After Liko's funeral, Beatrice went off to Cimiez, in the South of France, to recuperate. It was the first time in her life that she permitted herself a lengthy seclusion, one without the sheltering presence of a mother who had smothered her, not just in childhood but throughout her life. Louise came over to Cimiez to keep her sister company, as did two of Liko's brothers. Two empresses—the exiled Eugénie of France and the ever-wandering Elisabeth of Austria—interrupted journeys at Beatrice's villa to offer the princess their advice on how to deal with the loneliness she was now facing.

Finally, Queen Victoria herself came to see how her daughter was managing and to try to nudge her gently back to her former life. Skillfully drawing her back into the royal routine, certifiably dull, the queen reinstilled in the young widow a sense of purpose. At almost forty, Beatrice determined that what was left to her, beyond her children who would soon enough be grown and gone away, was to do her best at the job she was trained for and that had given her life meaning. For the next five years, Beatrice again became the royal servant who was closer to the sovereign than any other person.

In these last years of her mother's life, the last half decade of Victoria's reign, Beatrice commanded the best seat in the house on affairs that spun like a hurricane around the tiny monarch at its calm center. From corraling her mother through the exhausting Diamond Jubilee ceremonies to "remembering" for her the endless details of the court over which she determined to retain her usual control, Beatrice served faithfully as the elderly sovereign's eyes and ears. Perhaps unavoidably, she represented to much of the court and royal family a private casket that often couldn't be pried open. Ministers sighed banefully at the thought of this essentially uneducated princess "explaining" state papers to the queen, and the highly turf-conscious offspring of the monarch could only stand mute as Beatrice's influence with their parent seemingly far outstripped their own. Though Bertie often utilized Beatrice's services to bridge the divide that separated him from the sovereign, he would never in his own subsequent rein fully forgive his sister for her role as a royal confidante—Beatrice was never once invited to Bertie's private country home in the Edwardian years.

When her mother's death ended her service, not the least of her new problems was where she would make her home. After she was widowed, the princess owned no property of her own; she and Liko had always lived at her parents' three major residences: Windsor, Balmoral, and Osborne (the queen detested Buckingham Palace, and after Albert's death refused to live in it). Windsor and Balmoral would be her brother's properties by right of his sovereignty, and she would not be made to feel welcome, certainly not as a full-time guest. Bertie and Alix had spent the last forty years on the windswept broads of Norfolk, at their enormous Sandringham estate. The new king decided to refurbish Buckingham Palace as his London home, while his son George and daughter-in-law Mary took over his old residence, Marlborough House, in Pall Mall.

Though Bertie inherited Osborne House outright, he hated just about everything associated with it. Not only were the memories of being humiliated there by his mother painful, but even its fussy decor and the trouble involved in reaching the property from the mainland made it anathema to him.

But the estate became—like Windsor and Balmoral—the new

king's to do with as he wished. The only string tied to Bertie's inheritance of the place was that his own heir be offered the property
if he himself decided to reject it. George, the duke of Cornwall and
York (he wouldn't be created prince of Wales for nearly a year after
his grandmother's death), told his father that he and May had no
plans ever to live there. With that, Bertie resolved to turn Osborne
over to the nation for whatever good use the government might
make of it. The only obstacles were the objections he expected
might arise from one or more of his three younger sisters.

In her will, Victoria had made generous provisions for her daughters' living arrangements after her death. The Christians would have
two homes: Cumberland Lodge in Windsor Park and a historic old
crown property, Schomberg House, in Pall Mall, just down the
street from Marlborough House. Bertie knew Lenchen wouldn't
need or want Osborne, that she and her husband spent most of their
time in London anyway, and thus shouldn't—and didn't—raise any
objections to his plans to turn the estate over to the nation.

Louise and Beatrice were each bequeathed a "cottage" inside the
Osborne grounds. Kent House, designated for Louise and Lorne,
and Osborne Cottage, for Beatrice and her children, were, if not
palatial, at least amply proportioned Tudor-style villas. Each was
surrounded by its own small "park," really a large garden. Lorne and
Louise of course had their own homes as a result of inheriting the
Argyll dukedom and estates—though Lorne's money problems
meant that Inveraray Castle was virtually shut down under his own-
ership—as well as their lavish apartments in Kensington Palace. In
point of fact, Louise was about as fond of Osborne as was Bertie,
though she would soon redecorate Kent House, hiring Haynes Bad-
cock rather than Lutyens—the latter had become too expensive—
to carry out her improvements. Bertie expected and got little
argument from the Argylls as to his plans for the big house.

Beatrice wouldn't be so easy. The princess was shocked at her
brother's plan to dispose of what, with considerable justice, she
considered her home. Osborne had always been so interwoven into
her life that she couldn't imagine leaving the main house to take up
permanent residence in an outbuilding she considered a guest cot-

tage. She had been married at Whippingham Church on the estate; her husband had served as governor of the island (a position the queen had transferred to Beatrice on Liko's death); and her own private suite was comfortably situated on the top floor of the Pavilion, directly above her mother's old rooms. She frankly thought of Osborne as being somehow holy, a shrine to Queen Victoria's memory, and that furthermore it should be permanently maintained as a kind of family temple. When Beatrice learned that the government planned to make a boys' junior naval college and an officers' convalescent hospital out of the main parts of the estate, and that Bertie thought the idea capital, she was stunned. What was more, the grounds of Osborne Cottage were so limited that the plan would mean the end of her privacy. As co-executor of Queen Victoria's will—along with her brother Arthur[1] and Keeper of the Privy Purse Sir Fleetwood Edwards—Beatrice could have made it difficult for Bertie to hand over Osborne to the nation at least during her own lifetime; and at forty-three when the queen died, there was no reason to imagine the princess's life would not continue for many years more. Yet the unspoken reality remained that Beatrice could not afford to keep Osborne in its pristine state; and to expect the taxpayer to maintain it with her as sole resident would raise significant political problems.

In the end, she gave in—her brother *was*, after all, king, and Beatrice was nothing if not a respecter of royal prerogative—but only after Bertie promised to enlarge the grounds of her "cottage" so that importuning naval cadets or wandering invalids couldn't come looking in her windows. To further mollify his sister, Bertie made the household wing—the portion of the Osborne House complex in which the queen's court had lived and worked—into a public museum. In addition, the Pavilion, the part where their parents had lived out their private life, was turned into an exclusive royal sanctum, off-limits to any but the family and a few trusted staff and retainers.[2] On an afternoon stroll at Osborne, Bertie, Louise, and Beatrice came to an agreement over this disposition of the property, and the remaining bulk of the estate was accordingly given as a gift to the nation from its king, effective on the day Bertie and Alix would be officially crowned in Westminster Abbey. In the summer of 1901, six months after Queen Victoria's death, Beatrice packed up her belongings from the big house at Osborne and moved into Osborne Cottage, its grounds now generously enlarged by the king for the sake of his sister's privacy.

While Beatrice accustomed herself to the idea of a reduced existence in terms of both comfort and importance, her sister Lenchen and brother-in-law Christian continued what had long since been an existence best described as placid, the peaceful waters of their life only occasionally disrupted by family deaths and such anomalies as the unorthodox behavior of their ex-son-in-law, Aribert. Lacking the gravity of Vicky's position, the fulfilling artistic enterprise of Louise's life, or a status such as Beatrice had enjoyed at the center of the monarchy, Lenchen seemed to have little extrafamilial purpose or value beyond her patronage of nursing homes. In 1894, she had founded the Princess Christian District Nurses. By the year after her mother's death she had undertaken to expand it with a medical and surgical nursing home dedicated to the memory of Prince Christian Victor, the son she had lost in the Boer War. The result was the Princess Christian Nursing Home in Windsor, which opened its doors in February 1904.[3]

The Christians' greatest pleasure was their residence at Cumberland Lodge, which they were forced virtually to rebuild between 1911 and 1913 when dry rot was discovered; in the process, long-forgotten tunnels leading to Windsor Castle and Royal Lodge were uncovered.[4]

Bothered by the usual diseases of age—neuralgia and rheumatism, eye trouble that Dr. Reid assumed was the result of her nerves having been "shattered by stimulants and narcotics"[5]—Lenchen in the new century saw relatively little of her two remaining sisters. However, as was expected of all members of the royal family, Lenchen and her husband continued to take their ceremonial part in the monarchy. As merely a sister and brother-in-law rather than a descendant and son-in-law of the queen, the Christians' precedence had taken a significant step downward. Bertie bestowed the Royal Victorian Chain on Christian, in recognition of "personal services to the sovereign"—an honor that in reality represented little more than a coronation present passed out to most of his closest relatives.

From time to time, Christian was employed as a personal emissary of the king to family celebrations on the Continent, as when in 1906 he represented Bertie at Willy and Dona's silver anniversary party in Berlin. At that time, he carried a letter to the emperor, in which the king assured his nervous nephew that Britain "has never had any aggressive feelings toward yours, and the idle gossip and silly tittle-tattle on the subject emanates from mischief-makers and ought never to be listened to. . . ." In fact, Britain was building a huge and decidedly aggressive-minded navy with that one very realistic enemy in mind.

Like Prince Alfred of Edinburgh and Prince Charles of Albany, his first cousins on his mother's side, as a boy the Christians' son Albert also found himself forced to go to Germany. When it became apparent that his aged and childless cousin, Duke Ernest Gunther, was highly unlikely to produce an heir, which would spell the end of the Schleswig-Holstein-Sonderburg-Augustenburg title, Albert was uprooted from Cumberland Lodge and packed off to Germany, to be turned into a German and, when the time came, to propagate the family.

After war broke out in 1914, a now-Germanified Albert offered his services to his new country, as did all young male subjects of his Hohenzollern cousin, the German emperor. Hoping to escape serving on the same battlefields as his own English cousins, including his aunt Beatrice's two boys, who were serving in the British army, Albert asked for and received dispensation from serving on the western front. He was duly stationed in Berlin, where he was put to work building the city's defenses. Still, the middle-aged prince was not happy at having to wage war on the country of his birth, where his parents and sisters lived. Tortured that Albert was being made to fight on the opposing side, Lenchen—who could not communicate with her son, though she knew he was not on the western front—could only remark that Willy "must be *quite* mad to have lit such a conflagration." Albert survived the war to indeed inherit the Schleswig-Holstein-Sonderburg-Augustenburg title when cousin Ernest Gunther died in 1921—three years after German titles became useful for little more than impressing the impressionable.

As a sad coda to their lives, Lenchen and Christian had finally become grandparents, yet neither was aware of it.[6] Christle was dead; Helena Victoria a spinster in her thirties; and Marie Louise considered herself still married even after the hideous episode of her father-in-law declaring her marriage to Aribert "null and void." Of the Christians' four children, only Albert could give his parents a grandchild, which was exactly what he did on April 3, 1900. But the circumstances were neither the stuff of dreams nor of acceptable royal behavior.

When he was thirty-one, Albert had a love affair kept so secret that his mistress's name has never been learned. He would tell his sisters Marie Louise and Helena Victoria (probably the only relatives to whom Albert revealed any of the details) only that a resultant baby, Valerie Marie, was of "high birth," and born in what was then Hungary in a town called Liptovsky-Svaty Mikulas. Albert saw to it that respectable foster parents raised her, a couple named Schwalb who happened to be Jewish. Shortly before her father's death in 1931, Valerie Marie received a letter from Prince Albert in which he admitted his half of her parentage; but Schwalb would remain her surname until her first marriage in 1935.

After divorcing that husband, a lawyer named Wagner, in 1938, Valerie Marie undertook to marry the duke of Arenberg. She was assumed to be Jewish because of her foster parents, and the German authorities not surprisingly refused to approve the marriage of a Jew to a gentile German nobleman. Apparently at Valerie Marie's request, her aunts Marie Louise and Helena Victoria both sent letters attesting to the true identity of her father. The English princesses' word was evidently good enough that their natural niece was allowed by the Nazis to marry Arenberg, which event took place in Berlin in 1939.

Valerie Marie's marriage lasted until her death in 1953, when the illegitimate great-granddaughter of Queen Victoria bore the title of serene highness. Her aunt Helena Victoria had died in 1948, but the elderly Marie Louise attended the funeral in Enghien, Belgium.

Once husband, mother, and home of a lifetime were gone, the preeminent glory of Beatrice's widowhood became her enormously attractive daughter. As the new century turned, Ena—as Princess Victoria Eugenia was universally called—was unfolding into one of the most beautiful of Victoria's granddaughters; of her female cousins, only Ella and Alix of Hesse and Marie of Edinburgh matched or exceeded Ena's extraordinary radiance. Though her Battenberg heritage was still deprecated by many in Europe's courts, Ena had had the good fortune to inherit her father's tranquil charm and physical glamour. Excruciatingly shy, as were many of her palace-bred cousins, her provenance ensured that she nonetheless represented a highly valuable commodity on Europe's royal marriage market. The only cloud—admittedly a very dark one—shading her future was her genetic proximity to the bleeding sickness now wreaking havoc on Queen Victoria's widely scattered family. Her brothers Maurice and Leopold both suffered from the disease, just as had their uncle, Beatrice's closest brother.

At the time of her coming out at the age of seventeen, the man who would become Ena's future husband set out from his palace in Spain in a kind of steamroller mission for a bride with whom to beget an heir to his own desiccated dynasty. The young man had, literally, been a king for every day of the nineteen years of his life. But a less felicitous partner for the blossoming Battenberg rose would have been difficult to envision.

Alfonso XIII—the numeral proved a harbinger of troubles that would beset his entire life—was born a year before Ena. The circumstances of his birth were virtually unique in European history. His father, King Alfonso XII of Spain, had died without a male heir. At his death, however, his wife was two months' pregnant. If the child she was carrying turned out to be a boy, that child would inherit from the moment of birth his father's kingdom and titles—albeit under a regency headed by his mother until he attained his six-teenth birthday. (Had the baby been a girl, Alfonso XII's first child, his six-year-old daughter Maria Mercedes, would have been de-clared queen-regnant.) On May 17, 1886, the Lord Great Cham-berlain of the Spanish court ran frenziedly into the room of the royal palace in Madrid wherein had gathered the entire court. Called to the queen's delivery bed, the august assemblage held its collective breath. Without an extant monarch—and a male sover-eign was infinitely preferred to one of the opposite sex—many be-lieved that Spain would sink into anarchy or some kind of terminal torpor. The country had persisted centuries longer than most of the rest of Western Europe in a state of ignorance that was positively medieval.

The Lord Great Chamberlain cried out that the dowager queen had given birth to a boy: in its father's honor, ignoring the fear that the number thirteen wasn't a good idea, he named the child Alfonso XIII. It was pointed out to the superstitious that Pope Leo XIII was then reigning in Rome, and that he hadn't been in any way unlucky. Born weak, fatherless, and subject to convulsions, Alfonso's aca-demic training in his early years was sacrificed to every possible at-tempt to strengthen his body. He grew up into a pencil-thin young man, with a saturnine cast to his features, and an uncontrollable sexual obsession that would drive him to nearly every pretty female he encountered. Once his mother's regency officially ended, he began to search for a wife who would, first, appeal to his keenly pitched sexual radar, and, second, betoken a fertility that would look to the future of Spain's nearly exhausted dynasty.

Reckoning that Victoria's granddaughters would be his best bet, Alfonso in 1905 homed in on King Edward's court under the pre-text of a state visit. He had heard that the duke of Connaught's daughter, another of Bertie's nieces, was the best-looking of the En-glish princesses. But when he met the lovely Princess Patricia, he found that the young woman was serenely immune to his overtures. Since he considered himself irresistible to women—a conceit that had arisen not from any personal attributes but from a lifetime of being the object of mass sycophancy—Alfonso was nonplussed.

With Patricia of Connaught thus eliminated as a future queen of Spain, Alfonso's wandering eyes caught on her tall and elegant cousin, Ena of Battenberg.

Entirely inexperienced of men and of the world outside her closed existence, Ena was overwhelmed by the attentions Alfonso directed her way. In turn, the young king was himself genuinely dazzled by Ena's fresh beauty and her radiant wholesomeness, as well as by the evident delight she showed at having been noticed by the man whom all Europe seemed to admire.

The idea of marriage between these two was unsuitable in almost every particular, with the possible exception of the infatuation that overcame the young princess. For starters, Alfonso himself was too highly sexed to present her with any imaginable prospect of domestic happiness, though neither the Spaniard nor Ena could have been expected fully to realize this at the time. The question of Ena's religion—she was Protestant, he, Catholic down to his chromosomes—was a huge obstacle. Though she had always been fascinated by and attracted to the religion of her godmother and namesake, the empress Eugénie, Ena could not become queen of Spain without actually converting to Roman Catholicism. Even language divided the two: Alfonso spoke only a scrap of English, Ena less Spanish, and it was French that became their first language of communication. But the greatest, though most shadowy, misfortune in the whole affair was the matter of hemophilia.

Since Princess Beatrice was a carrier, as her two hemophiliac sons proved, her daughter hypothetically stood an even chance of passing on the gene as well. In 1905, there was still no effective treatment for the illness, nor any means of testing a prospective parent of its victims. If Ena were a carrier, then half her sons, statistically speaking, would have the disease. For a king who represented the tail end of the Bourbon dynasty, and whose country's future tranquility was thought to depend upon the continuation of that dynasty, such a marriage had to be seen as rashly irresponsible.

In spite of all these problems, Alfonso made up his mind that the broad-hipped, pretty, not-terribly-bright Ena would make the perfect queen for Spain. He was told about the possibility of hemophiliac heirs, but apparently chose to believe that someone who looked so healthy couldn't possibly be the agent of so devastating an illness. The couple became unofficially engaged five days after their first meeting in London.

The events that took place on their wedding day a year later, May 31, 1906, were an ominous portent against any chance of happiness Ena and Alfonso might have achieved in Spain. Having converted to Catholicism and been rebaptized, which infuriated many of her own countrymen when she had to declare that her former Protestant faith had been a grave offense (the words went: "I reject every error and heresy . . ."),[8] Ena set off with Alfonso for the church of San Jeronimo, near the Prado Museum. There Cardinal Sancha, archbishop of Toledo and primate of all Spain, pronounced the couple husband and wife at the climax of a fairytale if tedious three-hour ceremony. At its conclusion, the cardinal bade his king and new queen go forth in peace.

Every era is soiled by social plagues of one sort or another, vexations that serve to remind leaders as well as the common man of their vulnerability. At the time of Alfonso and Ena's marriage, much of the world was wracked by anarchism, a movement born out of oppression, poverty, and social inequality, whose chimerical goal was to eradicate authority. To the kings and emperors and presidents governing when the twentieth century was young, simply stepping outside one's palace doors could prove fatal.

After the church service, Alfonso and Ena's state carriage wended its way along with forty other equipages past the thousands of thunderingly ecstatic *Madrileños* who packed the old heart of the city. One Mateo Morral, who had just barely been kept out of the wedding ceremony itself and thereby lost the chance to blow up half of Europe's royalty with the bomb he was carrying, now took the opportunity to throw the same bomb from a third-floor balcony overlooking the procession.[9] It exploded almost directly on the wedding couple's carriage, somewhere just ahead of the front wheels and behind the rear pair of horses. A shard of the bomb hit Alfonso's uniformed chest, one of his medals blunting the bit of shrapnel. However, a mounted guard serving as an outrider outside the new Queen Ena's seat was instantly decapitated, his blood splashing from his headless corpse all over Ena's wedding dress as though a can of red paint had been overturned on her. She was, miraculously, uninjured—at least physically. Outside the carriage, thirty-seven people were dead, a hundred more injured.[10]

Evidently determined to show her new husband and Spain that she could be a real queen, Ena remained eerily frigid in her calmness. Taken to the palace in another carriage, she acted as if in what seemed to many to be a stupor, insisting that the wedding reception be held as planned. The English would have been dumbstruck in admiration at her fortitude. But in a country that expects mayhem when something like this happens, ordinary people took her composure as a very bad sign. She would have been better off had she gone into hysterics and stayed that way for a few hours. Alfonso, who had indeed been courageous throughout the entire ordeal, was *supposed* to act becomingly brave. Ena wasn't.

Off to a hideous start with her Spanish life, within a year Ena handed her husband and the crown another misfortune. Her first-born, the new crown prince—called the Prince of the Asturias—was, tragically but not surprisingly, a hemophiliac. Alfonso was devastated. Looking forward to an heir so he could loosen the bonds tying him to his wife's bed, his bedazzlement with his bride turned to bitterness. When a second son went deaf at the age of three from a case of mastoiditis, which also greatly hampered the boy's ability to speak naturally, the couple's romantic attachment essentially ended. More children—daughters and, finally, a healthy son,[11] followed by another hemophiliac son (one additional son was still-born)—did nothing to save the marriage. Ena came increasingly to realize that any joy she might experience in Spain would derive from her prerogatives as queen, which prerogatives she began to take up in spades in an increasingly lavish lifestyle. As for Alfonso, he expended a large part of his energies condemning the "infirmity which was carried by my wife's family." In truth, even had not hemophilia disabled his heirs, the marriage had probably been doomed because of his inability to remain faithful. But he surely would have been a happier man without the disease and Ena might have been able to carve out some kind of contented life.

The remainder of Ena's tenure as queen of Spain saw her nearly entirely estranged from Alfonso. Her husband would petition Rome for an annulment, which the pope logically viewed as presumptuous in light of the couple's large family. In 1931, the monarchy itself collapsed in the chaos of an economically ruined nation. Alfonso and Ena separated, informally but permanently. He died in Rome in 1941, she in Switzerland in 1969, having lived to see Generalissimo Franco seal her grandson's position as successor to the long-vacant Spanish throne.

After Liko's death, Beatrice had been determined to maintain the funerary obsequies for her husband fully as carefully as had her mother for the prince consort. She kept up these funeral rituals in her new home at Osborne Cottage, and while still governor of the Isle of Wight, elevated Whippingham Church (the little church on the royal estate where she had been wed and where Liko lay entombed) to serve as chief shrine commemorating their marriage. She hung the engagement rings that they had exchanged in 1885 on the chalice that decorated the altar. With such loyalty did she mourn the date of Liko's death that, when sailing in the Mediterranean with tea magnate Sir Thomas Lipton on one such anniversary, Beatrice asked to be put into port at Nice where she could take communion.

With the death of her brother Bertie in 1910, Beatrice—like all three of her surviving siblings—fell another substantial step down from the throne in terms of precedence. Being a sister rather than a daughter of the monarch had represented a major reduction in relative rank; but on becoming merely the aunt of his son, now George V, the new king, she was left very much on the fringes of the court. Unlike Louise, who despite her age was managing to retain a remarkably youthful presence, by the time George ascended the throne Beatrice was irremediably an old woman, even though she wouldn't turn sixty for another seven years. In 1912 it was probably a bad heart that convinced her to sell Osborne Cottage, and with it her link to the home she knew most intimately and loved best. Thereafter, visits to the island of which she would for the rest of her life remain titular governor were spent at Carisbrooke Castle, the island's ceremonial seat.

Beatrice was at Carisbrooke when war broke out in the summer of 1914. Her brother-in-law (as well as nephew by marriage) Prince Louis of Battenberg, who was First Sea Lord[12] when Britain went to war with Germany, advised her to leave for the mainland, the island officially deemed vulnerable to enemy action. The princess heeded the warning and returned to London, where she spent the war years. Beatrice filled those years soldiering on with the sorts of activities expected of elderly princesses. Money for war relief was raised at bazaars, and hospitals were visited where the patients could experience the excitement of being attended to by a real live member of the royal family. The princess established her own hospital for officers, something many rich women were to do during the war; she named her Hill Street establishment the Princess Henry of Battenberg Hospital for Officers.

World War I was a monstrously wrenching experience for the children and grandchildren of Queen Victoria. Most had been raised as virtually "European" rather than of a single nationality, the English and German connections so intertwined as to make the siblings and cousins constant visitors in each other's countries and homes; further afield, the family sat on thrones or were members of royal families of Russia, Greece, the Balkan states, Sweden, Denmark, and Spain. Yet in the war Victoria's grandchildren fought on sides opposing those of their parents or of their own brothers and sisters and first cousins. Willy, unsurprisingly, became to most of his English relations the embodiment of wickedness; other German descendants, however, such as Ernie in Darmstadt, were never hated by their English relatives. Ernie, in fact, refused to serve with the German Army, instead devoting himself during the war to hospital service. Arthur's daughter, the wife of the heir to the Swedish throne, was instrumental in neutral Sweden in passing private family messages between siblings and cousins on the opposing sides.

A tragically high number of Victoria's descendants died in fighting on the battlefronts or in the political carnage that came in the war's wake. Beatrice's youngest son, Prince Maurice, was the first on the Allied side to be killed. On October 27, 1914, the twenty-three-year-old field officer was leading an attack on the Belgian front lines when he was killed, nearly instantly, by a piece of shrapnel from an exploding shell. Because of the royal connection, an exception was going to be made by Lord Kitchener to the general rule that the battle dead be buried where they died, and the commander ordered Maurice's body home for burial. But Beatrice interceded, asking instead that her son lie among his comrades in Belgium. At the memorial service held for the dead prince in London, King George and Queen Mary, Queen Alexandra, Prime Minister Herbert Asquith, and two field marshals joined Beatrice in honoring Maurice's memory.[13] More happily, his two brothers—one the hemophiliac Leopold—also served on the western front and both survived.

However, as the hatred begot by the war's carnage poisoned the British nation, so too did the ill-will affect even the king's own family. In 1917, the name of the royal house itself was changed from Saxe-Coburg-Gotha to Windsor, in a small miracle of a public relations coup. (It might be kept in mind, as it surely was by the king's advisers, that Germany's so-called Gotha bombers were at the time dropping their bombloads over London.) No family members in Britain were so passionately identified as "enemy" as those descending from the Battenbergs of Hesse, most of whom were in fact thoroughly British by this time. Thus, Princess Henry of Battenberg became known once again simply as Princess Beatrice. Her eldest son, Prince Alexander of Battenberg, lost his royal status and became the marquess of Carisbrooke, in honor of the Isle of Wight castle with which his parents had been so intimately identified. Beatrice's only other son who survived until the 1917 wholesale name-changing, Prince Leopold, became Lord Leopold Mountbatten, his new last name simply the anglicized version of Batten-berg.[14] Alice's daughter, Victoria, saw her husband, Prince Louis, hounded out of the Admiralty because of his German origins and because his wife's sister was married to the kaiser's brother, which seemed to "prove" his disloyalty. The couple became the Marquess and Marchioness of Milford Haven, under the new family name of Mountbatten. Queen Mary's two brothers, both as English as stewed eel but tainted by the enemy as princes of Teck, became the Marquess of Cambridge and the earl of Athlone. Finally, even Lenchen and Christian, the latter a resident of England since 1866, dropped the Schleswig-Holstein title, becoming simply Prince and Princess Christian. When Willy heard about all this, he cracked that all future German performances of *The Merry Wives of Windsor* should be staged under the title of *The Merry Wives of Saxe-Coburg-Gotha*. His humor was rarely so subtle.

As for the Christians, whose son Albert was serving in the German Army, Lenchen kept herself busy and possibly her mind off Albert by engaging in every kind of nursing and war relief activity she could get into. As president of the Royal British Nurses' Association, the princess visited as many hospitals as her advancing years would allow. The octogenarian Christian did little except shoot, the activity at which he had already lost an eye. In 1916, the couple celebrated their fiftieth year of their marriage, their partnership the lengthiest of any of Victoria and Albert's children and the only one to reach a golden wedding anniversary. Since Christian was high steward of the royal borough of Windsor, the town marked the occasion by sending a deputation to the Thanksgiving Service held at the chapel in Windsor Great Park. At the tea that followed, Lenchen received a telegram from the kaiser that had been routed by her niece, the Swedish crown princess: Willy wanted his aunt and uncle to know that he desired them to have his "loyal and devoted good wishes"—even as the Battle of the Somme, the deadliest to date in European history, had been raging for almost a week.

In 1917, Lenchen's odd but lovable white-haired, white-bearded, and one-eyed husband—the last surviving son-in-law of Queen Victoria[15]—died peacefully, after a short illness, in Schomberg House, his London home. King George was there, and Christian's last words to his nephew were to ask about the progress of the ongoing Battle of Caporetto: "George, what about those damned Italians?"

With the close of the Victorian era, Louise, like Lenchen and Beatrice, had become part of the "old royal family," associated with an age that had been swept aside by their brother with what many viewed as unseemly haste. Bertie had determined from the moment of his accession to change the nature of the monarch and monarchy. As king, he forsook the primarily private and unseen institution whose head had for so long been obsessed with the daily minutiae of deskwork. He replaced the old style with public ceremony and appearances and social glitter, with himself and his wife at the center for all the world to see, in a way Victoria would have regarded as vulgar. Louise entered this new world with a gusto she had never shown in her mother's time. Close to Bertie and Alix, she and Lorne became enduring social fixtures of the Edwardian decade. The new king frequently consulted his sister on domestic concerns, as when he set out to renovate the old-fashioned private apartments at Windsor Castle. Drawing upon Louise's commonsense in such matters, Bertie solicited from her advice on how many bathrooms should be built and exactly where they should be installed in a complex in which chamberpots and portable tubs had hitherto sufficed, even for the royal family.

Yet Louise's rapport with the new king sprang in part from her and Bertie's shared political views. Both tended to take the French and Russian positions on issues affecting Europe, eclipsing the German orientation that had characterized Queen Victoria and so much of the extended royal family allied to the various German courts. Louise's closeness with her brother also hinged on their shared love of simply enjoying themselves, both of them able to laugh passionately and often. It was a style that Lenchen and Beatrice, heavily influenced by their mother's morbidity, never thought quite appropriate to royal life.

Alix, meanwhile, admired Louise's unique talents. The new

queen relied on her sister-in-law to advise her on the intricate costumes she would wear at the coronation in 1902. Though Alix refused advice from all quarters on her coronation dress itself, she
knew Louise's sense of artistry could be counted on to complement
her own spectacularly good taste. To obtain the intricately embroi-
dered fabrics destined for Alix's many other costumes, as well as for
those of the attendants and ladies-in-waiting at the Westminster
Abbey coronation service, yards and yards of handiwork in all,
Louise called upon the Ladies' Work Society, which she herself had
formed and still sponsored.

Lorne, anxious as ever to assert his independence, irritated much
of the family when, in the spring of 1901, he accepted an offer to
write a life of his mother-in-law called, clumsily, *V.R.I. Queen Victoria: Her Life and Empire.* He was paid £1,300 to create a serial-like
biography that the well-known publisher Spottiswood planned to
issue in monthly installments. Chary of the personal revelations it
might contain, the king thought the project inappropriate. Willy
weighed in with his own sense of astonishment that Lorne would
share with the world what should only be known to the family,
pompously asserting that no "life of Grandmama can be published
before the next twenty years are over." With skilled diplomacy,
Bertie told Louise that her husband should give such a decision
"more thought." Lorne nevertheless went ahead, but nobody need
have worried too much about embarrassment. As a reviewer remarked, the wholly uncritical birth-to-death narrative might have
been better had the author been able to write with "greater freedom
and less responsibility."

Though the royal family keenly disapproved of the new duke of
Argyll's literary activities, Lorne kept up his writing with a 1907 au-
tobiography called *Passages from the Past.* While it said a lot about
his youth and the Argyll residences, what the reading public really
wanted were stories about Louise, the royal family, Kensington
Palace—or at least something from his own political life. But that
was not what they got, and the book sank with little notice, the
Bookman calling it a "pitiable waste of good material"; the reviewer

might have added that it was also a pitiable waste of good connections. From *Passages*, Lorne proceeded to his family's history, in *Intimate Society Letters of the Eighteenth Century*. Another opera collaboration followed, but *Fiona and Tera* (of which he was lyricist) wasn't even produced. Lorne's last published book was *Yesterday & Today in Canada*, less successful than his 1885 *Canadian Pictures*, which had covered much of the same material.

In the Edwardian years, Louise gave less effort to maintaining her incognito and far more to showing herself to a nation again fascinated with the fripperies of a freshly designed monarchy. With a marriage that had long since failed to provide any substantial physical or intellectual joy, her public duties—tasks the king openly solicited and expected his capable sister to fulfill in return for the state income she received—and her continued sculpting commissions gave her more happiness than she had known in years.

The dark side of Louise's new prominence was that she would find herself physically drained by her duties, her health having never fully recovered from the sleighing accident in Ottawa a quarter century earlier. The long hours of standing at public ceremonies and receptions, though fulfilled with dignity and poise, were still too often followed by even longer hours of rest in darkened rooms, recuperating from headaches and exhaustion.

In these years, Louise employed an impoverished Viennese lady of gentle birth. It was Madame Klepac's job to see to Louise's well-being, including supervising her exercise and diet. Madame kept her charge on a regimen whose aim was to try to ensure that the princess wouldn't become a prematurely elderly, overweight woman such as both Lenchen and Beatrice had turned into. Bertie, dangerously overweight himself, joked about the efforts his sister suffered at Kensington Palace each day under Madam's ministrations—Bulgarian yogurt, clear Chinese tea, no sweets, early to bed—but Louise assured her brother that these precautions meant she would never look as their mother had looked. Louise did smoke industriously, but although this wasn't considered quite proper, at the time no adverse health implications were associated with the habit. The reward of her attention to fitness was that Louise retained her slim figure, lovely complexion, clear eyes, and a bounce in her step that only the vile headaches could dampen.

They stemmed from a particular source of torment in Louise's life. After her husband inherited his dukedom, he engaged in increasingly erratic behavior, often climaxing in stormy and embarrassing tantrums. The golden-haired youth with a seemingly unlimited future had turned into an eccentric (his meals often consisted solely of bowls of baked potatoes), seriously overweight, usually irascible, and often nasty old curmudgeon whose vast promise of decades past had turned, for husband and wife alike, to somber disillusion. Even his membership in the House of Lords brought little joy. In 1908, Prime Minister Asquith's new Liberal government threatened to squeeze Lorne's class dry by placing steep levies on the rich and drastically paring down the powers of the upper House, both of which moves were, of course, anathema to the Scottish duke. It was usually Louise who calmed her husband's rages, though, according to Madame Klepac, Lorne often performed the same service for his wife, subject to her own fits of anger. Often, Louise's demons were tied to money problems—the lack of it—as well as to too much time on Lorne's hands. She still professed affection for him during the times when he wasn't in one of his "regular bad moods"; but small incidents set off outbursts which even she wasn't able to control and which led to the headaches that nearly drove her insane in their intensity.

On leaving a theater one evening in the spring of 1910, Louise noticed freshly printed broadsides bannering the news that the king had been taken ill. She immediately rushed to Buckingham Palace, where Alice told her that Bertie's chronic bronchitis had taken a bad turn, and was in fact so serious that he could neither breathe freely nor speak. Shortly after noon the next day, Bertie suffered a series of heart attacks, bringing Louise hurrying back to the palace from her Kensington home. Giving what he likely knew were his last hours to those closest to him, Bertie had himself fully and formally dressed in a frock coat and propped up in a chair, where as king and head of the family he could receive relations and friends for a final good-bye. Louise remained close by her brother through this time, until just before midnight on May 6, 1910, when he died. With Bertie's passing, Louise's last substantive links to the monarchy were severed.

Still, she kept going, through more years of receptions and charity bazaars and patronages, and even the presidency of the National Trust. Most of the benevolent organizations she supported benefitted deprived youth. Downtrodden girls were her special interest in light of the paucity of opportunity for the female sex in Louise's lifetime. "The Upper Classes have to work *very very* hard to keep things going," she told her lady-in-waiting, a not uncommon sentiment for a woman of her class, yet one that a lifetime as a royal princess had made her believe with all her heart. In 1913, and approaching seventy, Louise carried out more public engagements than she had ever done before in her life. So long as the headaches stayed away, her stamina was extraordinary.

Lorne, alas, enjoyed no such comparable sunshine of the spirit in the winter of his life, senility or possibly Alzheimer's disease beginning to cloud his memory. In April 1914, the sixty-eight-year-old duke contracted pneumonia, which quickly overcame both lungs. At Kent House on the Isle of Wight, Louise tended to him as to a child, gently applying fresh water compresses to his forehead as he labored to catch a breath. At 10:45 in the evening of May 2, 1914, while his wife of forty-three years held his head, the ninth duke of Argyll died.

Leaning on the new duke's arm—that of her nephew, Niall, the son of Lorne's brother Archie[16]—Louise followed her husband's coffin as it was pulled up the hill from Rosneath to the churchyard at Kilmun. The *Sunday Times* that week best expressed Lorne's place in his country's history: as governor general of Canada he had manifested "gifts of statesmanship of no mean order," even though he "always seemed to lack that tenacity of purpose and concentration of thought" that a true statesman should possess. If there was any blessing in the timing of his death, it was that he had escaped by a few months the beginning of the cataclysm that would tear away so much of the world he had known.

Louise wrote a verse for Lorne's sepulchre, the last lines of which spoke of the affection the princess held for the man with whom she had lived, in happiness and its want, for over four decades: ". . . to make the Empire Nations one/His best was given to serve his country's cause/Loving, high-souled, and valiant, he now lives/In death, as in earthly days, Beloved."

There were, at least, no money problems now. Besides her quarters at Kensington Palace and at Kent House at Osborne, Louise retained the extraordinarily beautiful Rosneath Castle as her dower house as duchess of Argyll, and with it the connection to the Highlands she had known from her first halcyon days at Balmoral. Rent from duchy lands which Lorne personally owned would accrue to her for life. Without children, she was unconcerned about the necessity of providing for the next generation.

But for the twenty-five more years Louise would live as a widow, being without Lorne could be onerous. Though their relationship had more than once looked as though it might end in divorce, the companionship at least provided shared memories and the pleasure such sharing brings. Lorne and Louise had learned to depend on one another, to soothe each other's frustrations and tempers, and to simply be familiar faces always at hand. Disparate interests kept them apart much of the time, yet they always seemed willing and even relieved to end such separations. With first her mother dead, then her brother Bertie—two people who since her birth could be counted on to help or advise or support her—and now Lorne gone as well, Louise was simply lonely and alone, with nobody to lean on.

Like her sisters, she was eventually forced out of any self-pity by the national needs occasioned by the war. Louise performed an exceptional act of family kindness when in the winter of 1914–15 she gave Kent House to her virtually houseless niece and nephew, Victoria and Louis of Battenberg, the latter just booted so callously out of the Admiralty. This was no small sacrifice for Louise, who later often admitted to missing her old home. With her gift, there now ceased to be any connection for any of Victoria and Albert's children to their beloved Osborne.

Bringing special pride to the princess during the four years of the Great War were the Canadian units that came to Britain en route to the front. As she inspected and cheered them on, she exhorted the men with her late husband's message to defend the great imperial family. Seventy at war's end, Louise was elevated by her nephew, George V, to Dame Grand Cross of the British Empire in recognition of her contributions to its victory. A year after the war ended, he also appointed her colonel in chief of the Argyll and Sutherland Highlanders. Many Britons would long remember catching a glimpse of her, proud and standing straight as a flagpole, as she inspected her troops on their celebratory reviews.

Once peace was restored, Queen Victoria's three surviving daughters[17] were, unarguably, old ladies who belonged to a world now beyond retrieval. Though their nephew the king tried, perhaps anachronistically, to maintain the forms of his grandmother's and father's courts, a war-ravaged and democratized British nation had begun to regard the institution of monarchy with the first blush of skepticism. The sisters had become museum pieces. Of these last survivors, the first to go would be Lenchen.

In the spring of 1923, at the age of seventy-seven, Lenchen fell victim to influenza—then a worldwide killer—and, at the end of May, suffered a severe heart attack. On the morning of Saturday, June 9, Victoria and Albert's eldest surviving child died, cared for at the end by Lord Dawson of Penn, the king's personal physician.

The following Friday, Lenchen was buried at Windsor. Louise and Beatrice, their brother Arthur, Lenchen's two daughters—Marie Louise and Helena Victoria—and many younger members of the family attended the service at St. George's Chapel. It was a gray day, brightened only by the scarlet tunics of the Life Guards and Grenadier Guards. A troop of the King's Royal Rifles represented the regiment in which Lenchen's son Christle had fought and died in the Boer War; the khaki-clad troops were given the place of honor lining each side of the wide stairway leading up to the chapel's west door. The least known and most private of Victoria's children, Lenchen was taken in her coffin from the golden splendor of the royal family's signature church to the dark privacy of the tomb house below the Albert Memorial Chapel. There she would join the waiting Christian, the prince with whom she had passed a half century of contentment.

Though Louise's physique in her last years had remained that of a fit woman, the complaints of age hadn't passed her by; sciatica was the worst—"real vile pain that makes you shout," was the way she described it.

But there were still satisfactions. Throughout the twenties, Louise busied herself with charitable work and the methodical disposal of a lifetime of possessions. The princess always made herself available for the Kensington Dispensary and Children's Hospital, of which she had served for many years as patron. When the hospital outgrew its old buildings, she headed a relocation committee to find a replacement site, resulting in a new facility called the Princess Louise Hospital for Children, in North Kensington. In 1928, she was made Honorary Freeman of the Royal Borough of Kensington, the first recipient of that title.

As for her countless treasures, many of the fragile or especially valuable mementoes, some of great worth, were bequeathed to the Victoria and Albert Museum, while more personal objects were distributed to her family and friends: Lorne's scrapbook went to her niece, Lady Mary Glyn, because Louise could not "bear to think it . . . would be discarded or thrown away or got into the wrong hands." A large portion of her property—jewelry and sentimental keepsakes—she stored in a cupboard from which each piece would be handed out to its designated recipient after her death.

Generous as she was, she nonetheless once thwarted Queen Mary's notorious acquisitiveness. Her nephew's wife was famed for remarking on how much she liked some prize or another, successfully assuming its owner would feel obligated to hand it over. Louise was herself of sufficiently high birth not to be daunted. When the queen spotted a clock that took her fancy in her aunt's Kensington Palace flat, the princess stationed herself between Mary and the object of desire and avowed, "the clock is here, and *here* it will stay."

Louise spent most of her last years at Rosneath, passing a sort of "hermit existence." She wasn't, of course, literally alone, only that the servants didn't count. Sharing some of her niece's presumptuousness, she liked to prowl around the nearby village well into her eighties, making sure all was well and the residents safe. She thought her royal status meant she could walk into any cottage, unannounced, any time she wished, more than once catching people in situations not appropriate for a princess's eyes. Louise came from a family which believed that many of life's middle-class standards were meant only for those who were middle class.

The end neared in late November 1939, after a new war had started but before the bombs came. Ill and unable to talk for the first time in her life, the ninety-one-year-old lady wanted to simply stop living. Still lean and graceful to the very last, Louise clearly found that the infirmities she now faced made going on pointless. On December 3, at Kensington Palace,[18] she died, of old age, with very little fuss. The grass outside her windows had just been dug up for slit trenches; in retrospect, it was undoubtedly a mercy for this very elderly princess that she didn't have to see them put to their lamentable purpose.

Typical of her interest in things most of the royal family wouldn't have thought about, never mind become involved in, the princess left instructions that she be cremated. The idea appalled the Campbells, her nephew (Lorne's successor as duke) writing, "I dislike cremation and none of my ancestors have practised it and certainly none of the Royal Family either." Louise knew that Lorne wouldn't have approved any more than the rest of his family; when in 1910 the princess had first received a pamphlet from the Cremation Society, Lorne had been revolted at the idea. Nonetheless, her request was fulfilled. Her body was burned at Golders Green, in North London, and the boxed ashes put in a coffin and taken to Windsor for the funeral. To the gentle melody of "Flowers in the Field" piped and skirled by the Argyll and Sutherland Highlanders, and watched by many Campbells and members of the royal family alike, Princess Louise was laid to rest, not with her husband at Kilmun, but in the Royal Cemetery at Frogmore that lay at the heart of the British monarchy.

Of the five, it now came down to Beatrice alone. Her life after the Great War consisted in large measure of watching her relatives die. Most painful to her was the death of her own son, who had lived with her at Kensington Palace. In 1922, the musically talented Leopold— since the king's renaming spree in 1917 called Lord Leopold Mount-batten—died, at thirty-three, after emergency surgery at Kensington Palace. In truth, *any* surgery, no matter how minor, would have been dangerous for this hemophiliac. Neither his mother, who was in Sicily, nor his sister Ena could reach him before he died, the day after the operation. A violinist who had never married, the high point of his life had been the soothing effect his playing was said to have had on his grandmother, Queen Victoria, during the final hours of her life.

The last two decades of Beatrice's life were seriously impaired by rheumatism, bowing her frame and making her look much older than she really was. A fall at Kensington Palace in 1931 nearly killed her: after breaking two arm bones when she slipped on a mat, bronchial illness set in. Because her doctors expected the worse, Ena was called back to London from Madrid, where the Spanish queen was enduring the final chaotic days of Alfonso XIII's melancholy reign. Beatrice pulled through with her daughter at her side, and Ena returned to Madrid at the end of February, less than two months before Alfonso was to be forced off his throne.

Though Beatrice would live another thirteen years, they were essentially hollow years, passed under the constant care of her physicians. The only task she could put her hand to was the editing of her mother's journals, a trust Queen Victoria had willed to her youngest daughter, with the instruction that Beatrice should change or eliminate any passages in her thousands of pages of diaries that could prove embarrassing to the writer or to those she had written about. Tragically, the fully compliant Beatrice eradicated or bowdlerized massive portions of the monarch's daily notes, burning the original pages she had "edited," and transcribing the remains into her own handwriting. The 111 volumes that Beatrice reworked of her mother's originals are today preserved in the Royal Archives at Windsor.[19] Her loyalty deprived historians of much of one of the greatest historical treasures of the nineteenth century. Beatrice furthermore "systematically destroyed," in Lord Esher's description, some thirty volumes of her mother's letters to her second son Affie and to Princess Alice.[20]

After cataract surgery, her visits to the Isle of Wight, where Beatrice still officially served as governor, got her occasionally out of the gloomy confines of her Kensington Palace apartments. But the outbreak of World War II put an end even to these journeys. Beatrice's last task was the translating from German into English of the diaries of her great-grandmother, Augusta, duchess of Saxe-Coburg-Saalfeld (the duchess of Kent's mother). The princess selected extracts from Augusta's diary and turned them into a book called *In Napoleonic Days*, published in 1941, the proceeds going to war charities.

Beatrice became the last living child of Victoria and Albert on January 16, 1942, when her brother Arthur—the duke of Connaught—died at age ninety-one. Arthur had survived two of his three children: not only did his elder daughter, Crown Princess Margaret of Sweden, predecease him, but so did his heir, Prince Arthur of Connaught, who died three years earlier. The Connaught title passed to the younger Arthur's son, the twenty-seven-year-old earl of Macduff.[21] But the grandson did not long survive the grandfather; Alastair Arthur Windsor died a year later while on active duty in Ottawa, and with his death the male Connaught line and thus the title came to an end.

For the last two years of her life, Beatrice lived at the lovely Brantridge Park, in Sussex. The country house belonged to the earl of Athlone, her godson, and his wife, Princess Alice of Albany, Beatrice's niece (Leopold's daughter). Keeping his great-aunt out of wartime London meant less worry for the harried George VI, who had enough on his mind beyond the safety of the oldest members of the royal family. Beatrice remained entirely out of the public eye in her last days, but was joined at Brantridge by Lenchen's daughters Marie Louise and Helena Victoria.

At the end of October 1944, her health took a turn that the doctors knew would end in a quick death. Ena was notified but, living in Switzerland, had no idea how she was going to get to England with a war raging. The British government stepped in and sent a converted bomber to fetch the exiled Spanish queen back to London. Ena got to Brantridge just in time to be with her mother at the end. Princess Beatrice died in her sleep at 5:10 A.M., on October 26, 1944. She was eighty-seven. The next day, the bells of St. Paul's Cathedral tolled for an hour in her memory.

Because of the war, the obsequies were relatively simple, insofar as anything connected with Britain's royal family is ever simple. After the funeral at St. George's Chapel, Beatrice's body remained temporarily at Windsor, housed in the royal vaults. The following year, just two months after V-E Day, her son Alexander asked the king if he could transfer it to the final resting place that she herself had chosen. In accordance with the monarch's permission, a hearse arrived at Windsor, and on it was loaded the coffin bearing the remains of Queen Victoria's youngest child.

Its destination was Portsmouth. There a naval guard of honor stood at attention at the quayside, all the flags in the vicinity rippling at half-staff. Alexander received the hearse, and helped put the coffin onto a boat. The little craft, escorted by a naval contingent, took its load across the Solent and disembarked it at Cowes. The consignment was then carried to Whippingham Church. On that warm summery day, Beatrice was finally laid next to her beautiful Liko. The last daughter of Victoria had come home.

Notes

CHAPTER 1

1. The origin of the term "morganatic" is uncertain; some ascribe it to the German *Morgengabe* (the "morning gift"), others to *more danico* (marriage "Danish style").
2. The duke would in later years spend a large part of his time in Hanover in fulfillment of his duties as that small German state's king. On Victoria's accession in 1837, the Hanoverian crown passed to Cumberland because of the Salic law that barred women from its throne, thus breaking a link between Hanover and Britain that had existed since the Hanoverian George I inherited the British throne in 1710 on the demise of the last Stuart monarch, Queen Anne.
3. The princes of Leiningen lost their sovereign status when Napoleon subsumed the little state into Bavaria and Baden, even though they continued to rank as *ebenbürtig* (possessed of "equality of birth") and were thereby eligible to marry into Europe's sovereign houses.
4. His diplomatically formulated title was king of the Belgians rather than king of Belgium.
5. Locock, a native of Edinburgh, would after a few more royal deliveries become jocularly known as the "Great Deliverer of His Country."
6. The last princess royal before Vicky, King George III's daughter Charlotte (who became queen of Würtemberg), had died in 1828. Since there can be only one princess royal at a time, had Charlotte still been

living when Vicky was born, Victoria would have had to wait for Charlotte's death before being free to give the title to her own daughter.

7. His eldest daughter would inherit (or perhaps only emulate) this characteristic, which contributed to her later problems adjusting to the role of Prussian crown princess.

8. Lehzen had been created a Hanoverian baroness in 1826 by King George IV, who was king of both Britain and Hanover.

9. The tight corsets worn under the layers of her elaborate dresses remained in place even during pregnancies.

CHAPTER 2

1. This last factor more than anything else ruled out consideration of Brighton's Royal Pavilion as a getaway site. The holiday seaside confection, built by George IV when he was regent, ill-suited the conventional tastes of both queen and prince. Its associations with Victoria's distasteful Hanoverian uncles were, furthermore, far too fresh, and the building was—for a woman who felt people were always looking at her—far too public: the town's sidewalks came right up to the windows on one side.

CHAPTER 3

1. He would die two years later, and was taken to his funeral in one of the most spectacular ceremonials of the Victorian era.

2. "Duncan" was a complement to "dear Scotland," as the queen explained her reason for including it among the boy's names. His first name was, of course, given in honor of Uncle Leopold of Belgium.

3. Only a few female hemophiliacs—daughters of marriages between first cousins—have ever been recorded. None could have lived past puberty, as the onset of menses would cause them to bleed to death.

4. In Queen Victoria's case, it was only the last of her four sons who got hemophilia.

5. Research done by William Bullock for the Eugenics Society (1911). See Potts and Potts in the Bibliography for a greatly detailed expansion on the subject of hemophilia and Queen Victoria.

6. A title bestowed by Victoria on her husband in 1857, partly in lieu of the peerage Parliament never granted Albert.

7. Some historians say his condition was the result of disabling strokes; the king's bizarre behavior in his last years could have been explained by such mental incapacitation.

8. After its first year, the Crystal Palace was carefully moved to Sydenham, where it survived as a tourist attraction until burning to the ground in 1936.

9. "Electors" referred to the seven most powerful rulers in the Holy Roman Empire, who together formed an Electoral College to appoint the emperor; the rulers of Brandenburg had held one of these Electoral seats.

10. Called the *first* Frederick William because his predecessor of that same name had been only an elector, not a king.

11. The queen foolishly insisted Vicky's title should be both Princess Frederick William of Prussia and Princess Royal of Great Britain.

CHAPTER 4

1. Battenberg would cease to be part of Hesse when it was annexed in 1866 by Prussia in the latter's war with Austria, in which Hesse sided with Austria.

CHAPTER 5

1. David Duff in *Hessian Tapestry*, p. 74.

2. Unable to pass the bill, Bismarck simply closed down Parliament.

3. Unusual in this extended family, the girl would always be called by her real first name rather than by a nickname. In later life as the wife of Prince Louis of Battenberg (afterward Marquess of Milford Haven), Victoria became the mother of Earl Mountbatten of Burma and, via her daughter Alice, the grandmother of the present duke of Edinburgh.

4. Queen Victoria famously named a cow in the royal herd "Alice" after her daughter—the jest apparently the monarch's way of showing her distaste for a practice she found vulgar.

5. The New Palace was destroyed by the 1944 Allied air raids that created a firestorm in the heart of Darmstadt, nearly annihilating the city.

6. Of Louis's two brothers, William functioned as a Hessian staff officer on the grand duke's staff, while Henry served on the Prussian side,

though thoughtfully sent to a front on which he would not encounter Hessian forces under his own family members.

7. Today the Royal College of Art.

8. This principle was still invoked in the late twentieth century in Norway, when King Olav objected to his heir's marriage to a commoner on essentially the same grounds.

CHAPTER 6

1. The birth coming eight months after the prince consort's death, Vicky was honoring her father in naming this son.

2. This empire would incorporate the French-speaking provinces of Alsace and Lorraine, an action Bismarck took against the advice of many (including Fritz) who believed, correctly as it turned out, that this would generate long-lasting and unnecessary resentments on the part of the losing French.

3. Unlike the British prime ministership, the imperial chancellorship was answerable not to Parliament but to the sovereign. This difference would by 1914 fatally injure the German system.

4. Having been created a count in 1866, he was now upgraded to prince, a rank that was commonly used outside Britain as a nonroyal title.

5. Augusta would become German empress a few months later.

6. Part of Gladstone's speech in favor of passing the queen's requests for her children carefully pointed out how terrible it would be if London's parks were "cut up into building lots" by the queen. In theory, the royal parks belonged to the monarch.

7. Another son was born in 1876, but the boy, named Harold, died when he was eight days old.

8. This letter was found by Alice's biographer Gerard Noel in the State (formerly Grand Ducal) Archives in Darmstadt.

9. Noel writes that there is nothing in the Darmstadt State Archives to indicate what her mother had said that was so troubling.

10. Five years later the people of Eastbourne opened, through public subscription, the Princess Alice Memorial Hospital; the prince and princess of Wales cut the ribbon in June 1883.

11. The grandmother of Prince Philip, the present duke of Edinburgh.

CHAPTER 7

1. Prussia continued to exist in the empire as the most important of the constituent governments, and the German emperor and king of Prussia would always be the same man.
2. Vicky's eighth and last child had been born in the spring of 1872: Margaret, known in the family as "Mossy." Vicky asked her sister Beatrice to stand as godmother for the infant, a much-appreciated gesture for the fifteen-year-old who had felt left out of this aspect of her extended family's life.
3. Today, Cumberland Lodge is used by the King George VI and Queen Elizabeth Foundation of St. Catherine's, wherein students study Christian philosophy. The queen mother is the organization's Patron, Princess Margaret its Visitor.
4. A bill finally making such marriages legal was passed by Parliament in 1896, with the prince of Wales's support.

CHAPTER 8

1. Such was his title while he was serving in Canada; his earldoms would later be upgraded by the queen to marquess of Dufferin and Ava.
2. Sandra Gwyn's phrase in *The Private Capital* (see Bibliography).
3. Dufferin was going to St. Petersburg, where he would serve as ambassador. His career would climax in the viceroyalty of India, as well as innumerable British honors, including the inestimably chic Lord Wardenship of the Cinque Ports.
4. The painting is today reversed, on the outward-facing side of a door in the residence's principal private corridor.
5. Though Victoria had "raised" her son-in-law's rank to royal highness, this held only in Britain, and was unrecognized in Germany.
6. David Duff in *The Shy Princess*.
7. Not that Victoria herself now had any need of his services; the position was simply a royal sinecure and filled by one of the leading obstetrical practitioners in Britain.

CHAPTER 9

1. A year later, the Bulgars found another German prince to take up residence in the Sofia palace as their new ruler. Ferdinand of Coburg was reputed to use face powder and consult only female physicians to treat his delicate constitution. His dynasty lasted until the outbreak of World War II.
2. Frederick had been a moderate smoker.
3. The snare was electric; once in the throat, the electricity was turned on and the cold wire quickly heated.
4. The 1887 Jubilee was not officially called a "Golden" Jubilee, although that was what it in effect amounted to and how many writers since have referred to it.
5. The German press in an attempt to discredit Mackenzie would later assert that the British doctor had taken the tissue from the undiseased part of the larynx.
6. He wanted to call himself Frederick IV, thereby including a Hohenstaufen emperor from the Holy Roman Empire who had borne that name. Bismarck considered there was no connection between the Holy Roman Empire and the current German empire, and convinced Fritz he should call himself Frederick III. This episode appears to have been one of the few instances when Vicky agreed with Bismarck.
7. Puttkamer was later rehabilitated, in 1891 becoming *Oberpräsident* of Prussian Pomerania; he held the office until 1899, a year before his death.
8. The autopsy performed on Fritz by Rudolf Virchow—only the throat and chest were examined—showed that the entire vocal cord had been destroyed by cancer. Virchow wrote that "the Emperor had cancerous destruction of the larynx with secondary disease of a rather large lymphatic gland at the lower portion of the left neck and a cutaneous nodule at the right side near the wound. The esophagus was unaffected. Inflammatory destruction of the upper portion of the windpipe and the neighboring tissue. Numerous bronchiectasis with putrid contents. Near these, bronchopneumonic suppurating gangrenous patches."
9. Though it is said that the intended Gaelic name was Eua, not Ena, the mistake a misreading of the name on the birth certificate by the officiating cleric at the baptism.

CHAPTER 10

1. There had been speculation that Leopold might follow Lorne as governor general in Ottawa, his visits to the dominion having given him some claim to understanding the country. Though both Lorne and the Canadian government approved the idea, and even the queen liked the thought of her son representing her in Canada, there was never a realistic chance of such an appointment because of Leopold's hemophilia.
2. Lorne had sold their English country home, Dornden, just before leaving for his post in Canada.
3. After 1947, Earl Mountbatten of Burma.
4. As governor general of Moscow in later years, the full vent of the grand duke's steely retribution for his father's regicides would be employed with vintage Russian rigor.
5. Today the office of the federal chancellor of Germany.
6. The actual day of the anniversary of her accession fell on a Sunday, so it was decided to celebrate on a weekday when a Bank Holiday could be declared.
7. Prince Alfred of Saxe-Coburg and Edinburgh was heir to his father, Victoria's second son, Affie. Affie had inherited the Saxe-Coburg dukedom from his uncle Ernest in lieu of the normal succession to his older brother, Bertie, the prince of Wales; the arrangement was one of many years standing. Affie's son Alfred was brought up in the Coburg court. There the young prince fell in love with an Irish woman, a relationship his mother, the daughter of Tsar Alexander II, found incomprehensible. Alfred married the woman, but his parents insisted the union be annulled as illegal under the Royal Marriages Act of 1772, which encompassed the descendants of England's King George II. Suffering from venereal disease and acute depression, Alfred shot himself, almost but not quite fatally. Sent to recuperate at Meran in the Austrian Alps (against his doctor's advice but on his parents' insistence—the latter didn't want his presence spoiling their silver anniversary celebrations), he instead died—evidently from the effects of the move carried out against his doctor's advice. He was almost completely alone at the time of his death, without family members to comfort him, only a tutor and a medical attendant, circumstances which for a grandson of the queen of England seem hard to believe.
8. Lorne continued to be known as such even after inheriting the dukedom. Since he had no direct heir who would require the title, little

confusion arose from his using the subsidiary family title by which he had been known all his life.

9. The letters were edited and a selection published by Ponsonby in 1929 under the title *Letters of the Empress Frederick*.

CHAPTER 11

1. The duke of Connaught's small palace in London, Clarence House, had been transferred from his brother Affie upon the latter's death a year earlier, and he also maintained a country estate, Bagshot, southwest of London in Surrey.
2. The Pavilion was finally opened to the public in 1955.
3. After Princess Christian's death, her daughters Helena Victoria and Marie Louise took over sponsorship of the home, putting much of their energies into increasing its patient capacity.
4. In 1947, Cumberland Lodge became the home of the King George VI and Queen Elizabeth Foundation of St. Catherine's.
5. Dr. Reid, Queen Victoria's personal physician during the latter years of her life, maintained a friendship with Lenchen, Louise, and Beatrice long after the queen died.
6. The possibility exists that Lenchen may have learned the facts late in her life.
7. The actual wording of the letters went as follows: "We hereby acknowledge and declare that Valerie Wagner [her first husband's name] is the illegitimate daughter of our brother His Highness Duke Albert of Schleswig-Holstein, who died on the 27th of April 1931. We are entirely ignorant of the names and identity of Valerie Wagner's mother, but we understand that she was a lady of very high rank. Our brother in order to shield this lady's honor never divulged her name to anyone. Valerie Wagner's foster parents, in whose name she was registered, were of Jewish descent, but we desire to emphasize the fact that Valerie Wagner herself is *not* of Jewish birth. Our brother, the Duke of Schleswig-Holstein, in a personal letter to Valerie Wagner, deplored the fact that she had been entrusted to the family of a different race and faith to her own."
8. The fact that it was called a *re*-baptism was especially galling; her first baptism had been under Queen Victoria's roof, which should have been accounted (even in Spain) about as valid as any Christian service of this nature could possibly be.

9. Morral, called a "syphilitic maniac," was found two days later; after killing a policeman, he turned his gun on himself and committed suicide.

10. Affie's widow, who had been a Romanov grand duchess and was a guest, expressed lack of surprise as "these things happen all the time in Russia."

11. This latter son, Don Juan, is the father of the present king of Spain, Juan Carlos.

12. Uniformed head of the Royal Navy.

13. Maurice hadn't been the only or the first of Queen Victoria's descendants killed in the war. Two weeks earlier, her great-grandson Prince Maximilian, the second son of Vicky's youngest daughter, Mossy (Margaret of Hesse), was killed at a spot only fifteen miles from where Maurice would fall. Mossy's first son, Prince Friedrich, would be killed two years later in fighting in Romania. Maximilian and Friedrich, of course, fought on the German side.

14. It might be noted that there is in fact a place called Battenberg in England, a little headland overlooking the sea near Plymouth.

15. Lorne had died a few weeks before the war began (see below).

16. Archie had died in 1913, and thus missed becoming tenth duke himself.

17. One son still lived, too—Arthur, duke of Connaught.

18. Her sister Beatrice and niece Princess Victoria of Hesse (now the marchioness of Milford Haven, to whom Louise had in 1914 given her Osborne house) lived in nearby apartments in the same palace.

19. It is said that the portions of the journal covering the years 1832–61 were preserved by an order from King Edward VII and that they were typed from the originals. Beatrice is said not to have been aware of this act. If this is true, these copied portions have not been released to the public.

20. See James Lees-Milne's *The Enigmatic Edwardian*.

21. He bore this courtesy title in respect of his mother who had inherited in 1912, by special remainder, the dukedom of Fife.

Bibliography

From a family point of view, the most important sources of correspondence from Queen Victoria are the six volumes of letters between the queen and her eldest daughter. In chronological order they are: *DEAREST CHILD—Letters Between Queen Victoria and the Princess Royal—1858–1861* (1964); *DEAREST MAMA—Letters Between Queen Victoria and the Crown Princess of Prussia—1861–1864* (1968); *YOUR DEAR LETTER—Private Correspondence of Queen Victoria and the Crown Princess of Prussia—1865–1871* (1971); *DARLING CHILD—Private Correspondence of Queen Victoria and the Crown Princess of Prussia—1871–1878* (1976); and *BELOVED MAMA—Private Correspondence of Queen Victoria and the German Crown Princess—1878–1885* (1981), all edited by Roger Fulford and published by Evans Brothers, London. *BELOVED AND DARLING CHILD—Last Letters Between Queen Victoria and Her Eldest Daughter—1886–1901*, is edited by Agatha Ramm and published by Alan Sutton, Gloucester, 1990.

Other books containing the queen's correspondence include *Queen Victoria in Her Letters and Journals*, selected by Christopher Hibbert (New York: Viking/Penguin, 1985), and *The Letters of Queen Victoria* in three volumes—the first edited by A. C. Benson and Lord Esher, the second and third by George Earle Buckle (all published by John Murray, London, and all under Princess Beatrice's famous revising). A further source in this vein is *Letters of Queen Victoria from the Archives of the House of Brandenburg-*

Prussia, edited by Hector Bolitho (New Haven: Yale University Press, 1938).

For biography of Queen Victoria, three important sources are *Queen Victoria: Born to Succeed* by Elizabeth Longford (New York: Harper & Row, 1964); *Victoria—An Intimate Biography* by Stanley Weintraub (New York: Dutton, 1987); and *Queen Victoria—A Portrait* by Giles St. Aubyn (New York: Antheneum, 1992). The most powerful portrait of Victoria is Lytton Strachey's *Queen Victoria* (London: Chatto & Windus, 1921).

For Prince Albert, two principal sources are *The Life of HRH the Prince Consort* by Sir Theodore Martin (London: Smith, Elder & Co., 1882), and *Prince Albert—A Biography* by Robert Rhodes James (New York: Alfred A. Knopf, 1984).

Of the five women who are the principal subjects of this book, the biographies range from ample for Vicky to sparse for Lenchen. The most useful titles follow.

VICKY: Likely the most complete biography of Vicky is *An Uncommon Woman—The Empress Frederick* by Hannah Pakula (New York: Simon & Schuster, 1995); also good are *Vicky—Princess Royal of England and German Empress* by Daphne Bennett (New York: St. Martin's Press, 1971); *The Empress Frederick* by Princess Catherine Radziwill (New York: Henry Holt, 1934); and *The English Empress—A Study in Relations Between Queen Victoria and Her Eldest Daughter, Empress Frederick of Germany* by Egon Caesar Conte Corti (London: Cassell, 1957). Books of Vicky's correspondence include *The Empress Frederick Writes to Sophie, Her Daughter, Crown Princess and Later Queen of the Hellenes, Letters 1889–1901*, edited by Arthur Gould Lee (London: Faber & Faber, 1955), and *Letters of the Empress Frederick*, edited by Sir Frederick Ponsonby (New York: Macmillan, 1930). Sources on Vicky's husband Fritz include *Frederick III—German Emperor 1888* by John Van der Kiste (Gloucester: Alan Sutton, 1981); the scholarly *Frederick III—Germany's Liberal Emperor* by Patricia Kollander (Westport, CT: Greenwood Press, 1995); and *Death of a Kaiser—A Medical Historical Narrative* by Jain I. Lin (Dayton, OH: Landfall Press, 1985).

ALICE: *Princess Alice—Queen Victoria's Forgotten Daughter* by Gerard Noel (London: Constable, 1974); *Hessian Tapestry—The Hesse Family and British Royalty* by David Duff (Devon: David & Charles, 1979).

HELENA: No separate biography of Lenchen exists, though she is described in two books on Queen Victoria's daughters: *Queen Victoria's Daughters* by E. F. Benson (New York: Appleton, 1938), and *Victoria and Her Daughters* by Nina Epton (New York: W.W. Norton, 1971). Lenchen is also discussed in her daughter's book, HH Princess Marie Louise, *My Memories of Six Reigns* (London: Vans Brothers, 1956).

LOUISE: Far the most complete of Louise's biographies is *Princess Louise— Queen Victoria's Unconventional Daughter,* by Jehanne Wake (London: Collins, 1988); also good are *Darling Loosy—Letters to Princess Louise 1856–1939,* edited by Elizabeth Longford (London: Weidenfeld & Nicolson, 1991), *The Life Story of HRH Princess Louise, Duchess of Argyll* by David Duff (Bath: Cedric Chivers, 1971); and *Royal Rebels—Princess Louise and the Marquis of Lorne* by Robert M. Stamp (Toronto: Dundurn Press, 1988).

BEATRICE: *The Life and Times of HRH Princess Beatrice* by M. E. Sara (London: Stanley Paul, 1945). The best is *The Shy Princess—The Life of Her Royal Highness Princess Beatrice, the Youngest Daughter and Constant Companion of Queen Victoria* by David Duff (London, Frederick Muller, 1958).

Other works consulted for this book:

Alice, HRH Princess, Countess of Athlone. *For My Grandchildren.* London, 1966.

Anonymous. *The Empress Frederick, a Memoir.* New York, 1914.

Anonymous. *The Private Life of the Queen.* New York, 1897.

Aronson, Theo. *Grandmama of Europe—The Crowned Descendants of Queen Victoria.* Indianapolis, 1973.

———. *The Kaisers.* Indianapolis, 1971.

Auchincloss, Louis. *Persons of Consequence: Queen Victoria and Her Circle.* New York, 1979.

Baird, Diana, comp. *Victorian Days* and *A Royal Friendship.* London, 1958 (personal material about Helena expressed in letters to a friend).

Balfour, Michael. *The Kaiser and His Times.* New York, 1964.

Buchanan, Meriel. *Queen Victoria's Relations.* London, 1954

Cecil, Lamar. *William II.* Chapel Hill, NC, 1989.

Eilers, Marlene. *Queen Victoria's Descendants.* New York, 1987.

Friedman, Dennis. *Inheritance—A Psychological History of the Royal Family.* London, 1993.

Gwyn, Sandra. *The Private Capital—Ambition and Love in the Age of Macdonald and Laurier.* Toronto, 1984.

Hough, Richard. *Louis & Victoria: The First Mountbattens.* London, 1974.

Hubbard, R. H. *Rideau Hall.* Toronto, 1967.

Kenyon, Edith C. *Scenes in the Life of the Royal Family.* London, 1887.

Klepac, Madame. "A Royal Rebel" in Saturday Evening Post, Jan. 4, 1930.

Lees-Milne, James. *The Enigmatic Edwardian—The Life of Reginald, 2nd Viscount Esher.* London, 1986.

Leinhaas, G. A. *Reminiscences of Victoria, Empress Frederick.* Mainz, 1902.

Mallett, Marie. *Life with Queen Victoria.* London, 1968.

Noel, Gerard. *Ena: Spain's English Queen.* London, 1974.

Palmer, Alan. *Crowned Cousins—The Anglo-German Royal Connection.* London, 1985.

Pilapil, Vicente R. *Alfonso XIII.* New York, 1969.

Ponsonby, Frederick. *Recollections of Three Reigns.* New York, 1952.

Potts, D. M. and W. T. W. *Queen Victoria's Gene—Hemophilia and the Royal Family.* Stroud, U. K. 1995.

Reid, Michaela. *Ask Sir James.* London, 1987.

Röhl, John, and Nicolaus Sombart. *Kaiser Wilhelm II, New Interpretations.* Cambridge, U.K., 1982.

Salway, Lance. *Queen Victoria's Grandchildren.* London, 1991.

Taylor, A. J. P. *Bismarck—The Man and the Statesman.* New York, 1955.

Tisdall, E. E. P. *She Made World Chaos: The Intimate Story of Empress Frederick.* London, 1940.

Van der Kiste, John. *Childhood at Court 1819–1914.* Stroud, U.K. 1995.

———*Queen Victoria's Children.* Stroud, U.K. 1986.

Victoria, Princess of Prussia. *My Memoirs.* London, 1929.

Whittle, Tyler. *The Last Kaiser.* New York, 1977.

———*Victoria and Albert at Home.* London, 1980.

William II, Emperor. *My Early Life.* London, 1926.

York, HRH the Duchess of, with Benita Stoney. *Victoria & Albert: Life at Osborne House.* London, 1991.

Index